SOE8D-INTER

05333

D0042097

The
Foundations
of
Education:
Stasis
and
Change

Frank P. Besag
University of Wisconsin
Milwaukee

Jack L. Nelson
Rutgers University

Contributing Authors

H. Warren Button
Professor of the History of Education,
State University of New York at Buffalo

Richard Cummings
Professor of Cultural Foundations of Education,
University of Wisconsin, Milwaukee

Robert M. O'Neil
Professor of Constitutional Law, and President,
University of Wisconsin System

Random House
New York

The Foundations of Education: Stasis and Change

First Edition
987654321
Copyright ©1984 by Random House, Inc.

All rights reserved under International and Pan-
American Copyright Conventions. No part of this
book may be reproduced in any form or by any
means, electronic or mechanical, including photocopy-
ing, without permission in writing from the publisher.
All inquiries should be addressed to Random House,
Inc., 201 East 50th Street, New York, N.Y. 10002.
Published in the United States by Random House,
Inc., and simultaneously in Canada by Random
House of Canada Limited, Toronto.

Library of Congress Cataloging in Publication Data

Besag, Frank P.
  The foundations of education.

  Bibliography: p.
  Includes index.
  1. Education—United States—History.   2. Educa-
tion—Social aspects—United States—History.
3. Education—Political aspects—United States—
History.   4. Education—Economic aspects—United
States—History.   I. Nelson, Jack L.   II. Title.
LA205.B44   1983   370'.973   83–21132
ISBN 0–394–32817–5

Cover photograph © Elizabeth Crews/Stock, Boston.
Cover and text design by Elissa Ichiyasu

Manufactured in the United States of America.

To the 1962 and 1963 students of San Diego
High School who told me to keep
challenging the system for their sake if not
mine. Particularly the debate squad (Kent
Geddis, Bonnie Passenheim, John Battaile,
Cheri Storton, Sheryl Anderson, Randy
Moore, Sue Clark, Paul Levine, Landia
Peterson, and others remembered but too
numerous to name) and most especially
Stephen Shubert who has become a
confidant, friend, and colleague.
—F. P. B.

And to the corps of teachers and critics who
make the enterprise of education a subject of
fascinating study. Finally, to the future
students like three-year-old Megan, who
make the effort worthwhile.
—J. L. N.

Preface

We need good schools and good teachers. Do we have them? That is the subject of considerable debate from differing perspectives. There are significant disagreements over what to keep and what to change in schools. We offer, in this book, an introduction to the study of education from highly divergent perspectives, and we provide a series of different social science models which can be used to analyze schools and schooling. In addition, we treat topics like technology, multicultural problems, global issues, equality, and academic freedom in terms of their educational significance. The book is designed primarily for use by students in introductory and foundations courses preparing to become teachers, and for teachers who want to examine schools and non-teachers who want a better understanding of schools as social institutions.

Education has, once again, become a prominent public issue. The historic and continuing debate over what makes schools good is front-page news. Leading political figures identify education as the nation's number one priority. And a number of recent reports have drawn wide attention for their criticisms of the schools. This is a time of great turmoil in education, and a time when systematic study of schools helps to make sense out of the chaos.

Different national panels of important people produced differing analyses of the ills of education, and differing proposals for change. One panel was formed because of a "widespread public perception that something was seriously remiss in our educational system."[1] Another believes that "educational improvement is a preeminent national need."[2] And a third recognizes the special responsibilities of colleges and universities for improvements in secondary education.[3]

Proposals for change in schools are often conflicting. Some critics want more student rights, more humane environments, more nurturing, less competitiveness. Some want tougher standards, more homework, special treatment for high achievers, more competitiveness. Some say more emphasis should be placed on high technology, math, science, and vocational training. Some want more literature, arts, philosophy. Some want more drill and memory work; others say critical thinking is paramount. And some argue that the schools have a hidden agenda that maintains social class inequality, sexism, and racism. Others say schools should require more patriotism, more free enterprise, more religion. No one seems to desire bad schools and bad teachers, but clearly the perspectives and the models used in analyzing schools differ dramatically.

The purpose of this book is to provide a foundation for examining schools in their social, historic, political, and economic settings. The central theme of the book is the dialectic between stasis and change. We are interested in the struggle between forces which serve to keep things the way they are and those that seek change. We also provide a series of lenses through which schools can be examined—some models for analyzing the operations of schools. By using different perspectives and models it is possible to gain a rich understanding of issues in the continuing debate over schools. We hope to stimulate you to participate in the debate.

Since we recognize our own limitations in addressing the broad range of topics covered in this text, we asked three scholars to prepare specific chapters in their fields. In particular, we thank the following scholars for their contributions:

H. Warren Button, Professor of the History of Education, State University of New York at Buffalo (Chapter 3);

Richard Cummings, Professor of Cultural Foundations of Education, University of Wisconsin, Milwaukee (part of Chapter 11; Chapters 12 and 13);

Robert M. O'Neil, Professor of Constitutional Law, and President, University of Wisconsin System (Chapter 14).

We also thank Winifred Fairhaven Flisram, Cathy Nelson, Dana Hackenberg, William Stanley, and a variety of students and colleagues who criticized portions of the manuscript. Our Random House editor, Bertrand Lummus, deserves special credit for his support and patience. The constructive criticism of John Hardin Best, Stanley Wronski, and Maxine Green was particularly valuable in revising the manuscript. And we thank Dean Michael Stolee of the University of Wisconsin at Milwaukee, and the Rutgers University Research Council, for aid and support in completing the work.

F. P. B.

J. L. N.

---

[1] *A Nation at Risk: The Imperative for Educational Reform*. National Commission on Excellence in Education. Washington, D.C.: U.S. Department of Education, April 1983.

[2] Patricia Albjerg Graham. "The Twentieth Century Fund Task Force Report on Federal Elementary and Secondary Education Policy," *Phi Delta Kappan* 65:1 (September 1983): 19.

[3] *High School: A Report on Secondary Education in America*. A Report of the Carnegie Foundation for the Advancement of Teaching. New York: Harper & Row, 1983.

Contents

Flow Charts

The Foundations of Education: Stasis and Change

Introduction

We view society and the school as changing entities. There are enormous pressures in society and its institutions to maintain stasis, and simple inertia contributes to a feeling that things are relatively unchanging. But as a study of the history, sociology, politics, and economics of schools shows, change is constantly occurring. Much is very subtle and gradual; some is rapid and then slides back into the traditional; and some change is institutionalized and becomes the new stasis of future generations.

Assuming that not all stasis or change is progress, we propose that the study of education include the use of critical skepticism to weigh ideas and events. Evaluation of change and stasis depends upon knowledge and perspective. Institutional analysis assists in identifying potential areas of change, possible static reactions, and likely consequences. We do not take a deterministic stance that individuals and groups must submit to ongoing change or stasis. Rather, we note that society and schools have changed; that individuals have been responsible for change; and that change can be a productive challenge, not a fearsome disruption.

Individual and Institution

Among those who are interested in change, however, there is a division of opinion as to where to begin the process. In this country, which believes so strongly in the individual, most people hold that in order to facilitate change in an institution, we must first change the individuals who make up that institution. The phrase, "To have good schools, we must have good teachers" exemplifies this attitude. It assumes that the individual affects the institution more than the institution affects the individual. This is the traditional psychological, social-science approach.

This book takes a different approach. Rather than assuming that people make institutions, we assume that institutions make people. Punitive institutions generate punitive behaviors, while positive institutions generate positive behaviors. This changes the emphasis from an analysis of individuals to an analysis of institutions. The models presented in the book do not deal with how to look at the individual but rather how to look at the institutions that affect

3

the individual. There is a danger in this approach, namely, that the individual will be lost completely and that the institution alone will be discussed. To avoid this problem the text will focus on the individual in the institution.

In our examination of the foundations of education several themes emerge. The dominant theme is the tension between stasis and change. We propose that students of education need to consider the nature of society and the schools in terms of differing perspectives on stability and modification. A second theme is the concept of the institution and the variety of analytic tools for examining institutions. And a third theme is that of rational skepticism. We believe that the study of education demands rational inquiry—examining issues, considering evidence, drawing tentative conclusions—and the maintenance of a level of informed skepticism that permits us to entertain an outrageous idea, an alternative explanation, or opposing, provocative evidence.

This book is organized to provide a variety of perspectives, a number of issues, and some divergent ideas about education. The book's first section starts by looking at institutions in terms of stasis and change and moves to an historic overview of the school in American society. The second section provides several distinct models for analyzing the school. It includes views of the school from a Marxist orientation, as an administrative unit, as a political entity, as a total institution, as a labeling institution, and as a representation of culture. Section Three offers an examination of the social setting of the school and divergent views of the nature of society. Section Four looks at cultural and institutional issues that involve education and have implications for schooling. These include such topics as interdependence, technology, and multi-culturalism. The fifth section discusses equal justice and freedom of expression. The text is a general introduction to issues and ideas about schooling and society.

The book deals with specific questions under the following topics:

—Institutional and Historical Background to Contemporary Education
    What is an institution and what is the school as an institution? How have the schools remained static or changed over time? What traditional forms of utility, organization, and social values have dominated schools?
—Models for Analyzing Contemporary Schools
    Which perspective (social alienation, administrative, political, total, labeling, or cultural) provides the clearest or most intriguing analysis of the school? What manifest and latent forms of function, organization, and values are identifiable under each perspective? What roles for actors, sanctions, and ceremonies stand out when the school is analyzed under each perspective? How are change and stasis explained?

—Social Setting of the School

What is the relation between the social context of stasis and change and the schools of that society? How do institutions take on social utility and become different in their organization, sanction systems, symbols, and susceptibility to change? How do actors learn their social roles?

—Cultural Issues Involving Education

How do interdependence, technological development, and human relations in multicultural societies illustrate stasis and change in society? How is social change likely to influence the school?

—Equality and Freedom of Expression

What is the school's role in societal freedom? What battles still need to be fought?

On Observation and Perspective

An educator is, among other things, an observer. The classroom teacher keeps an eye on student behavior. The school principal tries to be aware of teacher morale and parent concerns. The guidance counselor is sensitive to student interests and their changing patterns. These require some skill in observing and interpreting. They also incorporate a perspective that provides the framework within which the observations are interpreted.

Observations and perspectives differ. For a trained auto mechanic, the sound of an engine or the feel of the clutch or the look of the maze of wires and equipment under the hood offers significant clues to the health of the car. A lawyer is educated to look for certain points in cases, and to ignore others. A parent becomes attuned to mood changes in children. The skilled mechanic, lawyer, or parent is the one who has developed keen observational abilities and who can interpret these observations from differing perspectives.

We want to assist you in refining your observations and perspectives in regard to school and schooling. That, we think, involves providing a variety of alternative observations for your consideration, and a number of different perspectives to use in interpreting observations of education. Nearly everyone has had a wealth of experience in schools by the time of college. Our concern is to stimulate you to consider this experience through differing lenses.

When is a school not a school, but a factory or a prison or a jungle? Are teachers moral and intellectual leaders, underpaid babysitters, dupes of capitalists, nurturing parent-substitutes, or work-a-day laborers? Is schooling designed to produce active citizens for a democratic society, robots for an industrial world, or a "rising tide of mediocrity"?

It depends on how you look at it. And how you look at it depends upon the perspective you adopt and what you look for. Certainly, pessimists and optimists and cynics differ in their interpretations of the same things.

We encourage you to explore this book and to reading further in testing your observations and perspectives.

Section One: Stasis and Change in Institutions: How We Got That Way

The first section of the text will define some of the critical terms used throughout the book. The first chapter places schools in their cultural context. Chapter 2 defines "stasis," "change," and "institutions." Both chapters do so in terms of sociology; that is, they consider the effect of the institution on the individual rather than that of the individual on the institution.

The third chapter is a social history of education in the United States. A social history is one that combines facts and dates with the social currents that accompanied them—in this case the quest for social justice, racial and sexual equality, and the freedom to know.

Section One tells us where we are and how we got here.

Chapter 1: Schools in a Cultural Context

Have you ever been to a class reunion for your high school? Or have you perhaps gone back to the school building for a visit? If so, you probably have noticed that some things seem quite different from when you were a student, yet much seems unchanged. Whether it is the first, fifth, tenth, or twentieth reunion, one usually finds things that change and others that remain the same. Although we may want and expect some elements of the school to change— Why did we have so many study halls?—we have nostalgic memories of other elements of school that we would prefer to keep static—Remember Mr. Stark and his great English class? You may have found, when you visit a school as part of your teacher preparation, that you often get a sense of *déjà vu*—a feeling that you must have been at that school before. Simultaneously, you may also get an uneasy sensation that some things about this school are quite different from your own student experiences.

A family exhibits a similar pattern of stasis and change. Your relatives seem to remain static in some respects and to change in others. Institutions, such as school, family, media, government, and religion, are subject to the pressures both of stability and of modification. And it is in the nature of institutions that stasis and change are in a continuing tug of war.

This book will examine one social institution, the school, within a cultural framework that experiences pressures for both stasis and change. The role of the school, education, permeates modern society. Virtually all of us experience it for large segments of our lives. The social, personal, and financial investment in education is very large, and schools are such public and pervasive institutions that they are subject to continuing cycles of debate over their purposes, practices, and results. Some want schools to return to a golden age of seeming stability. Others want dynamic alteration for a golden future.

THE SCHOOL DEBATES

Schools and schooling have been the subject of discussion and debate in societies throughout their histories. Certainly the current debates about schooling are not new, nor are they likely to disappear in the near future. Certain questions seem to come up over and over again whenever the subject of the school arises. Consider, for example, some of the following:

1. Who should be educated?
2. What knowledge, skills, and values should be taught in the schools?
3. What social, political, and economic views should be expressed in the schools? Which ones should be censored or ignored?
4. Are public schools better than private ones? Who should pay for schooling?
5. How do we assess the quality of schools?
6. How should schools address such social problems as racism, sexism, drug abuse, alienation, crime, prejudice, and illiteracy?
7. What role should teachers have in schools and in society? How should teachers be prepared?
8. Who should control the schools?
9. What expectations should a society have for its schools?
10. Do schools, and teachers, have a responsibility to maintain stability in society, or to try to make changes in that society?

The issues raised by these questions not only illustrate basic differences of opinion about schooling and education in society, they also illustrate the basic theme of this book. We will be examining both schooling and education in terms of the cultural framework within which they exist. *Schooling*, as a form of education, is given special treatment because it is the formal system that stimulates the most arguments about education. *Education* is a larger concept than schooling: it includes family influences, learning from peers, and individual learning. The *school*, however, is a particular institution in society that involves virtually everyone at some time of their lives and which is subject to public scrutiny.

Ways of Seeing A School

What is a school? It is a bit more complicated than you might think. In fact, you may be surprised at just how many ways it can be described. Consider, for example, this physical description of a typical suburban school:

> Our elementary school is a brick building with many windows and a large door in the center of the first floor. There is a driveway and small parking lot for the principal, the bus stop, and visitors in front, and a large parking lot on the side for the teachers. Some of the windows have paper cutout decorations in them; others are empty. Inside, the office, with its long counter, is next to the front door, and hallways lead off in two directions from the entry way. Each room has a numbered door with a window in it, although in some the window is covered. There is a gym, a multi-purpose room, a teachers' lounge, and a number of other special rooms.

But, of course, a school is more than the sum of its physical parts. Other descriptions might focus on human interaction in the schools as, for example, do these memories:

> BILL, INSURANCE SALESMAN: "I remember waiting on the benches in the office for the vice-principal to lecture me on my behavior and threaten to call my parents."
>
> BEVERLY, ACCOUNTANT: "My strongest memory is the feeling of panic because I hadn't done class assignments over the weekend."
>
> TOM, TRUCK DRIVER: "Sports. We had the best baseball team in the city and Coach Miller really took care of us."
>
> DENNIS, ASSEMBLER, TRI-X COMPANY: "Poor old Mrs. Parrington, trying to teach me English—even willing to take her free period to help me with grammar."
>
> BARBARA, OWNER, SUNRISE FLOWERS: "I liked to spend time in the library, and I liked the teachers who seemed to care."
>
> MARK, GRADUATE STUDENT: "I enjoyed discovering new ideas and having class discussions; not all the classes were interesting, but school was mostly fun and I learned a lot."
>
> SHELLY, MANAGEMENT TRAINEE: "I was bored in school, except for things like field trips or social activities."
>
> STEVE, ASSISTANT CITY PLANNER: "I remember our gang and some good times, but there was a lot of wasted time in classes."

Another description may use social-science jargon, as does this comment from a high-school senior reported in *High School Students Speak Out*:

We figure that our class once had three social strata. I'd call them the Untouchables, the Middle Group, and the Upper Echelon (the Nobility). Well, it was a matter of who went with whom, what kids you cut class with, what teachers you were rude to, things like that.[1]

And other descriptions might propose what ought to be, in this example placing the emphasis less on social life than on learning:

I think that somewhere along the line one or two teachers have a terrific influence on you, even though the rest of the school may not have any meaning. School should be concerned with intelligence. It doesn't affect the personality. You have school, then you go home and enjoy life.[2]

It is even possible to describe school as a process of sham:

Socialization in American Society is learning how to shuck, learning how to communicate the identity that brings about the biggest and best rewards. A car salesman acts as if the car he is about to sell you is an absolute steal. The more he is able to convince you of his lie, the richer he will become. School teachers and professors and students play the same game with variations that are particular to school life. . . . [I]n the classroom, the shucking game, as played by the teacher, becomes a process of molding the personalities of children through a series of mysterious shapings such as: "All right children, I want you to think of a color. Good, that's right, close your eyes and think. All right, Mary, now what color did you think of ?"
"Green, teacher."
"I'm sorry, Mary, that's wrong."[3]

Each of these descriptions is the result of a set of experiences and a perspective. The experiences and the perspectives, or ways of looking at experiences, may differ, but they all occur within a cultural context, which must be understood if we are to make sense of our experiences.

Culture and Culture

We have many words with multiple meanings. That is in the nature of language and permits some flexibility in communications. Unfortunately, this multiplicity also can lead to confusion and the muddling of ideas. One of the words most open to multiple definition and, therefore, to misunderstanding is culture, which, in our language, is used to mean such things as:

- The controlled growth of microorganisms, bacteria, or fungi
- The cultivation or growing of a particular crop, such as corn
- A stage in the growth of civilization, as in the Aztec culture
- The refinement of taste through education, where we speak of a sophisticated person as cultured
- The sum total of the experiences, traditions, and values of a people as reflected in their life-styles

We use *culture* in this book to refer to the environment in which individuals live and that continually provides them with ways of thinking and behaving. Culture, in this global sense, surrounds us and is part of us in ways that we seldom consider.

Our thought patterns, our criteria for what is right and wrong, and our ideas about nature are all influenced by the culture in which we live. Simple everyday activities like eating, reading, talking, and work are subject to cultural influences. The use of fork and spoon rather than chopsticks or fingers is a cultural phenomenon. Language is basic to culture; we read and speak a particular language that carries cultural values. And our work is judged in terms of its importance by cultural standards.

The other definitions of culture noted above are not wrong; they are actually incorporated into the larger definition. Culture as the sum total of experiences implies a static quality that we do not mean. It is, rather, a changing environment that assumes a continuing interaction between individuals and their historical and contemporary settings. We are the product of past civilizations and our own immediate surroundings, but we are not complete. Human beings change throughout their lives. And we have some hand in influencing our environment—it is not all imposed upon us. A culture changes as a result of interactions with other cultures and as a result of internal interactions. This is similar to the idea of culture as change in human organisms or the sophistication of people as they learn through interactions in life. The acculturation process, or *socialization*, wherein children learn the major values of a culture is an educational process. It begins at birth and continues throughout life. And school is one part of that process.

SUBCULTURES AND THE SCHOOL

We also live in *subcultures*. These are segments of a culture that possess relatively distinct characteristics but share in the larger culture. The subculture of school, for example, has a variety of characteristics that identify it. There are traditions and values like expected behaviors in classes and hallways, at school sports events, and when called to the principal's office. Closing schools on Saturdays and Sundays and certain holidays is simply part of a cultural tradition.

Subcultures also arise within schools. The following example is taken from a study of a particular school in which the researcher took the role of a high-school student for four months in order to get a firsthand view of the subcultures of the school. He was obviously young-looking enough to pass for a high-school transfer student, but he had been trained in anthropological research techniques like ethnography to examine evidence as an "insider" in the school subculture. Palonsky describes a number of different groups in the school and examines the nature of their interaction—or lack thereof. This was an integrated school, but there was limited contact between white and black students. Palonsky describes one illustrative incident:

> One day as we were eating lunch, Mel, one of the Hempies (a group of marijuana smokers), pointed to a group of black girls who were braiding the hair of some black guys. He asked me what they were doing.
> "I don't know," I answered, "why don't you ask them?"
> "Yeah, I will. There are a lot of black dudes in my three hour (vocational) block; I'll ask one of them when the time's right."
> "Are they friends of yours?"
> "Yeah, you could say that."
> Three months later, just before I was about to leave, I asked Mel if he had found out why the blacks were braiding their hair. He told me that he hadn't: "The time just has never been right." He had spent three hours a day, five days a week, in a class of five blacks and ten whites—yet the "time had never been right" to ask a "friend" why he wears his hair in braids.[4]

Schools are particularly good places to search for evidence of cultural traditions, multicultural patterns, and subcultural differences. In American society schools have several cultural dimensions. They are social institutions that have a special responsibility to implant selected parts of the culture in young people. We require all children between certain ages to attend school, establish what they are to learn, and who is to teach them. The accumulated cultural viewpoints on knowledge, skills, values, and behaviors, current in a society, are passed on to the young through schools. The socialization process is examined and questioned in a later chapter (see Chapter 7), but it is important here to see the school as a cultural transmission agent. Also, schools in a multicultural society exhibit a variety of examples of the pressures of stasis and change as these cultures interact or remain insulated within specific schools. And subcultures, as they exist in schools, are fascinating subjects of observation and very useful in understanding social relations and cultural processes.

This book offers a number of means for looking at these cultural foundations of education. It provides general background to a study of schooling in society, several models through which schools can be perceived, analysis of the social setting of schools, and examination of cultural issues that influence education.

LANGUAGE AND CULTURE

Language is a particular aspect of culture. It is not simply a means of communicating; it also conveys values and organizes thought. It provides signals and cues that identify parts of the environment. And those identifications are parts of the cultural tradition that schools, families, and others pass on to the young. Words and other symbols are not neutral; they are always value laden.

As you read this, you are most likely thinking in English, unless you are translating the words in your head. If this were written in Chinese, Russian, Arabic, Greek, or any other language, it could only be understood by someone who had been educated in that language, and many of the linguistic subtleties or idiomatic expressions would not be understood unless the person were very thoroughly educated in that language. The deciphering of a language code can be attempted with some success by finding culturally common roots of words—for example, the French *democratie* and the English democracy both derive from the Greek *demokratia*, which combines the roots *demos*, "the people," and *kratien*, "to rule." But knowing this is only of limited help. The definition of the word democracy is not static. Democracy means a variety of things in the United States and even more throughout the world. Virtually every country now in existence claims to be democratic, but they are certainly not similar in government.

We also label things, including ideas, with positive and negative words to convey values. Our self-descriptions tend to be positive, while terms used to describe those we oppose tend to be derogatory. Consider the language used to refer to certain human characteristics:

reasonable, fair, just, pleasant, thoughtful, considerate, irrational, dictatorial, hypocritical, mean spirited, boorish, nasty

Similarly, group self-interest is usually identified by positive phrasing and symbols:

the party of peace, the chosen people, the Allies, colleague, our flag, the brotherhood or sisterhood, defenders of the faith

And negative language is used to identify those groups with which we disagree or from which we would like to be separated:

warmongers, dregs of the earth, the unholy, enemies of the people, a cancer on humanity, ill-tempered and evil, ignorant savages

Schools are specifically designed to convey language to students. Yet, there is more meaning to that simple sentence than is expressed. Language is more than just the learning of words and sentences. Language conveys social acceptability or rejection, social status information, and cultural values. Some of these are obvious, as the social acceptability of "proper" grammar indicates — or the difference in social status that is evident in the spoken and written language of a person who has not had the social benefit of learning and using "proper" English.

Our determination of relative power in society is also tied up with language. We tend to define intelligence and knowledge in terms of language facility. Certainly, the common IQ tests are basically language tests. And one is not considered knowledgeable if one is unable to read, write, or speak fluently. Not only is social status indicated in these obvious differences in language facility, there are actual differences in political and economic power that are related to language use. People get promoted, in school and at jobs, because of their abilities in language. Professions like medicine and law command economic and political power partly as a result of the technical language used in these fields, and professional training consists in large part of learning to use that language.

Recent scholarship, examining the role of schooling in the allocation of social power, in exerting social control, and in the relation of schooling to knowledge and ideology, has included a concern for the use of language in these areas. These new sociologists of education tend to use a critical perspective that highlights the means by which schools are agencies recreating social inequalities. That is, schools are devoted to preserving and protecting the acceptable social heritage — including the gross inequalities among groups of people—and language is one of the main avenues that schools use to separate groups, to reward and punish members of different groups, and to allocate power. The definitions of knowledge that teachers use in classrooms, the nature of textbooks, the award system in the school, and many other obvious and subtle parts of schooling are examined by these critical scholars.

Frenchman Pierre Bourdieu uses the term "cultural capital" to refer to the high status given to knowledge, manners, and skills, which are developed and reinforced in social institutions, especially the schools, and which give some individuals much more power than others for succeeding in school and other institutions.[5] Englishman Basil Bernstein's multivolume work on the relation between language and social class is titled *Class, Codes and Control* and features a significant analysis of schools as tools for transmission of the culture.[6] He identifies educational "codes" in the language which signify what knowledge is considered valid and which govern the relations between pupils and teachers. He relates these learned educational codes to social class and to social control. Thus, schools become implicated in reproducing social inequalities and in training people to accept social control; they are not engaged in class-based protest.

Other critical, educational scholars have seen this link among schooling, social class, power, and ideology.[7] Some of their views are discussed more fully in Chapter 9. Here, our concern is to indicate that there is a tension between views of stasis and change even in such broadly used terms as culture and language. Henry Giroux, for example, points out that the concept of culture, which has been used traditionally in the United States, has "contributed little to an understanding of how power functions in a society," and that it has "tilted over into an apology for the status quo."[8] He argues that we should use the plural form, cultures, to indicate that more than one exists and that these cultures can be competing and in conflict. This use of language, in which the singular notion of culture suggests a pervasive and static condition to which people must adapt, and the plural term, suggesting change and dynamics, illustrates the influence of language. They also illustrate the divergence of view that is a theme of this book—stasis and change.

World Views

The cultures in which we live provide us with a *world view*, a large scale frame of reference, which we use to understand and to explain everyday events. World views are so well ingrained from childhood that they are virtually hidden; people operate on the basis of a world view without thinking about it. And certainly they don't question it.

At one time in human history it was widely believed that animal spirits inhabited all things and that they caused any good or evil. If there was a drought, flood, or a successful hunt for food, the spirits were believed to be responsible. This animistic world view offered answers for any happening. At another time, the world view was that the earth was flat and that one would sail off the edge if not careful. In parts of colonial America a harsh puritanism provided a world view that condemned most people to hell, with limited hope for salvation and severe punishment for religious transgressions.

Following the eighteenth-century Enlightenment a more recent world view developed, one that believed in the good of science and technology, the conquering of nature, and the continuing progress of civilization. Thinkers like Descartes, Newton, and Locke provided a new way of looking at the world that accommodated human ability to control their own physical environment, govern themselves, and pursue the improvement of the human condition. In Western societies we pretty much accept this world view without critical judgment. We believe that science and technology will provide answers to human problems like cancer, the depletion of resources, and transportation. We believe that democracy will provide equality and justice. And we tend to believe that things are better now than they were in colonial times, or during the Civil War or other previous periods.

There are some recent criticisms of our comforting world view. These include a concern that science and technology have created the conditions for total nuclear annihilation of the human race and have provided the basis for a rape of the environment through pollution and resource wastage. Prominent among these critics, Jeremy Rifkin points out defects in the current world view:

> Each day we awake to a world that appears more confused and disordered than the one we left the night before. Nothing seems to work anymore. . . .
>
> There are accidents at nuclear plants, shootouts in gas station lines over fuel allocations, the doubling and tripling of inflation figures, the steady loss of productivity and jobs, the increased danger of thermonuclear war. . . .
>
> We look around us only to find that the garbage and pollution are piling up in every quarter, oozing out of the ground and lingering in our air. . . .

> When the whole world begins to break down and fall apart then we must look at the way the whole world has been organized, because that is where the problem lies. . . .[9]

Other critics argue that equality and justice as perceived in the United States are a false illusion; that we have actually had no commitment to providing equality for minorities, women, or the poor. They point to the system of justice and note that our prisons are filled with nonwhite and poor people. They look at continuing income disparities between whites and blacks, or men and women. And they point to segregation and inequality in the schools more than a quarter-century after the Brown Decision, of 1954, which made racial segregation illegal.

SCHOOLS AND WORLD VIEWS

Schools are intertwined with the cultures they serve. They are among the most important social agencies for transmitting the culture — a world view — to the young. They are charged with the responsibility for preserving, organizing, and presenting the knowledge, skills, and values considered most important in a society. Schools are the only governmentally organized social institution that have this responsibility. Families, religion, peer groups, and media also transmit cultural knowledge, skills, and values, but they are not governmentally organized. Schools bear a special, and more controlled, relationship with the continuation of world views. It is unlikely that many schools or teachers in the United States would teach material that is anti-American, anticapitalist, or severely critical of the current American world view. The school is, thus, pulled toward stasis in world view.

At the same time, schools ought to be primary institutions to enlighten young people: to provide intellectual stimulation, to offer divergent ideas in the pursuit of knowledge, and to provide a place where academic freedom will permit a wide-ranging consideration of alternative world views. The essence of progress is the ability of people to comprehend and adapt to change. This requires understanding of a variety of ideas and possible alternatives. The schools of a democracy, educating children as thoughtful participants in their own governance, have a special obligation to raise questions about and pose challenges to an existing world view in order to keep that view vital. This school obligation pulls toward change.

Schools and Society

Consider the varieties of stability and change in society. Each day brings combinations of strong traditional patterns of behavior and new situations that have to be met. The tension between stasis and change in society provides daily challenge. We expect stability in certain habits of everyday life like arising, dressing, eating, going to school or a job, walking, driving, and operating electronic equipment. Yet we also anticipate change even in those habitual activities. Sleeping through alarms, breaking shoelaces, burning breakfast, misplacing car keys, stumbling over curbs, forgetting books or job equipment, or breaking a favorite recording are all events we occasionally must face and adapt to. Other changes may be more positive—arising eagerly, looking better than expected after dressing, find a new taste treat for lunch, getting better gas mileage than ever, or discovering a new insight about a class or a job task.

In nonroutine activities there is more expectation of change. When we attempt a new sport, start a new school or job, or visit a foreign country we anticipate, and even desire, change. Yet we seek certain forms of stability in new situations because change creates unease. We tend to look for clues in a new situation which relate to previous experiences we have had and that will give us some sense of confidence in coping with the changes we must confront.

It is these patterns of experience, and the ability to transfer experience in one setting to others, that provide a sense of stability. When there is no opportunity or ability to perceive patterns, one has a sense of chaos. At the other extreme from chaos is social control, where even the type and amount of change is determined and restricted. A spontaneous riot at a football game or a drunken brawl represents chaos, while a maximum security prison or severely restrictive institution represents a controlled environment.

There are aspects of each end of the continuum from chaos to control that have appeal, and aspects that are ominous. Tending toward chaos are the ideas of freedom, liberty, individuality, and innovation; tending toward control are ideas of security, common values, group spirit, and loyalty. Yet a shift

Figure 1.1

		Variations in Social Environments			
	CHANGE			STABILITY	
Chaos	Deviance	Current environment		Tradition	Control

in the environment toward chaos brings fears of reckless abandon, loss of morality, and lawlessness. And a shift toward control brings fears of authoritarianism, fascism, and loss of individuality.

Social Setting of the School

The social setting in which schools reside is subject to the pressures of stasis and change. Typically, societies do not change rapidly — evolution, not revolution, is the standard in society and education. Yet societies are always in a state of change, with pressures for stability.

The school is a social institution and is necessarily involved in activities of both a social and individual nature. The schools, as one form of education, are intertwined with their social setting. Social perceptions of stability and change have a direct influence on the orientation of the schools.

Schools are expected to provide a solid foundation in skills and knowledge the society believes are necessary to maintain social stability. Thus, American schools must stress reading, speaking, and writing English, arithmetic, loyalty to the country, and commitment to proper social behavior. Schools are also expected to prepare each generation to cope with social change. So, American schools include microcomputer and technological courses, goals of critical thinking, and electives on current topics. The great social debates about the failures and successes of schools tend to focus on the relative weight given to instruction in those areas considered static and essential and those considered innovative and progressive. The tension between stasis and change in society is reflected in the public arguments about the purpose and practice of schooling.

Those who favor stability include people who want to limit the school to teach only those things that have stood the test of time and which have been accepted as perennial or essential common values of the educated people within a society. It also includes those who believe that tradition and custom are important in society and, thus, in schools. These people often reflect on their own schooling as having been particularly good and want to have the same given to children.

At the other end are those who see change as the dominant element in society. This includes those who see the school as a place where young generations are given the opportunity to explore widely, inquire freely, and develop the ability to cope with change. It also includes those who see the necessity of changing society and who believe that schools can be used to improve the social system.

The following table illustrates in simplified fashion the debate over school purposes. While it should help you to separate the issues, you should realize that most people hold multiple views of the purposes of schooling that swing between traditionalist and progressive. There usually is agreement that the basic skills of reading, writing, and math should be required of all students, and there is also agreement that schools should provide freedom for children to explore and grow. Parents want their children to be happy and individual but also to learn certain socially acceptable knowledge and values.

The debate tends to resolve itself into one of emphasis, creating a pendulum effect represented by mass-media attacks on schools, at one time, for being too rigid and traditional and, at other times, for being too free and progressive. In fact, with a few exceptions, the schools change very slowly in basic structure, purpose, and approach to education, while changing rapidly in superficial teacher techniques and teaching materials as fads come and go. As social institutions, schools maintain a solid traditionalism; as political entities, schools respond to shifts in public perceptions. The idea that schools *should* operate this way, fitting people for socially approved roles and traditional values, can be called a "functionalist" perspective. The school fulfills a social function that is conservative and based on the idea of stasis.

Table 1.1:
The Debate Over the Purposes of Schools

		Illustrative Views
STASIS	ESSENTIALIST:	Schools exist to instruct the young in knowledge and values determined by authorities and society to be necessary for carrying on time-tested social ideas.
	TRADITIONALIST:	Schools should stress the common and basic social heritage, knowledge, and values, without criticism.
CHANGE	PROGRESSIVE:	Schools should provide freedom, guidance, and a variety of experiences to help young generations develop as whole persons.
	REFORMIST:	Schools offer an ideal place to provide informed criticism of social ills and to stimulate social activism to improve society.

The Critique of Functionalism

Recent criticism of the traditional view of the school as a place to prepare young people to fit into society has generated considerable interest. The issue is more basic than a mere dispute over the organization or operation of schools; it involves different world views and beliefs about the very nature of society. The issue is treated in depth in Chapter 9 but is of importance in this introduction because the perspective one has in examining a social institution like schools will have a direct affect on what is perceived. And the battle between functionalist and critical views of society and social institutions is part of the war between stasis and change.

In brief, the functionalist view assumes that there is consensus and cohesion in society and that social institutions function to maintain that consensus and cohesion. There is, according to the functionalist perspective, an order to society and that social order requires protection. Thus social institutions are established to preserve, maintain, and protect the social order and not to alter or criticize it. School is important to the social order because it reinforces the common values of society by passing them on to upcoming generations. School, by the functionalist perspective, is a conservative social agency that is expected to uncritically transmit the cultural heritage and to prepare students to "fit into" the society. The school is expected to require children to have socially acceptable knowledge, skills, and values. This is, of course, primarily a stasis position.

A critical perspective, as opposed to the functional, assumes that conflict is basic to society, that there are significant differences between social classes in their values and aspirations, and that society needs continual criticism in order to find improvement. Change is a major element in the critical view. The school, from the critical perspective, is too heavily tied up with social reproduction—reproducing the same social problems, like inequality, injustice, and discrimination, in new generations—because it fails to criticize or to offer opportunity for students to criticize the current society. Critical theorists see the school as maintaining dominant social class interests under a false idea that all members of society share those values. They charge that schooling contains a hidden social and economic agenda that protects the current elites and controls the masses. This hidden curriculum of the school is responsible for such things as separating the social classes, giving elites more freedom and opportunity, training nonelites to accept their lot and be punctual workers, and convincing students that their society and their economic system are the best in the world and that change comes slowly and only within socially approved mechanisms.

The critical perspective assumes and supports change and proposes that all social institutions should undergo continuing critical scrutiny.

In order to understand the significant difference between these perspectives let us consider their views of such a common school practice as testing students and then, on the basis of the results, separating them into different courses and curricula. The functionalist perspective sees testing as consistent with the order in society. We need some people to be assembly-line workers, others to be dentists. It is necessary for some to be leaders, and others to be followers to insure the optimal functioning of the society. Schools are a proper place to discover which students are best suited to which tasks and categories and then to assign them to different programs so as to produce the workers the society requires, according to standards already established. To do otherwise would lead to chaos and disruption.

The critical perspective sees the separation of students as class biased and protective of the dominant social class. As long as students are tracked in this way, the dominant class's view of which occupations (doctor, laborer, teacher, banker) and kind of schooling (college, preparatory, general, technical, vocational) have the highest status will remain the norm of the society. And the children of that class will predominate in the kind of schooling and occupations that have the highest social status. Thus the separation of students into different curricula is a part of a hidden curriculum designed to maintain class dominance. School reproduces class values.

The important thing to keep in mind at this point is that the functionalist and the critical perspectives are not simply abstract and intellectual. Holding to one or the other will have a great influence on how you see all operations of schooling—from the organization of the school, to the classification of students, to financial support for the schools and who should pay for them, and so on. And the beliefs you hold regarding teacher education, testing, teaching practice, and textbooks are significant, for they will, of course, effect the way you act in the classroom as well.

FOR CONSIDERATION

1. What is your strongest memory about school?

2. What examples of change and of stasis in society can you provide? What examples in schooling?

3. Ask people of differing ages, including some senior citizens, what they remember about school. How do their answers compare?

4. What examples of functionalism are evident in the schools you know?

Notes

1. David Mallery, *High School Students Speak Out* (New York: Harper & Row, 1962), p. 35.
2. *Ibid.*, p. 37.
3. Carl Weinberg, *Education Is a Shuck* (New York: Morrow, 1975), pp. 1, x.
4. Stuart Palonsky, "Hempies and Squeaks, Truckers and Cruisers," *Educational Administration Quarterly* 11 (1975):86–103.
5. David Swartz, "Pierre Bourdieu: The Cultural Transmission of Social Inequality," *Harvard Educational Review* 47 (1977):54.
6. Basil Bernstein, *Class, Codes and Control*. Vol 3, 2nd ed. (London: Routledge & Kegan Paul, 1975).
7. See, for example, Michael Apple, *Ideology and Curriculum* (London: Routledge & Kegan Paul, 1979); Brian Davies, *Social Control and Education* (London: Methuen, 1976); Ann and Harold Berlak, *Dilemmas of Schooling* (London: Methuen, 1981); J. Karabel and A. H. Halsey, eds., *Power and Ideology in Education* (New York: Oxford University Press, 1977); Paulo Freire, *Education for Critical Consciousness* (New York: Seabury Press, 1973); Michael F. D. Young, *Knowledge and Control* (London: Collier Macmillan, 1971).
8. Henry Giroux, *Ideology, Culture and the Process of Schooling* (Philadelphia: Temple University Press, 1981), p. 26.
9. Jeremy Rifkin, *Entropy: A New World View* (New York: Bantam, 1981), pp. 3, 4.

References

Anyon, Jean. "Social Class and School Knowledge." *Curriculum Inquiry* 11 (1981): 3–42.

Apple, Michael. *Ideology and Curriculum*. Boston: Routledge & Kegan Paul, 1979.

Berlak, Ann, and Berlak, Harold. *Dilemmas of Schooling*. London: Methuen, 1981.

Bernbaum, Gerald. *Knowledge and Ideology in the Sociology of Education*. London: Macmillan, 1977.

Bernstein, Basil. *Class, Codes and Control*. Vol. 3, 2nd ed. London: Routledge & Kegan Paul, 1975.

Cole, Michael; Gay, John; Glick, Joseph; and Sharp, Donald. *The Cultural Context of Learning and Thinking*. New York: Basic Books, 1971.

Davies, Brian. *Social Control and Education*. London: Methuen, 1976.

Freire, Paulo. *Education for Critical Consciousness*. New York: Seabury Press, 1973.

Giroux, Henry. *Ideology, Culture and the Process of Schooling*. Philadelphia: Temple University Press, 1981.

Jenks, Chris. *Rationality, Education and the Social Organization of Knowledge*. London: Routledge & Kegan Paul, 1977.

Karabel, Jerome, and Halsey, A. H. *Power and Ideology in Education*. New York: Oxford University Press, 1977.

Katz, Michael. *Class, Bureaucracy and Schools*. New York: Praeger. 1971.

Mallery, David. *High School Students Speak Out*. New York: Harper & Row, 1962.

Rifkin, Jeremy. *Entropy: A New World View*. New York: Bantam, 1981.

Russell, Bertrand. *Sceptical Essays*. New York: Barnes & Noble, 1928.

Spring, Joel. *The Sorting Machine*. New York: McKay, 1976.

Swartz, David. "Pierre Bourdieu: The Cultural Transmission of Social Inequality." *Harvard Educational Review* 47 (1977).

Trudgill, Peter. *Sociolinguistics*. New York: Penguin Books, 1974.

Weinberg, Carl. *Education Is a Shuck*. New York: Morrow, 1975.

Chapter 2:
Stasis,
Change,
and
Institutions

Stasis and Change Defined

Stasis is a word drawn from the German language that means "standing still." In physiology, stasis refers to a stoppage of the normal flow of fluids in organs of the body. More specifically, it is used to identify the slackening of the flow of blood and the creation of congestion. Most commonly, stasis has come to mean a slowing down or lack of change, a stability, as in homeostasis, "the tendency of a system to maintain internal stability." However, the word stasis can range in meaning from stability to restrictive stoppage.

Change can be identified as the total substitution of one thing for another, a mutation, a conversion, a fickleness, or a slight variation. It can incorporate a range of events from the complete obliteration of anything in existence to a mere alteration of opinion about food preferences. The atomic bomb changed Hiroshima and the world (both were changed physically, psychologically, and socially); an individual can change from a dislike to a preference for spinach. The range of meaning of the word change is remarkable.

Figure 2.1

Stasis —Change

As these definitions suggest, there are no clear and precise demarcation points between stasis and change. As any event approaches the extreme, the definition of it as either stasis or change becomes clearer. In the middle there is overlap (see Figure 2.1).

People's perceptions of events may differ according to individual perceptions of stasis and change. Often, we do not recognize large scale change as it occurs. People living in the Middle or Dark Ages did not think of themselves in those terms. Later historians named the period because, in some historians' view, the age was in the middle between ancient Rome and the Renaissance, and it was considered dark and unlearned. This concept changed in later scholarship. Similarly, we cannot have a complete grasp of our environments today. We may be in a period of long-term stasis or change but are unable to perceive the larger dimensions of it because we are so enmeshed in day-to-day activities. And we may change our views as events develop.

Another consideration in the definition of stasis and change is the value bias implicit in each. Some people seek stasis as the good side of the continuum. They want stability; it represents familiarity and firmness. Others prefer change. They want fresh opportunities and the challenge of the unknown. Both types consider their preferred positions to be "progress." Most people favor both dimensions, desiring some stability and some change in varying amounts and at varying times.

THE STUDY OF STASIS AND CHANGE

It is much easier to be a student of stasis than one of change. Learning information that is believed to be true and everlasting is a matter of repetition and review until it is committed to memory. Trying to master information that is subject to change appears to be inefficient and frustrating. The movements of the sun and earth have been so carefully detailed that one can rest assured that if a sunrise is predicted at 6:30 A.M. tomorrow, it will occur. This information is satisfying and complete, even though we know that the sun does not really rise, it is the earth in rotation. We do not expect change in the known relation of sun to earth. Such a change would be an event of the most enormous global proportions, presaging a new ice age or boiling temperatures destroying life.

Prior to the acceptance of the ideas of Copernicus, many (not all, by any means) people believed that the earth was the center of the universe and that the sun and stars rotated around it. This belief is now known to be false, but it was taken as an everlasting fact at the time. Only the mad or heretics would challenge it. What we now accept as everlasting fact may someday be overturned, but we shun the mad and the heretics who now raise challenges. This is not to suggest that all of the challenges to what we consider static knowledge deserve attention. Every year come dire predictions that the end is near, that civilization cannot survive, that a new apocalypse is on the horizon. These predictions have (so far) failed to come true, but people often take action based on the belief that a dramatic change will occur. For them, the belief in change makes a change in their lives.

Science and religion both offer explanations of stasis and change. The scientific search for truth has contributed a set of basic laws (more correctly, theories) by which it is believed the physical environment is governed. These are subject to challenge because science believes in theories, which are subject to disproval, and not absolute laws. However, the nonscientist has no credibility in the scientific world and is considered mad to raise questions; and the scientist-challenger is usually considered heretical. Thus even science provides beliefs about the physical world that are relatively static for long periods of time. It took years for the Copernican Revolution on the relation of the earth to sun to have large-scale effect in society, as it did for Darwinian explanations of human development, or atomic theory, or Einstein's relativity theory (all of which still have scientific and nonscientific challengers) to gain acceptance. Science has tried to explain change, but usually its explanations are based upon laws, theories, or principles that are relatively static.

Religion explains supernatural ideas by reference to everlasting ideas. The Bible, the Koran, or other theological documents provide static knowledge for believers. Yet theologians continue to reinterpret these documents and to explain change in terms of new interpretations. Situation ethics provided radically different views of religious beliefs than those of fundamentalist religions. Instead of supernatural laws to govern behavior, human situations would determine right and wrong conduct.

These two often competing realms of firm and stable knowledge, science and religion, are still subject to change. But other realms, like the arts, humanities, and social sciences, are even more susceptible to change, because, in these areas, there are fewer stable laws and basic principles. Ironically, one of the most stable principles that social science (particularly the nonpsychological social sciences) has contributed to human knowledge is that society is always in a state of change. In other words, the basic static knowledge is that change is a constant. This principle applies to science, religion, the arts, history, society, and individuals.

TIMES AND PLACES OF STASIS

There are, of course, periods of time when there appears to be no change. Feudalism must have seemed the everlasting way society would be organized to those whose lives were enveloped by a feudalistic system; a Chinese dynasty must have appeared static to those who lived in the center of the period. And now, most people believe that nation-states are static as a governmental system. It is difficult to contemplate that the nation as a particular body of people could be replaced by some other political structure. Yet nationalism is a phenomenon in existence for only the last three hundred years, a short episode in human history.

There are also specific segments of a society who accept stasis as the standard. To them change is forbidden and people live by custom and tradition. The Amish in the United States illustrate this concept. The most orthodox Amish do not use technology. They farm without modern vehicles, do not have electricity, maintain horse-drawn carts, dress in uniform simple clothing, and maintain a separate existence from the continually changing society around them. Some fundamentalist religious sects adopt literal and unchanging interpretations of dogma and do not permit any change in interpretations, (e.g., literally believing that God created the world in six days).

Society is constantly under tension created by the pull of stasis and the counter pull of change. Some people define conservatives and liberals according to this tug of war. They see conservatives as wanting stability based on principles derived from the past, while liberals desire change to correct social problems created in previous times. The difference may be in the speed and direction of change. Conservatives tend to prefer more gradual change, often toward prior conditions like unrestricted free enterprise and competition. Liberals tend to prefer more rapid change, often toward the alleviation of social problems like unemployment and inequality. Radicals of the right and left prefer revolutionary change at high speed.

STASIS AND CHANGE IN INSTITUTIONS

As suggested in Chapter 1, social institutions are subject to the cultural pressures of stasis and change. They also contain internal pressures toward stability and/or modification. Schools are involved in this social battle often through the issue of what should be taught to students. Forthright sex education is advocated in some areas to stem the problems of venereal disease and teenage pregnancy. In other areas any sex education is perceived as part of a communist conspiracy to undermine the morals of American youth. Teaching evolutionary theory in science classes is challenged by some who argue for the teaching of Creationist theories drawn from Christian fundamentalist religions. A return to traditional reading instruction is advocated by the Council for Basic Education. And new pressures to have dress codes and to reconstitute rules of conduct for students in school have arisen in opposition to the student rights movement. In each of these areas external and internal pressures have influenced the outcome in the school and this, in turn, has had an influence on stasis or change in the society as a whole.

As an institution of the society, schools exhibit the general characteristics of any institution. And, therefore, many of the actions and reactions of schools in regard to the pressures of stasis and change can be understood by consideration of the general characteristics of social institutions. The following examination of institutions is not an exclusive or exhaustive explanation of institutions, but it does offer a broad analytic structure that can assist you in looking at schools and the activities that go on in them.

Since things continue to change, one can understand that institutions— either specific ones or all of them—are also subject to change. Yet there are some elements of institutions that remain static over long periods of time. It is these general unchanging elements that we will focus on now.

Identifying an Institution

We can define an institution in several ways. Often we think of an institution in terms of its physical organization. The idea of a prison, for example, suggests a particular location, cells, walls, guards, inmates, and a set of organized rules of conduct. Thinking of a hospital usually conveys an image of a building, doctors, nurses, patients, and equipment in an organized system. And army stimulates the idea of a camp, soldiers, parades, and a hierarchy of organization. Certainly, many institutions can be defined as physical and organized.

There are many institutions, however, that are not physical or organized in the form that prisons, hospitals, and armies illustrate. Marriage, democracy, and certain patterns of behavior that are traditional and usually expected in a society are also institutions. These institutions have physical and organized aspects, but they are also composed largely of mental and perceptual segments. We behave according to some traditional—and institutional— patterns because we believe in them. For example, in Western culture the use of a plate, knife, fork, and spoon is part of expected and traditional behavior. These utensils are institutionalized in Western societies as part of a perception of etiquette and manners.

Every institution has some physical and some mental elements. Families consist of people, but they also incorporate many of the traditional behaviors and viewpoints within a society. So we are expected to treat parents with some respect; to exchange family greetings with certain relatives we may never have met but not with strangers; and to accept some activities in a family we would not accept outside it, such as lying and deception.

We can define *institution*, then, as any construct, organization, beliefs, or being that has become identified with an historically expected set of purposes and behaviors. An institution is something that is recognized by large segments of the society. Keep in mind that we are not speaking here of individual institutions, like a particular high school, but of general categories of institutions.

THE CHARACTERISTICS OF INSTITUTIONS

Another useful way to define an institution is in terms of its characteristics. Although many characteristics could be used to describe an institution, several are generally accepted as basic to an understanding of them. These are (1) utility; (2) actors; (3) organization; (4) share in society; (5) sanctions; (6) ceremony, ritual, and symbols; and (7) resistance to change. Each of these characteristics will be discussed at length below.

UTILITY   The first characteristic of an institution is that it has *utility*; that is, it has a purpose and it does something—it has a function. Prisons, for example, are supposed to restrain criminals and they do engage in a variety of activities to fulfill that social purpose. Schools are supposed to teach literacy and they do in general accomplish that purpose.

Functions or utility, however, can be either manifest or latent. *Manifest functions* include those overt, generally accepted purposes and activities that the institution is supposed to perform. They are the most obvious, visible aspects of an institution. What are school supposed to do? Teach, of course. That is their manifest function.

Latent functions include those purposes and practices that are not as obvious and generally understood. These are the hidden portions of the institution: the hidden agenda, the hidden curriculum. The latent functions of an institution are often performed more effectively and more pervasively than are its manifest functions because they are seldom under scrutiny. School understood as a baby-sitting activity, whose function is to take care of children while their parents do other things, is an example of latent utility. People don't recognize baby-sitting as one of the stated, manifest purposes of school, yet if a district decides to alter the starting time of its schools by only fifteen minutes, parents will react immediately, less because of the effect it has on their child's education than because it might affect the parents' schedules.

ACTORS   A second characteristic of an institution is that it has actors whose role is to carry out the functions. The *actor* is anyone (or anything) who has a position, role, or assumed status in an institution. An actor is normally considered to be anyone who is actively fulfilling some part of the manifest or latent function of an institution. Thus a salesman is expected to be engaged in selling, a student in learning, and a police officer in enforcing the law. There are, however, some inactive actors who hold assumed positions. One example would be the deceased owner of a business whose painting hangs in the board room and whose business views still direct the discussions of executives: "What do you think Mr. Inglenod would have done about this transaction?" Another example of a nonlive actor would be a computer, which is the primary actor in a computing center and which influences the behavior of other actors.

Actors as individual personalities are usually not as important to institutions as how that personality affects the position the actor holds. A school administrator who has a compulsion for excessive neatness and quiet is likely to issue rules and evaluate teachers on the basis of that compulsion. The neurosis may be individual, but it will have an influence on the institution.

ORGANIZATION   A third characteristic of an institution is that it has some form of *organization*. There is always some describable pattern of relationships among the actors. As with functions, there are manifest and latent organizational systems. We are most familiar with the manifest organization of institutions. Most of you will have seen an organization chart, clearly showing the hierarchy within a corporation—who is in charge of what and who reports to whom. The military is another good example: the president is commander-in-chief, followed by the Joint Chiefs of Staff, the generals and lesser officers, on down to the newest recruit. Decisions are supposed to be made at the higher levels and carried out at the lower. The latent chain of command, however, is less obvious and often far more effective. For example, a corporal who types out orders and keeps records may have much more power than his manifestly senior sergeants and lieutenants. In schools, custodians and secretaries are often sources of the greatest influence and information. A principal who seeks advice from a custodian, who has been at the school for years and whose brother-in-law is on the school board, is using the latent organization of the school.

Another factor important to the organization of an institution is *atmosphere*, or *climate*. Institutions seem to have a particular ambience setting them apart from other institutions, even ones that are similar. Schoools have common elements, but each school will have an atmosphere peculiar to it. What teachers think of the school and of each other; what students expect teachers to do; what principals think parents or the superintendent want are included in the informal organizational climate.

Brookover et al. found that differences among school climates had an influence on a manifest function of schools, the academic achievement of students.[1] School climate was measured by such factors as student sense of academic futility, perception of teacher expectations, and teacher perceptions of academic futility. A school climate that provided more class time in actual instruction was associated with higher achievement. And group rather than individual competition was more common in higher achievement schools.

SHARE IN SOCIETY   The fourth characteristic of an institution is that it shares sets of values, ideas, and attitudes dominant within the society. Institutions, then, do not exist separately, in a vacuum, but as part of a greater society. Institutions are interrelated with each other in a variety of ways. The school is related to the political and economic systems in a community, a county, a state, and a country. On a larger scale, schools are related to a culture through language, forms of knowledge, and beliefs.

Schools are also related to other institutions. Schools prepare doctors, nurses, and clients for medical practice. Business institutions often want to keep school costs down to save taxes but want schools to prepare well-behaved employees and consumers. Schools take on commitments like driver's education and sex education when the sentiment of society is that other institutions, like the family, can no longer do it effectively.

A set of core values and ideas permeate each institution. These are drawn from the world view of the culture, and usually include views on human nature, justice, equality, and morality. In practice this usually means that the dominant values and ideas are transmitted uncritically. In the schools, for example, we transmit values about capitalism, patriotism, evil behavior, and social protocols often without permitting critical analysis. The uncritical transmission of cultural values through schools has, in fact, been challenged by many writers. The general public view, however, is that that is just what the school is supposed to do—inculcate cultural traditions without raising questions.

SANCTIONS   A fifth general characteristic of an institution is that it is *sanction bearing*, that is, it has the ability to reward or punish actors. If an actor is defined as a misfit or misbehaving, a punishment can be imposed, ranging from a death penalty to such things as confinement, fines, withdrawal of privileges, or ostracism. If one behaves according to the institution's rules, there are rewards. The rewards may be money, prestige, honor, freedom, or the opportunity to participate in decisions.

The ability of an institution to apply sanctions is related to its sharing of societal values. A punishment or reward is evaluated for fairness by social as well as institutional standards. A teacher will not be put to death for refusing to recite the Pledge of Allegiance, but he or she is likely to be punished by reprimands or derogatory comments. Sanctions are used in institutions to produce conformity and control. A deviant actor will be negatively sanctioned at a moderate level to stimulate conformity to institutional norms. If that is not successful, increasingly harsh sanctions may be used, up to the point where the deviant is expelled.

In schools, sanctions are widely available: picking class monitors, giving grades, smiling or admonishing, putting exemplary papers on the board, ridicule or applause, suspense or honors, expulsion or graduation. For teachers, sanctions can come from administrators, board members, parents, other teachers, and students.

CEREMONY. RITUAL, AND SYMBOLS   A sixth characteristic of the institution is that it has ceremonies, rituals, and symbols which have meaning to the actors. A *ceremony* is a formal action that is recognized as conveying some status, knowledge, or value. Graduation is an example. A *ritual* is the standard process for conducting the business of the institution. Bureaucracies often operate on the basis of ritual behavior. And *symbols* are those signs or emblems that represent aspects of the institution. The title, principal, is a symbol of office; a school flag or motto is another symbol intended to represent the school.

Ceremonies, rituals, and symbols are ways to express social status and to convey sanctions within an institution. A dunce cap or the detention room is a symbolic means of applying a sanction and showing loss of status. The orientation of new students to a school is a ceremony that intends to express the values of the school, its rules, and the status of the different actors within it. A student sent to the office for misbehavior undergoes rituals in giving a form to the vice-principal's secretary, sitting on the bench, and being questioned by the vice-principal. The teaching certificate that licenses you to teach in your state is a symbol of status and is the result of rituals and ceremonies.

RESISTANCE TO CHANGE   The last characteristic of an institution is that it resists change. By its nature and establishment, an institution becomes self-justifying and reluctant to make dramatic alterations. There is a status quo orientation in an institution that is difficult to overcome. The institution was established for certain social purposes, has survived by doing things in certain ways, and the actors fear major disruption in that process. An institution tends to be conservative and self-protective.

At the same time, all institutions undergo change — as is true in society. And social change can create institutional change. War and depression stimulate change in institutions. Public criticism of the schools for being too rigid and authoritarian was part of the shift to open education. The criticism of open education contributed to the more recent back-to-basics movement in the schools. Member actors of institutions can also create change. A dynamic new executive may have significant impact on a major industry. A strike by teachers may change the schools. Student protest can alter school rules.

Institutions that undergo rapid growth or decline are more likely to engage in change activities to accommodate, though there is a tendency to try to keep the change superficial and limited. There are attempts to keep the traditional actor's roles, rituals, symbols, and sanctions, no matter what the situation.

Analyzing Institutions

The preceding overview of the general characteristics of institutions is meant to provide a way for you to better understand the working of the school in American society. You might consider taking the analysis a bit further: ask yourself the following questions about each characteristic, applying them to a specific school you know.

1. Utility: Which purposes and practices in the institutions are manifest? Which are latent?

2. Actors: What major and minor actors can be identified? What roles do they play?

3. Organization: What are the formal and informal organizational patterns? Who has power?

4. Share in Society: How does the institution reproduce or change dominant social values? How does the society affect the institution? Are there any deviations?

5. Sanctions: What are the rewards and punishments in the institution? Who gives and gets them?

6. Ceremony, Rituals, Symbols: What significant ceremonies, rituals, rites of passage, and symbols are evident? How do they work?

7. Resistance to Change: What indicators show that change is difficult to achieve within the institution? How does change seem to occur?

If you take the time to answer these questions as concretely and fully as possible, you should come to understand the institution of the school in a way that differs from your memories as a student. While for the purposes of this book, the school is the focus of our inquiry, and we have offered examples from practices in the schools to illustrate its characteristics, these questions, of course, may be applied to the analysis of any institution you may have interest in studying.

FOR CONSIDERATION

1. How would you define stasis and change? Provide some examples.

2. Using the seven characteristics of institutions identified in this chapter, describe the following institutions, using examples:

   Prisons
   Hospitals
   Military
   Your family

3. Which of the characteristics identified was most difficult to apply? Which was easiest? Why?

Note

1. Wilbur Brookover *et al.*, "Elementary School Climate and School Achievement," *American Educational Research Journal* 15 (1978): 301–318.

References

Bennis, Warren; Benne, Kenneth; and Chin, Robert. *The Planning of Change*. New York: Holt, Rinehart and Winston, 1969.

Brookover, Wilbur, *et al.* "Elementary School Climate and School Achievement." *American Educational Research Journal* (1978): 301–318.

Brown, Richard. *Knowledge, Education and Cultural Change*. New York: Barnes & Noble, 1973.

Fabun, Don. *The Dynamics of Change*. Englewood Cliffs, N.J.: Prentice-Hall, 1967.

Gordon, C. Wayne. *Uses of the Sociology of Education*. NSSE Yearbook. Chicago, Ill.: University of Chicago Press, 1974.

Karier, Clarence. *Man, Society and Education*. Glenview, Ill.: Scott, Foresman, 1967.

Martindale, Donald. *The Nature and Types of Sociological Theory*. Boston: Houghton Mifflin, 1960.

Nelson, Jack L., and Besag, Frank P. *Sociological Perspectives on Education*. New York: Pitman, 1970.

Wells, Alan. *Social Institutions*. New York: Basic Books, 1971.

Chapter 3: The History of Schools in American Culture

Inheritances

An understanding of our culture and of our schools depends in part upon knowledge of their pasts. The culture that is—for good or for bad—dominant in America is, as cultures generally are, the product of a long heritage. In the same way, most of the features of our schools have been inherited from a variety of historic origins. The history of our culture, of its generally shared values, beliefs, knowledge, and skills, has been in many ways a history of change. Our schools have changed in organization, in method of instruction, and in what has been taught. But, paradoxically, their history has been in another way a history of stability, of stasis, of lack of change.[1]

A distinctively American culture appeared when men and women began to think of themselves as "Americans" in the mid-1700s, somewhat more than two hundred years ago, after 150 years in which American culture had been in the making. Although schools were a part of American culture from its beginnings, they did not reach their present form until roughly a century and a quarter ago, some time after 1850.

COLONIALS, AMERICANS, AND THEIR WORLDS:
THE BACKGROUND FOR STASIS

Our culture came into being before our schools. It was not begun anew but incorporated elements of older cultures. Some elements of American culture came from the shared culture of Europe. One of those elements dated from the European Renaissance. In Europe in the fifteenth and sixteenth centuries, Renaissance scholars had rediscovered the knowledge, wisdom, and beauty of classical Rome and Greece and had become convinced that civilization would be reborn after, what they considered to be, centuries of dark ages and medievalism. (Renaissance translated means "rebirth.") A part of that heritage had never died in Europe, but the classics were re-emphasized at this time. Early manuscripts of classical authors were searched out. Erasmus and others had removed accumulated errors from the earliest Greek texts of the New Testament. Builders reintroduced classical motifs, columns, and domes into architecture. Sculptors turned from medieval to neoclassic presentations. In the formative years of American culture, classical knowledge, knowledge of the ancient world, was valued highly. Its language, Latin, was the language of the "well-bred" man (but not woman). Esteem for classical learning has lessened, but it still continues in American society. One of our national mottoes, *e pluribus unum*, "out of many, one," is in Latin. Our first secondary school was the Boston Latin Grammar School, where Latin was the curriculum. Public buildings still echo classical motifs, and such place names as Utica, Athens, and Syracuse echo classical history. Certainly, the schools still reflect Renaissance ideas and a European culture. We think of ancient history as Greek and Roman, not as Indian or Chinese, and we stress European ideas more than we do Asiatic. All of these cultural ideals reflect stasis and are past oriented.

Another pervasive and important part of the general European culture incorporated and shared by the colonists was the experience of the Reformation. Martin Luther, John Calvin, and others had said convincingly that unquestioning acceptance of the Roman Catholic Church did not guarantee salvation and that each person must undertake his or her own salvation. The history of the Reformation and Counter Reformation is a history of the strength of religious conviction. Even in the 1600s men and women died for their faiths. The first settlers were far more religious than are most of us now. The imminent possibility of being forever damned was most fearful. As Protestants, they believed that salvation, if it was possible at all, could come only from personal faith, knowledge, and judgment. It could not be gained without reading and studying the Bible. Therefore, salvation depended upon literacy. The Puritan Congregationalists of New England believed in this most strongly, although the Virginia members of the Church of England were only slightly less Protestant and less puritan. These were not the beliefs, naturally, of the Catholics living in the few and scattered settlements to the south.

THE PROTESTANT ETHIC   The colonists also brought with them what historian-sociologist Max Weber called the "Protestant ethic." Demonstrably not solely Protestant and in many senses not an ethic, the Protestant ethic is a set of interrelated values and needs, which includes a need to excel by diligence and hard work, the acceptance of delayed gratification, and seeing thrift as a virtue. Benjamin Franklin, that prototypical American, put the last into a pithy maxim in *Poor Richard's Almanac:* "A penny saved is a penny earned." The impact of the Protestant ethic may have lessened today, but for many of us it is still strong.

At the beginning, settlers brought with them parts of the culture of England. Most obviously, they brought with them the English language, which superseded Dutch in New Amsterdam, French in New Orleans and Saint Louis, and Spanish in Sante Fe, and, of course, often superseded the languages of Native Americas, the American Indians. There are Americans who do not now speak English, but they live on the margins of the prevailing culture of America. English-made iron ax heads made the first inroads into the forests. English tradition decided the size and shape and ownership of fields. Settlers brought with them English conventions of dress, according to gender, age, and station. They also had knowledge of a more formal sort, knowledge of medicine and of the natural sciences. Some of that knowledge may today strike us as quaint, for instance, the idea that migratory birds spend winters on the moon, which was accepted knowledge in the seventeenth century.

There were also parts of English culture and society left behind. The rich or noble English gentleman of leisure had no need to come to the colonies, and the colonies had no need of him. Some English gentlemen who did come to Jamestown starved, we are told, rather than work. The influential Englishman occasionally came as a government official, but he did not stay for long. At the other extreme, although some of the poorest Englishmen did come to the colonies as indentured servants, they were less likely to come than were Englishmen of the "middling sort." The very poor as well as the very rich were underrepresented in the English-speaking colonies, and society was consequently more egalitarian than that in England. Colonial societies tended to be more personalistic, and esteem and status tended to depend more upon the individual's worthiness than upon his occupation and post.

America Becomes American: The Inheritance of Change

The new American culture owed its uniqueness to a variety of influences. For Puritan New Englanders one link was cut early, when Cromwell's Puritan Revolution was ended in 1660 by the restoration of the King of England. The frontier with its cheap or even free land limited the economic, social, and political advantages in England that wealthy estate owners had. The unskilled laborer was better paid in the colonies, and often became a land owner himself. Further, almost from the beginning, other Europeans settled in the colonies: Netherlanders in New York (once called New Netherland), Germans in Pennsylvania, Protestant Scotch-Irish in Pennsylvania, and southward along the Appalachians, natives of every European nation. Blacks were first imported in 1619 and in great numbers after 1700. The other newcomers brought with them additional skills. For example, the technique of building the American log cabin was contributed by the Swedes. Crops, Indian corn the most important of them, came from Native American cultures.

A few seaports grew into cities, which became centers of a budding culture. There were subscribers for newspapers there, and customers for book stores, even listeners for musicians, and ideas for all. Vessels sailing coastwise and stage coaches made travel from colony to colony less difficult. Postmaster Benjamin Franklin directed an efficient postal system. Englishmen in the homeland less often made the distinction between, say, a New Yorker and a Pennsylvanian but saw the colonies as a unit. British laws, British taxes, British troops, and the Revolution provided common grievances and then common enemies. It is true that even after the Revolution some thought of themselves as, for instance, Virginians first and then Americans. But they were Englishmen no longer.

Even now, of course, American culture has ties with European cultures, and for a considerable time, those ties remained very strong. Far into the 1800s English authors were most avidly read here. Fashions in art, architecture, and dress followed European fashions. Distinctively American Hudson

River Romantic painting emerged almost by accident. Distinctively American architecture appeared only as designs were accommodated to American skills and materials. American social thought was shaped at the end of the 1700s by that of French revolutionaries and would be influenced later by Englishman Charles Darwin, German Karl Marx, and Austrian Sigmund Freud. Well into the 1800s science in America was little more than imported European science, although there were the usual exceptions in the scientific accomplishments of a very few, including Franklin, and in the American talent for practical inventions. In the twenty years after the Revolution more Americans went to European universities than before. But the continued tie to Europe is a qualification. America had an emerging culture of its own.

That culture was one which present American culture still very much resembles. Americans were materialistic, hoping and working for material possessions and wealth. They sacrificed today for the sake of tomorrow. They were "boosters," promoting their cities, counties, and states, and their own business enterprises. Compared with Englishmen of their time they were egalitarian, that is, democratic.[2] So while much of European culture was adopted without change into the young and growing American culture, we were, by the eighteenth century, in an environment that required change — the adaptation of European culture to fit distinctly American needs.

EARLY SCHOOLING

By the later 1700s there was a recognizably American culture, but there was not yet a recognizable system of schools. The standard pattern of schooling in America has emerged only in the last century and a quarter. There was no such pattern in early America.

As Englishmen the colonists were accustomed to schools, although schools were not for everyone, not even for everyone who would learn to read. Many boys attended Latin grammar schools; of mature New England men in 1645, perhaps one family head in twenty attended a university. Most of these attended Emanuel College of Cambridge University, since Emanuel was the most Protestant part of Cambridge, and since Cambridge was more Protestant in sympathy than Oxford, the other English university. Given the custom of educating young men in the home country, the recreation of England's schools in the new colonies was a matter of course.

There was an additional and most important consideration that furthered stasis — religion. To repeat, the Protestants of the 1600s strongly believed that nothing should come between the individual and the word of God, the Bible. Therefore, learning to read aided in salvation, if salvation were to be possible. But not all of the immigrants were members of Puritan churches, and only roughly half the children learned to read. Those who did learned at home, or in what was called a "dame," "petty" (little), or "reading" school, usually tuition supported, often taught by a woman in her home. Reading was taught from single printed pages, sometimes mounted on paddlelike boards and called hornbooks or battledores. There were also "primers," from which children learned the names of the letters and their sounds and rhymed alphabet verses and prayers. A Massachusetts act in 1642 required that children be taught to read; the famous "Olde Deluder Satan" Act of 1642 (so children could "delude Satan" by learning to read the Bible) required the establishment of schools, but not that they be public schools. Neither act required that children attend school.

The Boston Latin School was established in 1635, only five years after the establishment of Boston itself. As we now think of schools, Boston Latin Grammar School was a secondary school. Students were not admitted until they had learned to read. Much of their six years there was devoted to learning Latin, and most of the rest of it to learning Greek, from the same books that had been used in English schools. Latin grammar schools were for boys only. (Beyond instruction in reading there was little formal schooling for girls.)

About two dozen Latin grammar schools had been established in New England by 1689; there were also Latin grammar schools in Virginia, New York (rather briefly), Pennsylvania, and in several other colonies. There was no uniformity in their sources of financial support; it came from taxes, endowments, rents, tuition and fees, and gifts. The Latin grammar school masters usually taught for a few years before going on to the ministry or another occupation. Ezekiel Cheever, who taught for seventy years, the last thirty-seven of them at the Boston Latin School, was a rare and laudable exception.

The first college in colonial America, Harvard, was established in 1637. The first forty-seven graduating classes averaged only a little over eight students each. All subjects were compulsory, and most of the students' time was spent on the fine points of Latin and Greek. Instruction was in Latin. Religion was taught Saturday mornings and church attendance was compulsory, though, in keeping with the times, there was beer for breakfast. Arithmetic and geometry were subjects for seniors. Students attended Harvard because a classical education was still valued or considered gentlemanly or because they planned to enter the ministry. The second college in America, William and Mary in Williamsburg, Virginia, was not chartered until 1693.

In more than a hundred years schooling in America, of course, changed. In the mid-1700s "Great Awakening" evangelists preached of the dangers of hell, and Americans taught of these dangers in schools. Reading schools used the *New England Primer*, which after a page of alphabet began: "A: In Adam's fall/We sinned all." The Latin grammar schools, or at least some of them, continued to operate, but accumulated wealth and property made it possible for some parents to employ private tutors and governesses. Academies, private secondary schools where practical subjects and English rather than Latin were taught, made their first appearance. In the cities private owner-operated schools, some of them at night, taught an endless variety of practical and "decorative" subjects—penmanship, bookkeeping, surveying, navigation, fencing, and even guitar playing and dancing. New colleges, generally attached to religious denominations, also appeared. Great changes in schooling were taking place, and these were occurring more and more rapidly. Change had really come to American education.

Jeffersonian Democracy: Schooling for Americans

The American Revolution was in many ways a conservative one—the goal was independence but not other political or social changes. However, there were short-term dislocations. School masters—one of whom was Nathan Hale—were killed, and Loyalist masters hid or fled. Yale students left New Haven in fear of starvation. The Revolution also had longer-term effects. A new American needed new school books to teach American patriotism and American ways. The most widely used were Noah Webster's "Blue-Back Speller" (1783), of which tens of millions of copies would be sold, and Jedidiah Morse's *Geographies* (1784). (*McGuffey Readers* would not appear until 1836.) Naturally, patriotism could be taught through use of geography books. Webster's spelling books, and later his dictionaries, taught an American, not British, language (and incidentally contributed to the compulsion for correct spelling). Even an arithmetic book could teach patriotism: "The capture of General Burgoyne and his army happened in the year 1777, that of Cornwallis in 1781; how many years between these two events?"[3] Here is a patriotic example from an eighteenth-century elocution book:

> Columbia, Columbia, to glory arise,
> The queen of the world and child of the skies;

Thy genius commands thee, with raptures behold,
While ages on ages thy splendors unfold. . . .[4]

Of course, the child who had thoroughly mastered the school books of that day had learned much more than patriotism and the Protestant morality that seemed to accompany it. "Blue Back Spellers" taught Webster's standardized American spellings and pronunciation, Morse provided copious information about the United States and the world, and arithmetic books went as far as proportions.

Two Englishmen, Joseph Lancaster and Andrew Bell, developed the "monitorial," or "Lancastrian," school just before 1800. Pupils called "monitors" taught other less-advanced pupils. Skills and knowledge were divided into bits; for instance, recognizing and writing the perpendicular letters, *I, T, H,* and so on would be one task, or reading a single page from a dismembered primer. A monitor heard recitations. A monitor tested and promoted the pupils. A monitor took attendance. The master taught only the most advanced monitors and was the administrator of the school. Pupils competed for prize badges, medals, and candy. The monitorial school was popular in the United States during the early 1800s, because it was cheap and many pupils could be taught at one time. It was a logical form of instruction if pupils were the children of the poor and was successful if the instruction was coherent and valuable. The first assumption, that the pupil was poor and sinful, helped shape the student's role in later schools. The second, the subdivision of learning, would underlie later conceptions of mass production in the schools. Both assumptions are still with us to some degree, although the monitorial schools had disappeared in the United States by about 1850.

COLLEGES AND ACADEMIES

Although the academy had appeared before the Revolution, it was not popular until nearly 1800, when academies replaced nearly all the Latin grammar schools, and provided schooling for a wider variety of pupils. In the 1800s there were perhaps 6,000 academies, most of them small and short-lived. As we now think of such things, an academy was a private secondary school, usually associated with a religious denomination. There were Methodist academies, Quaker academies, and so on. Ideally the academy had an endowment. Actually nearly all academies were supported by tuition, as colleges were and to an extent still are. They offered an endless array of subjects, practical and ornamental, from the elementary to the college level. Their students usually boarded in houses nearby. Because they needed students, academies were responsive to the wishes of both students and parents. At best, they were an early analogue of alternative schools, although their opponents, the supporters of public schools, did not think of them in that way; rather they saw them as endangering public schools. Public high schools brought the academies to near extinction by the early 1900s.

Colleges also multiplied, from 1 in 1637 to 3 in 1700, 9 in 1776, and by 1860, 182. Other colleges failed, but their number is difficult to estimate. College students, in the college tradition, lived in the college under the control of paternal presidents, usually ministers, who were responsible to boards of trustees composed of laymen. College courses of study, also traditional, were largely classical, although mathematics and science were introduced more frequently than historians had thought. There were other new departures from tradition. Union College in Schenectady, New York, introduced French and American history, and then in 1829 a "parallel course of study" of science, modern languages, and mathematics. In the 1830s Union had more students than all but one or two other colleges. One reform that failed was George Ticknor's, who tried too soon to introduce German university rigor at Harvard, and in his discouragement resigned. In general, however, the colleges were conservative and small.

SCHOOLING FOR "FEMALES"

The republican spirit after the Revolution led to the establishment of academies, or seminaries, for "females," to use a term then popular. The first small female academies appeared before 1790. In New Haven, Connecticut, one of them was taught by geographer Jedidiah Morse. A later more important one was Joseph Emerson's academy in Byfield and Saugus, Massachusetts. The next logical development was of academies operated by women for women. In 1792 Sarah Pierce became principal of a female academy in Litchfield, Connecticut. One of its alumnae, Harriet Beecher Stowe, established girls' academies in Hartford, Connecticut, and in Cincinnati, Ohio, before she went on to greater fame and success as the author of *Uncle Tom's Cabin*. Zilpah Grant, who had already taught in country schools, attended Emerson's academy and became principal first of Adam's Female Academy in Londonderry, New Hampshire, then of Ipswich Female Seminary in Ipswich, Massachusetts. Emma Willard's female seminary (or academy) at Troy, New York (1821), and Mary Lyon's Mt. Holyoke seminary in Massachusetts (1836) would become the first colleges for women. Lyon had attended Emerson's academy and had taught with Grant at Ipswich before establishing her own seminary.

In spite of these developments, the provision of more than elementary schooling for girls was sporadic during at least the first half of the 1800s. The intent of this education was different, too. Schooling for boys was intended to make them good citizens and successful in their work; schooling for girls was expected to prepare them to be the helpmates of men and the mothers of boys who would be in turn civic minded and successful.

Jacksonian Democracy: Schooling for the Common Man

America was now truly ready for change, leaving many European traditions behind. Between Andrew Jackson's election as president in 1828 and the beginning of the Civil War in 1861, American public elementary education was "revived" in New England and firmly established in all but the Southern states. The "Common School Revival," as it was called, was, however, only one of many reform- and change-oriented movements that occurred during this period. For the first time, voting became the right of nearly every white male, which may have led to Jackson's election. There were reforms of other institutions—prisons, reformatories, and insane asylums. The same enthusiasms led to the building of utopias. Robert Owen's New Harmony in Indiana and the thirty-odd "phalansteries" established according to the theories of François Fourier were collectivist and socialistic. The Mormons' Salt Lake City was a most successful religious utopia. There were many other religious sects, most conspicuously the Millerites, sure the end of the world would come in 1843. Still other reformers were nonreligious, among them, the vegetarians, peace crusaders, enemies of "demon rum," feminists, and those most important reformers, the abolitionists. Zeal for reform was inspired by Romanticism, which was expressed in the literature, art, architecture, and Transcendental philosophy of the time. The Romantics believed in the individual above all, in the importance of his environment, in his worth, in his malleability, and perfectibility. Reform of the common school was only one major reform in an age of reformers, an age of change.

The first transformation of the United States aroused both anxiety and zeal. Canals, turnpikes, steamboats, and railroads had revolutionized transportation, which made profitable markets for farmers, merchants, and manufacturers. America was still rural, but cotton mills were already employing thousands, and industrialization was casting its shadow before it. Cities doubled in size every decade. Factories pulled from Europe the first floods of immigrants.

There was much in need of reform, and much to arouse anxiety. That anxiety came at the time of the religious reawakening. Although in the 1790s most college students had declared themselves atheists, in the 1820s college students attended revival meetings, then gathered together to pledge themselves to missionary work.

It was in this atmosphere that the role of the teacher was formed, and that the Common School Revival occurred. Before the Common School Revival, the colonial master, and his (at least ostensible) knowledge of the classics, had already been replaced by the teacher. The teacher had a calling, like the missionaries of his time. He—less frequently she—was to be an example of goodness and Godliness for his pupils. He was not to expect worldly rewards (which was to say that he should not complain because his salary was meager). He was to be expert in the knowledge and teaching of the "common branches": the three R's, spelling, geography, and maybe history. The gentlemanly knowledge of the classics was discarded and humbleness commended.

The Common School Revival took place in the same atmosphere. It was undertaken by the "friends of education," of whom Horace Mann of Massachusetts was most prominent. There were many others, including Henry Barnard of Connecticut (the first scholar of education), Calvin Stowe of Ohio (husband of the author of *Uncle Tom's Cabin*), Ninian Edwards of Illinois, and John Swett of California. Mann, a native of Massachusetts, was a lawyer. Before being appointed secretary of the new Massachusetts Board of Education in 1837 and becoming in fact state superintendent of schools, he had been a state representative, state senator, and president of the state senate. After his superintendency he became a leading abolitionist. Puritanical, compulsive, eloquent, and enormously energetic, Mann was a reformer both by conviction and by nature. For twelve years he wrote, spoke, debated, and edited in behalf of the public schools. He gave thousands of addresses. His twelve annual reports are bulky, small print volumes.

According to Mann the schools were to be improved by improving teaching, establishing state normal schools for teacher preparation, extending courses of study, improving school houses, and gaining community support. As advocate of the public schools Mann argued that they would right every wrong, turn away every danger, protect the rich against rebellion, rescue the poor from poverty, reduce crime and sin, even improve health. Schools were to be the cure-all, the "great panacea."

Of course there was opposition. The school masters of Boston fought every attempted reform. In Illinois an opponent of the schools said, "A human being may know how to read, and yet be a very stupid fellow. . . . Reading and writing are not magic arts; of themselves, they are of little value . . . and thousands of individuals with diplomas in their pockets are far inferior, in point of common sense and information, to the common run of backwoodsmen."[5]

At first schools were housed in cramped, dirty, cold, unsuitable places: in the cellar under a city market, in a long abandoned adobe mission, in a sawmill mess hall, in a log shed formerly a stable, in a rented house. Too many teachers were no more than elementary school graduates, and some were less than that. The "friends of the schools" were nevertheless successful, so successful that their accomplishments eventually would be taken for granted. That success did not come quickly or easily, but state superintendencies were established, normal schools organized, pupils won away from academies and other private schools, teacher qualifications somewhat improved. The number of unschooled children was reduced. In 1853 Massachusetts passed the first compulsory education law, although it only applied to child factory workers. The public schools were an idea whose time had come.

Because the schools had many different advocates and because many groups were to be won over, the purposes of the revitalized public schools remained blurred and unfocused. To gain support for the schools, Mann and other friends of education had made extravagant claims and promises. The schools had been oversold. In the future, public hopes would be frustrated, and the public schools burdened with tasks that were either inappropriate or for which there were insufficient resources. Nevertheless, by the time of the Civil War, there were public, tax supported schools in every state outside the South.

Schooling, however, was not for all. Immigrant Catholics were stigmatized, and many of them opted for schools operated by their church. In the South before the Civil War, teaching Black slaves to read was unlawful. Even in the North, there were segregated "African" schools for free Blacks, or none at all. When postelementary education for Blacks did appear after the Civil War, it was often largely vocational. What school existed for the native Americans was also vocational and "civilizing" in a way that made those pupils who returned to their tribes unable to readapt to their own culture. Probably fewer than twenty Blacks and American Indians had graduated from college before 1850. (It is to be added that a very few others, such as mathematician

Benjamin Bannecker, were nevertheless learned.) Secondary schooling for women was rare in 1800, as was college for women in 1850. In these ways schooling perpetuated inequality rather than reducing it. It really offered few opportunities for advancement and upward mobility. All in all, schooling for the disadvantaged was depressingly like that set up by imperialist powers to control their colonial subjects.

Centralization, Systemization, and Stasis

In the most general way, the centralization of control of the schools and their systemization was a consequence of changes in American technology, society, and culture. These had brought into being factories, often smoke belching, often dirty, often dangerous. The first major industrialization had been in the spinning and weaving of cotton, then of other textiles. Later factories grew up all across the United States, producing a thousand things for which there was a market, from mowing machines to cigars, from tableware to bathtubs (or at least a few bathtubs). The factories, and packing houses, had jobs, especially for unskilled workers. Immigrants came, millions of them, at first from Western Europe but later from the shores of the Mediterranean and from the lands of the Russian czars and the emperors in Vienna. They, especially the ones who arrived later, seemed very different to the old, established Americans. They spoke strange languages, wore strange clothing—babushkas, sombreros, yarmulkes—ate strange foods—borscht, enchiladas, knishes. A few of them even had strange and radical political beliefs. They practiced different religions. Some were Russian Orthodox, others were Catholic, still others were Jewish; few of them were Protestant. They lived with their own kind and seemed not to even want to be like others. To be succinct, they came from other cultures. But desperate as they were to establish themselves in this new culture, they would work for pennies and, therefore, could be easily exploited. Because the jobs were there, most of them settled in the swelling cities in slums, living in poverty and filth. The immigrants seemed not only strange but threatening. To the dominant classes, the traditional culture was in danger. To protect and accommodate it, new forms of schooling and school organization, which would maintain tradition and support stasis, were thought necessary.

Each of the old-fashioned, generally one-room country district schools was governed by public officials. That is, each school had its own feoffees, selectmen, trustees, or boards of education. In effect, the government of the schools at this time somewhat approached participatory democracy, through arrangements Michael Katz has called "democratic localism." For example, from 1824 until 1842 many New York City schools were governed by the New York Free School Society, made up of wealthy men who contributed their time in what Katz has termed "paternalistic volunteerism." Other such men participated in "corporate volunteerism," serving as trustees of private nonprofit academies, which were supported by gifts and endowments. But in the city's district neighborhood, schools were supported by unequal, unfair property taxes, and local board members seemed "not the best sort."[6] The New York Free School Society did provide schooling cheaply and without administrative costs, but it had the serious drawback that the schools for the poor were not controlled by the poor.

Each of these possible forms of school government had flaws that at the time seemed to outweigh its virtues. Corporate volunteerism was unsuccessful if for no other reason than that there was much more demand than benefaction. School reformers believed that centralization would speed reform. Their admiration for the schools of Prussia, which were centrally controlled, may have been a factor. The government of the schools, therefore, was centralized, rationalized, and bureaucratized. At the same time schooling was in many ways standardized.

SCHOOLING IN THE CITIES

Centralization, rationalization, and bureaucratization were the outcome first of city growth. City school enrollments grew enormously, faster proportionately than did the cities themselves. In Chicago, the fastest-growing city, public-school enrollments multiplied by 427 times between 1840 and 1890. Part of the growth was due simply to increases in Chicago's population, from 4,500 people in 1840 to 1,100,000 in 1890. But much of the growth in enrollments resulted from other causes. Schooling seemed to parents more important and, therefore, a larger proportion of children attended school and attended school for longer. The schools' potential clientele also increased as schooling was offered for both older and younger pupils. The first Chicago high school was opened in 1852, and kindergartens became part of the Chicago school system in 1892. Starting in 1854 there were classes to teach immigrants English, and beginning in 1865 night schools were opened for children who worked during the day. After 1852 Chicago had a "normal department" to train and supply at least some of the system's new teachers. The first vocational, "manual training," high school was opened in 1892.[7]

As many cities grew and their societies became more complex, the city fathers found it desirable for the city governments to assume control of services and to centralize control of them. Ward watchmen were replaced by city policemen; volunteer fire companies, which sometimes fought each other instead of fighting fires, were replaced by municipal fire departments and paid firemen. In some cities publicly owned water mains replaced private and neighborhood wells. Nearly all cities eventually provided public sewer systems. These changes were intended to improve service, to attract new residents, and to make the cities more pleasant — and, of course, more prosperous. To some extent the city school systems arose as a result of this booster spirit. The centralized, rational administration of the railroads, the first big businesses in the United States, may have provided a precedent for centralization of the schools. Possibly the army also did, although the army was itself a slow learner in matters of command and staff organization.

The centralization of control of the schools, and the replacement of numerous district boards by a central one, demonstrably had the effect of seating school boards whose members included proportionately more business and professional men and fewer from lower status occupations. It is quite possible that this made the school systems stronger supporters of middle-class values and of the status quo, which protected them.

As school systems grew larger and more complicated, there was greater need for control and coordination of their various parts. The increase in the division of teacher labor contributed to this aim. The most important and clearest example was the grading of the elementary schools, which made feasible teaching the class as a whole and reduced disciplinary problems in the primary grades. But the corollary was a need to coordinate, to assure, for instance, that second-grade pupils began in their readers where they had left off as first graders. Chicago Superintendent William Harvey Wells had graded the Chicago elementary school by 1861. His *Graded Course of Instruction with Instructions to Teachers*, first published in 1862, described carefully what was to be studied and learned in each grade, and it was used in many cities. (In the book there was also a series of essays on education and teaching, surprisingly liberal and progressive for their time. But those got far less attention.)

Since the time of Joseph Lancaster at the end of the eighteenth century, and even before then, influential educators had been convinced that there must be one simple best way of teaching, if only it could be developed or found. (This particular old and hurtful assumption unfortunately still survives.) There must be a best way of designing school buildings, a best way of grading schools, a best way of teaching reading. This conviction of the existence of a best way was a bastard offspring of eighteenth-century Enlightenment thought and belief in progress, and greatly appealed to Americans, with their penchant for practicality. The late-nineteenth-century version of this belief was a dedication to the grading of the schools, which was largely carried out by the superintendents of the nation's schools. These men knew of each other's schools and of each other's work. Many superintendents, for example, attended the Department of Superintendence's annual wintertime meeting and the meetings of the National Education Association, held each year the week of July 4. City superintendents' reports, bulky, copious things, were widely circulated. By 1890 both the schools and courses of study had been largely systematized. A few years later every pupil would read *A Tale of Two Cities* in ninth grade and graduate from high school only after three years' study of Latin. School books were graded, too, and largely standardized. City courses of study were made mandatory for the surviving country schools. Pupils were assigned to grades there, too. The cost there was a standardizing of instruction, without the compensating advantage of group instruction.

THE INDUSTRIALIZATION OF EDUCATION

It may be said that schools *are* like factories and that superintendents *are* like businessmen. This is a proposition from which testable hypotheses can be derived, to be proved or disproved. It may also be said that schools *should be* like factories and that superintendents *should be* like businessmen. This is a judgment, which is not immediately testable and, even in the long run, testable only by its consequences, whether good or bad.

That schools *should be* like factories and superintendents *should* be like businessmen was often said in the early 1900s. But this proposition was not new. A hundred years before, Thomas Jefferson, for all his rural preferences and democratic convictions, had been impressed by the first factories he saw in France. A contemporary writer saw monitorial schooling as "a new machine of immense power . . . rival to . . . the greatest acquisitions of mechanical operation."[8] To another writer at the time, "every boy seems to be a cog in the wheel—the whole school a perfect machine,"[9] and still a third wrote that "the principle of schools and manufactures is the same."[10] Teachers were sometimes referred to as "operatives." Factories had excited imaginations, and Lancaster applied the analogy to his school.

Even when monitorial schools were still popular, the industrialization of America, with its factories and division of labor, was making apprenticeship obsolescent as a method of occupational training. To repeat an example used in the early 1800s, if apprentice hatters spent all their time stirring vats of soaking felt, then they could not learn to make hats. The apprentice system, therefore, was used much less often. This process of industrialization led to changes in other areas of education as well, as educators concluded that schools should prepare children for factory work. William Torrey Harris, then superintendent of schools in Saint Louis and later U.S. Commissioner of Education, believed in this goal. In 1874 he and a coauthor wrote that "military precision is required in the maneuvering of classes. Great stress is laid upon (1) punctuality, (2) regularity, (3) attention, and (4) silence . . . for successful combination with one's fellow-men in an industrial and commercial civilization."[11] Whether or not one agrees with Harris, his dictum did accord with the realities of the time.

The years between 1900 and 1918, roughly, were the Progressive era, a time when many reforms were undertaken to gain effectiveness, honesty, and economy in government. Big corporations charged with monopolistic practices were brought to court. It was also a period of reform in education. John Dewey, then at the University of Chicago, developed the concepts and philosophical base for what came to be called "progressive education." However, its impact on American schooling was less than that of measures pushed by those Progressives most interested in efficiency and economy. Efforts to improve the schools along these lines were greatest after 1910.

Why school superintendents seized upon business management and efficiency then has been speculated upon by many. It did serve to increase their power more rapidly. It may also have allowed them to identify themselves more closely with the business magnates then so much admired. Some, undoubtedly, were simply swayed by the general enthusiasm for maximizing efficiency. For others it was protection against their vulnerability to the wrath and power of their school boards. At least a few, as in every calling, were simply opportunists.

BUSINESS MANAGEMENT IN THE SCHOOLS

A "business" and a "factory" are not the same, of course, nor are they run by the same principles. There are interconnections, but, if we are to understand developments in the schools in the early nineteenth century, it will be profitable to deal with business management methods separately. Management is oversight, choosing goals, distributing resources, and setting tasks and rewards. It may be by the owner, as was often true of the cotton plantations in the South or of the Mississippi River steamboats. That was satisfactory enough if the enterprise was not too large and if coordination was not called for.

The first elaborated management systems in the United States were the railroads. By 1860 there were ten railroads in the United States capitalized at $10 million and five for nearly twice that. For the period they were huge enterprises. Each railroad operated hundreds of miles of tracks—a freight train derailed in Buffalo, New York, could delay the arrival of passengers in Boston. In 1847 the Baltimore and Ohio adopted a new mangement system, with departments and lines of authority carefully defined, and the Erie Railroad adopted a refined version in 1855. Staff officials could be added as needed. This was the organizational pattern the Union army would emulate, and which perhaps was responsible for its victory over the less effectively organized Southern forces.

Stockholders know that the first purpose of a business is to make a profit, which can best be accomplished by keeping receipts high and expenses low. The earnings of a school or a school system are not in dollars, but its expenses are. Therefore, the businesslike management of a school was aimed at reducing its expenses. The first devotee of dollar savings was Frank Spaulding, superintendent of schools in Passaic, New Jersey, and then Newton, Massachusetts, who delivered an address on the matter as early as 1909. At the National Education Association convention of 1913 he spoke again: ultimate school earnings were unmeasured, but there was measurable "immediate outcomes," costs per unit of instruction. He had started by investigating the costs of coal for heating, which was greater for some school buildings than for others. He discovered, too, that some schools, the larger ones, had cost more to build per pupil. He applied the same method to determine the cost of school instruction on a per pupil per recitation basis:

> . . . I know nothing about the absolute value of a recitation in Greek as compared with a recitation in French or English. I am convinced, however, by very concrete and quite logical considerations, that when the obligations of the present year expire, we ought to purchase no more Greek instruction at the rate of 5.9 pupil-recitations per dollar. The price must go down, or we will invest in something else.[12]

For Spaulding, business management was economical management, management for cheapness. He allowed no other considerations, and he was respected and was successful.

EFFICIENCY IN THE MACHINE SHOPS   At the Philadelphia Centennial Exposition of 1876, a hundred years after the Revolution, American-made machines were the most interesting and most impressive of any on display. They were the best performing and most powerful in the world. British visitors were deeply impressed, even though England had been the home of the Industrial Revolution. At a minor display in the exposition's Machinery Hall, apprentice Frederick W. Taylor showed the industrial products of the manufacturer who employed him. Taylor was destined to make machinery still more productive and to make men perform like machines.

Taylor was at the same time prissy and profane, a prickly man difficult to work with and still more difficult to like. He was a misanthrope and, in his own neurotic way, a genius. The son of a prosperous Philadelphia lawyer, he had attended a famous New England prep school and then, pleading eye strain as a way not to go to college, had become a machine shop apprentice. In the machine shops of Midvale Steel, whose owner was interested in improved production techniques, he undertook the improvement of metal cutting machines.

He experimented quite capably with lathe speed, depth of cut, and almost a dozen other variables. Machining time was greatly reduced, and the experiments replaced craftsman know-how with that of the engineer. The engineer's know-how was replacing that of the craftsman, and the lathe hand became at most a semi-skilled worker; the work was to be planned by an engineer. Production was so speeded by Taylor's developments that a new shop management plan and much better and more detailed cost accounting became necessary.

Taylor was also interested in increasing the output per worker. If one assumed that the worker's motivation (and value) were only money, the worker could be thought of as no more than a money-driven machine. As another efficiency expert wrote in 1913:

> On a punch press costing $3,000, the yearly cost, on a basis of ten per cent for depreciation and five per cent for interest on the investment, would be $450.
>
> The operator of this machine would probably be paid $3 a day, a total of about $900 a year. . . . The only apparent difference is that the machine is paid for in advance, while the labor is paid in weekly, bi-monthly, or monthly installments.[13]

Like any other machine the worker could be readjusted. He could be trained, in somewhat the same way a computer is now programmed. The most famous man-as-machine was a laborer who Taylor called Schmidt. He was instructed in finest detail how to load iron ingots into freight cars:

> . . . [Y]ou will do exactly as this man tells you tomorrow, from morning until night. When he tells you to pick up a pig [ingot] and walk, you pick it up and walk, and when he tells you to sit down and rest, you sit down. You do that right through the day. . . ."

Schmidt started to work, and all day long, at regular intervals, was told by the man who stood over him with a watch, "Now pick up a pig and walk. Now sit down and rest. Now walk now rest," and so on. "He worked when he was told to work, and rested when he was told to rest. . . ."[14]

Schmidt was so well instructed that he loaded 47 tons of pig iron a day into a freight car, instead of the 12½ tons a day he had been accustomed to loading. His pay was increased $.60 a day to $1.85. Republic Steel had employed Taylor to increase profits, of course, and this he did.

EFFICIENCY AND MODERN SCHOOLING   The idea of efficiency had great public appeal. The word had long had positive connotations, but now, thanks to Taylor and others like him, it had a concrete means of attainment. Efficiency would aid in thrift, an old American value. In this setting it had an air of machines about it, and Americans were, as Americas still are, lovers of machines and gadgets. To many of the reform-minded Progressives, time efficiency was a "social invention," one more increment of social progress. Efficiency was popularized beginning in 1910, when Progressive Louis Brandeis brought efficiency experts to testify at an Interstate Commerce Commission's rate hearing. Newspapers covered the hearings at length, and there was a flood of articles on efficiency in popular, widely read magazines. One technology bibliography for the following year listed 219 entries under the heading "efficiency." The principles of efficiency, often misunderstood, were applied to every human endeavor, sometimes quite inappropriately. There was, for example, a small literature on the efficiency of churches, fully as ridiculous as one might suppose. Soon, as you might imagine, the concept of efficiency was applied to the schools. An educator writing of schools used the terms of efficiency engineers:

> *Definite qualitative and quantitative standards must be determined for the product. Where the material is acted upon by the labor passes through a number of progressive stages from the new material to the ultimate product, definite quantitative and qualitative standards must be determined for the product at*

each of those stages. . . . The worker must be kept up to standard qualifications for this kind of work during his entire service. [Italics in source.][15]

The child was the "material," the school's graduate was the "product," teaching was the "labor," the teacher was the "worker." The author was Dr. John Franklin Bobbitt, instructor in education at the University of Chicago. The quotation is from a 1913 yearbook of the National Society for the Study of Education, an organization of great prestige.

The efficiency of school systems could be judged by school surveys, which became fashionable at this time. (They were also effective public-relations devices.) The efficiency of schools would be judged by rating and by the achievement tests that were being developed. The potential of the child as material would be measurable a few years later by group IQ tests. The efficiency of teachers would be judged by the use of rating forms. There was some confusion among raters about what teachers should do and what teachers should be, but teacher rating nevertheless became all but universal. Bobbitt and others adapted machine shop job analysis to curriculum design. Curriculum development by that method was seen as a kind of engineering, beginning with exhaustive description of the task to be accomplished. The curriculum designer was to matter of factly describe what was, while maintaining a proud disinterest in what should have been. There was a list of 1,243 traits of good citizenship, for example, in one study Bobbitt directed. In a study upon which teacher-education sequences were to be based, exactly 1,001 "teacher activity statements" were compiled. As far as we know, no curriculum based upon this list was put into use. You should keep this in mind when looking at recent listings of "teacher competences," which seem if nothing else to demonstrate that "those who forget history are condemned to relive it."

THE ENDURING EFFECTS Business management and factory efficiency together had a variety of effects; they may even have made the schools more efficient. They became the basis of the prominent and long careers of Ellwood P. Cubberley, George D. Strayer, John Franklin Bobbitt, and others. They did shift the role of the school administrator, particularly of the superintendent, making him more businesslike (and hence, plausibly, more nearly an equal of businessman board members and community leaders). Presumably they saved the jobs of a few particularly vulnerable superintendents. Clearly, as Callahan has said, it diverted administrators and professors from the greater concerns of education.[16]

School administration was more centralized, or at least centralized more rapidly, in keeping with business practices. Administration acquired specialties of its own: finance, evaluation, even "child accounting" (attendance record keeping, but note the borrowing of business terminology). It became more businesslike, much more concerned with expenditures and budgets. Certainly the role of the teacher was constrained in the sixty years or so beginning with Harris's superintendency and continuing through the 1920s. The role of the pupil was further depersonalized.

A side effect was the strengthening of research and of the science of education. Educational research has its roots in the prior work of G. Stanley Hall, one of the American founders of psychology; Joseph Meyer Rice, onetime physician and reformer in the 1890s; and Edward L. Thorndike, developer of quantitative educational research methods. But efficiency and educational research were mutually supporting. One of the primary early concerns of the researchers was measurement, first because efficiency studies required measurement but also because measurement was one of the general scientific concerns of the time. So Albert A. Michelson had been the first American to win a Nobel prize, awarded for his measurement of the speed of light. Alfred Binet's method of measuring mental age (and hence IQ) was speedily imported from France and put to use in the schools. Normed achievement tests appeared in large numbers and considerable variety. Systematic evaluations were improved; we might almost say that improved measurements made them possible.

One drawback is that the press for efficiency predisposed educational research toward too great a concern with improving instruction in conventional school subjects, rather than a concern for underlying principles.

But we need not strike a final balance as to the contributions of business management and efficiency. What must be noted is that there were costs as well as gains. Even those generally critical of the conventions of school administration must concede that schooling could no longer be managed out of a superintendent's derby, or even out of his buggy boot. The enterprise had grown too big, too complicated for that.

New Deal to Great Society

At the beginning of the Depression in the fall of 1929, an era of business management ended as general confidence in business was eclipsed. In the depths of the Depression about 30 percent of all workers were unemployed. In some places the rate was higher: 40 percent in New England cotton-mill cities, 60 percent in East Saint Louis, Illinois, a Midwest railroad and meat-packing city. It was only after the election of 1932 that Franklin D. Roosevelt's "New Deal" took shape, which sought to aid the unemployed and impoverished, thus offsetting the social and economic impact of the Depression and opening the second reform era of the twentieth century. The New Deal precedent was that government should and would protect Americans against misfortune and adversity. That was an unparalleled shift. At the time, educators discussed building a new social order through the schools, but the schools were really only marginally involved in the New Deal.

Assuming that most pupils would have menial jobs or no jobs at all, educators proposed that schooling prepare pupils for low-income menial jobs, or for unemployment, by "Life Adjustment Education." In the early 1930s intellectuals generally expected a revolution and radical changes in society. A few influential educators, most of them at Teachers College, Columbia University, shared that belief. They felt that Roosevelt's New Deal reforms were trivial, and that far more general reforms were in order. Their most forceful spokesman was George S. Counts. His most widely noted argument was titled with a rhetorical question: "Dare the Schools Build a New Social Order?" The implication was that they should. Counts's influence may be responsible for the current assumption by some educators that social change should be one of their first concerns.

The Depression ended when the coming of war in Europe produced demand for American products, agricultural and manufactured, and for munitions and weapons. The United States entered World War II on December 7, 1941, Pearl Harbor Day, when the Japanese bombed the United States naval base in Hawaii and destroyed much of the United States' Pacific fleet. It is clear that the Depression, and World War II, which created more than enough jobs for all, produced a fundamental shift in American society and in the distribution of wealth. The rich became comparatively less rich; the poor, though still too numerous, were less numerous than before. Generally, the years after the war were prosperous. Demand for new homes, applicances, automobiles, and television sets and luxuries fueled prosperity, with only occasional lulls.

SCHOOLS FOR EXCELLENCE

World War II had increased America's respect for science and infatuation with technology. Science and technology gained further support during the cold war, when the United States felt increasingly threatened by Russia's rise to power. In the face of the Russian threat, there was a pressing need for excellence, for preparing scientists and engineers-to-be to defend their country, develop new technology, and aid in space exploration.

Life Adjustment Education was obviously inappropriate. What was needed was schooling for intellectual superiority and schooling for pupils who would be prepared to serve as the technologists of industry and of national defense. Admiral Hyman Rickover was a prominent and more or less typical critic of schooling at the time. After all, US atomic submarines could not be operational without technologists to design, build, and man them. Although the demand for education for excellence has not ended, it was most vocal and most influential during the fifties. One response was the development of new curricula, at first in mathematics and the sciences, by scholars rather than by teachers and other educators. There were summer programs for retraining teachers. New curricula, or at least new courses of study, appeared in most other fields. There were appropriations, modest at first, for research intended to increase the effectiveness of schools.

Before 1890, inventions were frequently the result of trial and error, and production increased largely by ingenuity. But scientific discoveries, at first relating to electricity, began to reveal the practical aspects of "pure" science, that is, theoretical science. By World War I, scientists were making major contributions—the development of flight and radio communication—and had a direct effect on the outcome of the war; during World War II, their contributions—the development of the atomic bomb and radar, among others—were crucial. Most of the pure research that resulted in these developments was undertaken at universities. After the war, such research became essential not only for defense efforts but for peacetime uses as well. Higher education had acquired a new function in the economy and in the culture, and the years after World War II were times of high prestige for science, scientists, and universities.

However, by the 1960s many people began to view science as a threat rather than as a promise. Dr. Strangelove, the mad and amoral scientist of the motion picture, became a pop symbol of evil. Opponents of science and advanced technology read with approval *The Greening of America*. The subsistence farm (abandoned a century earlier) became a hope. Concern for the education of scientists faded.

SCHOOLS FOR EQUALITY

With some exceptions, schools before the 1950s were segregated, either by law (*de jure*) or in fact (*de facto*). As early as the period after the Civil War

(1861–1865), some radicals had attempted to secure for Blacks schooling, the right to vote, and the end of racial discrimination, but their efforts were unsuccessful. The Supreme Court's *Plessy* v. *Ferguson* decision in 1896 held that segregation by race was constitutional. *Plessy* v. *Ferguson* was superseded in 1954 by *Brown* v. *Topeka* and subsequent Supreme Court decisions declaring racial segregation unconstitutional. But compliance with school desegregation decisions was slow. In 1957 the Arkansas National Guard was called out to prevent even nominal desegregation of a Little Rock, Arkansas, high school, although later the same year federal troops were brought in to enforce desegregation. In 1963 Governor George C. Wallace of Alabama attempted to prevent Blacks from registering at the state university. Throughout the 1970s and into the 1980s there were, and are still, all-Black public schools, especially in Northern cities, and nearly all-Black and all-white colleges and universities across the country.

A third era of reform was begun during the presidencies of John F. Kennedy and Lyndon B. Johnson. Johnson's "Great Society" attempted to bring to an end social and racial biases and discrimination. New laws protected voting and other civil rights, and the legality of residential segregation was ended. VISTA, a group composed of volunteers who worked in schools in depressed neighborhoods, was established, as was Head Start, a preschool program to prepare disadvantaged pupils to overcome cultural differences. Federal funds were appropriated for the first time to aid schools, especially schools with large minority and poverty-level pupil enrollments. As amends for past wrongs suffered, schooling for Blacks was to be compensatory—through Head Start and also through curriculum adjustments and special college admission services and procedures, such as affirmative action. The common thread in these reforms was the restructuring of the schools so as to restructure society and thus aid the dispossessed. This was the plan of Johnson, a one-time teacher, and a part of the dream of Martin Luther King. The schools, as Counts had wished in the 1930s, were to be a chief agency to reform society.

Looking back, it can be said that these measures were no more than partly successful. Segregated housing, long after it became illegal, still existed. The first Head Start programs seemed ineffectual. Equal job opportunity is difficult to achieve; equal pay for equal work is still unachieved. But there have been some gains. Larger numbers of Blacks do enroll in colleges, and larger numbers of Blacks have entered the professions. The middle-class Black community has been substantially enlarged.

SCHOOLS FOR FREEDOM

The efforts of Great Society reforms were blunted by United States involvement in Vietnam. The role of the United States in the Vietnam War was, even seen most favorably, a tragic error. Critics say it was criminal. During the war, the draft, compulsory military service, was bitterly opposed. That opposition, which was primarily voiced by the young, was joined by another thrust in the realm of education—the thrust for freedom.

Freedom as a goal of education, resting in part on faith in the innate virtue and potentiality of the individual, has been praised since Jean Jacques Rousseau's novel *Emile* was published in 1762. During the sixties, much was heard about freedom in education from diverse and sometimes eloquent writers. Edgar Z. Friedenberg wrote about the diminishment of freedom in *The Vanishing Adolescent*. A. S. Neill, longtime English schoolmaster and apostle of Sigmund Freud, described his school founded on freedom in *Summerhill*, a book that became as prominent as his earlier books had been obscure. American schools, the persuasive argument ran, mirrored American society, which was enormously constraining and damaging to the rights of the individual. Schools were cluttered with rules that were oppressive and which would have been unconstitutional if applied to adults. Dress codes, compulsory courses, and compulsory attendance were understood as infringements upon liberty. On college and university campuses students demonstrated against suppression of free speech, against the war, against the autocracy of administrators, against the draft. In high schools dress codes were abandoned or abolished. The number of required courses was reduced in high schools; in colleges they were sometimes nearly abolished. Students became members of what had been all-faculty committees at many colleges and universities. Courses—even on such intellectually disreputable topics as astrology—were offered to meet student interests.

The search for freedom led to what were called "free" schools, lamentably short-lived generally, and to communes. Flower children in search of freedom and love migrated to San Francisco's Haight-Ashbury and to the drug culture that flourished there. Free schoolers and flower children were really tiny minorities, although conspicuous and fascinating. Their impact was far greater than their numbers would have suggested. Unfortunately, the nature of some quests for freedom too easily led to the self-absorption and narcissism that Christopher Lasch described in 1979 and which led others to write of the "me" generation. The ebbing of prosperity made jobs seem more important and freedom seemed less so.

The urge for reform, for equality or for freedom, had its limits. At the polls conservative Richard M. Nixon defeated liberals Hubert H. Humphrey and George McGovern. Jimmie Carter's presidential administration was without the reforming intention of the New Society, and Ronald Reagan's administration was conservative in intent. Public devotion to equality and freedom seemed to have waned. Lasch wrote that public concerns had been replaced by private ones, that the intellectual impetus for reform had ended, and that public confidence was lacking.

A Summing Up: The Last Fifty Years

Over the last fifty years, the society has attempted to use the schools for social and cultural change. But it is now more certain than we had thought that schools by themselves or as agents of government are unable to produce sudden changes in culture. The limits of schooling in affecting the reconstruction of society are painfully obvious after witnessing the failure of the Great Society to implement its plans for social change. Most of the college and university demonstrators of the late sixties and early seventies have by now come to the same conclusion—the schools, even if they had been transformed, could not have transformed society. Counts's question of the 1930s, "Dare the schools build a new social order?" now seems purely rhetorical, if as evidence strongly suggests, they cannot. This has been a saddening, disillusioning experience for some educators.

We may turn then to a more general question. How successful have the schools been in other ways? But that question can only be responded to by other questions: By what standard? Compared to what? And the answers are somewhat disheartening, though not entirely bleak.

Compared to the hopes of idealists and idealistic reformers, the schools have been the most dismal of failures. They have done far less than was dreamed, far less than was hoped for them.

Compared to the expectations of the public, too, they have accomplished less than was expected. Perhaps this was particularly obvious in the days of the Great Society, but it has been true generally.

Nevertheless, compared to the schools of a hundred or of fifty years ago, the schools are successful, more successful than ever before. They have perpetuated the best in American culture as well as the worst. At the very least, they have attempted to serve an ever-broadening clientele and have been instrumental in widening the distribution of knowledge. As adjuncts for spreading of technology, they have been far more successful than could have been forseen. Universities have functioned in a similar capacity, that is both generating and distributing knowledge.

The schools have sometimes been discussed as if they are independent of all else. They are not nor have they ever been, of course. The schools have been shaped by the culture of which they have been a part, as they have been both more and less than mirror reflections of it. The schools are best seen within the context of culture, as shaped by the values, beliefs, knowledge, skills, and customs of their time and place.

Although the schools are a part of American culture, they do not and have not simply echoed that culture for a number of reasons. In some senses the schools have had subcultures of their own; their own organization, and sometimes their personnel, make change and adaption slow and difficult. Schools have their own traditions and their own entrenched interests, and ending them has sometimes been difficult. The schools have incorporated, perpetuated, and strengthened roles—of pupils, of teachers, and even of administrators. Nevertheless, the schools have changed in response to cultural changes: handwriting is less thoroughly taught now, for perfectly good and apparent reasons. When society has become more nearly equalitarian, schools and their curricula have been shaped for wider ranges of pupils. However, national politics has had little effect upon schooling, although there have been rare, interesting, and informative exceptions to the generalization, perhaps the most conspicuous of these being Lyndon Johnson's effort to create the "Great Society." Wartime has resulted directly in short-term belt tightening and teacher shortages, but the Civil War and World War II, especially, reshaped society, which in turn reshaped schools. Above all, schools have changed when the public mood, the temper of the times, or *Zeitgeist* has changed. Some feel that the Black riots and student uprisings at the end of the 1960s marked such a change, but it is still too soon for the historian to be convinced. Possibly the election of 1980 marked an opposite change in the direction of stasis, but here also, it is still too soon for the historian to have an informed opinion.

For those in school today, there are inherited roles, constraining even if less constraining than formerly. The child too often is still seen in the ways children were in the days of the monitorial schools—as without learning, without knowledge, without personality, and in need of charity and of Christian, or idealistic, reform. Nor has the teacher's role changed much from the way it was first formulated. He or she should be obedient but commanding, the exemplar and model to be copied, but is not entitled to much material reward. These roles, especially if not consciously considered, can badly inhibit, can imprison, can be static.

Schools are almost—not quite—impervious to intentional change and resistant to improvement. At a guess, this is due in all likelihood to interlocking, interacting roles and patterns of organization. The almost unshakable one classroom—one teacher, cell-like separation of teachers, the expectancy of teacher compliance, lack of teacher authority to make decisions, lack of information and perceptiveness where authority is centralized—have, in combination, brought the schools nearly to rest on dead center. But, as Philip Jackson has pointed out, the schools *have* changed, even though slowly and over long periods. Schooling is more practical. Less rote learning is called for; more learning is by doing. Punishment plays a smaller part; corporal punishment has almost been abolished. Schools are, even if the darker view is taken, less inhumane than they once were, giving us hope that more positive change is feasible for the future.

FOR CONSIDERATION

1. Select one period in the educational history of the United States, and explore the theme of stasis and change. Look for cultural influences on the schools. Indicate how cultural change or stability affected schools during your chosen period.

2. How has the concept of the "well-educated person" changed in the United States? What changes have occurred in the curriculum? What expectations of dress, manners, and teacher-student protocol have changed?

3. Visit a school to observe the idea of efficiency. What indicators would you use to describe it? What examples of attempts at efficiency did you observe? What examples of inefficiency were observed? How did efficiency in the school seem related to effectiveness?

Notes

1. For a more detailed historical account and further references, see H. Warren Button and Eugene F. Provenzo, Jr., *History of Education and Culture in America* (Englewood Cliffs, N.J.: Prentice-Hall, 1983).

2. This view of the forming of American culture follows that of Daniel J. Boorstin, *The Americans: Colonial Experience* (New York: Random House, 1958).

3. Daniel Adams, *The Scholar's Accountant; or the Federal Accountant* (Keene, N.H.: John Prentiss, 1810), p. 22.

4. Caleb Bingham, *American Preceptor* (Boston: Manning and Loring, 1799), p. 3.

5. James Hall, *Western Monthly Magazine*, I (1833):51. Quoted in Robert P. Howard, *Illinois* (Grand Rapids, Mich.: William B. Eerdmans, 1972), p. 173.

6. The landmark "revisionist" treatment of school organization is Michael B. Katz, *Class, Bureaucracy and Schools* (New York: Praeger, 1971, 1975).

7. Mary E. Herrick, *The Chicago Schools* (Beverly Hills, Cal.: Sage, 1971), *passim*.

8. John Foster, *Essays on the Evils of Popular Ignorance* (London, 1821), quoted in Carl F. Kaestle, *Joseph Lancaster and the Monitorial School Movement* (New York: Teachers College Press, 1973), p. 12. Kaestle is an excellent source for material on the monitorial schools.

9. *Edinburgh Review*, 9 (October 1806), quoted in *ibid*, p. 12.

10. Thomas Bernard, *Of the Education of the Poor* (1809), quoted in *ibid*, p. 12.

11. William Torrey Harris, *Seventeenth Annual Report of the Board of Directors of the St. Louis Public Schools* (1871), pp. 31–32.

12. Frank Spaulding, quoted in Raymond E. Callahan, *Education and the Cult of Efficiency* (Chicago, Ill.: University of Chicago Press, 1962), p. 73. Callahan's is the first and most important study of the introduction of business management and industrial methods into the schools.

13. Irving A. Berndt, "The Value of a Dollar's Worth of Labor," *Efficiency* (September 1913):13.

14. Frederick W. Taylor, *The Principles of Scientific Management* (New York: Harper & Brothers, 1912), quoted in Callahan, *Education and the Cult of Efficiency*, pp. 37–38.

15. Franklin Bobbitt, *The Supervision of City Schools: Some General Principles of Management Applied to the Problems of City-School Systems*, Part I of the 12th Yearbook of the National Society for the Study of Education (Bloomington, Ill.: n.p., 1913), pp. 11, 79.

References

Adams, Daniel. *The Scholar's Accountant; or the Federal Accountant*. Keene, N.H.: John Prentiss, 1810.

Bingham, Caleb. *American Perceptor*. Boston: Manning and Loring, 1799.

Bobbitt, Franklin. *The Supervision of City Schools: Some General Principles of Management Applied to the Problems of City-School Systems.* Twelfth Yearbook of the National Society for the Study of Education, Part I. Bloomington, Ill.: n.p., 1913.

Button, H. Warren, and Provenzo, Eugene F., Jr. *History of Education and Culture in the United States.* Englewood Cliffs, N.J.: Prentice-Hall, 1983.

Callahan, Raymond E. *Education and the Cult of Efficiency.* Chicago: University of Chicago Press, 1962.

Cremin, Lawrence A. *American Education: The Colonial Experience, 1607–1783.* New York: Harper & Row, 1970.

Friedenberg, Edgar Z. *The Vanishing Adolescent.* Boston: Beacon, 1959.

Herrick, Mary J. *The Chicago Schools: A Social and Political History.* Beverly Hills, Calif.: Sage, 1971.

Howard, Robert P. *Illinois.* Grand Rapids, Mich.: William B. Eerdmans, 1972.

Jackson, Philip. *Life in Classrooms.* New York: Holt, Rinehart and Winston, 1968.

Kaestle, Carl F. *Joseph Lancaster and the Monitorial School Movement.* New York: Teachers College Press, 1973.

Katz, Michael B. *Class, Bureaucracy, and Schools.* New York: Praeger, 1975.

Neill, A. S. *Summerhill, A Radical Approach to Child Rearing.* New York: Hart, 1960.

Lasch, Christopher. *The Culture of Narcissism: American Life in an Age of Diminishing Expectations.* New York: Norton, 1979.

Tyack, David B. *The One Best System: A History of American Urban Education.* Cambridge, Mass.: Harvard University Press, 1974.

Section Two: Models for the Analysis of Schools

S ection I introduced the basic themes of the book: statis and change, the major characteristics of institutions, and the social history of education. These provide background for the study of contemporary schools.

Section II offers five different models to use in analyzing schools. Some of the models contradict others. This is to be expected, since the models were not designed from the same perspective. The purpose here is to present a number of different models that can be useful in analysis of the school and education in different circumstances. For example, the Marxist model is an historical-alienation model, while the Hall model is an anthropological model. Although both could be used side by side, they investigate different types of institutions and analyze different variables. It is up to the reader to determine which model best fits a specific situation. Moreover, there are other models that could have been chosen for this book. Some may have been more graceful or more complete. However, we attempted to use those models that have seemed to be the most useful in the analysis of the school.

Each model provides a lens through which the purpose and practices of schools can be observed and understood. They are not presented as established truth; rather, they are offered as analytic tools to help obtain the most informed picture of what goes on in and around schools. They are applications from different theories to the practice of schooling. Experiment with each of them as a way of gaining insight into the schools you attend, the college you now attend, or your educational workplace.

The models, in order of presentation in this section, are based on the work of the following theorists:

1. Marx — to examine the school as an alienating process.

2. Guba and Getzels—to examine the school as an administrative institution with its impact on individuals.

3. Goffman—to examine the school as a semitotal institution.

4. Scheff—to examine the school as a labeler.

5. Hall—to examine the school as a cultural entity.

A Word About Flow Charts

In each of the models chapters, there are one or more flow charts that are designed to describe the way individuals move through institutions or the outcomes of interactions between institutions and individuals. Flow charts are used to give global pictures of relationships and inter-relationships in models and to describe graphically the way in which individuals pass through systems and what happens to them along the way.

As with any other picture, however, while it may be worth 1,000 words, it is still an oversimplification of the situation. These flow charts picture the way the model would describe the institution if the model exactly described the real world. That is very rarely the case. So, while these flow charts help us to understand the theory, they do have the danger of presenting the models in a simplified and ideal fashion. Flow charts are pictures and pictures help but do not completely describe. A written description accompanies each flow chart.

Within the flow charts themselves, symbols are used. Questions are contained in rectangles with pointed sides. Statements and decisions are contained in rectangles, and entrances and exits are contained in circles. Answers to questions are included on arrows which go from one cell to another. If an "or" appears on an arrow, it indicates that more than one alternative is possible. If an "and" appears on the arrow, it indicates that the statements at both ends of the arrow apply. For example, if institutional goals are in one box and institutional means are in the next box, and both have to be used for a third statement, the arrow would point from the goals to the means and an "and" would appear on the arrow. In most cases, the arrows will have either nothing written on them, indicating a forced choice, or will have "yes" or "no" written on them.

If you follow the arrows from cell to cell, you will have a graphic representation of the way in which individuals with particular characteristics proceed through institutions with particular characteristics.

Chapter 4:
The School
as a
Source of
Alienation

There are a number of conditions that differentiate this chapter from the other chapters in Section Two. While the other chapters deal primarily with how the institution maintains stability (stasis), this chapter presents a model of how institutions, and thus schools, change. Also, while the authors of the theoretical formulations presented in the other chapters are modern, this chapter is based on the works of Karl Marx, particularly *The Economic and Philosophic Manuscripts of 1844* and *The German Ideology*. Although the original formulation is 125 years old, the Marxian construct is one of the most important in the twentieth-century world, because half the world views Marx as a god and the other half views him as a devil. Both are wrong.

It is unfortunate that Karl Marx is known primarily as the father of Communism rather than as the social analyst he was. For as the father of Communism he is either defended or attacked on the basis of his economic theories. Marx was not a pure economist at all. He was an alienation theorist. His theory was that capitalism and assembly-line work breed alienation, while socialism and collectivism breed feelings of worth. According to Marx, the assembly line separated workers from their work — products of their labor — and he was interested in bringing workers and their work back together again. Both defenders and attackers of Communism miss the point that Marx and

Engels were among the first sociologists who systematically looked at society and its institutions as the causal factors in the behavior of individuals. They argued that "man is made by history, not history by man."

In recent years a number of scholars have rediscovered the value of Karl Marx as a social analyst. In particular, there has been a surge of educational theorists who have used a Marxian analysis to discuss the schools in relation to such factors as socioeconomics, hidden curricula, hegemony, and social reproduction. Although these factors are all very important, this chapter will deal specifically with the Marxian construct of alienated workers and how institutions can and do increase or decrease alienation. We will be defining the student or teacher as a worker on an assembly line and the school as the factory.

In this chapter five constructs are presented: (1) the essential construct of all Marxian theory that the history of a society or institution determines the behavior of all its member actors; (2) the alienated worker; (3) the construct of the ruled versus the ruling classes; (4) the construct of spheres of influence; and (5) the effect of the assembly line on people.

The Concept of History

In the Marxian construct of history, historical antecedents not only affect but are actually part of the present society. Each generation adds new constructs and new behaviors to the historical antecedents of previous generations and thereby adds not only to the history of the society but also to its present and future existence and store of behaviors. History is a continuous process affected by many influences.

Marx was the first really modern sociohistorian. He was the first to view history not as part of a dead past but rather as part of the living present and the future. Most nineteenth-century historians agreed that the past had an influence on the present, but Marx took the concept much further. In Marx we see history as a concept of change. Every historical event is a source of change in both the present and the future, and that change is personal as well as societal and institutional. We as individuals are shaped and changed by the institutions around us. Basically Marx would say that if we want good people, then we should have social settings that generate good people.

We are, in Marx's construct, not personalities that have formed ourselves, but rather, we are entities that have been formed by the institutions of which we are members. For example, many educators are fond of saying that if we could only have good teachers then we would have good schools, and are even more fond of saying that if we could only have good students then we would have good teaching and good schools. Marx would say that both statements are nonsense. In the Marxian construct, if the school is having trouble with the teachers or the students, it is because the school as an institution generates that type of teacher and that type of student (for example, a punitive school will have punitive students). The students don't make the school; rather, the school makes the students.

In brief, the Marxian construct of history is not the idle study of the past but the study of the effect of social institutions on people in the present. History molds a society, institutions, and individuals rather than the other way around. This is not to imply that individuals have no influence on their surroundings, for certainly they do, and Marx believed that individuals should influence their life conditions. However, the Marxian construct places the burden of present history not on individuals but on the society and institutions.

One thing must be admitted, Marx's construct is unsatisfying in that it does not place sufficient emphasis on the role of the individual. We, particularly those of us still tied to the Protestant, nineteenth-century, Victorian ethic, want to believe that each day we are getting better and better and that we are in control of our present and our future. That the past has an influence on us is quite clear and generally agreed upon. However, when we move to the influence of the present and the future, we Western Europeans and North Americans are not nearly so willing to accede to the Marxian construct. We have always been apt to try to control the present and the future. We have exploited both the present and the future in our thoughtless use of natural resources. It has only been in the recent past that we have seriously thought about our exploitation of each other and of our natural resources. We have always believed in progress and change as good things regardless of the consequences. During the period of the 1960s and 1970s in the field of ecology, for the first time in this century in any case, the United States seemed to be moving to the construct that indeed our past and future could and possibly should determine our present and that our present was indeed someone else's past and future. Marx said exactly the same thing in the 1840s, when he asserted that we must stop assuming that we can live our lives as though we exist in a time vacuum that has neither past nor future.

Despite its limitations, the Marxian construct of time and history implies some radical ideas about stasis and change. In particular it implies that we do not have nearly as much control over stasis and change as we would like, for we are controlled by the past, present, and future of our own society and those societies that infringe upon us. Further, if we take the construct seriously, then we are the guardians of the future just as our forebears should have been guardians of our present. It means that the unbounded exploitation of the right-wing radical ("rugged individualists") or the left-wing radical ("Do your own thing") are, by Marx's definition, not only totally irresponsible, but more importantly, show a lack of understanding of their role in history.

In brief, while Marx says that stasis is basic to any society throughout its own history, which will tend to determine its present and future, change is even more basic. Each of us is the determiner of the present and the future in the sense that as member actors of institutions we have an influence on them. That influence, when combined with the influence of other individuals in our communal lives (and we all live in communes or communities of life, marriage, school, and work to name just a few), will be part of the future, since we are the past of the future.

Basically, however, stasis is the institutional and societal norm. How then does change occur in institutions and societies? Most historians of Marx's time believed that change came from outside the society through conquerers, technological change, the process of history itself, and so on. Marx believed that change is inherent and internal to every society. Change begins and ends with the individual in a societal milieu.

Marxian Individualism

Marx was passionately interested in individuals. He had had great tragedy in his own life with the death of one of his children, not from any particular disease, but from poverty. What bothered Marx most was the miserableness of the workers of the world in the midst of plenty. This was as true of nineteenth-century England, where he did most of his work, as it was of many other parts of the Western world. Workers worked long and hard at dirty and demeaning jobs. The average work day was from fourteen to sixteen hours. The pay was miserable, and there were, of course, no benefits, no health standards, and no government protection of workers. This was the heyday of unfettered free enterprise, of Adam Smith's concept of *laissez faire*, the theory that government should intervene as little as possible in economic affairs, as described in his greatly influential work, *The Wealth of Nations* (1776). However, although the physical plight of workers in England appalled Marx, that was not what bothered him most. Rather, it was the futility of the life, the feeling of worthlessness on the part of the workers. This to Marx was the tragedy of nineteenth-century work and workers.

Marx harkened back to what he thought was a brighter day in the history of English industry, when the workers worked just as hard, the living conditions were just as bad, there was no government protection, and the work was long, hard, and often dirty. This was the day of the English cottage industries. If the work itself was just as hard, the life span was no longer, and the life itself possibly no better in terms of physical benefits, what then was the difference between the cottage industries of the seventeenth and eighteenth centuries and the assembly line industries of the nineteenth?

Marx idolized work and idolized the family and most importantly, he idolized the concept of the improvability of people. If people could be placed in right surroundings, they would be all right. The English cottage industries exemplified this right kind of work in the right kind of surroundings. A family, a village, or a group would decide that they had the natural resources and skills needed to produce a certain product. The family or group would divide the work among those who were available and capable of doing the work. Work was not divided evenly among all members, because all members were not capable of doing the same amount. Each member of the cottage had a task that was fitting for that person. The members of the cottage would collect the raw materials needed, fashion the product, produce it to completion, market the product, and bring the profits or losses back to the cottage to be shared by the members of the cottage. Again, the profits or losses were not shared on an equal basis or on the basis of who had done the most work. Rather, the sharing, as is true of most family or other close relationships, was done on the basis of need. If times and products were good, then the cottage prospered and there was much to share. If times or products were not good, then the losses would be shared. In any event, it was a familylike setting, which took from each according to his or her ability and gave to each according to need. As Marx said, "From each according to their ability. To each according to their need."

Marxian Alienation

With the coming of the assembly line, work itself changed. The workers were not involved in gathering the raw materials, producing the product, and merchandising it. Rather they were involved in only one aspect of the task, namely, their role on the assembly line. What the product was and the quality of the finished product were of less concern than getting out the piece work or putting in the required time. Pride in work and village, where the worker and all other members of the cottage were valued for their parts in producing the product, was replaced by the construct of the worker as mechanical cog in the wheel of progress.

From Marx's viewpoint, the industrial revolution was the ruination of the worker and of pride in work. It was his position that workers could not be expected to have pride in work when they had no direct contact with the product. They did not control what the product was to be, the quality of raw materials to go into the product, the quality of work that would be used to make the product, its price, or where and how it would be sold. The worker's task was to tighten one bolt on one nut all workday long.

This process is, of course, diametrically opposed to the work situation of the cottage industry, where the worker and the worker's family and friends are intimately involved with each other and with the product. The assembly line leads to a situation where the worker can no longer feel intimately involved with, or have pride in, the most important aspect of life, namely, work. With the end of the oneness with work, came what Marx called "the Estrangement from Labor." We would call this *alienation*. Marx predicted that workers would become so estranged from their work that they would become dissatisfied with their life and demand a return to the collective life of the cottage industries. The revolution of the proletariat, or workers, occurs, according to Marx, because the workers know that their work life is miserable and they want to return to a better one. The solution is a return to the form of industry where the workers have complete control over their own work lives, that is, the English cottage industries or a similar arrangement. This is where the construct of the commune or collective comes into being. Marx was not an economist, he was an idealistic, utopian thinker, who wanted people to be happy in the most important aspect of their lives, namely work.

Marx knew that his ideas would not be easily accepted because there was a great deal of money to be made through the industrialization of products and through the use of workers as mechanical units. Workers would have to revolt, not against the captains of industry, not against the capitalists, but against the system of industry and assembly lines that would not allow workers to feel good about themselves and their work. That is what the revolution of the proletariat is all about: workers changing their own history.

Flow Chart 1. The Marxian Assembly Line

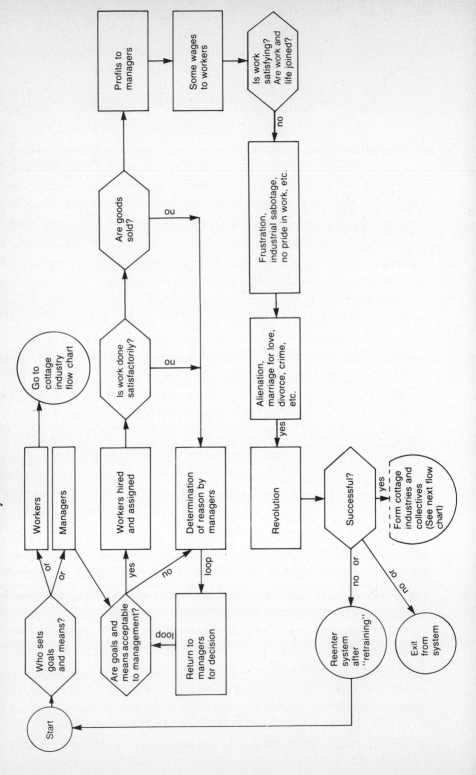

Description of the Marxian
Assembly-Line Flow Chart

There is a difference between Marxism and Communism. Communism, as practiced in countries today, is largely authoritarian with a top down administration of goals and means. Marxian socialism, however, calls for democratic communal ownership and control of industry and labor. Therefore, when the flow chart asks "Who administrates?" we are asking about the ideal Marxian institution.

The first question to be asked of any Marxian model is, "Who sets the goals and the means?" If the answer is that the workers determine the goals and means, it most likely is not an assembly line, and, therefore, the flow chart will indicate that we are to go to the cottage-industry flow chart that appears on page 88. However, if the goals and means are determined by the managers, although this does not guarantee that it is an assembly-line institution, we will recognize the first step in the assembly-line model. There are, of course, other institutions that have a top down organization, but at this point we are only interested in the Marxian assembly line.

If the goals and means are acceptable to the managers, then the workers are hired and assigned to tasks. The workers do not determine their tasks, nor do they have choice in their assignments. If they want the job, they do their assigned task as they are told. If the goals and means are not acceptable to the management or require changing for some reason, for example, through a change in administration or environment, then the managers must determine the reason for the unacceptability and continue in the loop until the goals and means are found to be acceptable.

After the workers are hired and assigned, a determination must be made as to whether the work is being done satisfactorily. If it is, the next question is whether the goods are sold. If either of the questions is answered no, then, again, the managers must again determine why. New workers may need to be hired, a different product may need to be manufactured, and so on. In any event, the managers must go back to the goals and means and begin over again. During this process, the workers are not involved in the decision making. This was largely true in Marx's time, since there were few labor guilds or unions. In our own time, there is some worker control over such factors as working conditions and health and safety standards, but there is still little or no control by the workers over the product to be produced or the way in which that product will be produced or sold. These decisions are for the most part in the hands of the managers.

If the work is completed satisfactorily and the product is sold, then the profits go to the managers, while wages go to the workers. In Marx's day, the determination of wages was almost totally in the hands of the managers. Now, with the advent of strong unions, workers bargain over the amount of wages to be earned.

The critical question for Marx, however, was not whether the product was sold or the workers received their wages. Rather, the question was whether the workers were happy in their work and fulfilled in their lives. What Marx saw in the 1840s was that workers were indeed not happy in their work and that there was an estrangement from work in their lives. This led to frustration, a lack of self-worth and pride in work, and industrial sabotage.

If the revolution were unsuccessful, the workers would either be retrained by the society to be more useful workers and members of society, or they would be "exited" from the system through banishment or death. If the workers' revolution were successful, the workers would want to reestablish the unity of work and life through the establishment of collective, group run, cottage industries. This leads us again to the cottage-industry flow chart.

The Changing Family

Marx predicted that certain things would happen if the assembly-line system were not changed to meet the emotional needs of the workers. The first was that the family, which had been so important to the cottage industry as a source of work companionship, would no longer be the place of work. According to Marx, with the rise of assembly lines, marriages would no longer be economic and social arrangements. Rather, workers would now pick their mates not with the approval of the community but because they wanted to get married. This led to, of all things, the concept of marriage for love. We are now so used to that concept that it would be foreign to us to think of any other. However, just for a moment, think of the disadvantages of the love marriage as opposed to the work and community marriage. It is a lot easier to fall out of love than it is to fall out of work or community. Further, since it is the individual's, not the community's, choice to get married in the first place, it can also be the individual's, not the community's, choice to get out of the marriage. This, of course, gives rise to the concept that divorce is all right because it is a person's own business, not the community's.

Most importantly, however, marriage becomes a place of solace for the worker. The family becomes that place where workers can find the emotional support that they cannot get in the work place. Here they are masters of their own fate and the rulers of the house. This put, and still puts, a tremendous strain on any relationship. Very few alliances, let alone the alliance between individuals as different as men and women, can withstand the pressure of continuous emotional support, combined with the day to day aggravations of just plain living together in a confined space. Marx predicted that love marriages would become the rule and further that the family would not be able to withstand the pressure and that divorce and family dissolution would become the rule.

The Consumer Society

With specific regard to industry, Marx predicted, and to some extent saw in his own time, that the emphasis in industry would shift from the importance of worker production to the importance of consumer consumption. Having someone buy something became more important than the production that goes into it. Every year American car companies produce a different set of models not because they are needed but because they can, or could in the past, sell them. There is a concerted campaign every year to get people to buy cars not because they are better than last year's models, but because the outsides are different. If the American car companies believed in the production model rather than the consumption model, they would leave the outside alone and change the inside. That way, if the product was a good one, people would be able to recognize it from year to year. As it is, we buy the outside changes without much being done to the insides from year to year. Volkswagen, for years, used a good production approach and forgot about consumption. The engine changed every couple of years, but "the Bug" was always "the Bug." Some of us miss it. It was ugly and honest.

We have, then, a construct from Marx which says that with the rise of the assembly line, there would be tremendous pressures on the family and tremendous pressures to consume largely useless products. Combined with this would be a general dissatisfaction with work, which would lead to tendencies toward industrial sabotage (adult vandalism); not working as hard as we should (cheating); and producing a product that we know has little or no value but that will be accepted by the consumer (taking tests, turning in homework, taking classes that are mandated by the state or the district). Finally, more and more of an emotional burden would be placed on the family or friends (social activities in the school) as a result of worker alienation.

The Marxian Model
Applied to the Schools

Although Marx did not discuss education, his concept of the cottage industry versus the assembly line can be applied to the schools. This analysis gives us the opportunity to look at the schools in a way that explains student behaviors in terms other than the traditional ones of academic ability, family background, previous achievement, and so on. Rather, the Marxian approach allows us to view both positive and negative student behaviors in terms of the behaviors and ethos of the institution itself. Again, the Marxian concept of the institution determining the behavior of individuals rather than the other way around is basic to this analysis. If we want good teachers and students, first we must have good schools.

In this section we will usually define the school as an assembly line with the teachers and administrators as bosses, the students as assembly-line workers, and school work as the product. Occasionally, when the context demands it, we will redefine the teachers as workers and the students as products.

To Marx the cottage industry, or cottage school, was ideal, and, indeed, as we have seen, there are a number of personal and societal advantages to the arrangement. The advantages will be more clearly appreciated in the context of the school if we enumerate the characteristics of the cottage industry and see how the school fits either the cottage-industry or assembly-line model.

First, in the cottage industry, the product was seen through not only to its completion but to its merchandising. This is a particularly important construct in industrial age education. Today, we as teachers are never sure of our effect on our product, namely students, since in our educational system, as opposed to the one-room school house, we are merely part of an assembly line that sees the child for a relatively short time during the twelve years of school. We do not see the product to its completion.

One of the frustrations often mentioned by teachers is this lack of product feedback. We are never sure of the effect we as individual teachers have on specific students. Occasionally we are given a glimpse of our role when a particular student either returns to the school or writes us and reports the effect we had on him or her. If that does not occur, we really have little or no information about our effect on students. We can say that a student graduated from our school, which may give us a general sense of having an effect, but it does not give us a specific feeling of accomplishment. That feeling of accomplishment can only come if we know what our part in the process is. If schools were run like English cottage industries, we would know what our part was, and we would be clear as to our role in the future of our students. However, because the modern school is more like an assembly line than like a cottage industry, we experience the same frustrations as do assembly workers.

Second, in the cottage industry each member of the cottage was responsible for the product because each member contributed to the product. Because the product was collective, neither the praise nor the blame was shifted to another. If a similar situation existed in education, college teachers could not blame high-school teachers for the ineptitude of students, high-school teachers could not blame junior high-school teachers, and on down the line to elementary-school teachers, who could not blame the lack of home training or bad home environment for the ineptitude of their students. Unfortunately, though, in our educational superstructure, there is little feeling of communality between various levels of the schooling, let alone between school and home.

Because of the assembly-line nature of the modern school, there is also little feeling of sharing between members of the staff. When a graduate becomes famous, or infamous, we say "That person was in my class." That phrase carries more status than does the statement, "That person was in our school." These statements are quite different in content and implications. They indicate very clearly that the classes in a school are not sharing aspects of the institution but rather are separate and distinct parts.

In most modern schools what one part does is of little or no concern to the other parts; each exists independently. This is most clearly indicated in our attitude toward curriculum. It is a true assembly-line model, even including a PERT (time-line) chart of sorts. The children are presented a prepackaged curriculum, which may or may not fit their needs. If they do not learn the material on grade level, then it will be difficult for them to learn the material on the next level. We should remember that in the assembly-line model (see page 82), the product, in this case the children, cannot be differentiated. In other words, the assembly line does not allow for handmade or unique items (if the fenders are not put in place at a certain point on the assembly line, it will not be possible to install the headlights at the next point). The only thing that makes the assembly line possible is that each product is exactly the same as the next. This can be applied to students as well. In assembly-line education, each level can blame the previous level because there is no mutuality of spirit between the various levels.

Third, because of the industrial situation of the cottage industry, the members of the cottage defined themselves in terms of their work. They iden-

Flow Chart 2. The Marxian Cottage Industry

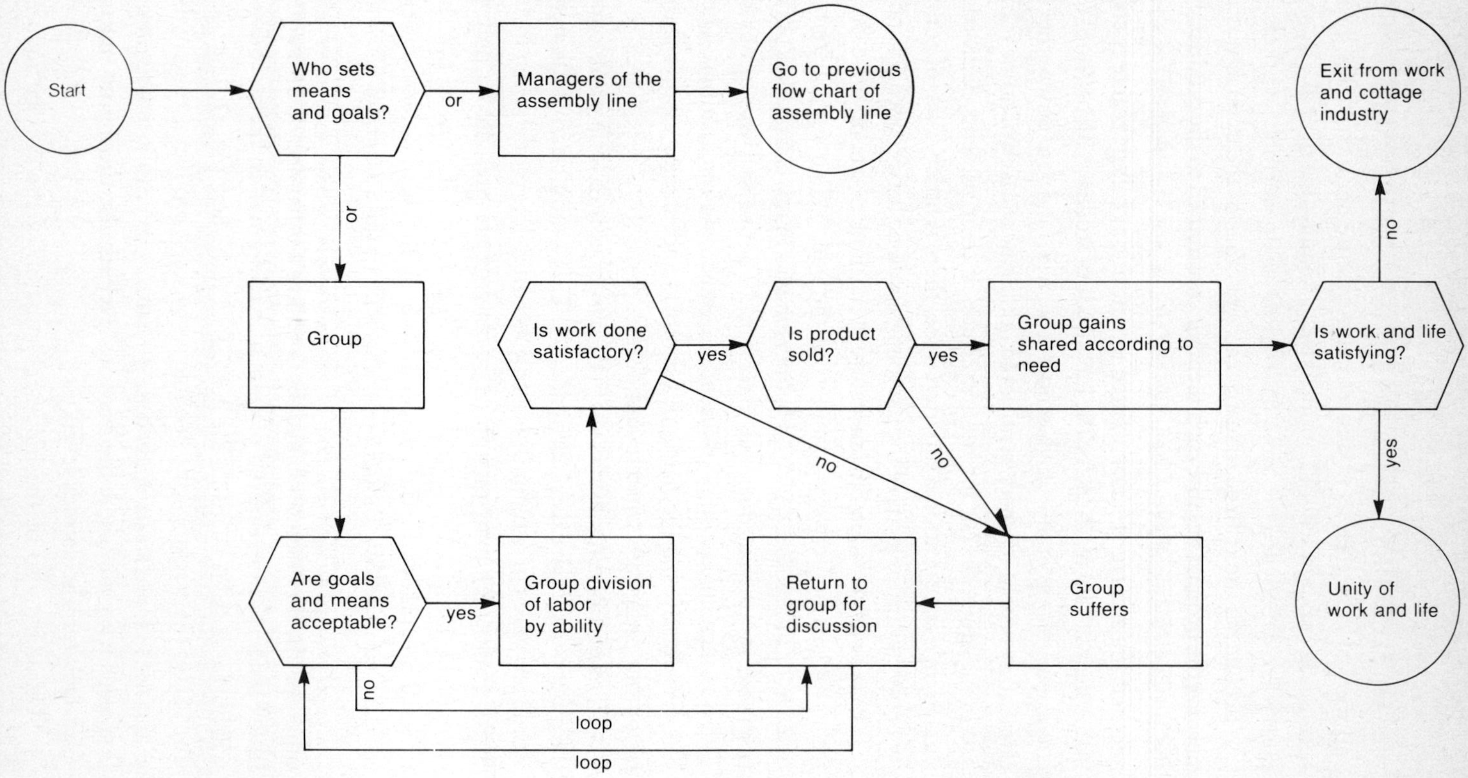

Description of the Marxian
Cottage-Industry Flow Chart

As with the Marxian assembly-line flow chart, this one also presents an ideal picture of the way things work. According to Marx, we would enter this flow chart by way of the workers' revolution predicted in the previous flow chart. The same first question is asked, "Who sets the means and the goals?" If the managers set them, then the flow chart tells us to return to the previous flow chart on assembly lines. However, if the group sets the means and goals, then we have started toward a Marxian cottage industry. Again, cottage industries are not the only institutions that have group-determined means and goals. However, for the Marxian cottage industry to function as planned, it must have group determination of means and goals.

The next question is to determine if the means and goals are acceptable. If they are not, then the decision must return to the group for further discussion and determination after which the question of acceptability is asked again. This loop continues until the goals and means are acceptable. When that occurs, there is a group decision on the division of labor. Although not shown on the flow chart, this process would also go through group discussion and, if necessary, rediscussion, until the division of labor is acceptable. In the cottage industry, this division of labor is on the basis of each person's ability to give to the group, not on the basis of equity. In other words, "From each according to his [or her] ability," not "From each the same amount of work."

The next two questions relate to whether the work is completed satisfactorily and whether the product is sold. If the answer to either is no, then there must be a return to the group for reexamination of the means and goals or the division of labor, and so on. If the answer to both questions is yes, then the group takes the profits from their labor back to the group. These profits are held by the group in common and used for the common good, or they are distributed to group members. However, just as the division of labor was not on the basis of equity but on the basis of ability, so the division of profits is not on the basis of equity but on the basis of need. That is, "To each according to his [or her] need," not "To each according to the amount of work done or the prestige of the work."

Again, the critical question for Marx is whether the workers are happy in their work and feel fulfilled, that is, if there is a unity of life and work. If there is not, then the worker should leave the cottage industry and exit the system, or the group should reexamine the goals and means to see if the worker can become happy in his or her work. Marx would hold that because of the unity of feeling of togetherness and the support of the family–work group and the feelings of involvement and control over decisions in the cottage industry, even if there were disagreements, there would be basic satisfaction with life and work.

In the cottage industry, then, the process of work is more important than the product. If the process involves the workers in their work, they will be happy in it and their lives and work will be in unity.

---

tified themselves as the village or cottage or family of millers, or coopers, or smiths. Before the seventeenth and eighteenth centuries, people were known in England not by a family name but by the family occupation or trade. There was a pride in that trade and that family. The members of the cottage industry could feel a part of something that was greater than any one individual. It was, indeed, a community of interest, a commune. Here they could feel secure, protected, and a part of past, present, and future.

In the assembly-line school, however, there is no pride in work because work is not rewarded. Instead, scoring high on tests and conforming to prescribed conduct is rewarded. Grades are the only reward that we really give to students, and that reward is extrinsic, that is, it has no real connection to the work performed and is not truly a result of the work. Pride in work and love of work is intrinsic, part of its very nature. Schools, in general, do not generate pride in work. At best they generate pride in grades. Sometimes there is as much pride in "conning the system" out of a grade as in working for it. School work is not important for itself any more than assembly-line work is important on the assembly line. Most assembly-line workers really do not care about the product. In point of fact, a number of studies have shown that assembly-line workers do not even buy their own product but prefer to buy the product of another assembly line. Why they make the assumption that workers on the other line are more caring than they are is not clear.

The situation is similar in the schools. Most students really do not care about the work at all. All they are interested in is the paycheck, in this case, the grade. Similarly, many teachers are less interested in the work of teaching than in the security of the job. If we were really interested in production quality rather than production quantity and consumption (for instance, people read test scores and tell us how good or bad our schools are), we would give rewards on the basis of degree of improvement, love of learning, and degree of willingness to share knowledge and ability with the rest of the class, school, and society. None of these is particularly measurable in the usual quantitative sense.

Fourth, and of great importance for Marx, cottage industries were production oriented and not consumption oriented. The products that were made, and the goods that were bought or traded for, were not superfluous goods. They were goods that were really needed and would be used. When production was not needed, then work stopped. There was no desire to work for the sake of work. During the winter, some types of work would stop altogether, and most types of work would slow down. There was no desire to create a market. Rather the desire was to produce a product that would be desired by others and, at the same time, to acquire goods from others that would be of use to the cottage. The purpose was a fruitful, meaningful, and reasonably happy life with work at the center.

Education in this country is incredibly consumption oriented. We care less about the quality of education than the quantity. Often those who say that they want more quality education will point to lowered test scores. But test scores do not indicate quality, they indicate quantity. Our quantitative roots go even deeper. There is a feeling, on the part of the schools, that children should always be busy, that there should be a minimum of idle time. As suggested in Chapter 3, this reflects our Protestant ethic and our belief in the cult of efficiency. These beliefs are part of the assembly-line model as well. If assembly-line workers are idle, someone will find something for them to do. Either the production rate will be increased, or fellow workers will make it very clear that the "rate buster" should slow down, so that the work rate will not be increased. The same thing happens in schools, where some students will tell the others to slow down, so that they will not be given more work to do.

This is not to imply that basic skills are unnecessary. Marx certainly appreciated skill and pride in work. His objection to our present schools would be twofold: first, he would object to the consumption mentality, that is, working not to learn skills but to keep busy; second, Marx would object to the externality of the rewards, namely grades. Marx would say that if the work were important, then the major reward would be emotional and moral, that is, the sense of satisfaction in a job well done. In brief, Marx should never be used as an excuse for not learning basic skills. Rather, Marx should be used as a rationale for making schoolwork meaningful.

Schools are justifiably famous for busy work and for giving those students who finish early more of the same. Ditto machines are the backbone of the assembly-line school. Free time is considered wasted time rather than creative time or rest and recuperation time. It is the assembly line at its prime.

THE SCHOOL AS AN ASSEMBLY LINE

The school can be viewed as an assembly line either from the standpoint of the student or the teacher. If the school is to be defined as an assembly line, it must have the same characteristics as Marxian industrial assembly lines, that is, (1) the school should turn out a product that has no intrinsic value to the worker; (2) the worker should not be directly connected with the product; (3) the worker should not have direct control over either the product or the quality control of the product; (4) the worker should not have control over the distribution and sale of the product; and (5) the worker should not be in control of the profits derived from his or her labor. The outcome of the school assembly line should be (1) a lack of interest in the product; (2) a desire for extrinsic gain from the work, since no intrinsic value is placed on the work itself; (3) industrial sabotage; (4) disruption of the assembly line as an indication of displeasure; (5) a need to maintain social relationships in lieu of a oneness with work; and (6) a desire to get as much as possible for the least amount of effort. In brief, if the school is indeed an assembly line, we would expect to find a good deal of work that the workers find meaningless and a good deal of alienation as a result. Further, there should be some rebellious activity from time to time from those who find the work situation most meaningless and alienating.

It may be somewhat difficult for us to view teachers as assembly-line workers because we are more used to seeing them as professionals. However, for the sake of this discussion, rather than looking at the profession let us look at the work itself. First, the product of teaching is students who are schooled. We are not going to use the word "educated," because it implies a whole different set of goals and means. Persons can become educated by themselves through reading, life experience, travel, and so on. Schooling, however, must take place in a school. Schooling implies a curriculum, a teaching staff, and an institution.

To this institution of schooling, if we define the teacher as the worker, then certainly the schooled student, at least schooled in that teacher's subject matter, is the product. If the assembly-line model holds, then each teacher should teach a specific subject matter or grade level without too much concern for the next grade level or the other subjects. Further, the teacher should not have final choice of the materials to be taught; the type of materials to be used in the teaching; the rate at which the materials are to be taught; what the finished product should look like; nor what the reward will be for the finished product. In brief, teachers should do their job of teaching those students who are assigned to them, using the materials that are prescribed and avoiding materials which are proscribed, and pass the product along to the next teacher so that he or she may do the same. The final result of this endeavor is not necessarily an educated person, capable of making intelligent choices in the modern world with an attitude of understanding and a tolerance of things different. Rather, the success or failure of the teaching process is measured by standardized tests that only show whether or not the product (student) has been schooled in the required amount of materials and has committed them to memory. The end products are students who have been schooled and who have been tested on their schooling. They may or may not be educated, intelligent, knowledgable, or functioning citizens of the modern world.

THE EFFICIENCY MODEL

For many of us who have taught school, one of the more irritating aspects of teaching has been our inability to allow students to learn. Learning is not a necessary product of teaching. It is possible to teach brilliantly or give a brilliant lecture without anyone in the classroom learning from it. Teaching and learning are separate activities that we hope come together for the benefit of both the teacher and the student. If learning is to be meaningful, it may, in fact, be necessary for each student, and for that matter each teacher, to operate in a different fashion, at a different pace, or even in a different setting. If automobile manufacturers chose to make cars this way, the results would be very expensive and in short supply.

As described in Chapter 3, at the turn of the century and up through the 1920s, there was a very great movement toward the concept of efficiency of education. It was part of the efficiency movement in industry. There was a move to stop such wasteful practices of the educational system as holding children back a year so that they could more completely learn the subject. Rather some children were moved out of the regular classroom and put into special education settings. Others were put into vocational education programs, since they were believed to be incapable of doing the work of the regular classroom.

Out of the efficiency movement came social promotion, tracking of children into ability groups, grading on the curve, and special education on a massive scale for groups in addition to the blind and deaf. It should be pointed out that the students who were most often identified as too dumb to go to regular school, not surprisingly, turned out to be the most recent immigrants to the United States: the Chinese, Poles, Russians, Jews, Italians, and to some extent the Irish. These immigrants were often lumped into a group called PIGS, which stands for *P*oles, *I*talians, *G*reeks, and *S*lavs.

We are the inheritors of this cult of efficiency. Ayers, who wrote "Laggards in Our Schools," would be delighted with the assembly-line model of education. He fought for years to initiate education into the assembly-line model. He compared efficient education to efficient industry, or sewage disposal, or milk purification. But education, as opposed to schooling, by its very definition is an inefficient enterprise. The prime goal of education is effectiveness, not efficiency. It takes time, and more importantly, each person involved in the enterprise will move at a different pace and will have different approaches to the process. So long as that is the case, if schooling is assembly-line oriented, then education will be, at best, an ancillary activity and, at worst, will be ignored entirely. Schooling is what American schools practice, and schooling is easily an assembly-line activity. As such, it is frustrating and irritating to both the workers (teachers) and to the products (students).

THE TEACHER AS WORKER

Not all teachers work in efficiency-oriented schools. However, those who do are assembly-line workers. The teachers as industrial assembly-line workers tighten one bolt on one nut on an assembly-line product all day long. They do not particularly care about the product when it leaves their work station, or about their fellow workers, or particularly about the quality of the product. The important thing is to get the work completed in the allotted amount of time. Teachers, as workers on a schooling assembly line, teach one subject to a passing group of students all day long. They are not particularly concerned about the product (student) when it leaves their particular work station. They are more interested in conditions than in the work itself, for example, asking how long the break is, what they will be paid, how much vacation there is, rather than how well the students are learning, what they can do to help, and so on. Teachers, if they are on an assembly line, see themselves as laborers, employees subject to the orders and whims of management.

That there is a great deal of alienation among teachers is quite clear. Not only are there continual complaints about students, parents, and the community, there are also continual complaints about the administration, stupid rules, and having to perform tasks that have nothing to do with teaching, such as hall duty and playground supervision. In many districts now, teachers are not allowed to volunteer their time to engage in extracurricular activities with students because of union contracts. In many districts the pattern is quite simply, "If we don't get paid for it on an hourly basis, we won't do it." This is certainly a far cry from the traditional role of the teacher as a lover of children who would go out of her or his way to aid the child's development in any way possible. And the job of management is to keep costs down, the employees busy, and the clients (taxpayers, *not* students) satisfied.

Whether we feel that the change in the professional attitude of teachers is good or bad is beside the point. The point is that the change has occurred, and the Marxian model gives us one explanation of why it happened and, perhaps more importantly, gives us a path to a solution. (However, we must always remember that it is not an objective model; it is a model that has a foundation in a utopian belief.)

THE WORK WORLD OF THE SCHOOL

Assuming that the school is an assembly line and that the teacher is the worker, what would that work look like? With the teacher as worker, then the students must be the product. What is to be produced is quite clearly defined. A curriculum guide is to be used by each teacher, so that there can be uniformity between classes in the same subject or grade level. Although there is some flexibility within the curriculum guide, there is also a good deal of rigidity. In most cases, the teacher-workers have not had a great deal of say as to what goes into the curriculum. They have almost nothing to say as to the quality of the final product, or even what the final product is supposed to be like, except for highly specific categories, such as be able to read, write, and count, or extremely general constructs, such as, be a good citizen, which is either undefined or is defined in terms of oversimplifications like going out and voting. (The act of voting, of course, does not show good citizenship or good education. Thoughtful voting does.)

By and large, teachers as workers are part of the ruled class in terms of their behaviors and their work. They are told how, when, and where to mold or remold their products. The teacher's bulletin gives them specific and general rules to follow for each day, just as district policy has given them general rules and policies to follow. Teachers often feel constrained by these rules and policies, but they feel largely impotent to change them. Some of the early teacher strikes of the 1960s were fought over these issues, rather than simply over bread-and-butter issues. Unfortunately, much of the union activity of the 1970s and 1980s deals only with the bread-and-butter issues and ignores such issues as academic freedom, freedom of choice, and experimental education.

Although this may seem to be a dreary picture (to some extent it certainly is) and there are many teachers who feel that teaching is a dreary, repetitious, and meaningless activity, the teachers at least have a sphere of influence at their

96

Flow Chart 3. The Teacher in the Marxian Assembly-Line School

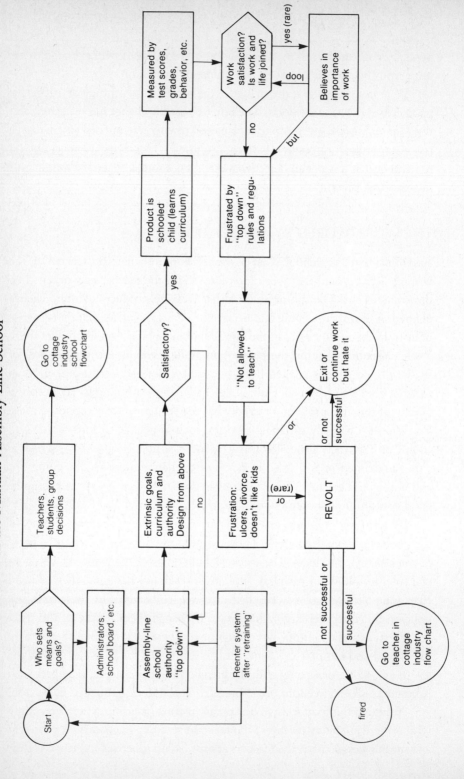

The Teacher in the Marxian Assembly-Line School

This is the first of the flow charts that directly applies a theoretical model to the school. In this case, we are looking at the Marxian situation of a teacher in the assembly-line school. Again, it must be remembered that the flow chart is an ideal picture which assumes that real life is exactly like the model. Because life does not work so neatly, the model will not fit exactly. There will be very few completely assembly-line schools or cottage-industry schools. Most will be combinations of the two. However, a particular school will tend more toward one model than the other. Another problem is that Marx did not discuss the school directly, largely because schooling was not particularly important in the 1840s. We are using a work model to describe the school.

If the teacher enters the assembly-line school, which is the most common situation, then there will tend to be a top down design of authority, curriculum, rules and regulations, and so on. That is, the teachers and staff will have little control over what they teach, the rules they will have to enforce, or how they will be expected to enforce those rules.

The product of the assembly-line school is the "schooled" child, the child who does well on standardized tests and examinations and who behaves according to the school rules enforced by the teachers and administration. There is no reward system for, or even a method of testing for, whether students learn to cooperate, become valuable members of society, learn to think independently, and so on. As products in the assembly-line school, these values are not measured. What is measured is mastery of predefined curriculum materials.

The critical question for Marx does not relate to the product (the schooled child), but rather to whether the teachers are happy in their work and whether their work is joined to their lives. It would be Marx's contention that since the teachers (workers) are not involved in the decision-making process and do not feel a part of the product, they will not have pride in their work. Furthermore, even if they feel that their work is important, they will still be frustrated by the top down nature of the institution. They will feel that they are not allowed to teach but rather must spend their time enforcing rules that do not make sense and teaching curricular materials that are irrelevant.

All of these frustrations lead either to exiting from the system or to continued frustration, with resultant emotional and physiological problems. All of this—including family disruption and social problems (alcoholism, divorce, and so on)—would be predicted by Marx in the assembly-line school.

Occasionally, teachers will revolt under such circumstances. However, teachers are not generally noted for their radicalism. If teachers go on strike or revolt in other ways, the issues are rarely work satisfaction but more often fiscal. Although more money can make people feel more secure, it rarely increases their work satisfaction. This is particularly true for teachers, who, as a rule, are quite dedicated people who would like to believe in the importance of what they are doing.

Flow Chart 4. The Teacher in the Marxian Cottage-Industry School

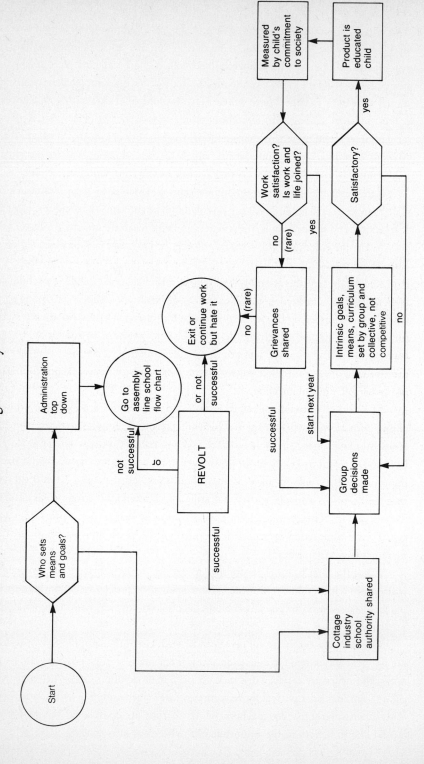

The Teacher in the Marxian
Cottage-Industry School

In the cottage-industry school the situation is quite different from the assembly-line school. Here, decisions are made in a group process, and the situation should be more like a family, with each person doing what he or she is most competent to do and with all work given respect because it is done well. The janitor who works well is as important as the teacher who works well, and the principal is given no more deference than is the student. Here, the goals and means should be set by the group. If they are found to be unsatisfactory, then they are returned to the group for further discussion. This loop continues until such time as the goals and means are satisfactory to the group. Ideally, the process should include students, who are the recipients of the process.

When the goals and means are satisfactory, then the product can be formed. In this case, the product is an educated student, as opposed to the schooled student of the assembly-line school. This product is not competitively compared to other students but rather is compared only to him or herself. Each student and teacher is expected to aid cooperatively in the collective product of the educated student. Everyone is responsible for the product, and if the product is a failure, everyone is to blame, including the janitor, teacher, students, administrators, and parents. The product is measured by the student's commitment to society at large. If students do not cooperate with one another while in school; do not develop a sense of the need for societal involvement and do not become involved in that society while they are in school; are not involved in society when they leave school; are not interested in continuing their education when they leave school; do not vote, and so on, then the school has failed. In short, although there is a need to test for skills (it is not possible to function in this society without knowing how to read, write, and count), the basic product of the school should be students and adults who can think and act for themselves.

The basic Marxian question, however, is not whether the product is successful, but whether teachers will feel fulfilled in this type of school. Marx would say that they would, because in this model they would be a part of the process of educating the child from the beginnning and would see that process to its conclusion and feel a part of it. They would have control over what the product is to be and how that product is to be shaped. If a teacher is not satisfied, then grievances would be shared and new group decisions would be made. This again would be a loop that continues until resolution or concensus occurs, or until those with grievances leave the system.

Although we could find pure cottage-industry or assembly-line schools, the more common situation is of a school that tends to be more like one than the other. In general, more of our society's schools tend to be top down rather than group oriented.

disposal. Within the classroom itself teachers are relatively independent and have a good deal of freedom of choice. While the curriculum may be set and the behaviors of the teachers and students prescribed by the district, individual style of presentation and materials is still allowed. Within limits there is a tradition of leaving teachers alone in their classrooms to modify the institutional requirements to fit both their own style and the styles of the students, so that the product can be more effectively molded.

Despite the requirements of the assembly-line school, there certainly are many, many teachers who feel a kinship both to the students and to the work. The only point of this chapter is that it is harder to maintain such a feeling of kinship with the product and the work in a school that is built on an efficiency assembly-line model. It is easier if we use a more collective model.

THE STUDENT AS WORKER

While teachers have both some power and some sphere of influence, the students in the school have almost none. The students are truly in the situation of working on something for which they have no rationale at all. The product that the students are supposed to turn out is schoolwork, or homework, or classwork. It should be pointed out that these tasks are never defined in terms of fun or leisure, that is, school fun, home fun, or class fun. School is a place where students work, and the work is often irritating and sometimes odious. If it isn't, then it can't really be work at all.

The product turned out by the student has a number of important characteristics:

1. The student-workers have had almost no say in what the product will be; what materials will be used to finish the product; the definition of what is and is not a valuable product; or the method of reward that will be used. They are truly the ruled class.
2. The reward given for completed work will have only extrinsic value, that is, the reward will have no value to the student-workers except as they have been convinced that it has value. Specifically, grades have no intrinsic value in their own right. Actually, they have little extrinsic value either. We can't really do anything with them—they are not currency, they are not tradable, we can't even bargain with them, except that some parents are willing to pay for high grades. The only thing that grades are good for is to enter the next level of schooling, where student-workers

will be expected to perform largely the same tasks again. If one wishes to continue schooling, this is indeed a value. However, a large proportion of students do not go on to higher education, and the value of grades is questionable for this group.

3. The materials worked on, that is, the subjects taught, may have little to do with life outside of the school–work place. There is therefore, an artificiality to the school–work place. Behaviors and work are expected here that are not expected anywhere else in the worker-students' lives.

4. The sphere of influence of the student-workers is severely limited in the school–work place. Even life and bodily functions are severely limited so that the student-workers, like assembly-line workers, must ask for permission to go to the bathroom, and unlike most assembly-line workers, must eat the food prescribed in the school–work place cafeteria.

5. The student-workers are definitely part of the ruled class. There is almost no sphere in the school-life area where they are the ruling class. This may be one reason that there is such as active underlife in most schools (see Chapter 6, The School as a Total Institution, for a fuller discussion of the underlife.)

STUDENT ALIENATION

According to the Marxian model what we should find in such an assembly-line school is rampant alienation; a lack of interest in schools; a tendency toward self-destructiveness, as well as violence toward others; industrial sabotage (that is, disruption of assembly-line classroom processes, for example, whispering, or note passing, behind the teacher's back); getting around rules and regulations; following the required goals through innovative means (cheating, and so on); and general negative feelings toward the school, the staff, and learning. And, indeed, these seem to be the primary complaints about schools raised by teachers, parents, the community, politicians, and almost everyone else.

The difference between most of the complainers and the Marxian model is that the blame is not placed on the students in the Marxian model. It is placed squarely on the shoulders of the institution itself. If the institution is alienation generating and develops estrangement from labor, then that is the behavior the workers who are member actors of the institution will exhibit. The Marxian alternative would be a collective school that would more closely resemble the English cottage industries.

Flow Chart 5. The Student in the Marxian Analysis

- Authority defined rules, curriculum, products, rewards, etc.
- Is work completed satisfactorily?
- yes → Extrinsic rewards (grades and satisfactory exit)
- no → Sanctions (grades, records)
- Education does not continue as an adult
- Student fits into social order
- Education measured by income it will bring
- Satisfactory exit
- Sanctions (grades, records)
- Frustrations, cheating, vandalism, violence, etc. — loop
- More work; remedial or EMR classes — loop
- or — Unsatisfactory exit
- or
- Societal sanctions (employment limits, jail)
- "?"
- Assembly-line school
- Student enters school type?
- Cottage industry school
- Group defined curriculum, product, reward, etc.
- Is work completed?
- yes → Is redefinition possible?
- no → Exit to other educational setting
- yes → Satisfactory?
- no
- yes → Intrinsic rewards (individual and group satisfaction)
- Education continues as an adult
- Education measured by commitment to society
- Satisfactory exit

102

The Student in the
Marxian Assembly-Line School

The model for the student in the Marxian assembly-line school is similar to that of the teacher. In the assembly-line school, the students, like the teacher, are faced with tasks over which they have no control and in which they have no say. The students do not set the goals or the means for their tasks. The only question raised is whether the work is completed satisfactorily. If the answer is no, the student is given more, sometimes remedial, work. Sometimes sanctions are also imposed. If the student continues with unsatisfactory work, there is a high likelihood that he or she will exit from the system in an unsatisfactory fashion (be expelled, dropout, certificate of attendance, and so on). This leads to a number of unsatisfactory societal sanctions, since many businesses and military service require a successful exit from the school. Therefore, the unsuccessful student often has a future that is a question mark.

If the student is successful in completing assembly-line schoolwork satisfactorily, then he or she is given extrinsic rewards, such as grades and a satisfactory exit. This satisfactory exit will lead to satisfactory societal relations. Education is often measured by the income it will bring when the student is an adult. One of the more common phrases heard in school is, "If you don't get good grades and graduate, you won't be able to get a job," which may be true but is still extrinsic to the goal of education. There is little or no concern with instrinsic values such as whether the student likes the work or develops a love for learning. As a matter of fact, in the assembly-line school, whether the worker (student) likes the job is of no consequence, since the worker (student) does not have anything to say about what the work, or the product, or the means to achieve that product should be.

All of this leads to frustration. The student may decide on an alternative to the conventional means and may decide to cheat, damage school property, and become violent—all of the characteristics of the assembly-line worker. Antisocial acts might even lead to revolution, although that is very unlikely with students, since they attend school only for three or four years and they have limited standing within the society.

What is more common in the assembly-line school is that the student (worker) will find other sources of emotional sustenance. Among the most common in the school are social and extracurricular events. All too often when students are asked what they like best about school, they say extracurricular and social events, not the schoolwork itself. This is the same pattern as that shown by the adult assembly-line worker, who uses the family as a source of emotional sustenance because the work itself is not satisfying.

Marx would say that all of the students in the assembly-line school are frustrated, it is just that some of them have learned to live with it. Those who are not good at the game of going to school will often be sanctioned in and out of school, will revolt in their own ways, and will usually be unsuccessful in those revolts.

The Student in the Marxian Cottage-Industry School

In the cottage-industry school, the goals, means, and curriculum, as well as the rules, would be communally determined. If the work is completed satisfactorily, so much the better; if it is not, then the problem is not to force the student into a pattern, but rather to redefine the goals and means to meet the needs of the student as well as the school and the society. If that is not possible, then the student will have to find an alternative school setting, perhaps even a traditional assembly-line school.

Success for a student, however, would not be measured in terms of such extrinsics as grades or adult income. Rather, both love of learning and whether the student becomes a worthwhile member of society become the measures. Does the student continue with education as an adult? Is the student an intelligent and valuable producer and consumer? Is the student politically active? In brief, the cottage-industry educated student becomes an active participant in society and his or her education continues for life.

Again, we are speaking of the ideal situation. In the assembly-line school, the students (workers) are not involved in the work and are frustrated and eventually rebellious. Or they rely on school social events as an emotional release, just as the adult assembly-line worker uses the family as a release. In the cottage-industry school, students (workers) are directly involved in the decision-making process, helping to determine what the work will be, how it will be done, and what the rewards will be.

THE SCHOOL AS AN ENGLISH COTTAGE INDUSTRY

There are a number of industries in the world that have moved to a more collective industrial model. Some Volkswagen and Volvo plants do not have assembly lines. Rather, a group of workers are given all of the parts of a car and are told to put it together from beginning to end. Industries have noted that it takes about 15 percent longer to put the car together in this fashion. However, the savings in an absence of industrial sabotage and incorrectly assembled cars, and an increase in quality control in general, more than make up for the loss. This is obviously not Marxian collectivism, where the workers would determine the raw materials to be used, the type of car to be made, the price of the car, and where and to whom the car would be sold. However, there are some aspects of the English cottage industry in this model. The workers themselves determine who will perform what task and who their leaders will be. They decide when the work will be done (day, evening, or night shift). Further, and perhaps of greatest importance, the workers see the product to completion, are together during the entire process, and are able to socialize while they are working. They are able to take breaks together, leave the job for short periods when they wish, and, in general, work in a more familial atmosphere.

Certainly schools have used this model and could do so again. The one-room school house, with all of its disadvantages—a lack of offerings, particularly in science; the necessity of dealing with one teacher all the way through school; and the lack of exposure to people different from the students —did have the advantage of being a familial situation. Here individual tastes and preferences could be accommodated, the community had a direct influence and involvement in the school (sometimes too much influence and involvement), and the teachers and the students were known to each other. Even if the teachers and students did not always like one another, at least they knew each other as three-dimensional people. Assembly-line teachers who are seen in grocery stores and are accosted by surprised students with, "Gee, I didn't know you shopped for food," are not exhibiting personal so much as institutional characteristics. Teachers are not real people to students, and students are often not real people to teachers in the assembly-line school.

Given the mass society with its large population centers, informal patterns, high geographical mobility, lack of extended family units, impersonal behaviors, and so on, what can the school as an institution do about estrangement from schoolwork? How can the cottage-industry model realistically be applied in our modern schools.

Before reasonable answers can be given from a Marxian, or for that matter from any sociological point of view, a number of homilies have to be put to rest:

1. Good teachers do not make good schools. Rather, good schools make good teachers.
2. Good students do not make good schools. Rather, good schools make good students.
3. Good curricula do not make good schools. Rather, good schools make good curricula. In point of fact, the curriculum type does not make any

difference at all. The only thing that matters is whether the institution has established itself as an alienation-producing or an alienation-reducing institution. Open education can be done using an assembly-line model ("All children will now be open, whether you like it or not."), and back to basics can be done in a collective fashion ("Johnny you are good at reading. Why don't you help Jimmy who is good at math but not reading?")

What then should the Marxian school–work place look like? First, it would be a place with some shared rulership. This is not to imply that the children should be given full control of their education, but that, on every level, the children with their parents should be included in the process of planning and executing their educational goals and processes.

Second, while schooling can be accomplished on a quantitative, assembly-line model, education cannot. Education, because it is an attitude toward life-long learning, not just memorizing the subject matter before a test, cannot be measured in the usual way. The great bane of the educational system, as opposed to the school system, is the concept of efficiency. Education has always been expensive, time consuming, sometimes exasperating, and absolutely essential for a democratic society. The Marxian school would not condemn one child for doing less well or particularly praise another for doing better. Each child would work to his or her capacity, and each would give to the collective class his or her ability. One of the first items to go would have to be competition between students; cooperation and sharing would become the model.

Third, how the student-workers choose to learn would be less important than that they do learn. If the student-workers work best in a noisy environment, then so be it. If some students wish to work alone and others in groups, then that would also be acceptable. Each would perform in his or her own way and would take from and give to the group in his or her own inimitable way as well.

Another Application
of the Marxian Model

Of particular concern to educators today is an understanding of history and alienation in relation to their influence on school conflict. One of the difficulties that has most recently come to the fore is student-school conflict. In the past students were willing to assume the values of the school. Recently, however, students and the community have gained a greater interest in their education and are therefore ready to challenge the authority of the school. Because of recent history (which has emphasized the importance of education among students and in the community), the clients of the school are no longer willing to remain in the ruled class. The school, however, is largely unwilling to give a greater voice to students and the community, and sometimes seems to understand neither the conflict nor the genesis of it.

This chapter, through its application of Marxian principles to analysis of the school, may also indicate a method of analyzing areas of potential conflict within the school. It discusses the way in which change can occur within institutions without interference from an outside, noninstitutional force.

There are many areas of potential conflict in the assembly-line school. Whenever the workers, teachers, or students are kept from uniting with their work, they will feel frustration and alienation from that work. So long as that frustration continues, conflict will be generated taking the forms of violence, vandalism, or withdrawal.

These outcomes are products of the system itself. There are no outside agitators in the Marxian model. There may be outsiders who take advantage of the turmoil within the institution. However, if there is no turmoil within, no one can create agitation.

The basic construct of a Marxian analysis of the school is that if the students or the teachers are violent and alienated, it is because that school is the type of institution that generates that type of behavior. Punitive schools generate punitive behaviors. Accepting schools generate accepting behaviors.

FOR CONSIDERATION

1. Prepare a list of examples that you think would illustrate either side of the argument that the history of a society or institution determines the behavior of its members. (For example: A school that has a reputation for academic excellence will cause its teachers and students to behave as though the reputation were true.)

2. How do you define alienation? Have you ever experienced it? Have you experienced alienation in the schools? What are the causes and characteristics of alienation as you know it? How do these compare with Marx's analysis?

3. Apply the Marxist model described in this chapter to a school you know. Along one side of a sheet of paper, list the characteristics of the model:

ruled class versus ruling class
alienation
cottage or assembly-line industry

Opposite each characteristic, provide one or more school examples that illustrate the characteristic.

4. How well does this model provide a suitable analysis of schooling? What are the strengths of this model? What are its limitations?

References

Calahan, Raymond. *Education and the Cult of Efficiency*. Chicago: University of Chicago Press, 1962.

Fromm, Erich. *Marx's Concept of Man*. New York: Ungar, 1966.

Goffman, Erving. *The Presentation of Self in Everyday Life*. Garden City, N.Y.: Doubleday, 1959.

Marx, Karl. *The Economic and Philosophic Manuscripts of 1844*. Translated by Martin Milligan. New York: International Publishers, 1964.

————. *The German Ideology*. New York: International Publishers, 1939.

Chapter 5: The School, Administrative Style, and the Individual

This chapter will teach teachers how to survive in the institution we call the school. But more than just survive, the model will attempt to show how teachers can prosper in the school. Conflict is inevitable in any institution, but the conflict can at least be made rational and task oriented if we understand that a good part of it is not over substantive issues but over the way in which the issues are institutionally and individually presented. Teachers who come into extreme conflict with the school and who are fired are not fired because of incompetence. Incompetence is almost impossible to prove. Rather, they are fired because of behaviors that the institution considers inappropriate. Some may sound inconsequential but turn out to be irritating to someone in enough authority that they become reasons for conflict. Causes of conflict can range over a wide variety of noneducational and educational issues, from not turning in keys at the end of the day, to speaking out during faculty meetings, not liking football, or having the wrong political or academic beliefs and behaviors.

Usually dismissal occurs for a combination of reasons falling under the general heading of "not being a member of the team," or "not understanding the way we do things around here," or "just not being able to get along with others." If we try to define these statements in terms of specific behaviors, we will be hard pressed, because there are very few specific behaviors to which we can point. The reality of what has occurred is that the individual and the institution are in conflict not over specifics but over the general attitudes that the institution feels it has the right to expect from the individual and the behaviors that individuals feel they have the right to expect from the institution. The problem is one of confused definition and confused expectations. The individual and the institution have differing definitions of the behavior that each should be expected to perform.

The Guba-Getzels Model as Applied to the Schools

Specifically, in this chapter, we will be looking at a model that allows us to view this conflict between the school and the individual from the standpoint of each. In general, individuals want more freedom and personal satisfaction; on the other hand, institutions, in general, want stability and peace and quiet. The model developed by Egon Guba and Jacob Getzels posits three types of relationships between individuals and institutions: (1) ideographic relationships; (2) nomothetic relationships; and (3) transactional relationships.

IDEOGRAPHIC RELATIONSHIPS

In *ideographic relationships* individuals feel that the institution is not maintaining standards and roles for individuals to follow. There are not enough rules and regulations, which results in what sociologist Emile Durkheim has called *anomic normlessness*, or alienation. This describes the situation of some teachers who feel uncomfortable because they are not quite sure what is expected of them, or that there is not enough structure in the school, or that both the students and many teachers are allowed too much freedom. Ideographic institutions, then, are seen as either having no roles or leaving role definition to the individual actors. In the ideographic institution the actors feel that they are too free to establish the parameters of their own behaviors and roles after they have entered the institution. If there is a chain command, it tends to be loose and not followed with any great care. If ends are established, they are usually determined by group discussion or by the individual actors. The means are equally fluid. Again, the ideographic institution appears to the actors to be too loose and formless; it is not a comfortable open institution. It should be kept in mind that ideographic relationships are not "true" in any absolute sense. They are subjective: it is the way one individual views the institution, or vice versa. Another individual or institution may view the relationship quite differently. This is true of nomothetic and transactional relationships as well.

NOMOTHETIC RELATIONSHIPS

In *nomothetic relationships* the individual feels that the institution has entirely too many rules and regulations. Here the complaint of teachers is that they cannot get their job done because every time they turn around someone is telling them to do something else or to follow some unnecessary rule. *Nomothetic* (norm-based) institutions, then, are those that cause the actors to feel that there are many oppressive rules and regulations which have been established for them without consent or even their knowledge. The primary characteristic of this kind of institution, in the mind of the actors, is that their roles have been determined prior to the individual actor's appearance (these are called antecedent roles). The chain of command is relatively determined and rigid and moves from top to bottom. Both the ends and the means are preestablished, exist apart from the actor, and antedate the actor who is asked to achieve the ends. Again, there is no question of fault; there is only the viewpoint of the individual and the institution. While one teacher may object to curriculum as confining and thereby say that the school is too nomothetic, another teacher may feel that the curriculum does not go far enough, would prefer to have direction, and generally believes that the institution is too ideographic. It is not the institution or the individual that makes the institution nomothetic or ideographic. It is the relationship between them and how that relationship is viewed.

TRANSACTIONAL RELATIONSHIPS

In a *transactional relationship* both the individual and the institution are satisfied with the behavior of the other. This is a situation that we very often do not even notice. Everything is going so well that the rules and regulations of the institution do not intrude into the actors' awareness. Transactional institutions fall somewhere between the other two in the actors' minds. While actors in such institutions feel that some of the ends and means are given, they also feel that many are left open and fluid and that they may exercise choice in these open areas. It is a comfortable place. There may be many established

Flow Chart 6. The Guba-Getzels Model

Individual enters

Role expectation met (effective behavior)

Role expectation not met (ineffective behavior)

and

and

and

and

Need disposition is met (efficient and effective behavior)

Need disposition not met (inefficient and effective behavior)

Need disposition met (efficient and ineffective behavior)

Need disposition not met (inefficient and ineffective behavior)

Individual happy and productive (adjusted and integrated)

Individual unhappy but productive (underintegrated, adjusted)

Individual happy but unproductive (overintegrated, underadjusted)

Individual unhappy and unproductive (underintegrated, underadjusted)

Institution happy and productive

Institution happy and productive

Institution unhappy and (too open) productive

Institution unhappy and unproductive

Transactional relationship

Nomothetic relationship

Ideographic relationship

"Anti-transactional" relationship

Interchangeable through Merton's reactions

Description of the
Guba-Getzels Flow Chart

The first division in the flow chart is the one that is of most concern to the institution, namely, whether or not role expectations are met. The upper half of the chart assumes that role expectations have been met (effective behavior), while the lower half assumes that they have not been (ineffective behavior).

If the role expectations have been met, one goes to the next division and asks whether or not the individual's need dispositions have been met (efficient behavior). In the uppermost row, both the role expectations and the need dispositions have been met (effective and efficient behavior). Here the individual's behavior is both integrated and adjusted. The upper row, therefore, describes the ideal situation, wherein both the institution and the individual are happy and productive. This is the transactional institution, where there is harmony and conformity without conflict.

The second row shows the situation where the institution's role expectations have been met (effective behavior) but the individual's need dispositions have not been (inefficient behavior). Here, the individual is unhappy but productive (that is, does what he or she is supposed to do). The institution is both happy and productive, since it really is not particularly interested in the worker's need disposition unless it effects productivity and role expectations. Here the individual is adjusted or even overadjusted but underintegrated. This is the nomothetic institution.

The lower half of the flow chart describes the situation in which role expectations are not met (ineffective behavior). In such a case the institution will always be unhappy. In the third row, we have the situation where although role expectations have not been met, the individual's need dispositions have (ineffective but efficient behavior). The individual, therefore, is happy in his or her work, since it is not taking a great deal of emotional energy to perform. However, not much work is getting done. The individual's behavior is overintegrated but underadjusted. The institution is unhappy because of the lack of production. This is the ideographic relationship.

The bottom row of the flow chart describes the situation in which neither role expectations nor the need dispositions of the actors are being met (ineffective and inefficient behavior). Here both the individual and the institution are unhappy and unproductive. The individual is underadjusted and overintegrated, while it would appear that the institution is not in tune with either its roles or the needs of its workers. This is what we have chosen to call the "anti-transactional relationship." It does not appear in the Guba-Getzels model, perhaps because this type of institution would certainly die.

Again as we emphasize throughout this chapter, no institution is any particular type. Institutions are perceived to be a type by individuals. Further, the perception of an institution by an individual can, and often does, change.

goals and means, but the individual actors do not notice them because there is tacit agreement between the institution and the actors. It is a pleasant place to be. However, this state of equilibrium can be easily disturbed either if the institution changes or if individuals come into the institution who feel that it is not transactional but either nomothetic or ideographic.

Situational Perceptions

The one thing that should always be remembered is that no institution is ideographic, nomothetic, or transactional. Rather, it is the relationship between the individual and the institution that is central to the construct. The unit of analysis in this model is the way in which the situation is viewed, *not* the situation itself.

Teachers often get into trouble in the institution because they misread the level of relationship that is expected. If a teacher wants more or less structure than the school is willing to give, a conflict will ensue. Often the conflict is resolved when one or the other party yields. Usually, it will be the teacher, who, in general, has less power than does the school. At other times, the suspect teacher may be willing to take the heat from the institution and fellow teachers in order to make a point. However, more often than not, neither the teacher nor the school will be quite clear as to the precise nature of the conflict, which is simply perceived as a vague feeling of dislike. The conflict is not a conscious choice on the part of the individual or the institution but rather a lack of understanding of what each expects of the other.

In the last chapter we developed a model that would allow us to look at the genesis and growth of deviance and disruption in the school. The present chapter gives us the opportunity to look at a functionalist model that describes how we can better survive as teachers. At the same time, the chapter puts forth a model that shows how the school, or any other institution, maintains stability while the individual attempts to maintain selfhood within that institutional stability. While the Guba-Getzels model is concerned with conflict, in the Marxian model conflict is open, and it assumes that the workers will want to revolt or at least show their displeasure in some overt fashion. The Guba-Getzels model does not; it assumes conflict that is manageable within the institution. In fact, this model does not even assume that the conflict will ever come out into the open.

STASIS AND CHANGE WITHIN THE INSTITUTION

The first purpose of any institution is self-preservation. However, existence by itself is not enough. Rather, a situation of stasis is desired; that is, institutions want to stay pretty much the way they are. Institutional self-preservation implies stasis as well as mere existence. Most institutions are willing to allow change in the environment around them. Indeed, some institutions are specifically designed to foment change in their environment. However, the institution itself most often does not want to be changed. Revolutionary councils are notorious for demanding changes and then institutionalizing those changes in order to prevent further change. Once in power, the revolutionaries want stasis. Counterrevolution is not acceptable to most revolutionaries.

At the same time that most institutions, including schools, want stasis, or at least institutionally controlled and deliberate change, many individuals will enter an institution with some ideas as to what they would like to change. This is particularly true of creative activities such as teaching. It is both common and gratifying to see new teachers come into a school setting with enthusiasm and new ideas. They want to improve both teaching and the schools. Unfortunately, both the enthusiasm and ideas are curbed, not because they are wrong but because they are misinterpreted by senior peers or by those in authority. Many new teachers, therefore, become very disheartened and frustrated.

Within any institution, there must be a balance between these expectations of the institution and the needs of the individual. If the expectations of the institution are never met, then the institution must either change or cease to exist. If the needs of the individual member actors are never met, then those individuals will eventually revolt or leave. Effective institutions, in this model, find ways to maintain their own primacy and stasis, while still sufficiently meeting the needs of their individual member actors. It must always be remembered, however, that the institution's purpose is not to meet the needs of its member actors. Rather, it is to maintain itself and its functions. This is, then, a functionalist perspective.

In the rest of this chapter, we will view the school as an administrative unit. However, we will be taking the viewpoint of the teacher. The teacher will be understood as the individual, while the administration, rules and regulations, state laws, and so on will represent the institution. Sometimes the institution will be represented by examples that sound like the actions of a principal or other single adminstrator, while at other times the examples will be more general.

Conflict in the Guba-Getzels Model

Just as there are three types of individual-institutional interactions, so there are three basic conflict dichotomies, or dialectics. These are:

1. The institution versus the individual
2. Institutional roles versus the individual's personality
3. Institutional role expectations versus the individual's need dispositions

Each of these dichotomies will be discussed in some detail because they describe the way in which we as individuals interact with institutions. We will also discuss some role theory, so that we can see more clearly the kinds of roles necessary for successful functioning within any institution. Last, we will describe Robert Merton's analysis of conformity to institutional norms so that we may more fully understand how each of us can learn either to conform or to fight conformity more effectively. Since we must all live in institutions, it cannot hurt us to learn to exist in them with greater skill.

Every institution is part of the greater social system. The members, as well as the institution itself, respond to the pressure, norms, and values of the greater society. Indeed, this is where all behavior, individual and institutional, begins. Most individual behavior, however, is effected or even modeled by the institution. The various forms it can take are shown in Table 5.1.

It should be emphasized, again, that all institutions are subjectively defined by the actors themselves as being nomothetic, ideographic, or transactional. No institution is objectively one or another, and different actors may define the same institutions differently, or the same actor may define the same institution differently at different times.

While it is impossible to categorize any given institution as nomothetic, ideographic, or transactional, since the definition depends on the perspective and the attitudes of the actor who is doing the defining, we can agree that some institutions are more nomothetic than others. Prisons, for instance, are more restrictive (nomothetic) than are artists' colonies.

With this extremely important distinction in mind, we can discuss nomothetic, ideographic, and transactional institutions and the styles of leadership

Table 5.1:
Selective Categories of Institutional Modes

Institutional Mode	Center of Attention in Each Mode	Character of Roles and Personality in Each Mode	Behavior Within Roles in Each Mode
NOMOTHETIC	Role and role expectations of institution	Role: Defined in terms of role expectation; dynamic organization outside the actor	Overadjusted Underintegrated
			Adjusted Effective
TRANSACTIONAL	Roles and needs of both institution and individual	Balance of role expectation and need disposition	Integrated Efficient
IDEOGRAPHIC	Personality and need disposition of individual	Personality: Defined in terms of need disposition; dynamic organization within the actor	Overintegrated Underadjusted

within them. In this discussion our primary interest is in the behaviors of institutions toward their member actors and the response of the actors to the institution.

All behavior within an institution begins within the social system. No behavior is performed in a vacuum. Behavior is based on the norms and values of the society in which the individual or institution performing them resides, and grows out of the milieu in which it is perfomed. When the behavior is performed, it adds to that social milieu and becomes part of the mass that is the groundwork and the base for future behaviors. All behavior emanates from, and adds to, the social system of which it is a part.

THE INSTITUTION VERSUS THE INDIVIDUAL

The institutions formed within a social system have *utility*, that is, they perform functions needed by that social system. Because they do have functions and are interested in effective behavior, institutions tend to be nomothetic and stasis oriented. Within the institutional structure, however, there is a countervailing force that causes the institution to modify its nomothetic behavior. This force is the individual, who may be opposed to the roles and expectations established within the institution. Individuals tend to want to establish, or at least have a hand in establishing, the ends and means of their own roles.

There will always be some conflict within any institution. Individuals feel that their needs are not being met, or that they cannot do the kind of work they feel is important. Institutions, on the other hand, are rarely satisfied with the level of performance of the actors and almost always would like more work performed for an equal or lesser amount of renumeration.

In the school setting, for example, many students find the school to be nomothetic, while the school itself often finds students to be too ideographic. But if there is a conflict, it is the student who will change or leave, not the institution.

ROLE VERSUS PERSONALITY

While the individual and the institution are the two basic elements of the interaction, role and personality are the basic units to be studied. Without going into a complete discussion of role theory, there are certain aspects of roles that we should be familiar with before continuing. A *role*, simply stated, is the sum of the behaviors expected of an actor by the institution. For example, a teacher is expected to teach in the classroom, not to dig ditches. That is obvious. However, things get a good deal more complicated when we delve into some of the hidden aspects of the role. Teachers, for example, even today, are expected to lead somewhat more exemplary lives than does the general population. This is even more true of the clergy. Such a requirement is not explicitly stated in the contract for either teachers or clergy, but it is part of the role nonetheless. Teacher roles are discussed further in Chapter 10.

Roles have certain characteristics. First, they are most commonly established by the institution. Sometimes, the member actors do have a say in the establishment of a role, but most commonly the institution has already established the parameters of the role. Second, in most cases, the roles antedate the actors who will assume the roles, that is, the roles were there before the actors enter the institution. The roles will most likely be there after the actors leave as well. Roles, therefore, tend to be consistent and institutionally oriented.

ROLE THEORY   A *conventional role* is a prescribed pattern of behavior expected of actors in a given situation by virtue of their positions. A garbage collector is expected to act like a garbage collector, not like a baseball umpire; a baseball umpire is expected to play his role, not act like a garbage collector. The *audience* (other actors in the immediate vicinity who can observe the actor's behavior) and observers would feel cheated if the two were to interchange their roles. In brief, a conventional role is what we are expected to do because we inhabit a particular role.

Role obligations, or role expectations, are specific acts that the actors feel are required of them because of their roles. Society has socialized actors to believe that it is important for them to act out their roles. Another factor influencing actors is the social pressure of the audience, which expects them to maintain *role consistency*, that is, to perform their role always in the same way. The reason that role consistency is important to the entire institution and, for that matter, the society, is that so long as consistency is maintained, the behavior of a particular role incumbent will be predictable. If each role incumbent were to establish his or her own ends, means, and behavior, no one would be able to predict the behavior of anyone else. This would make both societal and institutional functions complex and even unworkable—if some people decided that green traffic lights meant "stop" and red ones meant "go," things would get pretty dangerous for the rest of us.

As opposed to an obligation, a *role claim*, or need dispositon, is what actors may expect others to do for them because of the role status they occupy.

For example, teachers are obligated to teach, but they also have a right to claim respect. There is an obligation to meet classes, and a claim to be called by an appropriate name. As with many other roles, the role claims of teachers are somewhat determined by how well they have fulfilled their role obligations.

Role playing involves the ability of the actor to live up to the claims and obligations of the role. The actors do not really need to believe in the value or justification of the role; they merely need to follow it. The institution is concerned only that the actor play the role with enough skill that necessary functions can be fulfilled. In a mass society it is entirely possible to play one role at one time and a totally different role at another. For example, the shop foreman who is a traditional working man to his fellow workers may be a typical middle-class suburban resident when at home. The roles may be quite different, and the actor may believe in both roles, in either one, or in neither. The actor's belief is unimportant, in that the main interest of the institution, fellow workers, spouse, children, and neighbors is the effectiveness with which the role is performed.

Goffman, in *The Presentation of Self in Everyday Life*, makes the distinction between sincerity and cynicism in role playing. In the former case the incumbents believe in the role, while in the latter they do not. No value judgment should be placed upon this distinction, since at times sincerity can be bad and cynicism can be good. We would all object to the open display of hostility by a teacher who sincerely did not like a particular child or the display of excessive favoritism toward a like student, no matter how sincere. Instead, in this situation, we expect a form of cynical behavior that will guarantee equal treatment for each student. Goffman's point is that we all play roles. Sometimes we believe in them and sometimes we do not.

Role taking refers to the ability of one actor to see the situation through the eyes of another. For example, the ability of labor leaders and industrialists to see the situation from the other's standpoint is necessary if contract negotiations are to be fruitful. The same is true for school administrators, teachers, parents, and students. Much of the difficulty in relations between them is due to a lack of role taking. Cooperation is based upon this ability to see a situation from the standpoint of the other actor. Although role taking does not assure concensus, certainly it cannot be achieved without it.

A final distinction which should be made is that between impersonal and personal roles. In *impersonal roles* the claims and obligations remain the same regardless of the actor's personality; in *personal roles*, on the other hand, the personality of the actor will help determine those claims and obligations. An example is the difference in the handling of curriculum materials on the high-school and university levels. In general, the high-school teacher is expected to follow a preestablished curriculum. The curriculum itself may vary from very demanding and time consuming, leaving the teacher little time for innovation, to greater flexibility. But in either case, the general curriculum usually is followed quite closely and the teacher's personality plays little part in determining the parameters of the curricular role of the teacher. On the university level, however, quite often the only curriculum guide presented to the teacher is the title of the course. The teacher is expected to improvise in the development of the curriculum and personality will greatly affect the results and how the curricular role is fulfilled.

PERSONALITY   As institutions are juxtaposed to individuals, so roles are juxtaposed to personality. *Personality* is that portion of a person's behavior that, though it does change over a long period of time, is still more or less constant from one situation to another. It is what makes individuals different, even though they may have the same kinds of roles. One person tends to smile and laugh more than another regardless of the situation. This person is said to have a "happy" disposition or personality. Of course, this definition of personality is neither complete nor exclusive. Personality theory fits more justifiably within the domain of psychology than it does here. For the purposes of this discussion, however, the above incomplete definition will be sufficient. For the model of institutions under discussion, the primary characteristic of "personality" is its opposition to the "role" established by the institution. Personality's primary function is to imbue the role with the individual, that is, to allow individuals to put part of themselves into the role, even while performing the function that the institution has established.

In all cases, both personality and role are involved, although some institutions are traditionally more role oriented and others are traditionally more personality oriented. Mental hospitals are almost totally role oriented, since the inmates are allowed little if any freedom to express themselves. To a lesser extent the same can be said of the armed forces. On the other hand, artists' colonies and retreats place far greater value on personality characteristics, on individual differences and freedom, than on function.

Personality orientation is not necessarily better than role orientation, since, as with all nomothetic and ideographic categories, what is good, better, or best is determined through the perspective of the individual. Some people do not wish to emphasize their own personalities; they prefer an established role. Others find the established role limiting and prefer personality orientation.

The terms used in this discussion are operationally defined, that is, they are defined in terms of the behavior associated with them, not in any absolute sense. For example, personality is not defined in terms of some innate set of characteristics (though perhaps it could be) but rather in terms of the individual's behavior. A happy personality denotes happy role playing, not necessarily a happy inner self. The same operationalism holds true for the description of roles. A role is not described as an absolute set, but rather as a set of expected behaviors that can, and often does, change through personalization or change in societal attitudes.

From an operational viewpoint, then, a role is the dynamic organization of behavior outside the individual actor. It is dynamic in that it is constantly changing, but it is organized, since there is a set of expected behaviors that are joined to make up the role. It is outside the actors, since the role antedates the actors and will exist after they leave it. A personality is the dynamic organization within the individual actor. The personality is also both constantly changing and a conglomeration of patterns forming a whole. Unlike the role, however, the personality arrives at and leaves the institution with the actor.

ROLE EXPECTATION VERSUS NEED DISPOSITION

The closer one comes to behavior, the more complex the discussion becomes. This is because we move from the theoretical structure of the institution to a more operational discussion of the interaction between the institution and the actor. In discussing role expectation versus need disposition, we must consider conflict within the institution and how and why it occurs. Role expectations and need dispositions are, as we have said, opposites.

Role expectations are the specific behaviors expected of actors because they occupy a role. Whereas the role defines the actor's position in general terms (the teacher's role is to teach), the role expectation defines it in specific operational detail (the teacher's role expectation is to maintain order, teach history, and so forth). These are the role obligations. Similarly, while personality is the general construct ("I want to be happy"), need dispositions are the specifics ("My work should be happiness producing"). *Need dispositions* are those internal satisfactions that actors expect to receive from their participation in the institution. They are the role claims.

Both role expectations and need dispositions are defined in terms of adjusted and integrated behavior and in terms of efficient and effective behavior. *Adjusted behavior* is behavior that meets role expectations, that is, behavior adjusted to the preexisting role expectation. *Integrated behavior* is behavior that meets the need dispositions of actors. In many cases a rapprochement between integration and adjustment can be achieved by compromise between the actors and the institution. In such a case the individuals would be said to be effectively performing their functions — doing what they are supposed to do — and doing so efficiently — using the least possible amount of emotional energy. *Effective behavior*, then, is doing what is expected; *efficient behavior* is doing it with a minimum of energy expenditure. Efficient behavior refers to emotional, not physical, energy, since the amount of physical energy expended seems to make little difference in terms of either the amount of work completed or the satisfaction to the actor.

Although the balance between adjustment and integration is often maintained, sometimes the pattern shows overadjustment or overintegration. In *overadjustment*, the individuals subjugate themselves completely to the institution. Often they will even forget the end for which the institution was designed and maintain a slavish dedication to the institutional means. The teacher who slavishly follows the course curriculum day by day without thought as to whether the students are learning anything, or the student who slavishly maintains a perfect attendance record without regard to whether or not school is a meaningful experience, is illustrating overadjustment. The amount of overadjustment will, of course, vary with the individual and the institution; but to the extent that actors overadjust, they have subjugated their own needs to institutional roles. Overadjusted behavior is often very *effective* in that the actors do exactly what is expected of them, but their *efficiency* suffers in that need dispositions are not satisfied and the actors are either emotionally "dead" or distraught. Overadjustment meets the definition of the current term "burnout."

The other extreme is *overintegrated behavior*. In this case the actors flaunt the institution and sacrifice *effectiveness* and roles for their own internal *efficiency* and personal needs. Their behavior is underadjusted and overintegrated. The institution often attempts to eliminate such actors. (See Figure 5.1 for a graphic illustration of these terms.)

The concept of efficient and effective behavior is an important one. Teachers' complaints seem to be less about the amount of work than about the amount of emotional energy required to complete the work. The alcoholism, ulcer, and heart-attack rate among teachers is entirely too high and does

Figure 5.1 The Guba-Getzels Dialectic

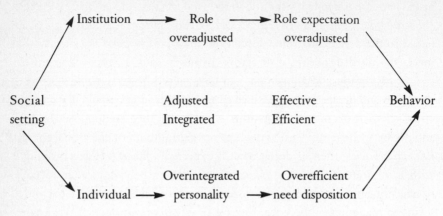

not show any appreciable signs of going down. This is not because of any lack in student learning, that is, the production rate. Rather, it is because of the emotional energy required to teach, maintain discipline, and follow guidelines and instructions, and because of the unsuitabilty of some curriculum materials for the particular population of students. Ulcers are a sign of inefficiency, not of ineffectiveness.

In terms of institutional interactions, however, difficulty occurs when individual adjustment takes too much energy (is too inefficient) or when the integration of the individual diminishes effectiveness. At that point, the institution views the individual as overintegrated or under- or maladjusted, while the individual views the institution as overadjusted or underintegrated. At this point we have reached a conflict situation. Robert K. Merton has developed a model that shows individual reactions to that conflict, which we shall discuss in detail in the next section.

THE MERTON CONFLICT RESOLUTION MODEL

We are now at the focus of stasis and change in the institution. The Guba-Getzels model has shown us how the institution and the individual come into conflict. The Merton model will show us how individuals react to that conflict. Some of the reactions lead to increased stasis, which makes the institution happy. However, in any conflict, there is also the potential for change. This may or may not make the individual happy, but it most certainly will not make the institution happy.

Table 5.2:
The Merton Conformity Model

	Goals	Means
CONFORMITY	+	+
INNOVATION	+	−
RITUALISM	−	+
RETREATISM	−	−
REBELLION	±	±

The Merton model is couched in terms of institutional means (the methods used to achieve the goals) and goals (the functions of the institution). In each of the individual responses to institutional pressure for stasis, the goals and means are handled differently. Both the goals and means are institutionally established; it is the problem of the individual to respond to those means and goals.

The first individual response is *conformity*. This is the ultimate stasis response. Here the individual accepts both the goals and the means of the institution. Merton assumes that the individual is sincere about accepting the goals and the means, that is, the goals and the means are truly internalized and believed. Goffman, on the other hand, would be perfectly willing to accept the idea that the individual assumes the role of believer while in actuality not believing at all. Merton is interested in how individuals in an institution alleviate their alienation. A cynical role playing will not alleviate alienation, but true conformity will since individuals can now believe that they are part of a greater whole, namely, the institution. They, therefore, willingly identify with it.

The second major individual response to alienation and conflict with the institution in Merton's model is *innovation*. Here the individual accepts the goal of the institution but does not accept the means. Innovation is generally viewed as a positive function in our society. The word itself has a pleasant connotation, and, in general, innovation is viewed positively by the school. Teachers who work within the system to try to change it usually have accepted the goals of the institution; they only want to make some revisions in the means. So long as the revisions are not too great, the institution will often be quite accepting. In fact, the definition as well as the connotation of innovation imply that the innovator is still in the system and wants to remain there. So long as the innovation does not go to far, the institution will most likely not only find the behavior effective but may even praise it as being more effective than the old means. The individuals may find that with the innovation accepted and allowed, their personal need dispositon is met and that they feel integrated. Innovation then can be a positive form of conformity for all concerned.

We should be clear, however, that innovation can also be negative if it goes beyond the bounds of what the institution is willing to accept. The student who wants to get good grades and is willing to cheat to do so is accepting the goal of good grades but is not accepting the conventional means suggested by the school. The juvenile delinquent who accepts the goal of wealth without the conventional means for achieving wealth is an innovator, as is the embezzler, the tax fraud, and so on. Innovation, just as is true of any of Merton's other responses, is neither positive nor negative in itself. Its value is neutral until the institution places a value and a sanction upon it.

The third response to alleviate alienation and ineffectiveness is *ritualism*. Here the individual has assumed that there is little that can be done about either the goals or the means and, while still not accepting the goals, decides that the means will be followed without much thought. If the individual truly believes in the means, and has merely lost sight of the goals, then we have true ritualism. Ritualism is exemplified by the "we've always done it that way" mentality. Form is given priority over the substance.

The fourth response is *retreatism*. Here the individual rejects both the goals and the means of the institution and either withdraws from the institution or is asked to leave. The institution, no matter what institution it is, will not accept an individual who rejects both means and goals. These are the true dropouts of the school or of the society. These people are not interested in either changing the institution or in setting up their own alternative. They are merely in the position of rejecting what exists.

The fifth response is both the most difficult and the most interesting— *rebellion*. Rebellious individuals both reject and accept the goals and the means. How is that possible? Very simple. Rebellious individuals think the goals and the means of the institution are more or less all right. They just feel that the wrong people are running the institution, that is, the present leadership should be replaced by the rebels.

Rebellious individuals, while they are terribly ineffective from the standpoint of the administrators of the institution (the rebels want the administrators' jobs after all) might, in fact, be terribly effective in terms of the institution. Rebels rarely find sufficient support to become a force in the institution unless the institution has some things wrong with it. If rebels gain an upper hand in an institution, there is good reason to believe that the institution needs some changes in leadership anyway. If the rebels do not gain the upper hand in the institution, they will very often retreat from the institution, thereby both eliminating the institution's power over them and, at the same time, eliminating any influence that they might have had on the institution. Unsuccessful rebels may also assume any of the other possible responses, assuming that the institution is willing to accept such a response from them.

There are two groups that are not included in the Merton model at all. These are the two groups in our society who do not have to follow any of the rules if they choose not to—the very rich and the very poor. The rich and powerful can and do make many of the rules but do not feel any particular obligation to follow them, while the very poor and powerless feel that they have nothing to lose by disobeying the rules and nothing to gain by following them. Both of these groups could fall into either the retreatist or the rebellious response modes, however. Neither particularly respects either the goals or the means and does not feel any obligation or guilt about it. Neither the railyard bum who cares not a wit about integration, nor the United States senator who votes for integration and sends his children to private segregated schools has any interest in the goal or the means of integration. This is left to those who are neither in the position of making the rules or of disobeying them. These two groups are nonconformist because they do not need to conform.

Transactional Behavior: The Ideal

The transactional category has not been discussed fully because it is the ideal. A transactional institution is one in which the actor and the institution have arrived at a balance that is mutually acceptable. This is not to imply that transaction is a middle path; it, too, can be quite extreme. As has been mentioned, every large institution needs certain people who slavishly follow the prescribed pattern: "There is a right way, a wrong way, and the Navy way; and we do it the Navy way." Their behavior may be considered slavish and overadjusted by some observers, but the institution could not exist without these workers. Their role may indeed be transactional if it meets their needs as well as those of the institution, even though most of the audience may feel that their behavior is overadjusted and nomothetic.

An example of transactional behavior at the other end of the scale stems from an institution's need for new ideas if it is to grow. These ideas may come from the highly unconventional and overintegrated actor, but they are still important to the institution. Thus they are transactional in that they meet the needs of both the institution and the actor, even though each may irritate the other.

FOR CONSIDERATION

1. Identify three social institutions that you feel are either nomothetic, transactional, or ideographic. What are the reasons for your choice?

2. Provide examples from your own experience that illustrate nomothetic, transactional, or ideographic behavior. Describe the roles and role expectations you had in each example.

3. Apply the administrative-style model discussed in this chapter to a school that you know. List characteristics of the model (roles, role expectations; individual personalities; need dispositions; adjustments, integration, overadjustment, and underadjustment). Then, present examples of each. Classify the school, as nomothetic, transactional, or ideographic. Classify the examples you have chosen as nomothetic, transactional, or ideographic.

4. How well does this model work in analyzing the school? What are its strengths? its weaknesses?

References

Getzels, Jacob W. "Administration as a Social Process." In *Administrative Theory in Education*. Edited by Andrew Halpin. Chicago, Ill.: University of Chicago Press, 1958.

————, and Guba, E. G. "Social Behavior and the Administrative Process." *School Review* 65 (1957):423–441.

Goffman, Erving. *The Presentation of Self in Everyday Life*. Garden City, N.Y.: Doubleday, 1959.

Shibutani, Tomatsu. *Society and Personality*. Englewood Cliffs, N.J.: Prentice-Hall, 1961.

Chapter 6:
The School
as a
Total
Institution

There are some who would contend that the school is the single most powerful agent for stasis in our society. The school controls the child's behavior for a period of 6 to 8 hours per day for some 180 days per year for 12 years. During that time, the school does a great deal more than just "school" a child in subject matter. That may be the least that the school does. At least as important is the school's role as educator in the life styles and mores of the society at large. This is the school's citizenship role. That it is important is without doubt, but there is nothing necessarily evil or sinister about this role. Every society tries to socialize its young into the societal rules, roles, taboos, prescriptions, and proscriptions. In our society the primary agency of acculturation is the school.

As is true with most socializing institutions, the values to which the children are socialized in the school are not new and innovative. Rather the patterns are traditional and represent societal stasis. This chapter deals with the power of the school as a socialization agent into those traditional stasis values.

This chapter is not an attempt to describe all the values that are learned in school. Rather, we shall concentrate on the process by which the values are learned. Here we will be dealing with power—specifically the power of the school over its students. The model of analysis we shall use will discuss the source and continuity of this power not only during the student's in-school life but also its extension into the student's post-school life.

By power, we do not mean political power in the broader sense. The school is not known for its influence over society or, in any case, has not exercised its potential power there. Most changes in our society and in our schools have not come from within the schools but rather have been products of other institutions, such as the courts, space technology, media, or legislative actions. The type of power with which this chapter deals is not the power of the institution over the society, but rather the power of the institution to mold individuals. We seek to examine it so that we may understand the relationship of the school as an institution to its members.

Conformity to Society

The Goffman model, which is the basis for this chapter, describes those institutions that have total power over their member actors. The purpose of these total institutions is to bring the member actors into conformity with behavior consistent with the role expectations of the institution or the society; that is, they attempt to impose *homeostasis*. The total institution does not give the individual the opportunity to choose either stasis or change. All of the other models in this book assume some level of freedom on the part of member actors. In the Goffman model of total institutions, the institution determines what pattern it wishes for the individual and then forces that pattern on him or her. The institution determines the form and content of the role to which the member actor is to acculturated.

People in total institutions are there because the society feels that either they are dangerous to themselves or others, or that they are in need of specific training to make them appropriate members of society. As will be shown in Chapter 10, while the society does not consider children to be dangerous members of society, it, in general, does maintain that they are in severe need of acculturation. Children are not really considered members of society — they are malleable souls in need of molding. Schooling and education in this or any other society has always played a major role in this acculturation process. What makes the school a total institution, initially, is that the recipients of the acculturation have little to say either about the pattern of the culture to be learned or about the process and procedure that will be used in the learning process. Children are sent to school to learn societally predetermined subjects and societally acceptable behaviors. This chapter will show how the school proceeds with that process in its role as a permeable total institution, that is, a total institution open to some outside influences.

The schools are expected to teach children to be quiet, clean, neat, passive, polite, punctual, bright, pleasant, and obedient. Obedient and passive may be the most important values to school personnel. Many of these school virtues may be of little worth outside of school. It is certainly true that in our society, where boys are raised to be more aggressive than girls, some of them may actually be dysfunctional outside of school. Even in school, it is sometimes true that poor and minority children, particularly boys, have more difficulty in adhering to these standards of behavior and, therefore, more often get in trouble with the school. Girls, in our society, are more commonly expected to show innocence, passivity, and reserve, so it may be easier for them to fulfill the school's expectations of good behavior. If they do not, they are often placed under severe pressure in school.

It should be pointed out that although the term total institution might seem to have a negative connotation, it should not be conceived in this light. In certain types of schools, the behavior of the students is of great importance. For instance, a highly academic setting requires that all the students follow the role prescribed by the teacher and adopt the silence necessary to hear the lecture. In such a school, the aspects of the total institution might so conform to the expectations of students and parents that there is little or no concern over what more progressive educators might consider harsh treatment. In any case, it is important to remember that the purpose of this chapter is not to chastise the school for being a total institution but rather to analyze the school in the light of the model of a total institution, so that it may be easier to understand the school and those who populate it.

The Goffman Model

Erving Goffman's analysis of the total institution as presented in his book *Asylums* will be used as the model to examine the school's power. As is the case with any model, it must be used with caution, since any one model for the investigation of institutions will not fit all cases. In *Asylums* Goffman discusses a particular type of institution, the mental hospital, which has almost total control over its inmates. The institution tells the inmates what and when they may eat, with whom they may speak, and even when they may fulfill their bodily functions. The total institution is, in short, an institution that

Flow Chart 7. The Goffman Model

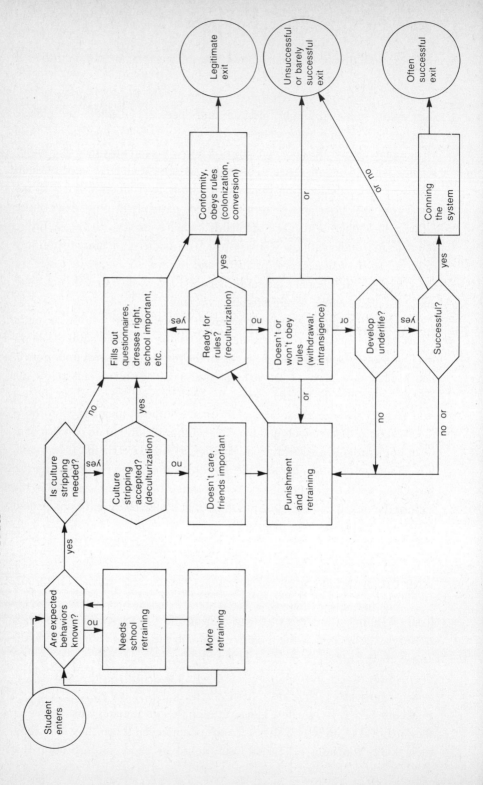

Description of the Goffman Model Flow Chart

The student enters the model in the upper left-hand corner of the chart. The first question asked is whether the student is aware of the expected behaviors. If yes, the next question asked is whether or not culture stripping has been accepted. Again, if the answer is yes, the student and his or her family fill out questionnaires, dress properly, behave according to accepted principles, and generally accept the school, its rules and regulations, and its ethos. A student of this sort finds it easy to conform and most often exits from the system with a minimum of complaint from either the individual or the school.

As can be seen from the chart, the child in need of behavioral training or retraining follows a far more tortuous path. This child either does not know the culture of the school or does not choose to follow the rules prescribed by that culture. If the rules are not known, the school attempts to retrain the child through stripping him or her of the outside world culture. If the student accepts this process, he or she is ready for reculturization. If not, the child is punished and then retraining often is reattempted. This loop continues either until the child accepts both de- and reculturization through colonization or conversion, or until the child unsuccessfully exits from the system.

There is, of course, an alternative path for those who are shrewd, bright, or lucky enough to use it—namely, the underlife. If the underlife is successful, it may be possible for the student to successfully exit the system without conforming to the culture of the school. If the underlife is unsuccessful, however, the punishment is often quite severe, since not only have rules and regulations been violated but there has been a direct attack on the authority of the school and the school may have been made to look ridiculous.

In brief, the Goffman model presents three possible exits from the system: (1) conforming to the school's culture; (2) subverting the school's culture and exiting successfully without conforming, via a successful underlife; and (3) exiting unsuccessfully through a lack of conformity to the school's culture.

governs the basic civilian functions of the individual member. The Army is a more familiar total institution, but Goffman finds the mental hospital a better example. Though our primary emphasis in this chapter is, of course, on the power of the school over the individual, we shall retain Goffman's example of the mental hospital here because of its clairty. Once his theory has been stated, we can investigate its implications for the school.

THE DECULTURIZATION AND RECULTURIZATION PROCESS

The previous background of particular inmates is of little or no importance in studying the total institution, since the purpose of the institution is to mold an individual into a member who may differ markedly from the same individual as nonmember. If the institution is wise, of course, it will take into account the background of inmates, so that it will be able to control and analyze their behavior more effectively. The point to remember, however, is that the background is taken into account only in order to make the task of indoctrination easier. If, for instance, one of the goals of the school is to teach a particular behavioral pattern to the students (for example, punctuality or cleanliness), it will make little difference whether the child is a boy or girl, or from a lower- or upper-class family. The purpose is to teach the behavior, not to take into account the previous biography of the student. The school will take the children as they are and attempt to mold them into "members." This is the purpose of the total institution.

Since most actors are either not willing or not able voluntarily to give up their individuality and previous cultural standards, it is the task of the institution to socialize the potential inmate into acceptance. Though this process continues for as long as the inmate remains in the institution, the process is begun through *stripping*, or *deculturization*, whereby, the noninstitutional culture of the individual, which may contain practices at variance with the desires of the institution, is eliminated.

This deculturization process begins with admission procedures. Here the initial attempt is made by the institution to change the inmate from nonmember to member. First, physical objects connecting the inmates to their noninstitutional self are removed. In the mental hospital inmates are informed that they may not retain their personal belongings, clothing, cosmetics, razors, and so forth. These are to be left with the authorities. The ostensible reason for this is to prevent the inmates from harming themselves or committing suicide.

According to Goffman, the actual reason is that individuality is connected with the front of personal belongings, and the institution must initiate the "de-individualizing" of the potential inmate. As another part of the stripping, inmates are often told to undress in the company of others, although they may never have done so before. They are then given physical examinations, where they may be asked embarrassing questions about their personal and medical history. Inmates then receive a uniform that is exactly the same as, or at least similar to, the uniforms of all other inmates. In all these processes, the individuality of the inmates is broken down so that they will be more receptive to the reculturization of the institution.

Reculturization is usually begun as part of the orientation, where inmates learn that they will not be successful members of the institution unless they conform to the definition of acceptable behavior presented by the authorities. *Reculturization* is the indoctrination of the individual with a new culture intended to replace the individualistic one stripped away. In the case of the mental hospital, it is implied not only that conformity is the only way to be acceptable to the authorities but also that the inmate will not get out of the hospital except by conforming to the authorities' definition of sanity. Inmates, therefore, have a double reason for negating their own personality in favor of the personality definition presented by the institution—reward or nonpunishment, and release from the institution.

Thus, through a process of stripping or deculturization and reculturization, the institution achieves a level of conformity and a sense of membership among its inmates. In this way it achieves not a cure but rather inmates who can be controlled with the least amount of effort.

INMATE RESPONSES

According to Goffman, the inmate takes one of four possible courses of action in order to counter the effects of the deindividualizing patterns of the institution:

1. *Situational withdrawl*, in which inmates apparently withdraw their attention from everything not directly concerning themselves and define themselves differently than does the institution.
2. *Intransigence line*, in which the inmate refuses to cooperate with the staff and is labeled a troublemaker. This is often the initial reaction of the inmate in response to inundation by the institution.

3. *Colonization*, in which inmates take what remains of their outside life and define their situation in terms of it. They redefine the norms of the total institution to fit their picture of what life was like on the outside. They deny that there is any difference between the institutional life and the life outside, or they indicate that their present life is better than the one outside.
4. *Conversion*, in which inmates assume the value structure of the institution as their own. They become model patients, recruits, or students.

Regardless of which course of action inmates take, one of the themes that permeates their lives in the total institution is that of the *underlife*. The basic function of the underlife is to give inmates the feeling that they are still maintaining some semblance of their individuality. This is accomplished by the development of a series of procedures through which the less important rules, and ones that are difficult for the institution to enforce, are broken. Thus inmates may make obscene noises that cannot be traced to any one member of the group but which are distracting to the speaker and amusing to the other inmates.

Institutions can assume more or less total control. For example, a mental hospital controls more of the everyday activities of its inmates than does the Army, even though both are considered total institutions. The thing that distinguishes these two institutions is their *degree of permeability*. Permeability here refers to the degree of outside influence on the institution and its inmates. Even though there may be few outside influences that affect soldiers, they do have periods of absence during which the Army has little control over their behavior. Therefore, the Army may be considered a more permeable institution than is a mental hospital.

The Power of the Schools

Schools, excluding restrictive boarding schools, are by no means so totally powerful as either the Army or a mental hospital. Yet there are enough similarities that the model of the total institution can be useful in analyzing the school's power over individuals. As in the total institution, there is an initial process of deculturization or stripping followed by reculturization, the imposition of a set of norms and rules that may or may not have anything to do with outside norms. Although perhaps to a lesser degree, the four response patterns identified by Goffman as open to mental hospital inmates are also characteristic of the student population. And the student population exhibits patterns of the underlife. This is particularly true of those students who are at odds with the patterns presented by the school authorities but is true, to some degree, of all students.

In the sections below, we shall discuss each of the characteristics of the total institution as they specifically apply to the schools. We shall begin with the processes of deculturization and reculturization, which begin, in fact, before the child enters the school itself.

DECULTURALIZATION AND RECULTURIZATION IN THE SCHOOL

Weeks or months before they finally enter a classroom, and regardless of their backgrounds, the process of acculturation begins. First the children's parents are told to fill out a series of registration forms. These forms ask for information about the children's parents; their occupation, if any ("If unemployed, for how long?"); the children's physical and medical history (including any and all diseases); the parents' physical and medical history; the number of siblings in the family; how many of these have attended the school; and so forth. These questions ostensibly serve the purpose of giving the school needed information regarding the children's academic ability. In many cases, however, they also give the school a great deal of information that will help to pigeonhole or label children. It also gives the parents a first sign that the school is watching their behavior as well as that of their child.

Once students have passed the entrance requirements, they are placed with a group of children who may or may not be part of their peer group. In some schools there is a definite, though often unwritten, policy that children in the same peer group (often called gangs) are to be separated as much as possible. This is done so that the teacher will have less trouble in handling the children. Within the class group, children are informed, either formally or informally, of the rules and regulations of the institution. They are also informed that if these rules are broken, certain sanctions will be placed upon them or the group. These sanctions vary—from writing a note to the parents, to having the offending child put his head on the desk while the other children play, or even to sending the child home.

Some of the rules and regulations will run counter to the behavior of the child in the nonschool setting. For example, toilet habits become a ritualistic pattern involving requests for permisson (usually granted). Separation of the sexes by the creation of two bathrooms requires the child to memorize which room is correct and which is taboo (this creates a code of modesty). At the same time codes of modesty are broken down within the sex group by having the child go to the bathroom in the presence of others. All three of these patterns may be opposed to home behavior, where many children go to the bathroom in the presence of family members of the opposite sex but never in the presence of strangers.

Children may also be told that they are to remain silent during the milk period, that they are to have a rest period, and so forth. Many of the rules and regulations presented to the primary-school child are less designed to enhance subject matter schooling than as a breaking in and socialization procedure. This procedure is not nearly so severe as is the deculturization of the mental-hospital inmate, but it serves many of the same functions: to mold individuals into team members who can be handled easily by the institution.

If the school finds that it cannot form the child into a member, the parents are called in. They are informed of the school's opinion of the child's behavior and are given pessimistic predictions for the future should this behavior continue. The kindergarten teacher will inform the parents not only of the consequences of the behavior for the child's chances in the first grade but also of its consequences if it is carried over into adult behavior. The behavior and the parents' attitude will be duly noted in the child's cumulative folders, which follow her throughout her academic career, even if she moves from that school. This leads to the looping process described by Thomas Scheff, whereby behavior in one situation will be brought to the child's attention in another (looping and labeling concepts will be more fully discussed in Chapter 7).

The processes of de- and reculturization discussed so far have all dealt with entrance into elementary school, particularly kindergarten. Though the examples given by no means exhaust instances of total behavior on this level, they are sufficient to indicate that one of the primary purposes of the early elementary school is to mold children into members. As children progress through school, the total institution reculturization increases rather than decreases. For one thing, kindergarten children spend less time in school than do older children; for another, parents are still considered supreme by children at this stage. The influence of the school, therefore, has not reached its peak.

When children reach later elementary school, junior high, and high school, they discover that their behavior and production rate are judged on the basis of how well they have adopted the school's cultural values. This is not to say that evaluation does not go on in lower elementary school but only that it is not as extreme or overt. Whereas children in elementary school are told that they will not do well in reading, high-school students are told that they will not get into college, will not graduate, or will not be able to get a job with the kind of recommendations that the school will give. This makes the negative sanctions and the need to reculturate immediate.

Some educators have gone so far as to suggest that all high-school students be given a plastic card listing their grades, attendance, and so forth. This would merely make official what is now open practice: the use of the school as an information depository for business and government. Since even with such practices students know the school is used as a source of information (they are often told so by their teachers), it is no surprise that they rarely come to their teachers or counselors with serious emotional, ethical, or personal problems. Further, students know that the consequences of negative behavior go far beyond the school.

Not only do their records follow them after they leave school, but the school also in large part can determine the single most important factor in that record: the method of egress from the school taken by the student. If students have either broken enough of the school's rules or broken the same one often enough, they can be expelled or suspended. This process depends, of course, on the power of the parents to bring pressure of countersanctions upon the school. Regardless of parental power or other extenuating circumstances, however, the school, like the mental hospital, has the power to enforce its regulations by threatening to withhold the proper egress papers.

Taking all these reculturization considerations together, we might at least tentatively call the school a semitotal institution. During the time that children are in school, the influence exerted on them is sufficient to force them to conform to the school's pre- and proscribed patterns or accept the consequences. They are forced to become members of the institution.

THE COURSES OF ACTION
OPEN TO STUDENTS

If the model of the total institution is to hold for our purposes, the students in the school should respond to the processes of deculturization and reculturization according to one of the four courses of action developed by Goffman. And, indeed, if we look at student responses to school, we find that they do.

The first course of action open to students is *situational withdrawal*. Here, students, for one reason or another, do not accept the definition of the situation presented by the school but rather than fighting it, ignore it. For example, gang leaders who recognize their own abilities to lead a gang but who are placed in a remedial class may reject the concept that they are stupid or even uneducated. They may merely withdraw from the sanctions of the school by indicating that they do not care what the school says and that the remedial class seems to be the easiest way to get out of school without doing any work. What they have done is to negate the power of the school over them by refusing to recognize that anything which the school does to or for them is of any significance in their lives. This is the "sit out" as opposed to the dropout. Such students merely sit out the time until they graduate, neither causing anyone else any trouble nor allowing the school to cause them any. These students may be irritating and unrewarding, but they are generally of little concern to the adult staff since they are conforming to the role of the "typical lazy remedial student."

There is, however, another type of withdrawn student, the kind who has withdrawn due to a sense of failure. These students say, in effect, "Don't try to teach me anything; I'm too stupid." They appear listless and unaware of their surroundings, with the exception of the bell that signals the end of the period and, hopefully, the day. Another distinguishing characteristic of this type of withdrawal is that it may not extend to all subject matters; the withdrawn English student may be expressive in shop, on the athletic field, or in history class.

Intransigence is a more open attack upon the authority of the school or particular class. Here a student refuses to obey, openly flaunts, or simply breaks the rules of the school and dares anyone to take action. In some cases, students may recognize that they have greater power (for example, a parent on the school board) than does the school. At other times, they may wish to defy the school openly for personal reasons. One of the dangers here is that the students' occasional "sounding" (insults designed to be taken in a half-joking fashion to see how far they can go without punishment) may be taken as defiance.

Colonization may be the most common response by students who feel they have nothing better to do than go to school. Here students recognize that the school has little to offer them in terms of basic desires and needs, but that it is better than walking the streets. The general attitude is "live and let live." Often such students use the school not for its manifest function of attaining knowledge but rather for a latent function such as social contact.

Conversion occurs when students simply accept the definition of their role as presented by the school. This is easier for some students than it is for others.

For example, as Paul Goodman has pointed out in *Growing Up Absurd*, the school is a predominantly feminine, middle-class institution, and so girls find it easier to accept the definition of the situation as presented by the school. If statistics regarding discipline are any indication, it would appear that more boys than girls, more lower-class students than middle- or upper-class students, and more minorities than majority students are referred for disciplinary matters.

For heuristic reasons the four characteristic responses have been separated, but in actual practice pure types of reaction will be less common than will mixtures of some sort. Most students do not recognize that they are adopting a set of roles in school, since many of the roles have become part of the societal expectation of the school and are adopted without the students awareness. It must also be remembered, however, that regardless of the course of action taken by students, they, like the inmates in a mental hospital, will attempt to keep part of themselves inviolate. This will be particularly true of those students who come into conflict with the institution. This attempt to maintain individuality within the institutional structure makes up the underlife.

THE UNDERLIFE IN THE SCHOOL

The purpose of the underlife is to enable inmates to maintain portions of their own individuality in the face of the institution's power. The connotation of the underlife is that this is done through covert attacks on the institution for which the inmates cannot be punished. This gives them a double feeling of self-worth, since they have been able to break the institution's rules and at the same time "put one over on them" in that, if the attack is well-planned and well-executed, they will not be punished.

For example, a student is sent to the office and arrives some forty-five minutes later. When asked what took her so long, she replies that she had to go to the bathroom. The student knows that it is a lie, and she knows that the administrator knows that it is a lie, but they both know that there is little or nothing that can be done about it. This is a reasonably simple form of the underlife. It can be far more complex. The complexity of the specific act is in part determined by the amount of control exercised over the individual by the school. The greater the control, the more complex and, in many cases, bizarre the behavior will appear. For example, students in a social-adjustment class are far more closely watched than are their counterparts in a regular class, and they must, therefore, resort to making strange noises or belching or the like in order to indicate their individuality in the face of the institution's power.

The underlife can sometimes become endemic in a school. For example, a group of students may discover that one of their teachers does not pay attention during tests. Both in order to show their disregard for the values held by the school and to get good grades without studying, students may then cheat in any way possible. If out-group members of the class indicate displeasure, they will be convinced through social pressure that they should hold their tongues and cheat with the rest of the class. Sometimes the brightest students in the class, who could obtain a good grade without cheating, will seem to cheat so that they will not be ostracized by the group. If the students respected the class, school, or teacher they might decide not to cheat. Then there would be no underlife. Despite this occasional endemic form of underlife, individual acts that elicit support from the rest of the class in the form of sympathetic laughter are more common.

Is the School a Total Institution?

The "totalness" of the school depends upon the permeability of the school. Permeability refers to the amount of cross-contact between the larger culture and the institution. Certainly the school is a far more permeable institution than is the mental hospital, but the armed forces are more permeable than the mental hospital, too. The problem here is to determine whether there is so much cross-contact that it does not make sense to call the school a total institution at all. One example of cross-contact is the encouragement parents are given to take an interest in the school and the welfare of their child within that school. Parents are urged to join the PTA, and in some cases pressure may be brought to bear upon children if their parents are not members of the PTA.

If we look more closely at the relationship between parent and school, however, we see that there is not nearly the permeability we may have originally suspected. It is difficult for a parent to "just look around" the school. There are particular times when parents are allowed to enter the school, talk to teachers, and review their child's work. Open houses, PTA meetings, and father's nights are examples.

Viewed from the standpoint of the school as a total institution, the purpose of these gatherings is not to make the school more permeable but rather to make it less permeable while seeming to make it more so. If parents have a complaint or just want to learn more about the school, they are told to become active in the PTA or a similar organization. If they become active, they may feel that they are getting close to the workings of the school. But if they analyze the degree of school contact, they will soon realize that they have spoken only to the principal or to the faculty PTA representative. If the schools were permeable, any interested parents could go to the school and talk to the people involved in teaching their child. Whether a permeable school is desirable is not, however, the point at issue; we merely conclude that the PTA and other such devices are often used to keep parents and the public from directly intervening in the school. This may not be the intended manifest function of the PTA, but it is a latent actual function.

All in all it seems feasible to assert that the school bears a sufficient similarity to other total institutions to make the construct of the total institution valid. And, in fact, this construct is basic to the theoretical formulation of this book. An instrinsic part of the role of the school is that it does have power over the behavior of children in the present and in the future. The school does change the behavior of children from whatever it was before they entered school to a behavior that conforms to the value structure of the school and the society; it does attempt to change the nonmember to the member.

If the society is particularly interested in academic achievement in school and a compliant citizenry when they leave school, then the main purpose of the school is to impart knowledge to the young. In such a society, the more total the school, the better. This type of school is a stasis school—it repeats the knowledge of the past and forces children to learn it. If, on the other hand, the society strives to teach independence of thought and action rather than compliance, then the school will allow as much freedom as possible to individual students, so they will learn to make choices. This describes a change-oriented school.

The purposes of these two schools are quite different (stasis for one, change for the other), so the method of training children is quite different. Correspondingly, the role expectations for the children are different (obedience and conformity versus independence and innovation).

FOR CONSIDERATION

1. Using Goffman's concept of the total institution, classify the following social institutions according to how total they are. Rank order the list from the most total to the least total. Explain your rankings in terms of the institution's degree of permeability.

Media
Family
Health care
Military
Religion
Peer group

2. Pick a particular example of each institution in item 1 above (for example, your own family or the local newspaper). Then discuss it, using specific illustrations of permeability (that is, what factors outside the institution influence inmates' behavior and ideas?).

3. Apply the total institution model to a school. Using the following characteristics, identify examples of school life that either illustrate or refute the characteristics.

Deculturization
Reculturization
Inmate response patterns:
    Situational withdrawal
    Intransigence
    Colonization
    Conversion
Underlife

4. How well does this analytic model fit the school you have examined? How does it compare with models discussed in other chapters in its ability to provide explanations for or to predict school events? Which model offers you the best insights for understanding stasis and change in schooling?

References

Friedan, Betty. *The Feminine Mystique*. New York: W. W. Norton, 1963.

Friedenberg, Edgar A. *The Vanishing Adolescent*. New York: Dell, 1959.

Goffman, Erving. *The Presentation of Self in Everyday Life*. Garden City, N.Y.: Doubleday, 1959.

Goodman, Paul. *Growing Up Absurd*. New York: Random House, 1956.

Scheff, Thomas J. "The Role of the Mentally Ill and the Dynamics of Mental Disorder." *Sociometry* 26 (1963):436–453.

Shanley, Fred; Alzobaire, Jalil; and Lefever, D. Welty. "Comparative Analysis of School and Behavioral Data for Aggressive, Well-Adjusted, and Underachieving Students." Youth Studies Center, University of Southern California, Los Angeles, 1964.

Chapter 7:
School
Definitions,
the Student,
Socialization,
and Equity

All of the previous chapters have dealt with stasis and change as processes on an institutional level. This chapter will show institutional affects on individuals. A society's institutions define individuals and attempt to maintain stasis in terms of these definitions. For example, males in our society traditionally have been expected to maintain a macho image while women were supposed to be ladylike and demure. Both of these images, which happily are changing, were defined in rather specific detail, although no one wrote out the definitions and handed them to children as they were born. Rather, societal definitions are ingrained in the societal fabric and are informally learned in daily interactions.

The primary agency sponsored by the society that consistently and intentionally trains children in their role definitions is the school. (The family is not directly sponsored by the society.) Society expects the school to teach more than academic subjects. Certainly one major task is to teach behavior and role definitions that are acceptable to, and sponsored by, the society. The school occasionally has fought some societal definitions. For example, the idea that blacks and whites could not go to school together was effectively fought by many educators. Our focus in this chapter, however, is not on the school's influence in such broad social areas. Rather we shall concentrate on the school's influence on the commonly used definitions of children—as good student, bad student, neat, clean, punctual, nice, troublemaker, and so on—and on how these definitions affect children on a day-to-day basis. The way children are defined by the school will determine many of their behaviors and attitudes as adults. Furthermore, the school is a primary influence in the way future adults define themselves and each other.

How children are defined by the school is not constant or static, but instead continually undergoes change. The meaning of good or bad behavior in the schools has changed radically over the past twenty years. Many educators think current definitions are better; others think they are worse. But the fact of change is not the critical issue for this chapter. The important question here is to determine how the school, or the society, generates and maintains generally accepted and acceptable definitions. We will also want to consider how the society, or institution, assures acceptance of the definition by the individual, once the definition had been inculcated.

Transience or
Permanence of Role

The process of accepting the societal definition of the self has been discussed by various writers, but none has dealt with it more systematically than Thomas J. Scheff.[1] Scheff is interested in two related considerations: (1) the societal pressures that cause transitory eccentricities to become permanent deviant behaviors; and (2) how people become labeled as deviant.

Though Scheff does not discuss it, it is possible to deduce that the patterns which cause transitory deviance to become career deviance are the same as those that cause transitory positive behaviors to become permanent positive behaviors (such as becoming a "good student," or a "good citizen").

Also, by implication, labeling theory can be used to analyze any form of career behavior by an individual within an institution. Therefore, even though Scheff is primarily concerned with deviance and makes no mention of the institution of the school, his theory may be applied to the school and the process of labeling that goes on within it. Specifically, Scheff's theory may be used to ask two questions of the school:

1. Under what conditions do various forms of deviant or conforming behavior become stable and uniform, that is, when is the school's definition accepted and internalized by an individual student?

2. To what extent are symptoms of deviant or conforming behavior the result of conforming to societal definitions of stereotypic behavior, that is, have "bad" and "good" students been taught how they are supposed to act by the society? For example, "bad" students fail, cheat, don't do homework, and so on, while "good" students pass, succeed, do homework, and so on.

Residual Deviance

Scheff begins his discussion by distinguishing between nonresidual and residual deviance. *Nonresidual deviance* refers to recognized categories of deviant behavior with specific traits; *residual deviance* includes all forms of deviant behavior for which there is no specific category. For example, catatonic schizophrenia is characterized by certain psychotic behavioral patterns that distinguish it from other deviance. Mental illness, on the other hand, may include everything from psychosomatic disorders (undefined), to nervous breakdowns (undefined), to keeping too many house pets. Catatonic schizophrenia is a nonresidual category, while mental illness is a residual category. Fist fights in schools are nonresidual because they are relatively clearly defined. But the definition "bad student" is a residual category, which is poorly defined. Residual deviance is what is left over when the defined categories are removed. Scheff is interested in residual deviance—those disorders that are defined differently by different people (including experts) and that affect behavior by the way in which they are defined. For example, the child who scores poorly on a standardized test may be defined as "having a bad day" or as "stupid," depending on his or her past record and, unfortunately, on possible racial or socioeconomic bias. Both "bad day" and "stupid" are undefined residual categories. The effect of each label, however, is very different.

LABELING AND THE SELF-FULFILLING PROPHECY

To understand just how extreme the effects of labeling can be, and to better understand the concept of residual deviance, it is useful to look at an experiment on children undertaken in the early 1960s by Rosenthal and Jacobson and reported in their book *Pygmalion in the Classroom*.[2] In this rather controversial experiment, school children were placed in one of two categories without regard to their ability or previous learning achievement. The teachers were told that the children had been tested. One randomly selected group was arbitrarily labeled late bloomers, who were now ready to jump ahead, and the other group was arbitrarily tagged as not capable of doing much academic work. There was no difference between the two groups, but the teachers were told that there was. By the end of the year, the late blooming children had advanced dramatically, while the non-academic children had not improved appreciably, or had even declined in achievement. The self-fulfilling prophecy had been fulfilled: those children who had been labeled smart became smart, while those who were labeled stupid became stupid.

The students in the stupid group and their parents were justifiably angry at the study, since at the end of the year the children in this group were a year behind. In fact, one of the results of the study was the establishment of a new set of guidelines on the use of human subjects, because the researchers did do something that was not in the best interests of those children unlucky enough to have been placed in the stupid group. Unfortunately, this was the only way the researchers could prove their point—that children will learn as much or as little as they are expected to learn. The teacher who expects little will receive little and the teacher who expects much will receive much. This is a point that is rarely made in teacher-training institutions. We teachers and teacher trainers would prefer to blame anyone but ourselves for student deviance.

Scheff's Nine Propositions of Labeling

Sheff's theory presents nine propositions to show the effects of labeling on the definition of deviance. These propositions are as follows:

1. Residual deviance has varied sources.
2. The rate of unrecorded residual deviance is extremely high.
3. Most residual deviance is denied and is transitory.
4. The sterotypes of deviance are learned in early childhood.
5. The sterotypes of deviance are reaffirmed, inadvertently, in daily interaction.
6. Once the society has labeled the deviants, they are rewarded for playing the deviant role.
7. Deviants are negatively sanctioned for attempting to leave the role.
8. When the institution attempts to label individuals, they may feel that no other option is open to them except the institutional definition.

9. In residual deviance, labeling is the single most important factor contributing to career deviance.

Each of these propositions may be applied to the school and help us find answers to such questions as how the child becomes labeled and defined as "good" or "bad" by the school; how the child comes to accept that label; and how the child is maintained in that label, definition, and role. Although the theory does hold for conformity, as well as for deviance, for the sake of simplicity, we shall be concerned in the discussion below with those children who are negatively sanctioned for their residual deviance.

RESIDUAL DEVIANCE HAS VARIED SOURCES

It has been shown that definitions of mental illness differ according to their source, be it genetic, physiological, nutritional, or the traditional psychological. Likewise, we learn what it is to be a "good" or "bad" student from diverse sources. The definition of student is a great deal broader than just getting good or bad grades. It also includes the idea of acceptable or unacceptable behavior. The source for the definition of good and bad student behavior is clearly diverse in nature. Books, movies, television, school-board definitions, teacher demands, and peer pressure all help to define both the good and the bad student. The definition is complex both because it is not specific, that is, it is residual, and in that it comes from so many diverse sources.

THERE IS MUCH UNRECORDED DEVIANCE

Scheff's second proposition, that there is a high rate of unrecognized residual deviance, is of less concern in relation to the school than are the others. We should note simply the tendency on the part of the institution to ignore deviant behavior. For example, if the preconception of the school is that boys tend to get into innocent mischief, there is greater likelihood that misbehavior will be denied as a major problem area. The same behavior might be defined as delinquency in another setting. The determining factor is not the behavior itself but the desire of the institution to ignore or not ignore behavioral implications contrary to accepted definitions. The Rosenthal and Jacobson experiment is classic in this relation. Whenever a late bloomer scored poorly on a test, it was assumed that the child had had a bad day. On the other hand, if a nonlate bloomer did well on an exam, it was assumed either that the child had cheated

150

Flow Chart 8. The Scheff Model

Student enters

Is student behavior O.K.?

Does O.K. behavior continue? (conformity)

Student defined as O.K. (primary deviance)

Is definition accepted? (career deviance)

Definition confirmed

Successful exit

Is institutional definition doubted?

"Had a bad day, tries to be bad for friends," etc.

Definition not confirmed

Does not O.K. behavior continue? (nonconformity)

Defined as not O.K.? (primary deviance)

Is definition accepted? (career deviance)

Does not O.K. behavior continue?

Is institutional definition doubted?

Cheated, lied, tried to "con" system

Is career deviance accepted?

no (rare)

Definition not confirmed

Definition confirmed

Unsuccessful exit

yes

no

Flow Chart of the Scheff Model

This is the most individually and behaviorally oriented of the models. Here the focus is on the institution's response to the individual behavior of the student. The first question asked is whether the student's behavior is OK as defined by the institution. If the behavior is OK, then the next question asked is whether the OK behavior is continuing. If it is, the student is defined as OK by the school (primary deviance). If that definition continues, the student will most likely also accept the definition of him or herself as an OK student (career deviance).

Naturally, it is more pleasant to be defined as an OK student than as a not OK one. However, once that definition is confirmed, it is as difficult for OK students to leave their definition as it is for the not OK students to leave theirs. Up to the point at which the definition is confirmed, the OK students can still redefine themselves as not OK by engaging in acts that the school thinks are not OK. However, once the OK definition is confirmed, even not OK acts will be interpreted positively. For instance, if an OK student fails a midterm exam, his teacher might say, "He's just having a bad day." Even in a positive case, then, there is still a requirement to conform to the definition.

As usual, nonconforming students have a more convoluted path to follow. Since the institution has more difficulty with those students, there are more cells in the chart dealing with them. Let us assume that the not OK student enters the school and that his or her behaviors are not OK. The next question asked is whether or not the not OK behavior continues (nonconformity). If not, we revert back to the original question of whether or not the student behavior is OK. If it is, then the pattern of the conforming student begins. If it is not, then the question of the continuance of the not OK behavior is asked again. This is a continual loop until the behavior either gets better or continues to be not OK. If the not OK behavior continues, the student is defined as not OK (primary deviance) by the school but has not yet accepted it within him or herself. If the definition is accepted, then it becomes career deviance.

It is more difficult for a not OK student to break with the confirmed definition than it is for the OK student to do so. There is a greater tendency on the part of schools to believe that OK students can get worse than that not OK students can get better.

Once the definition is confirmed, the question is whether or not the not OK behavior continues. If it does, then the definition continues to be confirmed. This is what the school expects and really encourages, just as it encourages definitional consistency for the OK student. If the student does not confirm the definition, however, it may be necessary for the school to reevaluate its definition. It does this by asking whether or not the definition should be doubted. If it is decided that it should not be, then the defined not OK student is accused of cheating or conning the system. Thereby the student is forced to maintain the not OK definition even if he or she has been honestly trying for redefinition. This most often leads to continued career deviance and usually an unsuccessful exit. More rarely, the student will again attempt redefinition. On the other hand, if the school doubts its own definition and accepts that the student might be trying to redefine him or herself, then the process would have to start all over again with the initial question of whether the behavior is OK, or, at least, whether or not the OK behavior is continuing.

It is more convenient for the school, or any other institution, to maintain its definitions of students, whether good or bad. If the administration and the adult staff constantly have to be on the lookout for changing definitions, things will tend to be unstable from day to day. Students who can be counted on to be good could become bad, and what is worse, the opposite could also be true. Definitions would break down, and each day's definitions would be different.

The point of this model is to show that definitions are hard to break and that labeling is a primary function in the process of definition. Further, the definition process has at least two steps, namely, primary deviance, where the institution defines the individual, and secondary deviance, where the individual accepts the definition. Once the definition has been accepted, it is difficult, if not impossible, for the individual to break with the definition.

---

or had learned that particular subject well for that week, or the teacher remarked, "Wasn't it nice that they could achieve occasionally." Test results are not nearly so important as is their interpretation by the person or institution in authority.

MOST RESIDUAL DEVIANCE IS DENIED

The third proposition, that there is a relationship between denial of the symptoms and the ephemerality of the disorder, is central to Scheff's thesis. In effect, if you do not mention the disorder, it will go away. Indeed, in the case of stutterers, if the infirmity is not mentioned and if nothing is done, stuttering in young children often will pass. If the parents become concerned and make a fuss over the stuttering, however, there is some reason to believe that it will continue. Scheff points out that a number of forms of deviant behavior occur in children, such as temper tantrums, biting, thumb sucking, or imagining nonexistent playmates or ghosts. Yet these behaviors are normally transitory. Adults, too, engage in transitory deviant behavior; they may talk to themselves, daydream, or steal from libraries, but unless the behavior is reinforced, it does not become a career pattern. Again, in the Pygmalion study, the patterns the teachers expected were those that were reinforced. The patterns that were not expected were either ignored entirely or were understood as unimportant anomalies. In this way, unexpected symptoms were denied and eventually went away. No matter what, the "smart" students could not be "dumb," and the "dumb" students could not be "smart."

A particularly striking instance, which bears out Scheff's proposition that any form of deviant behavior will tend to be transitory if the behavior is not reinforced, is Eysenck's study[3] of a large number of diagnosed schizophrenics, only half of whom could be treated immediately. The others were required to go through their normal daily activities for a period of up to a year. At the end of that year, much to everyone's surprise, those who had not been treated for schizophrenia were in no worse condition than those who had been treated. According to Scheff's propositon, the ones who were being treated for schizophrenia had been reinforced in deviance by being treated, whereas those who were not being treated did not have their behavior reinforced. They had to learn to live with it, and their deviance not only did not increase, but they actually adapted to the new situation with some facility.

Again the basic question is raised as to the difference between factors that allow deviance to remain transitory and the factors which seem to make deviance permanent. Scheff postulates that the primary factor involved is social reaction to the behavior. He discusses Glass's experiments with battle fatigue in Korea[4] to illustrate his point. Glass discovered that when men who sincerely thought they were suffering from battle fatigue were told that their symptoms were nothing unusual and certainly nothing to worry about, the rate of withdrawal from the front lines dropped appreciably. The theory is that since the symptoms were denied, the mental disorder disappeared. To hypothesize a more familiar situation, what would be the effect of reinforcing success in students who had a history of failure in class. Is there a relationship between being failed in a class and considering oneself an academic failure? What would be the result if we expected everyone to pass?

STEREOTYPES ARE LEARNED EARLY

Scheff's fourth proposition is that the imagery of mental disorder (or mental and social health and stability) is learned in early childhood. Through the mass media, remarks of adults, bizarre farces of the insane in the media, and so forth, the child picks up a series of cues that form the basis for a definition of mental deviance. For our purposes, the same communication forces present cues that define schools, students, teachers, and administrators. Judging by studies of the public's sterotyped role expectations for teachers, it would seem that the process of presenting cues about the school to children may be more advanced than are the cues about mental disorders. The role and definition of the school and the teacher are both highly stereotyped. The imagery of the school is learned and firmly imprinted from early childhood.

It is surprising how consistent the definition of the "well-adjusted," or "good" student is. In a number of studies teachers have pointed out those children in the classrooms who are "aggressive," "well-adjusted," and "underachieving" without being given the definitions of those terms. There was unspoken agreement as to what the terms mean. The well-adjusted student is generally quiet but does speak; is polite but can get angry; gets relatively good grades but not necessarily so; gets along well with others; is cooperative, and so on. The point is not the specifics of the definition of this residual category, but that it is so easy to come to agreement on the definition. Just as there is an imagery for the mentally ill, so there is an imagery for the "good" or "bad" child in school. The school's definitions are pervasive in the society, and children are saddled with them from an early age.

STEREOTYPES ARE REAFFIRMED

Scheff's fifth proposition indicates that stereotypes are reaffirmed in daily life. For example, many schools and school professionals have preconceived notions about the abilities of various types of students. These sterotypes are reconfirmed by mass media, informal communication with other teachers, and so forth. In terms of achievement, teachers tend to equate family background and socioeconomic status with academic ability. However, as early as the fifties and sixties, the Lynds in *Middletown*[5] and Riessman in *The Culturally Deprived Child*[6] have shown the equation to be fallacious. The lower-class children have great interest in learning, and their parents, though they may be uneducated themselves, share the American faith in education. Nevertheless, the stereotype of uncaring lower socioeconomic parents is so entrenched that the data are denied, and the school continues to operate on the assumption that lower-class children have neither the ability nor the home encouragement to learn.

THE REWARDS AND PUNISHMENTS
OF DEVIANCE

Scheff's sixth and seventh propositions indicate that once the society has labeled individuals as deviants or conformists, they are rewarded for playing that role. For instance, if teachers expect poorer performance from the lower socioeconomic status students, they will have a tendency to lower the academic expectations for these students. If the teachers assume that the lower-status students in a remedial class are incapable of writing an essay, they will not be required to write essays. Since many students are pleased to get out of work, the lower socioeconomic status remedial students are reinforced in their role of being poor students. On the other hand, new teachers who do not feel that these students are incapable of doing work may blithely assign essays every week and receive them every week. Negative school rewards (that is, not having to write essays) positively reinforces the residual deviant role of the poor student.

With regard to negative sanctions for attempting to leave the deviant role, what would happen if a teacher believes her students are not capable of writing essays, but one student denies the role and turns in a well-written one? If the teacher's preconceptions are sufficiently strong, she will assume, perhaps, that the student had someone else write it for her or that it was copied out of a book. The teacher may believe that she is punishing the student for cheating when, in actuality, the student is being punished for leaving the deviant role.

THERE IS A LACK OF OPTIONS
FOR THOSE LABELED DEVIANT

Once deviants or conformists feel that other avenues have been closed, they may consider that the only option open is to accept the deviant role. In the example used, students may come to accept the school's definition of them as poor students. This is Scheff's eighth proposition: When individuals attempt to adopt the conventional role, they are often negatively sanctioned for trying to leave the deviant role. They thus assume that deviance is the only option left.

Up to this point, we have been stressing the school's attempt to label the student. Most of this labeling is external to the student's self-concept; that is, the individual's definition may still be quite different from that presented by the institution. Many students do not accept what the school says about them. If the labeling practices of the school are sufficiently effective, however, students will eventually incorporate the institution's definition into their own self-concept and become career deviants. For example, when the school defines a student as a "failure" a sufficient number of times, gives him report cards to prove it, and calls in his parents to discuss it, the student will come to think of himself as a failure, unless he has the strength or support to deny the school's definition. If he internalizes the definition, then primary deviance will become career deviance.

CAREER DEVIANCE IS THE RESULT OF LABELING

Scheff's last proposition, and his major conclusion, is that labeling, rather than any actual offense or behavior, is the single most important factor in the establishment of career deviance. The extent and direction (positive or negative) of labeling is determined largely by the school's reaction to specific behaviors or to student stereotypes. Part of this reaction is determined by the history of interaction between the student and the school and the preconceptions and points of view developed on the basis of that history.

The severity of any negative reaction, however, will also be based on three factors inherent in the specific situation. The first factor is the visibility, amount, and degree of deviance—that is, the degree of overtness of the behavior. The definition of visibility, of course, depends largely on the institution. For example, being three minutes late to a social engagement is certainly acceptable. On the other hand, being three minutes late to a junior high school class is not acceptable. When students walk in three minutes late, they are highly visible in that everyone in the classroom is fully aware that they are late.

The second factor is the power of the individual students and the distance between them and the agent of social control. The more powerful or the more distant the deviant students, the less will be the effect of labeling. For example, if the deviant student's parents are members of the school board, the deviance may be ignored or glossed over rather than systematically punished. In this case, the student may have greater powers than do some of the teachers or administrators in the school.

The third factor is the tolerance level and preconceptions of the institution. The school's tolerance level determines, to a large extent, the behaviors that will be considered deviant. An open-education school will accept more noise than will a traditional school. The behaviors may be the same, but the school's response will be different.

Certain students are more prone to the labeling process than are others. Lower-class, minority-group male children are often more visible in terms of color, speech habits, and poorer dress. They, their families, and their particular community have the least amount of power of any group in the society. Furthermore, because they are children in an adult-run institution, their power is further decreased when the distance from the authorities (teachers, administrators, and counselors) is diminished. Because of the preconceptions of the school, the tolerance level may be lowered, so that deviant behavior, which is sometimes called "good clean fun" in other schools or at other times, now is seen as malicious mischief. All this indicates that the power of the school to label individuals and the individual's acceptance of the label will be different with different types of students. Nevertheless, the basic hypotheses that the school is a potential labeler and that such labels can effectively change the behavior of students still holds.

Stasis, Change, and Labeling

This chapter has presented an analytical approach to labeling in the school. The school's role as labeler can have positive as well as negative effects upon students. It is true, however, that much of the school's labeling is negative in nature—there are always fewer honor students than "bad boys" and "bad girls."

Regardless of the specific outcome, the school can and does label students and can obtain acquiescence to its labels from them. The labeling process is a primary source of the school's power as an institution. Once the school can get students to accept its definition of their roles, then it is in a position of great power in relation to them.

All of Scheff's propositions seem to be born out by the Rosenthal and Jacobson experiment. The definitions of good and bad or smart and dumb are not clearly defined categories, that is, they are residual. The definitions do not hail from a specific place but are general in the society. The definition is an incredibly powerful inducement for the student to do what is expected. In brief, labeling is a process that goes on continually in the school and which is largely unstudied by the school. Children are subjected to it, but neither the subjectors nor the objects are aware of it or understand it.

The implications for stasis and change are, of course, immense. As was pointed out in Chapters 1 and 2, the school has often been the primary force in keeping children in their place. Keeping them in their place means more than just treating them as children. It also involves treating them as lower- or middle- or upper-class children; as minority or majority children; as the children of the ruling class or the ruled class; as good or bad; as smart or dumb; as nice or not nice.

These definitions are much more than individual problems of individual children. They are the problem of society. If we in education believe that the schools should make the society more free and just, then part of our role should be to show children how they can change that society and their places in that society. If children are taught, and reinforced in the belief, that they are what the society believes about their skin color, socioeconomic status, sex, or behavior pattern, then we are implying that the school is and should be a force for stasis. Defining children into residual categories is a strong force for stasis.

However, if the school believes in change and the right and responsibility of every child to become what he or she is capable of becoming, then the process of labeling is dysfunctional. If a child is left educationally undefined and is allowed to determine his or her own self-definition, could this not lead to greater achievement and feelings of self-worth? The school is not equitable in its definitions. Verbal and female behavior patterns and definitions are generally more acceptable to the schools, as are those of members of the majority and the upper-socioeconomic classes. What labels do we place on the male, minority, nonstandard-English or dialect-speaking, lower-socioeconomic child? Is this child doomed to educational failure because of lack of ability and desire, or should we also look at the preconceived definitions and labels of the school?

Labeling itself may be a great part of the problem in the relationship, or lack of it, between some communities and the school. Many communities hold highly negative stereotypes of the school, and many schools hold negative stereotypes of the community. While both may be wrong, this book is aimed at teachers, administrators, and all others who are charged with running our schools. We, therefore, hope that the school can investigate and possibly alter its process of labeling. It may be that the community would be willing to respond in kind.

FOR CONSIDERATION

1. Suggest some examples of social role definitions (such as male and female; old and young; tall and short; large and small). Indicate how these expec-

tations are ingrained in the social fabric. That is, illustrate how these role definitions are reinforced by such entities as TV, peer groups, and neighborhoods.

2. Provide examples of behavior that is deviant from the typically defined role, for example, machismo. Discuss this behavior in terms of the nine propositions of Scheff. Focus on residual deviance.

3. Apply Scheff's model to a school. Identify examples of residual deviance in the school. Examine this deviant behavior of individuals in terms of labeling and Scheff's nine propositions. Exemplify how this deviant behavior is reinforced in the school. Consider whether this deviant behavior is transitory (primary), or has become a permanent career pattern (secondary) for the individual.

   How well does this model of behavior fit an analysis of schooling? Does it give better insights than do other models? What are its strengths? its weaknesses?

Notes

1. Thomas J. Scheff, "The Role of the Mentally Ill and Dynamics of Mental Disorder: A Research Framework," *Sociometry* 26 (1963):436–453.
2. Robert Rosenthal and Lenore Jacobson, *Pygmalion in the Classroom* (New York: Holt, Reinhart and Winston, 1968).
3. H. J. Eysenck, "The Effects of Psychotherapy: An Evaluation," *Journal of Consulting Psychology* 16 (1952):319–324.
4. L. J. Glass, "Psychotherapy in the Combat Zone," Symposium on Stress, Army Medical Service Graduate School, Washington, D.C., 1953.
5. Robert S. Lynd and Hellen Merrell Lynd, *Middletown*, Harvest Books, (New York: Harcourt, Brace & World, 1956).
6. Frank Reissman, *The Culturally Deprived Child*, (New York, Harper & Row, 1962).

Chapter 8: The School as a Culture

Each of the previous chapters has dealt with the school as an institution, albeit a different kind of institution in each case. The present chapter, in many ways, combines the perspectives of the previous chapters in an anthropological model. Anthropology tends to be *holistic* in its approach, that is, it looks at the whole system, institution, or society at once rather than looking at its component parts.

The Silent Language, by Edward T. Hall, is the result of Hall's work for the Peace Corps. Hall's original task was to develop a method whereby Peace Corps volunteers could quickly and accurately "get a handle on" the cultures of the countries in which they were working. The Peace Corps had a number of instances where volunteers made serious errors in judgment, not because of carelessness or ill will but because of cultural ignorance. The volunteers violated cultural taboos because they did not understand the culture they were working in. Hall's methodology attempted to ameliorate this problem through the development of a model for analyzing culture that could also be used as a training tool. The model stresses the need to understand the way individual cultures distinctively handle modes of interaction. Many of the conflicts and difficulties that arise between groups occur because one group does not understand the interaction pattern of the other.

If we can learn the cultural patterns of others, or at least recognize that they are different, we will better be able to communicate. Since the Hall model is specifically designed to facilitate intercultural communication, we have chosen it as our anthropological analysis model. There are many other more academic models, but this one has immediate practical application and has proven its use.

In this chapter we will apply the Hall model to the school, though we are not used to looking at the school in terms of its cultures. Generally speaking, we think of the school as a unit not as a cluster of cultures. Specifically, we will discuss the cultural patterns of administrators, teachers, and students to show how different cultural patterns can lead to unnecessary conflicts among them. As was true of the four previous chapters, our goal is to present a method of analysis so that different patterns may be recognized and understood and so that readers can generalize the model to their own situations.

The Three
Reaction Patterns

According to Hall, there are three general patterns of interaction between people in a society; formal, informal, and technical. These patterns describe the general way people react to one another. *Formal patterns* are those behaviors performed for traditional reasons. For example, few of us wonder why we usually do not work on what we call the weekend. We just don't. In point of fact it really isn't even the end of the week. It is both the end and the beginning of the week, since on most calendars Saturday is the last day of the week and Sunday is the first day of the next week. Individuals rarely question their rationale for formal patterns. Formal patterns are performed because "we've always done it this way."

An example of a formal pattern in the school would be summer vacation, or the Christmas and Easter breaks. Although summer vacation may have made some sense when we were a predominantly agricultural society, the logic behind a three-month vacation in the summer is less tenable in a largely urban society. But even those schools that have gone on the quarter system and have a summer quarter have found it difficult to change people's habits. The summer quarter is still viewed as the vacation quarter. Christmas and Easter present different formal problems. Both of these vacations are Christian in origin, and public schools and colleges would be in violation of the separation of church and state if they celebrated them. So the Christmas vacation has been changed to winter break and Easter vacation to spring break. The formal pattern of school vacations was too entrenched, so we made a technical change—we changed the name.

Formal patterns are the most resistant to change. They have the weight of history behind them and the tremendous weight of custom. They support stasis. When they are challenged, there is usually quite an upheaval, which often leads to change. For example, when teachers began to unionize, the society questioned whether teachers could be good teachers if they were no longer dedicated, loving "task masters" to children. Unionization would be "unprofessional." None of these terms were defined but everyone seemed to have some idea as to what they meant. The union movement in education forced a redefinition of "professional" and "teacher." Of greatest importance to our discussion is that because teachers in some areas of the country were able to secure sufficient power, they were able to force an "out of awareness" formal definition to become a technical "in awareness" discussion of what the definitions should be. Although this has caused conflict, it has also caused a re-evaluation of the role of teachers, administrators, and the school.

Informal patterns of behavior also generally exist out of our awareness. For example, we learn to speak by imitation. There is often no conscious effort in learning to speak, we simply imitate those around us and thereby learn the sounds common to our culture. Most of the significant learning of children occurs in this fashion. Speech, walking, running, many of the games children play, and basic interaction patterns with peers are all learned in this out-of-awareness fashion. In the school, learning is largely a formal activity, while it is largely informal outside of school.

Actually, many patterns in this country are relatively informal: we do not require a formal introduction to meet people, we learn by watching or doing, we tend to be independents rather than to belong to a particular political party. In our highly informal and technical society, one of the few predominantly formal institutions is the school. The school's formal style is in direct contrast to most of the other institutions with which students, teachers, or administrators come into contact. While all three groups may find it difficult to maintain formality in an informal society, teachers and administrators have a vested interest in maintaining formal power and status relationships, while students do not. It may be that when students say that school is irrelevant, they are speaking less of its content and more of its style or pattern. This may be the source of some student-school conflict.

Technical patterns are distinguishable from both formal and informal patterns in that the individual practicing the pattern is fully aware of how it is learned, why it is learned, and why the behavior is performed. For example, though children learn to talk informally, they learn to use the telephone technically; that is, they must be taught which end to speak into and which end to listen to (some of this is also learned informally through imitation). They are taught that it is possible to speak to people even when they cannot be seen and when they are at a great distance from the speaker. Because we are a technical society, our educational practices are also often technical. Schools technically define everything from cheating to tardiness to sexual behaviors. The definitions are relatively clear and concise and understood.

Two problems arise with technical patterns. First, someone else may have a better rationale and want the definition changed. This often occurs when there is a conflict between an authority figure (such as a principal) and a nonauthority figure (such as a student). In this case there is often an appeal to the formal pattern by the authority or power figure, for example, "You'll understand when you are older," while the nonauthority figure appeals to the technical pattern, for example, "That doesn't make sense. My way is better." Second, technical patterns are in greater flux because they can be challenged without fear of violating a formal or informal pattern. Logic and power are the keys to technical change. If you have the power, however, your logic can be somewhat weaker.

All societies will exhibit Hall's three reaction patterns, but each will tend to be characterized more by one than by another. So, for instance, Japan is a more formal country than is the United States, though both are highly technical. Even within the same society there will be a variation in patterns. Adults in the school are likely to be formal, while the students will be informal, and the influence of the federal and state government on local education tends to be technical (they supply the money to make the school function.)

When people change roles they may also change their reaction pattern. A teacher on the tennis court is likely to be less formal than in the classroom. Finally, reaction patterns change over time. Often these changes are from the technical or the informal to the formal. As the technical or informal pattern becomes commonly accepted within the society, it becomes tradition bound and formalized. Often, interestingly enough, the formal pattern may no longer reflect the reality of the situation. For example, the sentence "It's a quarter past twelve" makes good technical sense if we are wearing a watch with a face and hands. But if we are wearing a digital watch and still say, "It's a

Flow Chart 9. The Hall Model: Teacher and Student Outcomes

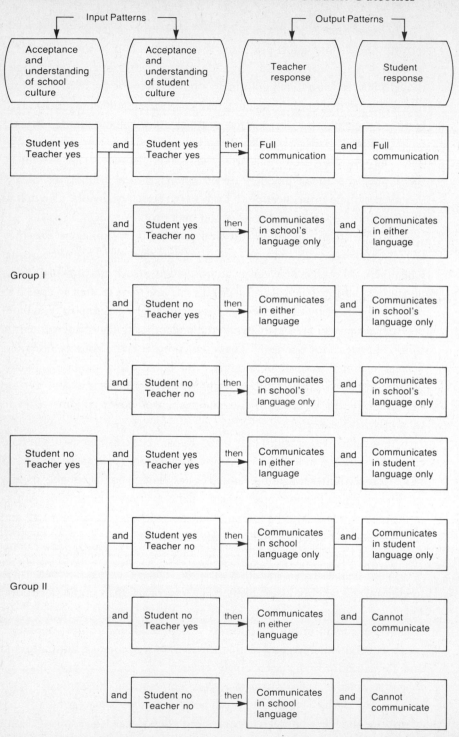

Flow Chart 9. (*Continued*)

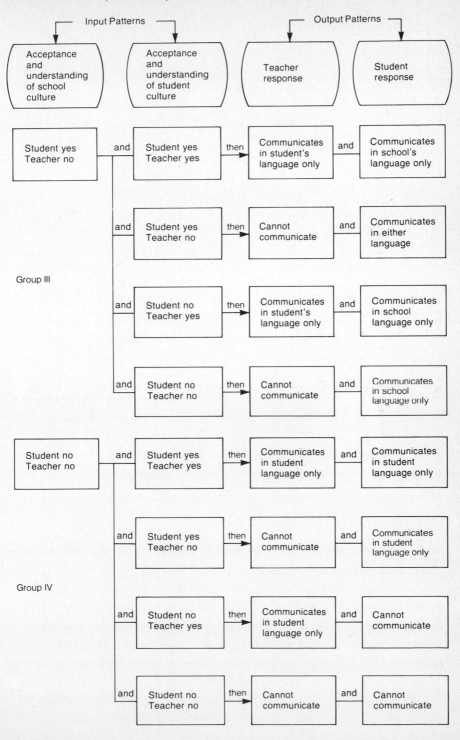

165

Flow Chart 10. The Hall Model

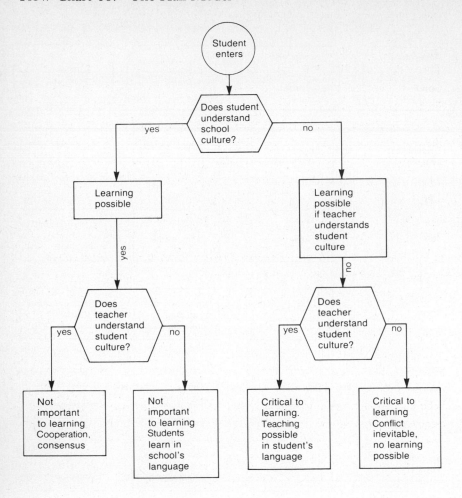

Description of the Hall Model Flow Charts

Flow Chart 9 describes the Hall model itself in terms of the possible outcomes of teacher and student understandings of both school and student cultures. It describes the communication flow that will be possible given the level of understanding by the teacher and the student of the school's and the student's cultural languages. Each group (Group I, II, and so on) refers to a cluster of possible situations and their behavioral outcomes. The Hall model is a communications model. Flow Chart 9 on pages 164–165 indicates the possible combinations of those communications patterns.

Group I describes situations in which both the teachers and the students understand the school's cultural language. This is the situation in most suburban schools, where both the students and the teachers are aware of the purpose and language of the school. This does not mean that both groups accept all of the cultural language and behaviors, but at least they understand them.

Group II simulates situations in which the teacher understands the cultural language of the school and knows what the school expects, but the students do not. This is the case whenever the traditional school comes into contact with nontraditional students, for example, in a Spanish-speaking community, in many inner-city situations, and so on.

Group III is quite unusual. Here the students understand the cultural language of the school and the teachers do not. This might occur in school districts that have unusual schools which are directly atuned to the students and the community but where a new teacher may find it difficult to adjust. For example, an Anglo teacher in a Native American school, a traditional teacher in an open-education setting, an urban teacher in a small rural community, and so on might experience the situation described in Group III.

Group IV is even more unusual. Here neither the teachers nor the students understand the cultural language of the school. This could occur if a school district went through a radical change in policy, instituting new curricular approaches that are unknown to both teachers and students. This did occur in some cases when desegregation came to some schools and neither teachers nor students were prepared for it.

So long as students understand the school's cultural language and abide by the cultural patterns of the school, everything can proceed without much difficulty. It is when students do not understand the school's language that it becomes critical for the school to understand the culture and language of the students. It is under these circumstances that the school finds itself pressed, because teachers have rarely been trained to communicate in the student's language. Most teacher-training institutions do not even indicate to future teachers that they may find students who do not understand the cultural language of the school. But in such a situation conflict will often arise. Since the student cannot communicate with the school, the school often abrogates its teaching responsibility and stops trying to teach the student, or demands that the student learn the school's culture. However, we should always remember that the fact that students cannot communicate in the school's language is neither surprising nor particularly significant. It is, after all, one of the purposes of the school to teach the child the language and patterns of the school.

In Flow Chart 10, which is more conventional in format, two questions are asked: (1) Does the student understand the school's cultural language? and (2) Does the school understand the student's cultural language? If the answer to the first question is yes, then learning is possible. This describes the most common situation in the school, where the students in general know what is expected of them.

If students do understand the cultural language of the school, then the question of whether the school knows the student culture is really not of any great importance. Teaching and learning can take place even without knowledge of the students' cultural language. Of course, it is more pleasant if the school does understand the students' cultural language, since this can lead to cooperation and consensus. But it is not critical to the teaching and learning process.

In the situation where students do not understand the cultural language of the school, however, it is far more critical that the school understand the students' cultural language. Here the children are not culturally prepared for the school experience and do not understand either what is expected of them, or sometimes even what is said to them. In this situation the only communication possible, at least until the children have learned the school's cultural language, is if the teacher understands their language. Unfortunately, it is a very rare situation for teachers to understand the culture of nontraditional students. If the teacher does not understand the child and the child does not understand the teacher, conflict would seem to be inevitable and learning will be at a minimum. It is in such a case that multicultural teacher education is so critical.

---

quarter after," when asked the time, our reaction pattern has become formal. Digital watches, after all, only show the numerals "12:15," not the sweep of the minute hand. Though the reality of the situation has changed, the behavior has not.

The Primary
Message Systems

Besides the three patterns of reaction there are, according to Hall, ten primary message systems: interaction, association, subsistence, bisexuality, territoriality, temporality, learning, play, defense, and exploitation. It is Hall's contention that if we learn the ten primary message systems and understand the reaction patterns of each of them, as they occur within a particular culture, we will then be able to understand the culture fully and, thereby, live in harmony with it.

Since he was constructing an anthropological model Hall, of course, did not deal with the school. But as the three reaction patterns could be applied to the school, so may the primary message systems. Understanding how these work within the context of the cultures of the school should enable us to take a necessary first step toward communication among students, teachers, and administrators.

Each of the ten primary message systems will be analyzed in relation to the three reaction patterns discussed above. Each primary message system can elicit one of the three reaction patterns; that is, it may be used formally, informally, or technically by the society, institution, or individual. Furthermore, each primary message system may combine elements of the three reaction patterns. It is unlikely, in fact, that any message system will fall neatly into one or another category, since few societies or individuals are either all formal, all informal, or all technical.

Table 8.1:
Matrix for Cultural Analysis (from Hall) Applied to the Schools

PRIMARY MESSAGE SYSTEMS	Examples: Basic Reaction Patterns		
	Formal	Informal	Technical
Interaction	In-class questions and answers	Peer discussion at at lunch	Computer-assisted instruction
Association	Elementary and high schools	Principal's powerful secretary	School bus assigned, sent notes home
Subsistence	Grades	Personal social success, cheating	Records, transcripts
Bisexuality	Sex education curriculum	Teasing, showing off	Contraception
Territoriality	School desk, locker use	Unassigned illegal smokers' area	Our school, my class
Temporality	Summer vacation	"See you later"	School starting time
Learning	Homework systems	Listening, watching others	Programed textbooks
Play	Organized gym class	Horsing around	Rules of sports
Defense	Report to office to explain absence	Writing own excuse	Illness excuse for absence
Exploitation	Older student privileges	Useless homework	Teacher at low salary

INTERACTION

The first of the primary message systems, *interaction*, refers to the general way in which we relate to or treat one another. Interaction patterns tend to be individual, that is, person to person or person to institution. (Association, the second primary message system, deals, on the other hand, with the way we aggregate into groups.)

Interaction, as is true of the other primary message systems, exhibits the three reaction patterns. Although we all know people or societies that tend to be more formal, informal, or technical, which reaction pattern is used will often depend on the situation. A student called into the disciplinary vice principal's office will tend to use terms like "yes, sir" and "no, sir" more often than he or she would with friends or relatives. The situation requires more formality and so the interaction becomes more formal.

Societally, some cultures are far more formal than others. For example, in China of the fourth century B.C., patterns of interaction were highly formalized. Everyone knew exactly what his or her roles were and how these roles related to others, to institutions, and to the society. A father knew exactly how to treat his children, and his children knew exactly how to treat him. In each case, the role was highly formalized and traditional, and there was little if any deviation from it. Although no society is entirely formal, informal, or technical, ancient China was certainly an example of a largely formalized society. Teachers and administrators in our society also have highly prescribed roles that are difficult to break. In other words, they, too, have highly formalized interaction roles, though, of course, not as formal as were roles in China.

An example of informal interaction would be the way in which children tend to interact in school when not under adult supervision. Although there are some formal patterns, such as boys sitting near other boys and girls sitting near other girls (children are taught sex biases early on in our society), by and large the patterns are informal; that is, children sit largely where they find it most convenient to sit. It is when the students are under adult supervision in school that their language, behavior, and general response pattern become more formal or technical. So, for instance, in a traditional classroom, the students are often placed in row desks in some technically convenient (for example, alphabetical) order without regard to the students' personal preferences. This is ordering is a pattern that is both technical and formal.

The United States abounds in technical interaction patterns. One of the reasons Americans tend to interact as they do is because of the technical elements involved in the interaction process: the telephone, television, newspapers, letters, and other means of communication. Even very young children learn that it is sometimes more convenient to communicate with friends or acquaintances over the telephone than in a face-to-face encounter. Children in our society learn early to interact technically, that is, via technical means of one sort or another rather than informally or formally.

Furthermore, our technical society has enabled us to become geographically highly mobile. This has its effect on interaction patterns. It is so common to move from one place to another (one out of four families moves every five years) that friendships must be developed that can be broken on relatively short notice. In this context transitory friendships are formed. Correspondingly, whereas in nontechnical societies it is important to be able to get along with one's immediate neighbors, in a highly technical society, with its freeways, thruways, and mass transit, it is not particularly important, since one's friends and one's neighbors may be entirely different people.

In the days of the one-room schoolhouse, formal relationships were maintained not only because students had the same teachers for eight to twelve years (if they stayed in school that long), but also because teachers were members of the community and were treated as teachers outside of school as well as in school. In today's highly mobile situation, teachers and students rarely see each other outside of school because they usually do not live in the same community. In schools where the cultural patterns of teachers and students are different, such as the inner city or in bilingual situations, this lack of out of school communication can be a particular problem. If students and teachers interact only in a school setting, without having the advantage of seeing each other in a nonschool environment, there is a far greater probability of interaction conflict due to interactive ignorance.

This audience separation is the most common aspect of interaction in modern American urban life. We separate our work audience from our social audience and our social audience from our family audience. We perform to different groups and can wear different faces in each group. This has some advantages in terms of freedom of action. However, in relation to the school as an institution and a place where children learn, there is a tendency for this separation to mean that children have to learn from people who are rarely seen as three-dimensional people in three-dimensional settings.

Another major source of interaction problems occurs when one person expects one pattern of interaction and another person expects another. For example, if a child's pattern of interaction is one that the teacher generally considers to be far too info mal, while the teacher's pattern of interaction is one that the child considers far too formal, conflict will occur. The child may expect the teacher to acce t joking behavior, a certain amount of physical body contact, and so forth, while the teacher may demand respect in the form of psychological distance, as well as no body contact, and, generally, a more formal recognition of role differentiation. Unless one or the other is willing to change the pattern of interaction, the distinction between the formal and informal will continue to be a source of conflict between teacher and student.

Interaction is the most basic of the primary message systems. Not only is interaction the most important of the primary message systems, it is also the one frought with the greatest dangers. Without an understanding of the interaction patterns in the school, we are left with a situation in which full communication and understanding exist only when the adult and student cultures have the same make-up, that is, where adults and students agree on their mutual roles. Since this, in reality, is often not the case, a knowledge of interaction patterns in the schools is crucial to the avoidance of conflict.

ASSOCIATION

The second primary message system is association. While interaction deals with the way individuals relate to one another, *association* deals with the way in which we act as part of institutions and the way in which institutions themselves interact. For example, elementary schools, junior high schools, high schools, and colleges are not just names. These institutions are related to each other in an organic way that is a great deal more important than the simple fact that most students pass from one to the other. One of the characteristics of the school curriculum is that it is not set independently on each level but that rather it is influenced very heavily by the level immediately above. The colleges and universities determine a great deal of the curriculum of the high schools. Students are required to take two years of math and a foreign language, some laboratory science, a number of years of English, and so on, because it is believed a preparation for study on the next level, in college or university. The high school in turn sends messages to the junior high school, which sends them to the elementary school. What is interesting for the present discussion is not only that this association exists, but that most people accept it as perfectly reasonable. In point of fact, it is just "the way we've always done it." There is no particular reason to assume that the curriculum appropriate to college preparation is of much value to the majority of students who will not be going to college. This is an example not only of institutional association but of formal association. Teachers make up the curriculum and downgrade the value of the noncollege preparatory programs in the schools because that is what we have come to expect.

Individuals also associate with institutions, when they fulfill the roles required of them. Roles, as described in Chapter 5 on administrative styles, are those expectations and claims that the institution can make on individuals and vice versa because they are member actors of the institution. For example, teachers have the right to expect some courtesy and respect from students, so long as teachers behave in a way that is expected. Students, on the other hand, have the right to certain expectations, ranging from respect to being taught the subject matter. These associations are not determined by the individuals through interaction, but rather are determined by the association or relationship that the individual actors have with the institution. The roles exist before the particular actor arrives and will still exist after the actor leaves. Teachers have certain roles to perform over which they have minimal control; students also have roles. When either teachers or students break with the institutional roles, they are attempting to associate in a new way, and conflict will often result.

An example of conflict is the relationship of American nuns to the Roman Catholic church. During the past ten to fifteen years, many nuns in the United States have stopped wearing the habit or veil. This rather extreme break with formal patterns was relatively well accepted in the United States where the pattern became either technical (habits are very inconvenient to wear if you are coaching basketball), informal ("We would like to make our own choices"), or a new formal association was substituted ("We have the RIGHT to FREE CHOICE"). The major conflict did not come on the level of interaction, that is, nun to layperson in the United States, but rather between the nuns and the rest of the world where the church tends to be more traditional than in the United States. The comments of Pope John Paul II supporting the wearing of habits by nuns were greeted with applause in much of Europe and with significant silence from many American nuns. Here the associational conflict was between a formal authority and a group of member actors who would wish to change the formality of the institution or move it to a more informal pattern.

Whether the association is institution to institution, or between the individual and the institution, it can occur on the formal, informal, and technical levels—or in any combination of the three. Formal association occurs most often in such structured institutions as the army or the school. In the army, the formal organization runs from the general down to the private; in the school, from the school board to the superintendent, the principal, the teacher, and down to the student. Even though the general may not be smarter or better equipped to administrate than the private, and the school-board president may be no more intelligent than the student, this organization has been established and maintained and is the formal pattern.

Informal patterns of association often exist outside the formal structure. The staff sergeant who understands the system may be more powerful than the general, and the school janitor who is related to the president of the school board may have more influence than the superintendent. To return to our curricular example, the formal association between the college and the school is relatively clear if we are thinking of the traditional school. However, the association becomes much more informal in less-traditional school settings, for example, in an open school. Here, in theory at least, the students are directly involved in the planning and execution of activities, and although the same general subjects are to be learned (reading, writing, and arithmetic), the emphasis is quite different. It has shifted from the curriculum, and particularly from the training of students to meet the curricular needs of the colleges, to a more informal and flexible pattern in which the students determine at least the methodology to be used in their learning. Even in the open school, the interaction patterns may still be the same as in the traditional school. So teachers and students may still be expected to maintain their traditional roles, even though the association pattern will have been made more informal.

Possibly the best example of a technical pattern of association is urban life. Though urban life has developed some formal patterns of association (such as the habit of people living in apartment houses not speaking to their immediate neighbors in order to maintain a semblance of privacy), by and large the pattern of urban dwellers is a technical one. People come together not because of a pattern handed down from their ancestors but because it is technically more convenient to live in a city close to where one works and plays. Implicit in this technical pattern of association, as is true of interaction, is that it is possible to segregate audiences. We may belong to a work audience, a play audience, and a school audience, and we often perform differently to each one. We can, and often do, lead more than one life.

This concept will become clearer if we consider the example of Harold, an urban teenager, who lived at least two lives and was seen in different ways by each of his audiences. Although he was in many ways a true leader, the teachers and administrators at his school could not see him as a school leader, because he did not share the characteristics of a school leader as defined by them.

"School leader," as defined by the adult school staff, is a far more complex construct in an urban than in a rural setting because of the segregation of audiences and roles. In a small town or rural setting, schools see the student as a family and community member as well as a student. In the urban setting, the school often knows little of the student's home, community, or play world. The school associates with the student as student only, and it establishes roles not for the individual student but for "students" as a group or class of individuals. The urban school staff traditionally defines leaders in terms of school activities. Leaders are the students who tend to behave themselves in class, get relatively good grades (not too good), are active and participate in school activities, and are "well-adjusted."

One of the enlightening experiences of the school disturbances of the late 1960s and early 1970s was the reaction of the adult staff to the riot leaders who seemed to have a great deal of support from the students. These leaders were not the leaders that the adult staff expected; they were not school leaders. During a disturbance in Buffalo, New York, where the students of one school had organized an assembly and were writing their own Declaration of Independence without benefit of school approval, this classic comment was overheard, "My God, how can Harold be running that meeting? He can't even spell!" Well, it was true that Harold could not spell, did not get good grades, was not "well-adjusted" to the school, and was not active in sports or other activities in school. He did not perform well to his school audience. However, he was recognized as a gang leader of great ability outside of school, was socially very adept, and was aiding (paralegally) in fiscal support of his mother and five siblings. He was highly respected outside of school as a man and inside of school as the leader of the underlife. He performed well to his nonschool audience. He was, in brief, known as a friend of students in trouble and a leader of the opposition.

Because Harold led more than one life through audience segregation, and because the school saw only one of those lives (namely, the in-school one, at which Harold was not very adept), the school both missed the opportunity of using Harold's very great leadership skills to avoid the school riot and was further amazed and incapable of response when Harold took over the riot.

So many of the association patterns in modern urban life are technical at their base. This leads to a good deal of confusion in an institution that is as traditional and formal as the school. Because we continue with our formal patterns regardless of the technical situation, we tend to disregard many of the students who might wish to be associated with us. If the school demands that all associations for both teachers and students conform to formal role expectations, then we will be missing many of the talents of those who remain in school, and we will lose many students and teachers who choose to leave.

In summary, association is the way in which institutions interact or the way in which individuals interact with institutions. Basic to a discussion of association are roles and role expectations. One great difficulty with modern American urban school associations is that the institutional power is poised to maintain the formal pattern of association between the institutions and the individuals. Everything from the curriculum to the relationships of students and teachers is part of a formal pattern. Conflict occurs because most of the clients of the system, both adult staff and students, do not live in formal associative patterns but rather in informal and technical ones. So long as the school insists on maintaining largely formal patterns in this technical and informal world, conflict and confusion are bound to result.

SUBSISTENCE

The third primary message system relates to the way people handle *subsistence*, that is, the eating habits, employment, and other patterns needed to survive in society. As an example of a formal subsistence pattern, religious practices are often connected with the planting of crops, the consumption of food, and so forth. In many societies there are still both planting and harvesting feasts, and prayers or grace are said at meals. Some of these formal patterns are performed out of habit, without the people who are directly involved knowing their original purpose.

Many city dwellers tend to deal with subsistence patterns in an informal fashion; that is, subsistence is on a catch-as-catch can basis. There is no set time for eating meals, there is no particular place where meals are eaten, and there are no definite people with whom meals are eaten. With whom we eat, with whom we work, and what our employment is becomes less important than the fact that we have jobs and that we can find a place to eat. In modern industrial society it is no longer a great chore to cook at least marginally palatable meals. We can go to the freezer and prepare a full-fledged meal in a half-hour, or if we choose, we can stop for a meal at a fast-food restaurant, where there is little concern either for us as individuals or for our culinary habits. We are simply objects to be fed, and what is placed before us is an object to be eaten. Whether what is eaten is particularly palatable is almost beside the point, since the purpose is to eat as quickly and as efficiently as possible, so that we can get back to the business at hand.

Within the school, subsistence takes on a particular meaning for students. At the basic level, subsistence is just making it through. Grades are the most common example of the formal subsistence level. Grades are what we "pay" students for the work they do—good grades for good work and bad grades for bad. Grades themselves have no intrinsic value. They have only slight educational purpose, since even if they are an incentive to students, that incentive is to learn those things that the student hopes will be on the test. Grades do not facilitate general learning or love of learning. Attempts to eliminate grades, however, even though most educators agree that they are not particularly useful educationally, have met with very little success. Once again, the definition of a student's subsistence in terms of grades continues because "we've always done it that way."

Informal subsistence in the school tends to be on the social level. Grades and citizenship may be important to the adult staff of the school, but many students define subsistence in terms of success in sports, social activities, sexual prowess, and so on. The specific rules and roles for success are not clearly defined and tend to vary a good deal from school to school and from situation to situation. Although these patterns are informal, this does not mean that they are less important. Indeed, as we saw in the association section, the informal patterns are very often critical ones.

But perhaps the technical pattern is again the most important one. For technical subsistence in the school is not bound to the school years but extends into the adult life of students. One of the major technical roles of the school is record keeping for the military, business, and educational institutions with which students will later come into contact. In this case, the records of the present subsistence pattern of students will follow them for the rest of their lives. This is what makes grades extrinsically important. One aspect of technical subsistence, therefore, is both extremely important and extremely powerful. In brief, if students do not "make it" according to the formal pattern of school subsistence, the technical pattern of record keeping will follow them outside the school. In other words, the grades they have received for scholastic achievement (or failure) or good (or bad) citizenship, their attendance records, and details about their school activities will forever be on file. This technical looping pattern from the present to the future is now coming under some attack by parents and students.

BISEXUALITY

Bisexuality relates to the way in which males and females treat one another. Where formal patterns of bisexuality exist, the individuals involved have less choice over their own behavior than they do in informal contexts. In the formal pattern, the traditions of the society determine what the formal behavior will be. Weddings are arranged; premarital relations either do not exist or exist only as the society dictates; bisexual patterns between two people often are the concern of the extended family and, in some cases, the entire community; and the relationship between husband and wife is determined largely by societal decisions.

In informal patterns there are few formalized or traditional rules and regulations. Modern bisexual behavior in the United States is a good example of this. Since the formal patterns of arranged marriages and codes of ethics regarding premarital and extramarital sexual behavior have broken down, a more informal pattern exists, in which individuals or couples can determine their own behavior.

Again, as with other primary message systems, there is direct interaction between the informal and the technical patterns of bisexual behavior. The greatest single technical influence on bisexual behavior has been the increase in reasonably sure and safe contraception. With such technical advances there have been increases in marriages without children and trial marriages. The primary stigma and fear of pregnancy has been taken from premarital and postmarital sexual behavior and has changed the entire sequence of events leading to courtship and marriage, as well as many marital and extramarital sexual patterns.

The school tends largely to ignore bisexuality, except in terms of sex education, on the one hand, which is dealt with in a formal traditional academic setting and fashion, or, on the other hand, in terms of formal sexual morality or technology, wherein the school says either, "Thou shalt not," or "Not when you are in school and don't get caught when you are out of school." The problem, of course, is that students deal with bisexuality informally because formal patterns are either nonexistent or diffuse and confusing. Students are looking for answers to their informal questions, but the school gives formal answers to formal questions. So long as the school deals with the vibrant informal questions of bisexuality in sterile formal or technical fashion, students will tend to ignore most of the advice given. In brief, bisexuality is important and informal to students and embarrassing and formal or technical to the school.

TERRITORIALITY

Territoriality refers not only to the way in which a society handles land rights but the way in which it handles all property rights. For example, some societies have no sense of personal property at all, since they have no concept of formal property rights. All things are held in common. Other societies, such as most Western cultures, have tended to believe that property rights are extremely important—"A man's home is his castle." Examples of formal patterns of territoriality are such ideas as the divine right of kings and the primacy of law, both written and unwritten. Informal and technical patterns, on the other hand, include the belief that "finders keepers," or "possession is nine-tenths of the law." Within informal and technical patterns, boundaries tend to be fluid and ill-defined. And within the technical pattern, there is often greater reliance on sheer power, that is, the one who has the greatest power will maintain the greatest amount of territory.

The school aids greatly in teaching children the importance of looking at property and territory formally and technically. Children are taught to respect the property of others and of the school and to maintain property rights over their own possessions. Everything within the school belongs specifically to someone. Even performance in academic areas and citizenship is personal property; it does not belong to the entire class. We say, for example, "your grades, your test, your work, your behavior," and so on. If a child fails in either citizenship or in academic studies, it is his or her personal responsibility alone, even if it could be shown that group effort and cooperation would be educationally more advantageous.

In other cultures, such as the People's Republic of China, if a child fails either in citizenship or in academic areas, it becomes the concern of the entire class. If any person fails, it is the responsibility and the shame of the entire class, since the class is understood as a communal unit. For this reason, China attempts to see to it that every person passes every subject. The emphasis is upon communal rather than upon individual territoriality.

TEMPORALITY

A relatively easy message system to diagnose, and one of the most important to the school, is *temporality*, or time. One of the serious difficulties facing many schools is that although the school tends to handle time very technically (school begins at 9:00 A.M., not 9:05 or 8:55), the students may handle time quite informally, though not quite as informally as do the Navajo or Hopi Indians of the American Southwest. Among these Native Americans things begin when they are ready to begin, and not before or after. This may mean that school will open at 10:15 one day, 9:00 another, and not at all on a third day.

Conflict between various patterns of temporality often makes school difficult for children, since they must learn a technical method of handling time. To some extent they, of course, have learned these patterns at home through having to be home for dinner on time, but the definition of "on time" is different at home. At home there is a leeway of a certain number of minutes or even hours, depending on the particular pattern within the home. At school there is very little leeway within the "on time" system. One of the most common reasons for discipline in schools is not that the student is absent but that the student is late. Because neither the school nor the student recognizes that there is a conflict in culture, or the school is culturally myopic and demands its pattern be accepted, the conflict is not understood and remains unresolved until the less powerful of the two parties involved, the student, either changes or is eliminated through suspension or expulsion. To resolve the conflict, understanding of the pattern is needed; then the school, the child, or perhaps even both can respond appropriately to the other.

Formal patterns of temporality deal with traditional methods of handling time. For example, the English custom of having tea at four o'clock regardless of the circumstances is a formal pattern. Whether it makes sense to have tea at 4:00 P.M. in the middle of the Arabian desert is a moot point. The same is true of temporal patterns of sleeping. Whether it makes any particular sense for an individual to work during the daytime and sleep at night in a modern urban setting is again disputable. For an artist who needs the natural sunlight, obviously the daylight hours are extremely important (a technical problem); but for a writer who needs quiet and solitude, the night may be a far more convenient time in which to work (again, a technical problem). The writer, however, will be forced into a daytime life to some degree, simply because the rest of the society, through a traditional, formal pattern, uses the day to work and the night to sleep (a formal pattern). The school has a number of formal time periods, the most obvious of which is the waste of the school buildings at night, during vacations, and much of the summer, when they remain closed. To eliminate the waste, we would have to change our formal patterns regarding the hours when we will attend school. This, in fact, has been tried but without much success.

LEARNING

Learning, broadly defined by Hall as the incorporation of any information, also differs greatly in terms of formal, informal, and technical patterns. An example of a formal pattern of learning is the traditional didactic approach. Students are given a recitation to learn, recite, and be graded on. There is very little interchange within this highly formal pattern. The rules and regulations for teacher behavior, such as the maintenance of a psychological and/or physical distance between student and teacher because "familiarity breeds contempt" or "the quiet classroom is a good classroom," are part of this formal pattern. Whether there is any demonstrable relationship between neatness, quiet, and distance and good teaching is questionable, but the formal tradition connects these norms of learning with it.

Whereas the school has many formal patterns of learning, children have learned largely through informal patterns. Children learn language not by being systematically taught how to speak but by listening to those around them and finding that it is more convenient to ask for the milk than it is to shout or mumble something incomprehensible. They also learn informally how to play with peers, about nature—in brief, many things necessary in order to interact, associate, or play adequately in the society. Most often no one specifically teaches children these things; they learn them through observation and emulation. When children enter school, however, they are, in effect, told that they must change their pattern of learning from an informal to a formal one. The first job of the school, then, is to change the pattern of learning. This immediately means that there will be a conflict between the children and the school, until the children have changed their pattern from the informal to the formal and have come to accept the change.

With the increase in teaching machines and programed text books, and the advent of computers and so forth, technical patterns have greatly increased in the schools. These machines can be used to teach children basics in a self-paced, nonthreatening environment. Further, teachers should have more time to interact with students, since some of the basic skill teaching can be done by machines. However, another pattern has been introduced, which in spite of the positive benefits, will often lead to conflict. While teachers teach formally and children often learn informally, the machines teach technically and can do so without human contact at all. We still have very little research on the effect of computers and programs on learning attitudes, but we do know to expect frequent conflict between patterns. How the particular conflict between computers and teachers will be resolved may be a central theme of the next decade.

PLAY

The eighth primary message system deals with the way in which people *play*, or entertain themselves. Examples of formal patterns of play characterize much of the play or entertainment of the Orient, such as flower arranging or forms of karate and jujitsu. All have a very definite formal philosophical basis as well as an entertainment base. Informal patterns of play are those largely adopted by children in western culture, such as sandlot ball games, making sled runs on a convenient hill, or choosing teams on the basis of who happens to arrive rather than on the basis of skill.

Technical patterns of play include such things as Little League baseball (which has almost became a formal institution), where the informal sandlot game is turned into a highly structured team sport with a great deal of competition both for the children and for the parents. Spectator sports also fall into this general category of technical play. Since we are a largely technical society, we tend to engage in technical kinds of sports, primarily team sports. Unfortunately, much of the team-sports activity that we teach in the school is of little value to individuals when they leave, except as they become technical spectators as adults.

It is unfortunate that traditionally school is considered part of the formal subsistence, or work portion, of a child's life rather than part of the play section. Except for sports, play is one aspect of schooling that has been almost completely excluded from the school. School is understood as a work activity that is required for a certain number of hours every day with the weekends off. This is a formal pattern without any particular rhyme or reason. School is part of the language of work. There is "schoolwork" and "homework" and "classwork." "School play," "home play," and "class play," if they are considered at all, are viewed as ancillary and unimportant. This may be one of the reasons that lunch and recess are two of the favorite activities listed by students and explain why students can hardly wait to get out of school so that they will not have to learn anymore. Learning is not considered a lifelong activity, since learning is not a hobby but a job. This partitioning of school into the subsistence-work primary message system is at best unfortunate and at least highly dysfunctional for learning as a lifelong activity.

DEFENSE

The ninth primary message system is *defense*. Hall defines defense in the broadest sense. We need defense against the fates as well as against our enemies. One of the most common formal patterns of defense is religion. Religion is used in a traditional sense to defend us from storms, the attacks of enemies, or even death. An example of informal defense is the citizen soldier, traditionally the Minuteman of the United States, who is not a soldier in his everyday life but becomes one when he or his country feels that he is needed. Formal defense patterns in the military would include full-time professional soldiers, though professional soldiers generally have less formal status in this country than they do in many others. This is partially true because of our formal and traditional subordination of military power to civil authority, that is, the president is the commander in chief of the military, not the other way around. Technical patterns of defense include such weapons as today's guided missiles and nuclear weapons.

Difficulty occurs in the school situation with regard to some formal and informal patterns of defense, since students have many formal patterns of defense and offense that the school may or may not recognize. The boy whose mother is called a name may feel that he has been directly attacked and therefore must defend himself (a formal pattern). If he does not defend himself, he will be considered a coward and will be subject to constant future attacks (a technical pattern). He, therefore, physically attacks the person who has blasphemed or defamed his mother. This pattern is recognized by the students. On the other hand, the school, which also has its formal and technical patterns, does not recognize the students' formal pattern of defense as being legitimate and says that verbal attacks cannot be answered by physical attacks (a formal pattern). Therefore the student who engages in this behavior must be suspended or expelled (a technical pattern). In this particular example, the conflict is not just between different types of patterns but also between different definitions of formal patterns.

EXPLOITATION

The last of the primary message system is *exploitation*, defined as the way we use objects in our world. Formal exploitation again has its basis in tradition, law, or veneration. For example, there are a number of legal ways for individuals to exploit one another within American society. A particularly vivid example of this is the small loan, for which it is perfectly legal to charge a higher interest rate than for larger loans. This has been formalized in law and tradition and has become accepted within the American framework. Only recently has the lender even been required to state how much the annual interest is. Another example is the sexual behavior of the American male, who traditionally is expected to exploit his female counterpart to the greatest extent possible. The American male who wishes to marry a virgin but to have intercourse with as many eligible females as possible previous to his marriage exemplifies this type of exploitation. Indeed, in many aspects of life, it has become almost a formal pattern within the American society to get as much as possible from others and, at the same time, to give as little as possible of oneself—"Never give a sucker an even break."

There is also a good deal of informal exploitation, exploitation that is largely unintentional. For example, the Southern plantation owners who planted cotton and then, when the land was depleted, moved on to new fields, burned off trees, and again planted cotton were not systematically exploiting the land. In many cases they did not realize what they were doing to the land. Theirs was a more informal, unconscious pattern of exploitation.

Technical patterns of exploitation have been the most common within the United States. As the United States has become more technically oriented, it has exploited both its natural resources and its people on a technical level. One example of this is the assembly line, where the workers do the same thing day in and day out. The work is dreary, but it must be continued in order for the product to be produced. In this case, a human being has been exploited for the sake of technical efficiency.

American society also has exploited, and continues to exploit, natural resources. Redwood trees are felled, even though it may take three thousand years to grow a redwood tree. Major canyons, such as the Glenn Canyon in Arizona, have been partially destroyed to build dams for electric power. The conflict here involves a balance of power between conservation and technical exploitation. This is not to say that technical exploitation is not necessary; the point is that where some societies (Native American, for example) have greater respect for nature, and thereby might exploit it in a far more understanding fashion, the (non-Native American) United States traditionally has exploited its natural resources without thought to the future.

The Interplay of the Systems Within the Schools

Now that we have analyzed the ten primary message systems, we can turn to the interplay of these systems within the context of the school. Table 8.2 has been prepared in order to indicate how administrators, teachers, and students handle selected primary message systems.

The administration handles interaction and association in a highly formal and technical fashion; it maintains a distance from students and faculty, and relies heavily on rules and regulations. The teachers tend to be somewhat informal with both administrators and students. They tend to speak less in terms of rules, regulations, and traditions. The students, on the other hand, relate to one another in an even more informal fashion; their interactions and associations are based largely on who sits next to them in class, who walks to and from school with them, and who shares their common interests. The one formal pattern existing within student culture is that associations tend to fall along socioeconomic status lines. This is largely due to parental, peer, and neighborhood pressure.

Table 8.2:
Reaction Patterns for Four Primary Message Systems

PRIMARY MESSAGE SYSTEM	Administrative Pattern	Teacher Pattern	Student Pattern
Interaction and association	Highly formal	Somewhat formal	Informal
Subsistence	Technical and informal	Technical and informal	Informal
Bisexuality	Technical	Technical and formal	Informal: exploratory, or formal ("going steady")
Temporality	Technical	Technical	Technical: curricular, or informal, i.e., extracurricular

Subsistence can be defined as "making it" in school, or the ability of the student to pass courses and get out. The administrators tend to define subsistence according to technical and formal patterns. A technical pattern is based largely on the administrator's formal role as grade-giver, diploma-granter, and disciplinarian. An informal pattern of subsistence on the administrative level is based largely on the pressure and influence of the community. Those parents who have great influence within the community will be able to exert pressure on administrative decisions, whereas those parents who have little or no influence in the community will not.

Teachers tend to deal with subsistence on a technical and informal level. They are also governed in part both by their formal roles as teachers, in terms of grades and discipline, and the informal pressures of the community. Because of their closeness to the students, however, they are also governed by an informal pattern of likes and dislikes.

Students, on the other hand, are far more governed by their informal patterns. While they may be concerned with the technical extrinsic rewards or sanctions of grades or discipline, they are also very interested in the informal intrinsic patterns of their social leaders and of their personal interactions. When teachers were asked to indicate the leaders in a class, they almost always chose the academic work leaders; when students were asked to pick the leaders, they almost always picked the social leaders. The patterns among students are far more informal than they are among teachers and administrators.

Bisexuality is also dealt with in different ways by administrators, teachers, and students. Administrators tend to deal with bisexuality in a highly formal-technical fashion, by telling students that bisexual behavior is not acceptable in school. Bisexual behavior may be defined as holding hands, walking together down the halls, sitting together in classrooms, or intercourse. Whatever the definition, it should be remembered that the principals' primary interest here is the maintenance of order and the absence of scandal and publicity. Administrators are not primarily teachers of morals; they are technicians of a formal pattern.

Teachers, on the other hand, are not only technicians but also formal teachers of morals. That is, teachers are not only required to say that under no circumstances should bisexual behavior be allowed in school (technical pattern, to avoid scandal), but they are also to teach such mores as that sexual relations previous to marriage are not acceptable under any circumstances in the society at large. This is a formal pattern.

Students have a number of sexual patterns that they follow at various times. One is an informal exploratory and exploitative pattern in which both males and females attempt to find out as much as they can about bisexual relations without endangering themselves and, in some cases, with little concern for any danger to their partner. There are also a number of formal patterns in bisexual behavior that include going steady or being pinned. A formal pattern still often expected of students by parents and by the school is that of chastity. As mentioned before, however, a number of technical patterns that have come into play during the last several decades may be changing the formal pattern of chastity. Two of these are contraceptives, which make sexual relations "safer," and the automobile, which enables the children to get away from their parents and the school. Students, then, may have quite a different set of rules within their own group than those put forth by administrators, teachers, or even parents.

In terms of temporality, the administration and the teachers both handle time in a highly technical and formal fashion. It is precise and it is exact (technical) and breaking the temporal rules carries many negative sanctions (formal). The students, on the other hand, have to maintain two patterns. One is the technical pattern that they have learned in school in order to function within the school, and the other is the informal extracurricular pattern that has a great deal more leeway and involves their peers.

Stasis and Change in the Hall Model

This chapter has presented one cultural method of analysis for the study of the school. Particular emphasis has been placed on Edward T. Hall's concept of the primary message systems as a tool to aid in the specific analysis of culture and of the school as a setting for cultural conflict.

As can be seen from the discussion of the relationship of the three reaction patterns to each of the primary message systems, where there is more than one culture present, there is potential for conflict between reaction patterns. This implies that the seeds of change exist within the culture of the school, or, indeed, of any other institution that has more than one culture within it. While the cultural conflicts in the school are the seeds of change, there is also a formal structure within the school that will attempt to maintain stasis. So long as the different cultures define the primary message systems differently, or have different reaction patterns, there is little doubt that conflict, overt and covert, will continue.

Overt conflict is relatively rare in schools because it is difficult for students, who are temporary residents in the school, to organize against the adult staff, which is more or less permanent. The students are in a largely powerless position without many rights or privileges. Further, the society has taught all of us to respect both the school and the teachers in it. However, this does not prevent covert hostility and conflict from being present. Everything from cheating and vandalism to attacks on teachers and administrators (verbal and physical) to unexcused and unexplained absences points to a general dissatisfaction with the school.

In each of the chapters presented in Section Two of the book, the problem has been the same: How can we, as professional educators, learn to be more knowledgeable about and responsive to educational problems and pressures? This chapter has discussed the way in which the cultures of the school can be analyzed so that the conflicts and pressures within them can be alleviated, not just "to keep the natives quiet," but, more importantly, to make the school a place where students will want to be and where they will develop the skills and attitudes to keep them learning after they get out of school. So long as there are multiple cultures in the school and so long as the power structure of the school recognizes only one basic pattern, the conflict will continue. Many students will attend school only under duress and will leave school with the belief that schooling and learning are both odious. This will, indeed, be unfortunate.

FOR CONSIDERATION

1. Explain the difference among formal, informal, and technical patterns of interaction. Use examples from your own recent experience to illustrate the differences.

2. List the ten primary message systems (PMS) on one side of a page. From current newspaper and magazine articles, provide an illustration of each PMS. For example, a story about a reunion of sisters who have been apart twenty years could be used to illustrate interaction and/or temporality.

3. Apply this communications model to a school. Analyze the organization and operation of the school in terms of the three patterns of interaction. Do the same with the ten primary message systems. One way to do this is to construct a matrix, listing the interaction patterns across the top and

the message systems down the side. Try to find a school example to fit each box in the matrix.

	Formal	*Informal*	*Technical*
Interaction	Faculty meeting	Teachers' lounge	Memos to faculty
Association			

4. How well does this model fit the school? Does it provide more perceptive insights for understanding schooling than do the other models we have discussed? Compare it to the other models used.

References

Hall, Edward T. *The Silent Language*. Greenwich, Conn.: Fawcett Books, 1959.
McLuhan, Marshall. *Understanding Media*. New York: McGraw-Hill, 1964.

Section Three: Social Milieu of Education

S ection One included a general introduction to the study of and history of stasis and change in the institution of the American school. Section Two presented six models for use in analyzing contemporary schools. They ranged from socioeconomic to political to cultural models.

This section is devoted to a consideration of the social context of education—the setting in which the schools operate. The chapters here deal with divergent views of society and how they influence our perspectives on schools. The section also includes an examination of the process of socialization.

Schools are shaped by, and also shape, the social environment in which they exist. Similarly, individuals are shaped by, and shape, their environments. These chapters provide a framework for understanding the social environment and the role of the school in socializing young people. Socialization may be ideologically loaded as a term, but at very least, it is a description of what happens to each of us. Our interaction with our environments is socializing. The process of socialization occurs throughout life and includes, therefore, socialization into occupations such as teaching. Finally, Section Three includes a consideration of the social perceptions of teaching.

Chapter 9:
Social
Milieu
of
Education

The Traditional versus
the Progressive View

The dominant mission of schooling is the development of adults possessed of the knowledge, values, and behaviors considered appropriate by the society. So American schools teach information about numbers, letters, and national history because this is considered useful by our society. The values of competition and material success, as well as the superiority of Americans throughout history and behaviors considered appropriate to society, such as punctuality, neatness, and obedience, are also stressed.

   These citizen-developing activities of the school represent a basis, or rationale, for the existence and operation of formal schooling. Developing knowledge of reading, writing, and arithmetic has been a primary basis of the schools for centuries and is not subject to argument. There may be broad disagreements on how and when it is to be done, but none on the need for such knowledge. The acquisition of values that support the extant society is a subject of some debate, but is also an historic goal of schools. The debate is not actually about whether the schools should engage in value development, but what values should be taught by whom, when, and how. Similarly, long tradition and common consent affirm that schools should participate in the development of student behaviors; the issue is which behaviors, how, and when.

Transmitting socially acceptable knowledge, values, and behavior is the basis for traditional approaches to schooling. In light of this John Dewey's criticism of traditional education almost fifty years ago is still apt:

> The subject matter of education consists of bodies of information and of skills that have been worked out in the past; therefore, the chief business of the schools is to transmit them to the new generation. In the past there have also been developed standards and rules of conduct; moral training consists in forming habits of action in conformity with these rules and standards.[1]
>
> Since the subject matter as well as standards of proper conduct are handed down from the past, the attitude of pupils must, upon the whole, be one of docility, receptivity, and obedience.[2]

The indoctrination of selected knowledge, values, and behaviors in a society is potentially counterproductive. It presumes that the selected characteristics to be transmitted represent reality in the existing society. It requires learning that tends to be class-based and nation-specific. It imposes learnings necessarily derived from looking backward rather than from contemporary situations or from projections of the future. And it encourages students to passive receptivity rather than active participation in the process of schooling. Thus, society pressures schools to transmit selective socioeconomic and patriotic perspectives drawn from narrow historical views and to expect conformity to a society presumed to be static.

Yet, one of the few principles on which social scientists agree is that change is a constant social phenomenon. The counterproductive quality of traditional schooling lies in the school having virtually contradictory goals: to produce citizens who passively conform to traditional expectations and to produce those who can actively participate in progressive transformations. As long as the schools concentrate on training people to fit into a past society, they create obstacles to freeing human intelligence for thoughtful social change.

One answer to this dilemma is to shift dramatically from traditional passive education to social activism—an appealing approach to those who have a particular agenda for social change or to those who believe progress comes from social tension created by opposing activists. While there is some reason to incorporate activist ideas in schooling, it is unsatisfactory as a basis for education. Activism on its own has no inherent rationale. Obedience to it can be as blind as adherence to traditional education. It is as easy to produce unexamined activism as it is to produce unexamined passivism. The Inquisition, Nazi Germany, and the Ku Klux Klan represent activism coupled with uncritical allegiance. The mob, whether organized for things considered socially desirable or destructive, is not a thoughtful group. Training people to be more skillful as activists without developing skills for making autonomous judgments is as counterproductive for contemporary schools as the cloistered conformity of traditional education.

Dewey addresses this problem:

It is not too much to say that an educational philosphy which professes to be based on the idea of freedom may become as dogmatic as ever was the traditional education which is reacted against. For any theory and set of practices is dogmatic which is not based upon critical examination of its own principles.[3]

The key principle in combatting dogmatism identified by Dewey is critical examination: criticism not only of specific subjects studied, but continuing criticism of the educational approach itself and, by extension, criticism of society. Social criticism can be perceived as an appropriate, perhaps the most appropriate, basis for schooling. Schools should teach critical thinking and students should engage in social improvement in light of that criticism. Criticism incorporates the best features of traditional forms of education, utilizing basic skills of language and mathematics and requiring continuing sophistication in reading, writing, speaking, and listening as well as the interpretation, analysis, and evaluation of evidence. It goes beyond traditional education by encouraging active participation in the process and breaking down the barriers of dogmatism about knowledge, values, and behavior. Criticism is dependent upon access to information and ideas, but does not accept them without question. Concern for the improvement of human welfare should be a goal of society, and certainly a goal of schooling. Thoughtful and critical decision-making is necessary in an enlightened democracy. Thus, exposure to and encouragement in rational decision-making should be a strong component, if not the primary activity, of schooling in societies that aim toward democracy. Criticism is basic to that concept.

T.B. Bottomore writes:

Social Criticism, in one form or another, has had a place in most human societies. . . . The force of custom and tradition is very great, life is altogether precarious and difficult, and the established ways of behaving are not to be lightly altered or upset for fear of total disaster. It is only in societies which have become literate, possess economic reserves, have developed an urban life and in some measure a professional intellectual class, that any sustained criticism of the working of society is possible.[4]

Obviously, American society fulfills Bottomore's conditions. We are literate, have economic reserves and urban life, and we have a professional intellectual class composed of philosophers, writers, teachers, and other thinkers. Clearly, not all philosophers, writers, and teachers are social critics, but Bottomore's point is that social criticism is only possible where some members of society have the privilege of systematically reviewing social conditions and recommending change. This privilege is not limited to those with a certain level of education or a particular job. The intellectual social criticism of such people as Eric Hoffer, a longshoreman with virtually no formal education, and a host of other critical leaders who lack advanced degrees and status in "professional class" positions, have brought significant changes in American social, economic, and political life.

A major point of agreement among sociologists of education, and the most obvious comment to anyone who has contemplated the school as a social institution is that the school is related to the society in which it resides. The nature, purpose, and operation of the relationship between school and society are the subject of somewhat more debate.

There is disagreement among analysts about the subleties, causes, and results of the school's social agenda, but no disagreement on the description of the school as reflective of the values and goals of the society. At the prescriptive level, suggesting what the school ought to be doing or proposing resolutions of the ills of society and schooling, arguments about the manifest and latent functions of schools become more pronounced. Some of them follow.

SCHOOL AS REFLECTOR OF SOCIETY

Some consider the reflective school-society relationship as a natural state of affairs, impossible to alter. This view condemns the school to a continuing existence as a reactive organization, following the commands of the society. It suggest that what is is what ought to be or that what ought to be cannot be, so one must accept what is. It also locks the teacher in the role of servant. There is much evidence to support this position; virtually the entire history of education argues for it. Society proposes and the school uncritically disposes.

SCHOOL AND SOCIETY IN A BILATERAL RELATIONSHIP

Another view of the school and society is that the relationship is bilateral, with society organizing and directly influencing the purposes and practices of schools, and the schools exerting influence on society as a result of their size, resources, and long-term effects on individuals who move from being students to become adult members of society. Schooling involves the largest profession in the country, some 3 million educators; schools employ a sizable proportion of the educated people in society; schools utilize significant amounts of financial resources, often the largest proportion of local public budgets; and schools have some effect on virtually all young people in a society for an extended period of their lives. In this view the school and the society influence each other in differing domains. Society formalizes, controls, and directs what happens in schools; schools and those in schooling become a political and economic force in the society.

SCHOOL AND SOCIETY IN A TRANSACTIONAL RELATIONSHIP

A variation of the bilateral view is that the relationship between the school and society is transactional, that is, that school and society influence each other in ways that transcend simple explanations of one acting on the other. Each influences and is influenced by the other at the same time in a constantly changing environment. Thus, it is more complex than a straight-forward relationship where society legislates the operation of schools and teachers vote for legislators. Instead, there is a dynamic in which school legislation, as an example, results from a variety of pressures from individuals and groups representing schools and society in a particular time and place setting. Similarly, school practices like the hiring and firing of teachers and decisions about curriculum and teaching materials are intertwined with the economic and political situations of the society.

A RECONSTRUCTIONIST OR REFORMIST PERSPECTIVE

One analysis of the school and society is critical of the school as a reflective agent. The reconstructionist perceives that society has a number of deficiencies, like injustice and inequality, and that the school is a primary social agent to address and attempt to correct these social ills. This, as was pointed out in Chapter 2, was a sympathy of the Johnson administration. Since the schools have a well-educated cadre of professionals, an unequalled opportunity to influence each generation, and a responsibility to improve society, they are the most likely institutions for reconstructing the society. The reconstructionist perspective inverts the traditional relationship between schools and society by making schools the dominant member. This position requires the reformist or reconstructionist to have a particular vision of the preferred society and an agenda for change. It also requires some agreement on that vision and agenda.

These varying views of the relationship of schools to society do not exhaust the possibilities, but they describe a spectrum of accounts—from the concept that schools are in a relatively static position, pushed and pulled by forces in the society and reacting to them, to a mutually dynamic position, to a view that the schools can build a new social order.

There are advocates and detractors among those who adopt each of these stances. Advocates among those who see the school as reactive suggest that that is a fully appropriate role. Schools are created by the society for certain purposes and the schools must properly fulfill those purposes. The schools have to be responsive and responsible in the training of young people to become full citizens of the society. Detractors in this camp decry the fact of reflective schools because of the social limits imposed upon education, the censorship and the false morality required by society, but they note that schools have always been—and always will be—the tools of the powerful groups in society. They are critics but resign themselves to the situation.

Advocates of the bilateral or transactional view of influence propose that this offers the opportunity to accommodate change and to extract the best ideas from society and from schools. The tension created provides a cauldron for testing ideas and developing critical abilities in students. Detractors identify the chaos and confusion resulting from the lack of unified purposes and the inconsistent planning when times and circumstances change. The pendulum merely swings between conservatism and liberalism in school and society, and criticism swings in an opposing arc.

Advocates of a reconstructionist position perceive recent student revolt and activism as an example of the possibilities for social change inherent in the school setting. Detractors perceive that the period was short-lived, dominated by self-interest related to staying out of the war in Vietnam, and relatively ineffective in redirecting the society.

Differing Perspectives on Society

Social scientists argue about what determines the nature of society, how it has been established, how it can be changed, and what it should be. A number of differing perspectives, or theories, on society are important to consider in a text on school and society because the perspective that we adopt on the nature, operation, and values of society influences our views of social institutions, including the school. From one perspective, the school performs a proper social function in its efforts to produce individuals who share common social values but at the same time attempts to plan for change; from another, the school's efforts are perceived as pernicious and contradictory.

EXAMPLE: MAX WEBER
AND BUREAUCRACY

A particular view of how society works influences individual and group attitudes and social behaviors. It informs and controls our sense of social reality and change. It also provides a basis for attitudes, prejudices, and explanations of events. Alvin Gouldner uses the example of Max Weber's theory of bureaucracy to illustrate this point.[5] Gouldner suggests that the idea of increasingly more complex social organizations and the inevitablity of expanded bureaucracy described by Weber strikes a sympathetic chord in people and underscores their pessimism about large-scale social change. That is, people who accept the theory of expanding bureaucracy will have a ready explanation for social alienation and will consider efforts to alter society dramatically to be futile. They may complacently accept bureaucratic requirements and responses, and the social control that follows. As Weber states:

> Once it is fully established, bureaucracy is among those social structures which are hardest to destroy. . . . The individual bureaucrat cannot squirm out of the apparatus in which he is harnessed. . . . The ruled, for their part, cannot dispense with or replace the bureaucratic apparatus of authority once it exists. For this bureaucracy rests upon expert training, a functional specialization of work, and an attitude set for habitual and virtuoso-like mastery of single yet methodically integrated functions.

. . . More and more the material fate of the masses depends upon the steady and correct functioning of the increasingly bureaucratic organization of private capitalism.[6]

For many people, including teachers, Weber's comments make sense. He seems to describe a virtually inevitable expansion of bureaucracy, which resonates with the lives of most of us. Whether Weber is correct or not, the perspective of increasing bureaucracy in the social order can create a self-fulfilling prophecy. We assume that bureaucracy will encroach more and more on individual lives and we accept the encroachment without question or protest.

In addition, the Weberian analysis of bureaucracy implicates education, since bureaucracy requires "expert training" and the development of social attitudes related to the specialization of work. Educational institutions provide the expert training and instill the attitudes necessary for operation of the bureaucracy. Specialized degrees, certificates, and training programs (illustrated by the growth in degrees like the M.B.A., certification for insurance and real-estate agents, and training programs for dental assistants and paralegal professionals) are part of this process. Weber notes that democracy is threatened by the increasing bureaucratization through education because this education is class-based. The relation of class to education is important enough for treatment in a later section of this book. It is raised here to indicate Weber's concern about the antidemocratic nature of capitalist bureaucracies.

To follow Gouldner's point that pessimism about large-scale change can result from this perspective, consider schools and teachers. Teachers tend to accept the rule of bureaucracy in schools. They may complain to each other about particular record-keeping or other bureaucratic regulations, but they are unlikely to believe that any major change in the organization and operation of the school bureaucracy is possible. The believing teacher does not challenge a bureaucracy in a large school district even though some edicts and regulations are obviously preposterous. A shrug, showing belief in the inevitability of expanding bureaucracy, may be the only outward sign. This teacher then becomes part of the bureaucracy, defending it and imposing it on students. The teacher rationalizes bureaucratic actions, supports the need for order and control, and expresses these views to students: "We must not move our chairs because the principal likes neat rows." "Only one person may have a hall pass at a time; that is a school rule."

The school bureaucracy becomes an easy reference point for teachers. It can be blamed for virtually every problem in a school but not confronted directly. It provides a faceless excuse for inefficiency or ineffectiveness. And it is a basis for the acceptability of stasis and control, and an argument against change. Imagine the following conversation in a teachers' room of a local school:

> NEW TEACHER: I'd like to take my 3rd period class to visit city hall? How do I make the arrangements?
>
> SENIOR COLLEAGUE: The board doesn't like us to take students out of the building. There's something about insurance.
>
> ANOTHER SENIOR COLLEAGUE: Well, you can do it; but the principal's office will make you find a teacher to handle your other classes, and you have to get parent permission slips signed. It's not worth it.
>
> THIRD SENIOR: Even with parent permissions, you are still legally responsible; and you have to make bus arrangements and get your students out of after-school activities.
>
> NEW TEACHER: Why do we need parent permission slips if we are still responsible?
>
> THIRD SENIOR: That's just the rule.
>
> NEW TEACHER: Maybe I can just bring in some newspaper story about local government.

The example of a belief in bureaucratic expansion illustrates one perspective on society. There are other perspectives that have been identified and through which we can analyze schools.

FUNCTIONALISM VERSUS THE CRITICS: CONSENSUS VERSUS CONFLICT

The "coming crisis" identified by Gouldner in his book centers on the disparity in views between those who can be classified as functionalists in their analysis of society and those who are critical of the functional view.[7] There are a number of ways of describing the differences; among them the distinction between a social order dependent upon consensual values and one based on conflict is clear.[8]

Functionalists tend to see a common core of social values and to present a view that preserves and protects the existing social order. Marxists, as one body of critics, perceive conflict as basic, using dialectical analyses to strip away superficial social conventions and examine the root structure of the society. In this context, Gouldner argues that the "ideological character of Functionalism is conservative in nature,"[9] while Marxism and other critical views are radical because they are concerned with continuing criticism of the roots of social ills.

Donald Hansen, analyzing the critical ideas of George Herbert Mead, Karl Marx, and Max Weber, notes that there is a "fundamental rift in the images of the individual and society that informs our social and economic actions and which support and challenge our social order." He goes on: "The dominant 'schools' of American sociology continue to embrace 'normative' images, emphasizing consensus, cohesion, and the social bond—to the comparative neglect of questions of conflict, coercion, negotiation and change."[10] Hansen sees the writings of Mead, Marx, and Weber as avenues to explore disturbing questions about self, other individuals, and society. Gouldner identifies the work of Erving Goffman, Harold Garfinkel, George Homans, and "New Left" sociologists as important in challenging the functionalist concept of social consensus. An exploration of functionalism and its influence on the way we perceive schooling is an appropriate starting place.

THE FUNCTIONALIST VIEW   Many ideas of functionalism are drawn from a variety of sources in anthropology, sociology, education, biology, economics, and other disciplines. Many differences exist among those classified as functionalists, but they share some basic concepts about society, its institutions, and the relation of society to individuals. It is possible to trace functionalism to Greek social thought, but current functionalist ideas derive from August Comte, Herbert Spencer, Emile Durkheim, and Branislaw Malinowski.[11] Their views coincide in trying to explain the nature of society in terms of the integration of several parts into a functioning whole. Spencer and Durkheim drew inspiration from ideas in biology that stressed the functional relationship of parts of an organism to its whole. Malinowski, a cultural anthropologist under whom Talcott Parsons, one of the leading theoreticians of functionalism, studied, is known as the creator of the formal theory of functionalism.

Functionalism includes the following basic concepts:

1. There is an order to society.
2. Each social system must account for the biological, economic, and psychological needs of its members.
3. Each society has a set of common core values and norms of behavior.
4. Mechanisms of socialization and social control must be successful to limit deviance and encourage social motivations of individuals.
5. Social institutions are functionally related to each other in an integrated society.

Donald Fisher, in a recent analysis of the role that American philanthropies had in establishing conservative functionalist views in the social sciences in Great Britain, wrote:

First, the foundations, past and present, have occupied a mediating role between the economic structure of capitalist societies and the other social institutions. Further, that their mediating influence has tended to reproduce the existing social structure rather than alter it.[12]

Fisher sees the tax-free foundations in the United States as gatekeepers, controlling the type and quality of sponsored research. He notes that the Rockefeller Fund refused support to the "diffusionist" school (Elliott-Smith) in anthropological research, while the functionalist school (Malinowski) was given extensive support.[13] He quotes from the 1953 Annual Report of the Rockefeller Fund a segment written by Dean Rusk, who was the foundation's president, on the definition of the fund:

It is private in that it is not governmental; it is public in that its funds are held in trust for public rather than private purposes. As a social institution, it reflects the application to philanthropy of the principles of private initiative and free enterprise, under public policies which have long recognized the benefits of such activity to a free society.[14]

The conservatism of functionalism is, according to Gouldner, primarily its acceptance of master social institutions and its commitment to the maintenance of order in a society. Functionalism, then, is not engaged in basic criticisms of society or of social institutions. Functionalists try only to describe and analyze the workings of the social order. They are willing to solve social problems within the framework of existing social institutions and protocols. Social change is explained in terms of the ongoing consensual values and gradual modificaton.

Actions that support the social order are functional; deviations from the accepted social order are treated as dysfunctional. That is, a disruption in the status quo is seen as something that interferes with the functioning of the social order. This concept of dysfunction permits functionalists to explain a social movement, such as student protests, or a deviant individual in socially negative, but sterile and neutralizing, terms.

Since the society and its social institutions, like the family and the school, are already functioning on the basis of a common core of values, it is the individual who is to be adjusted. This is fundamental in the functionalist view. Although Parsons and other functionalists indicate that there is an interaction between the individual and the society, there is still the assumption that the ongoing social system will implant itself on the individual.

THE SOCIAL ORDER ACCORDING TO FUNCTIONALISM   Social organization simply refers to the condition that permits reasonably accurate predictions of what will occur in typical situations. These predictions are based upon traditional patterns of socially acceptable behavior and an assumption of stasis. Under an assumption of change, or without adequate experience in social tradition, predictions about behavior become much less accurate. The stronger the force of stasis and tradition the more predictable is the behavior of individuals and groups, up to the point of complete control. Functionalism assumes a relatively strong force of tradition as basic to social order.

Maintenance of the social order involves several ongoing problems. Parsons identifies four of them that need resolution as follows:

1. Adaptation: there is a need to make adjustments to a changing environment of people, things, ideas, and traditions.
2. Goal identification: a minimum level of agreement on relatively clear social goals is needed to guide general behaviors.
3. Inculcation and reinforcement: mechanisms and institutions are needed to produce among children an understanding of and agreement with social values, norms, and customs, and to reinforce those agreements and behaviors for adult members of the society.
4. Coherence: there is a need to integrate the variety of individual and group interests in a society into a workable whole.[15]

A legal American horse race illustrates the elements of control and deviance. The location and size of the track, the time and operation of the race, the number of horses, their age and general physical condition, the manner and operation of betting, certain requirements on the owners, trainers and jockeys, and related factors are controlled. Within these limits, however, the speed of any horse in any particular race, the weather, and the legal handling of a horse by any particular jockey are not controlled. Those gamblers who are relatively successful understand the social order of the track, the legally prescribed conditions of track length and race operation, the tradition of particular horses and jockeys in certain kinds of races, the likely effects of weather and track conditions, and any specific information about horses, jockeys, and conditions that might influence a particular race. There is the distinct possibility of change in the race — a scratched horse, a moderately ill jockey, a stumble, illicit drugs, or simple chance.

Predictions about behaviors in regard to the time, location, and general operation of the race will be highly accurate because these factors are controlled. If a race is fixed — thus, controlled — it is also subject to highly accurate predictions and betting by those who know of the fix. Otherwise, betting is mainly among those who base their predictions on tradition and stasis, those who predict on the basis of change and chance, and those who do some of each.

Knowing the traditions, legal controls, and general operations of horse racing in the United States would not yield accurate predictions of horse racing with distinctively different traditions. If the object of the race were to see which horse could last the longest over variable terrain, without size or weight controls on riders and with no understood rules about fairness in the race or in the betting, an American horse handicapper would have much less predictive power than would someone who lived in the society where such races were commonplace. The more control, the more predictability.

Social order, then, can be defined very simply as those social controls, norms, and expectations that usually govern and can reasonably predict be-

Table 9.1:
Illustrative Elements of the Social Order

Controls	Norms	Expectations	Deviations
Laws	Dress	Parent, family role	Civil disobedience
Regulations	Greetings	Work roles	Criminal acts
Requirements	Language use	Peer group roles	Aberrant behavior
Binding agreements	Body language		
Dominant morality or ethics	Time usage	Institutional roles	Antisocial acts
Specific institutions: Prisons, military, school, work	Defintions: Social roles, e.g., work, play, cooperation, sanity		
Pressure			

havior in routine situations. The simplicity of the definition, however, masks the complexity involved in subtleties and nuances of controls, norms, and expectations. It also masks the necessary occurrence of social change and chance factors that alter situations and behaviors.

The social order exists in the continuing compromise with the tension between stability and change. As Shils suggests, this comparison between restraint and freedom, and between the interests of individuals and the shared goals of society, is what creates the social order.[16] It is always in flux, dependent upon tradition but subject to change. The pull of extremes toward chaos or complete control is threatening, but enticing. The balance point shifts over time.

SCHOOLING IN THE
FUNCTIONALIST PERSPECTIVE

The school is an institutional element in each of the problems identified by Parsons. Schools are charged with a responsibility for providing skills and knowledge that assist young generations to adapt to their environments; that stress socially approved goals; that inculcate and reinforce belief in those goals; and that assist in the integration of individual and group interests.

Following are some examples of stated goals of education drawn from several sources. Note how these commonly expressed goals illustrate the perceived role of the school in support of the social order.

Massachusetts Bay Law of 1642:

This Court, taking into consideration the great neglect of many parents and masters in training up their children in learning and labor and other employments which may be profitable to the Commonwealth, do hereby decree and order that the elected officials . . . have the power to take account from time to time of all parents and masters, and of their children, . . . especially of their ability to read and understand the principles of religion and the capital laws of this country.[17]

Aristotle (Fourth Centry, B.C.):

We conclude that from one point of view governors and governed are identical and from another different. And therefore their education must be the same and also different. For he who would learn to command well must, as men say, first learn to obey. . . .

No one will doubt that the legislator should direct his attention above all to the education of youth, or that the neglect of education does harm to states. The citizen should be moulded to suit the form of government under which he lives. For each government has a peculiar character which originally formed and which continues to preserve it.[18]

Noah Webster (1790):

Our constitutions of civil government are not yet firmly established, our national character is not yet formed; and it is an object of vast magnitude that systems of education should be adopted and pursued which may not only diffuse a knowledge of the sciences but may implant in the minds of the American youth the principles of virtue and of liberty and inspire them with just and liberal ideas of government and with an inviolable attachment to their own country.[19]

National Education Association (1918):
      (Basic Objectives for Secondary Schools)

Education in the United States should be guided by a clear conception of the meaning of democracy. It is the ideal of democracy that the individual and society may find fulfillment each in the other. . . .

1. Health, health instruction, physical education, sports
2. Command of Fundamental Processes (reading, writing, arithmetic, oral expression)
3. Worthy Home Membership (home as fundamental social institution, coeducation, responsibilities to home, household arts for girls, home appreciation for boys)
4. Vocation (career education, vocational training)
5. Civic Education (community welfare, civic duties, national loyalty, sympathy for international problems)[20]

Schools as major social institutions have many manifest and latent functions in regard to the social order. Some of these functions are complementary, like preserving selected social values and instructing students in the dominant language. Other functions are contradictory, like producing citizens who have a national patriotic bias and producing global citizens who think critically. Basically, the schools are formally expected to protect, preserve, and teach the core values of a society. The most significant manifest function of schools is to continue the existing social order by teaching it to new generations.

In modern societies that intend to be democratic, schools are often given another manifest function: to prepare young people to be thoughtful decision-makers. This function incorporates the concepts of change and critical thinking. It assumes that societies change and that a democracy can only survive if its citizens can cope with change and make informed decisions.

This duality of major functions has created continuous debate about and often vicious attack upon the schools. Those who believe the school should be essentially a static institution that inculcates students with the social order do not want schools to provide opportunities for students to be critical of that order. At the other end of the continuum are those who believe the schools must produce critical citizens.

FITTING INDIVIDUALS INTO SOCIETY

From the functionalist view, schools serve a number of necessary functions in maintaining and extending the shared values of a society: Schools convey the cultural heritage to new generations; schools provide basic skills to masses of the population; schools inculcate a belief in the common core values of a society; schools help assimilate young people and immigrants into the society; schools offer a means of social mobility; schools offer preparation for work; schools develop habits of value to the society; schools provide a semblance of the outside society; schools develop a respect for authority. As in the horse race example described earlier, schools function to assure that people learn and follow the rules in predictable ways.

A major purpose for schooling, for functionalists, is to fit the individual to society. Their argument is often that the continued existence of the society and the stability of the social order depend upon the schools preparing young people to fit in. Parsons emphasized the malleability of individuals within the larger group.[21] The process of socialization, examined in depth in Chapter 10, involves the stamping of individuals with the marks of the society. In the functionalist view, such socialization is tantamount to producing social conformity.

School, then, functions as a major social institution to preserve and continue the values of the existing social order. Schools, teachers, or students are dysfunctional when they challenge that social order. This perspective affects the school in many overt and subtle ways, including:

> school organization—hierarchy and authority patterns consistent with those in the society; in the United States a business or corporate model is apparent[22]

school operation—a bureaucratic and technical orientation drawn from corporate styles[23]

norms for teacher behavior—models of decorum, American values; conservators of morality; controllers of the class; conveyors of truth; employees in the labor market[24]

norms for student behavior—learners of good working habits; proper respect, appropriate knowledge, national values[25]

curriculum—predetermined, socially acceptable knowledge; required courses reflect dominant national or social interests; curriculum separates social classes into academic and vocational[26]

extracurricular activities—athletics to build competitive spirit; clubs related to vocational interests or socially responsible activities; student government to learn patterns of standard political life[27]

teaching materials—reflect dominant socially acceptable ideas; bland, middle of road content; moralistic; nationalistic, biased toward corporate interests[28]

testing—screening system to fit students to social models; separates, segregates, and classifies students; presumes competitive structure as in capitalism[29]

teacher education—based on socially traditional knowledge; attracts students interested in security and maintenance of social order; nonradical content[30]

THE CRITICAL VIEW

Functionalism has many forms and competing ideas expressed by those identified with it, but it has a common basic view: maintenance of the social order. Similarly, critical perspectives have many forms and competing advocates, but a certain common basis for analysis of society. Much of the critical perspective includes dissatisfaction with functionalist theory. Such dissatisfaction is sometimes based on problems in logic for functionalists (the existence of something does not explain its cause); sometimes based on substance (functionalism fails to account adequately for social change, and stresses harmony rather than dissent); and sometimes based on ideological grounds (functionalism is essentially conservative and supports the power of existing elites).

Critical views of the nature of society share the following elements:

1. Conflict is basic to society.
2. Dominant classes in society strive to project the illusion of social cohesion based on the values of those classes and to coerce others into agreement.
3. Significant differences in values and interests exist between and within groups in society.
4. There is a tension between social actuality and social potential.
5. Society consists of a set of situations in which individuals find themselves; it does not exist separately.

CRITICISMS OF FUNCTIONALISM   The conflict model of social analysis argues that the functionalists cannot adequately explain rapid change, because change threatens stability in society. The idea of "equilibrium" that functionalists use to explain minor deviations in society, and the implied pull of social forces back toward conservative stability, is seen by conflict theorists as an attempt to create a self-fulfilling explanation to avoid revolutionary ideas. Equilibrium is the mechanism that permits the ongoing social order to adjust to change without dramatic alteration.

Another criticism of functionalism is that the social cohesion the functionalists describe is actually a myth designed to perpetuate the interests of the dominant classes. Conflict theorists present the view that a minority of the society's corporate interests, families with traditional wealth and social status, and the managerial classes control the society and create the illusion that it has a common core of values. In fact, according to this criticism, the differing classes are in conflict in values and interests.

The false consciousness that there is a consensus in social goals and values, say the conflict theorists, hides the more brutal aspects of reality in society. Thus, in functionalism there are hidden social and economic agendas, illustrated by such things as class-based consumer advertising, controlled newspaper treatment of political issues, tax-law provisions that help the rich, disparate operation of the criminal justice system, protectionist international affairs, and socioeconomic differences in health care. There is also a hidden curriculum in the schools that produce conformity to the mythology of social order. The very nature of schooling, according to critical analysts, hides the broad social and economic agenda that maintains the power of elite groups.

H. L. Neiburg describes the political setting where one set of values dominates others:

The formal institutions of state authority reinforce (the values) through socialization, consensus and ultimately, a monopoly on legal violence. This enables dominant groups to determine the choices available to the lower orders of the hierarchy. They organize and manage social policy, resources and the environment in such a way as to reflect their own values of order, which limits the choices that remain open to groups with competing value systems.[31]

Among major "formal institutions of state authority" are such agencies as the police, legislatures, tax systems, and schools. These provide protection, enforcement, and reinforcement through education of the values of the dominant groups. Even in the political structure of a democracy, based on general values of equality and justice, there are inequalities and injustices that are maintained by social institutions. Conflict analyses of society point out these disparities and look for root causes.

MARXISM AND THE CRITICAL VIEW   Not all critics of functionalism are Marxists; neither are all who hold other critical perspectives of society and schools. But Marxism provides a theoretical rationale and relatively consistent viewpoint for analysis for systematic examination of the social condition of humans. Marxists, among other things, are noted for considerable self-criticism and vehement arguments over which faction promotes truth. Even Karl Marx would have difficulty deciding which Marxist views are compatible with his own. Still, there is agreement on the need to subject society, social institutions, and the socialization process to continuing critical scrutiny, based on general tenets of Marxism. These tenets include:

1. a critique of capitalism in its exploitation and oppression.
2. a theory of continuing revolution of the masses against the elites, a class struggle.
3. use of a dialectic method of analysis (thesis–antithesis–synthesis) based on analysis of opposing forces in society.

Erich Fromm (as well as Chapter 3 of this book) states that Marx is misinterpreted widely throughout the world. Fromm holds that Russian communism is a distortion of Marxist theory, especially in the Soviet contempt for human dignity and humanitarian values. The essence of Marx, according to Fromm, is that humans make their own history, they are their own creators. Thus, active individuals involved in social and political relationships constitute society (for the functionalists, society implants itself on passive humans).

Marxism suggests that humans can change society, can alter situations, and can have freedom. To Marx, then, most of what people think of consciously as true, is actually a "false consciousness." It is ideology and rationalization rather than truth. The traditional social organization traps people and prevents them from being conscious of certain information and experiences.[32] Critical analysis must, therefore, strip away the ideology and falsity.

The process advocated for stripping away is a form of dialectic reasoning. Herbert Marcuse, a noted philosopher identified with neo-Marxist ideas, suggests that dialectic thinking is to "distinguish the essential from the apparent process of reality, and to grasp their relationship."[33] This comes from Hegel, who held that appearance and essence are different. The dialectic approach takes appearance as a thesis, poses an antithesis, and attempts to arrive at a synthesis. For example, the thesis that the school is a place where everyone has an equal opportunity to learn is examined from the antithesis that school is a class-based structure where inequality of opportunity to learn is dominant.

As Samuel Bowles argues about inequalities in schooling:

> That schools have evolved in the United States not as a part of a pursuit of equality, but rather to meet the needs of capitalist employers for a disciplined and skilled labor force, and to provide a mechanism for social control in the interests of political stability; . . . that the U.S. school system is pervaded by class inequalities. . . . Thus, unequal education has its roots in the very class structure which it serves to legitimate and reproduce.[34]

Capitalism, in Marxist terms, is to be criticized because it produces an interest in money and private gain as the primary motivation in humans. Capitalism obstructs human freedom. It presumes a competitive structure with a ruling class, the bourgeoisie, and a working class, the proletariat. The ruling class exists as a result of profit from the labor of the proletariat, and not from its own productive labor. The bourgeoisie also try to preserve and protect their status in society by controlling its legal, political, and economic institutions. They prefer that the proletariat be controlled by a variety of social restraints, including the idea of dominant social values, passivity and docility, acceptance of social roles and norms, and ignorance. Schools are a means of social control and socialization.

Thus, Marxism holds that functionalist interpretations only assist the dominant class in social control and in holding back change that would improve human conditions and free people.

PRACTICAL EFFECTS OF FUNCTIONALISM FROM A MARXIST PERSPECTIVE
Marxists are not only critical of functionalist theory, but of the significant
practical effects of functionalist thinking on schooling. These practical effects
include the following:

1. Schools become mechanisms to control social deviance. School is intended
   to maintain equilibrium.
2. Normative social behavior is reinforced and rewarded. Conformity is
   especially important.
3. Traditional ideas about curriculum continue to dominate.
4. School is seen as a training center, separate from society.
5. Teachers are expected to inform and prescribe for students. Teachers
   maintain authority and convey social norms.
6. Controversial topics or activities are to be avoided or shielded from view.
7. Criticism of society is severely limited and does not appear in texts, films,
   or teacher discussions in public.
8. Individuals are not expected to develop autonomy or independence of
   mind.
9. The school reinforces a set of values that maintains and reproduces unequal social classes (e.g., grouping, selective courses, guiding some students to college and others to vocational training).

This discussion of Marxism has been relatively brief since Chapter 3 presents a more extensive picture of Marxist perspectives on education and
schooling.

SUMMARY

This chapter describes the social setting of the school and notes divergent perspectives on the nature of society. Stasis and change are significant aspects of
the cultural framework within which education functions. The world view
that we bring to an examination of society and social institutions virtually
foretells the results. A functionalist view stands ready to explain the social system and schools in terms of relatively static influences of the social order on individuals. A critical view challenges the idea of individual passivity and the
hidden social agenda which functionalism supports. Certainly, these views
differ on the importance of stasis and change. They also differ extensively on
the purposes and practices of schools in society.

In schools the difference between functionalist and critical views of society becomes apparent in the debates over basic purposes, curriculum, teacher activities, expectations of students, teaching materials, and a long list of issues like:

basic skills versus critical thinking

behavior modification versus individuality

conformity versus autonomy

authority versus freedom

behavioral objects versus social criticism

management by objectives versus participatory democracy

FOR CONSIDERATION

1. From your experience as a student and as an observer of schools, identify important groups in the school's social setting. How does that setting reflect the tension between stasis and change? How do the groups influence the school?

2. Present an argument on one side or other of the idea that schools *should* emphasize stasis or change. What are your assumptions? What evidence do you have? What are the probable consequences of your view?

3. Describe a school using the functionalist perspective, that is, in terms of its functions in perpetuating the social order. Describe the same school from a critical perspective, that is, the social class interests it serves, its hidden social agenda.

Notes

1. John Dewey, *Experience and Education* (New York: Collier, 1938), p. 17.
2. *Ibid.*, p. 18.
3. *Ibid.*, p. 22.
4. T. B. Bottomore, *Critics of Society* (New York: Pantheon, 1968), pp. 3–4.
5. Alvin Gouldner, *The Coming Crisis of Western Sociology* (New York: Basic Books, 1970), p. 40.
6. H. H. Gerth and C. Wright Mills, *From Max Weber: Essays in Sociology* (New York: Oxford University Press, 1958), pp. 228–229.

7. Gouldner, *op. cit.*

8. Colin Lacey, *The Socialization of Teachers* (London: Methuen, 1977).

9. Gouldner, *op. cit.*, p. 331.

10. Donald A. Hansen, *An Invitation to Critical Sociology* (New York: Free Press, 1976), p. xii.

11. Percy S. Cohen, *Modern Social Theory* (New York: Basic Books, 1968).

12. Donald Fisher, "American Philanthropy and the Social Sciences in Britain, 1919–1939," *The Sociological Review* 28 (May 1980): 177.

13. *Ibid.*, p. 302

14. *Ibid.*

15. Edward A. Shils, *The Torment of Secrecy* (New York: Free Press, 1956).

16. Talcott Parsons, *The Social System* (New York: Free Press, 1951).

17. Massachusetts, *Record of the Governor and Company of the Massachusetts Bay in New England* (Boston: William White, 1853).

18. Aristotle, *The Politics of Aristotle*, trans. Benjamin Jowett (New York: Random House, 1943), p. 320.

19. Noah Webster, *A Collection of Essays and Fugitive Writings* (Boston: I. Thomas & Andrews, 1790), p. 1.

20. National Education Association, Commission on the Reorganization of Secondary Education, *Cardinal Principles of Secondary Education*, Bulletin 35 (Washington, D.C.: Government Printing Office, 1928), p. 1–10.

21. Talcott Parsons *et al.*, *Family, Socialization and Interaction Process* (Glencoe, Ill.: Free Press, 1955); and Parsons, *The Social System, op. cit.*

22. Raymond Callahan, *Education and the Cult of Efficiency* (Chicago: University of Chicago Press, 1962); and Martin Carnoy, ed., *Schooling in a Corporate Society* (New York: McKay,. 1975).

23. Joel Spring, *The Sorting Machine* (New York: McKay, 1976); and Samuel Bowles and Herbert Gintis, *Schooling in Capitalist America* (New York: Basic Books, 1976).

24. Jack L. Nelson and Frank Besag, *Sociological Perspectives in Education* (New York: Pitman, 1970).

25. Audrey J. Schwartz, *The Schools and Socialization* (New York: Harper & Row, 1975); and Clarence Karier, "Testing for Order and Control in the Corporate Liberal State," in *Schooling and Capitalism*, ed. Roger Dale, G. Esland, and M. MacDonald (London: Routledge & Kegan Paul, 1976), pp. 128–141.

26. Henry Giroux, "The New Sociology of Curriculum," *Educational Leadership* 37 (December 1979):248–253.

27. Jacquetta Hill Burnett, "Ceremony, Rites and Economy in the Student System of an American High School," *Human Organization* 12 (Spring 1969):1–10.

28. Jean Anyon, "Ideology and United States History Textbooks," *Harvard Educational Review* 49 (August 1979): pp. 361–386; and Jack L. Nelson, "Nationalistic Versus Global Education," *Theory and Research in Social Education* 4 (August 1976):pp. 33–50.

29. Karier, *op. cit.*

30. Harmon Zeigler, *The Political Life of American Teachers* (Englewood Cliffs, N.J.: Prentice-Hall, 1967); and Jack L. Nelson and Thomas Linton, *Patterns of Power* (New York: Pitman, 1974).

31. H. L. Neiburg, *Culture Storm* (New York: St. Martin's Press, 1973), p. 82.

32. Erich Fromm, *Marx's Concept of Man* (New York: Frederick Ungar, 1966).

33. Herbert Marcuse, *Reason and Revolution* (New York: Oxford University Press, 1941), p. 146.

34. Samuel Bowles, "Unequal Education and the Reproduction of the Social Division of Labor," in *Schooling in a Corporate Society*, ed. Martin Carnoy (New York: McKay, 1975), pp. 38–39.

References

Anderson, Charles H., and Gibson, Jeffry. *Toward a New Sociology*. Homewood, Ill.: Dorsey Press, 1978.

Anyon, Jean. "Ideology and the United States History Textbooks," *Harvard Educational Review* 49 (August 1979): 361–386.

Aristotle. *The Politics of Aristotle*. Translated by B. Jowett. New York: Random House, 1943.

Bottomore, T. B. *Critics of Society*. New York: Pantheon, 1968.

Bowles, Samuel, and Gintis, Herbert. *Schooling in Capitalist America*. New York: Basic Books, 1976.

Callahan, Raymond. *Education and the Cult of Efficiency*. Chicago: University of Chicago Press, 1962.

Carnoy, Martin, ed. *Schooling in a Corporate Society*. New York: McKay, 1975.

Dewey, John. *Experience and Education*. New York: Collier, 1938.

Fisher, Donald. "American Philanthropy and the Social Sciences in Britain, 1919–1939: the Reproduction of a Conservative Ideology," *The Sociological Review* 28 (May 1980): 277–315.

Fromm, Erich. *Marx's Concept of Man*. New York: Frederick Ungar, 1966.

Gerth, H. H., and Mills, C. Wright. *From Max Weber: Essays in Sociology*. New York: Oxford University Press, 1958.

Giroux, Henry. "The New Sociology of Curriculum." *Educational Leadership* 37 (December 1979): 248–253.

Gouldner, Alvin. *The Coming Crisis of Western Sociology*. New York: Basic Books, 1970.

Hansen, Donald A. *An Invitation to Critical Sociology*. New York: Free Press, 1976.

Karier, Clarence. "Testing for Order and Control in the Corporate Liberal State." In *Schooling and Capitalism*, edited by Roger Dale, G. Esland, and M. MacDonald, pp. 128–141. London: Routledge & Kegan Paul, 1976.

Lacey, Collin. *The Socialization of Teachers*. London: Methuen, 1977.

Levitas, Maurice. *Marxist Perspectives in the Sociology of Education*. London: Routledge & Kegan Paul, 1974.

Marcuse, Herbert. *Reason and Revolution*. New York: Oxford University Press, 1941.

Massachusetts. *Records of the Governor and Company of the Massachusetts Bay in New England*. Boston: William White, 1853.

National Education Association, Commission on the Reorganization of Secondary Education. *Cardinal Principles of Secondary Education*. Bulletin 35. Washington, D.C.: Government Printing Office, 1918.

Neiburg, H. L. *Culture Storm*. New York: St. Martin's Press, 1973.

Nelson, Jack L. "Nationalistic Versus Global Education: An Examination of National Bias in the Schools and Its Implications for a Global Society." *Theory and Research in Social Education* 4 (August 1976): 33–50.

————, and Besag, Frank. *Sociological Perspectives in Education*. New York: Pitman, 1970.

Parsons, Talcott *et al*. *Family, Socialization and Interaction Process*. Glencoe, Ill.: Free Press, 1955.

Parsons, Talcott. *The Social System*. New York: Free Press, 1951.

Schwartz, Audrey J. *The Schools and Socialization*. New York: Harper & Row, 1975.

Shils, Edward A. *The Torment of Secrecy*. New York: Free Press, 1956.

Spring, Joel. *The Sorting Machine*. New York: McKay, 1976.

————. *American Education*. New York: Longmans, 1978.

Webster, Noah. *A Collection of Essays and Fugitive Writings*. Boston: I. Thomas and Andrews, 1790.

Zeigler, Harmon. *The Political Life of American Teachers*. Englewood Cliffs, N.J.: Prentice-Hall, 1967.

Chapter 10:
Socialization,
Schooling,
and the
Teacher
in Society

Socialization

The means by which the social setting is transmitted to new generations is called "socialization." Other terms, like "acculturation" and "enculturation" are often used in a way that is virtually synonymous with "socialization." These other two terms convey the idea that the young are initiated into a culture, larger than a society. This, of course, is true since a child learns a language, customs, rituals, and ceremonies that often transcend a particular society. But "socialization" includes the learning of specific social roles and expectations and is a term that is more often used in the social science literature.

Chapter 9 discusses divergent views of the school in the social setting. The present chapter deals with the process by which the assorted ideas, bits of information, values, and attitudes of society are absorbed by members of a society. Certainly, not everyone learns to believe the same things or behave in the same way. But general patterns of thought and behavior in a society become the dominant patterns in a majority of people. There are individual differences and dissidents, but socialization occurs in most of us for most of our lives.

Merton defined socialization as "the process by which people selectively acquire the attitudes, the interests, skills and knowledge—in short, the current in groups to which they are, or seek to become, a member."[1] Merton's definition of socialization would appear to be positive, that socialization is in the interests of individuals and the social order. A different perspective is presented by C. Wright Mills, who writes:

> The ideally adjusted man of the social pathologist is "socialized." This term seems to operate ethically as the opposite of "selfish." It implies that the adjusted man conforms to middle-class morality and motives and "participates" in the gradual progress of respectable institutions.[2]

Thus, a term widely used in the social sciences is ideologically loaded. In Mills' view the use of "socialization" to describe the process is itself socializing readers toward maintenance of the social order. In this text, because of the widespread use of the term in educational and sociological literature, "socialization" will be used to define the process, and the reader is advised to remain skeptical. Socialization can be, and usually is, devoted to the preservation and protection of traditional ideologies, and against change; socialization can also occur in the transformation of people into revolutionaries and believers in a cause that aims to radically change society.

Socialization, then, is larger than the learning of certain information, or the acquisition of personal habits or the adopting of particular behaviors. It is considerably more complex because it involves the general view of the world that one comes to have: a value perspective, a concept of knowledge, a framework of interests, and a set of skills.

A person who grows up in the group known as the Tasaday, a society discovered to be living a Stone Age existence, will have values, interests, knowledge, and skills very different from a person who grows up in San Francisco. And someone who grows up in a family of wealth and power in San Francisco will likely differ in views of the world from one brought up in poverty in another section of the city. There may be some shared values, like the preservation of life, among all societies, but attitudes toward life, ideas about what knowledge is of importance, interests that influence life goals, and determination of which skills to develop are likely to differ.

Similarly, socialization occurs within societies in preparation for certain roles. Family roles like mother, brother, and uncle are learned. Children are socialized into roles like peer leader or follower, student, adolescent, youth, adult, and senior citizen. People learn the roles and expectations of being a criminal, a prisoner, a politician, an undertaker, and those of all other occupational groups. Becoming a teacher involves socialization to the attitudes, knowledge, interests, and skills identified as fitting that profession.

An important point about socialization is that it is a process, not an end state. It is continuous. Although socialization is more obvious at the earlier stages, when a new individual is being brought into the group and has the most to learn, it continues to act upon those who have been in the group for a long time. Socialization, including role expectations for all members of the group, continuously modifies people's behaviors and attitudes. Long-term leaders of a group, like a labor union or a hospital staff, are subject to role pressures to accommodate new developments, differing expectations of the society or members of the group, and self-perceptions.

Socialization is a process by which the young learn the ideas, the ethics, and the behaviors of a society. These aspects of society are learned; there is nothing innate about them, save the physical and mental capability to comprehend and respond to the learnings. This in an important concept. As Marx stated in the *Introduction to a Critique of Political Economy*, "It is not the consciousness of men that determines their existence, but, on the contrary, their social existence determines their consciousness."[3] The existence, or order, of a society is implanted very early on members of that society and reinforced throughout their lives.

Differing Views
of Socialization

As Chapter 9 noted, there are major differences between functionalist views of society and critical views. Since socialization is the process by which the dominant concepts and values of society are transmitted to individuals, opposing views of society would suggest differing perspectives on the nature and operation of socialization.

The functionalist concept of the socialization of individuals emphasizes fitting into the social system. It is a major function of various social institutions, for example, the family and the school, to develop in children the ability to conform to the ongoing social order. The final product of socialization is the mature individual who has assimilated the ideas, values, and behaviors of the dominant social system. Some functionalists argue that such socialization is required in order to preserve and protect the social order. The individual, in functionalist terms, is a relatively passive recipient of society's will. As a book of blank pages, each person becomes inscribed with the values, concepts, and knowledge deemed appropriate by society.

Dennis Wrong, however, speculates that socialization is considerably more complex, incomplete, and fragmentary than the typical functionalist view of it.[4] A critical view of socialization would point out that it is not a neutral, or beneficial, process. The critical position is that social cohesion is based more on "the economic power of capitalist and managerial classes"[5] than on a well-integrated set of social values like justice and equality. The inherent conflict between socioeconomic and other sectors of society suggests that socialization may be more difficult and potentially disruptive than functionalists believe. Socialization into a group that is in conflict with other groups is not likely to lead to social order. Families and neighborhoods may socialize children to anti-Semitic, antiblack, antiwomen, or other conflict-based ideas. Children from working-class homes, teachers from middle-class homes, and prep school students from upper-class homes have been socialized differently and have differing world views.

Critical theorists would be expected to examine socialization processes in terms of the extent of intergroup conflict, individual reaction and creative response to imposed socialization, and opportunities to effect social change through socializing agencies. Functionalists are more likely to stress overarching traditions and stability in socialization. Functionalism relies on established structures to implant the cultural heritage on the young, while critical theorists challenge the ideological content of those structures and the socialization process.

As Eric Carlton describes socialization, it is a process that inhibits "tendencies towards deviant behavior by the inculcation and internalization of norms which reflect the essential 'rightness' of the system."[6] He argues that socialization is linked to social order and social control, but that it is not always passively taken on by the individual. Many are willing to pursue fundamental social change and challenge traditional ideology, despite the strong influence of socializing agents like school and work. This suggests that socialization is an interactive process in which the individual is capable of self-initiated action and selective reaction in regard to the forces of social control.

Agents of Socialization

Social existence is expressed to young and old through a variety of agencies, including schools. Figure 10.1 illustrates the interactions and complexities of these agencies.

Figure 10.1 Agents of Socialization

Family

Clients   Parents   Siblings   Foster Home   Aunts   Other Relations   Friends

Enemies

Lawmakers

Means

Language

Customs, traditions

Rituals, ceremonies

Class status

Laws, regulations

Sanction systems

Models

Playmates

Authorities

Police

Peers

Schoolmates

Clergy

Teachers

Workmates

Bosses

Agemates

Media   Schools   Prison   Military   Unions   Family

Institutions

As Figure 10.1 indicates, there is a variety of agents of socialization. To illustrate the pervasive quality of socialization only a sample of them are shown. The figure diagram includes four nonexclusive categories of family, peers, institutions, and authorities. These overlap and interrelate. Family is one kind of social institution; some family members may also be peers and others authorities; and institutions include both peers and authorities.

School, of course, as a major agent of socialization, is at the center of debate. It is not a question of whether or not socialization occurs, but rather a series of questions like:

What forms of socialization are the responsibility of schools?

Who should be able to decide? The public? teacher? students? parents? board members? administrators?

Should schools reinforce or challenge the social order?

To what extent should schools be an agent of stasis or an agent of change?

How does the socialization purpose of schools effect the hiring of teachers, selection of curriculum content, accountability practices, rules of student conduct, and relation of school to community?

These agents of socialization utilize the means shown in the center of Figure 10.1 to inculcate and reinforce the social order.

LANGUAGE

Language includes formal and informal systems of conveying meaning.

Language includes words, tones, symbols, and body stance. A child soon learns the meaning of a stern look, a smile, a loud "No!" A student learns to "read" a teacher for authoritarianism, looseness, rigidity, and cue words. A teacher stands near a classroom troublemaker, raises or lowers her voice to control whispering, casts a knowing eye about a classroom during test. A student teacher learns classroom management tactics designed to elicit certain socialized responses from students. These are all examples of language used in socialization.

CUSTOMS, TRADITIONS

Another means of socialization is custom and tradition. We use a knife, fork, and spoon to eat, and we train young children to use them. A person's first confrontation with chopsticks, after fork and spoon training, is often fearful and embarrassing. Variations with fork and knife are seen as peculiar; in Europe people often use the knife as a pusher to put food onto the back of the fork for eating, while the knife is held in the other hand; in the United States the knife is used for cutting or spreading, then it is put down before taking a bite of food from the fork. Of course, there is no right way or right utensils for eating, there is only custom. We drive on the right side of the road while the English, Irish, and others drive on the left.

Further, socialization incorporates the learning of traditional beliefs and behaviors in families, at school, at play, and at work. In some families, being a Democrat is the expectation. At some schools there is a tradition of athletic achievement that students are expected to share. In play, a child learns the traditional rules and permitted behaviors in games from hide and seek to Monopoly to courtship. At work the traditional roles of new worker, complainer, sycophant, and boss are learned. Custom and tradition are strong forces in socialization.

RITUALS, CEREMONIES

In the pattern of socialization in any society there are a variety of rituals and ceremonies that are well understood by members of that society. Initiates to the society—young generations and immigrants—usually come to know and internalize these rituals and ceremonies. Some of the rituals are rites of passage through which members must go to signify a change in status. For example, secret ceremonies for adolescent males and females of some tribes include tests of skill, endurance, and knowledge before they are permitted adult status. Confirmation rituals in certain religions represent a rite of passage. The ceremonies surrounding graduation from a school celebrate student success in rites of passage.

One is socialized to accept and participate in rituals and ceremonies, and one is socialized by those rituals and ceremonies. Much socialization occurs without understanding or reasoning. The ritual of flag salutes in American schools is intended to build patriotic loyalty to the flag without any particular understanding on the part of children. Studies have shown that most primary grade children do not understand, or often misunderstand and misstate, the pledge of allegiance. They do become socialized to it and participate in the daily school ritual regardless of understanding.

Children quickly pick up the rituals and ceremonies of families and schools, without raising questions or critical judgments. Birthdays, religious holidays, weekends, silent tributes, and certain times of the day or season have rituals and ceremonies to identify them. Children learn these early. They recognize special decorations, meals, dress, and settings. Jacquetta Hill Burnet examined high-school athletics for evidence of rituals and ceremonies, and identified such activities as cheerleading, bonfires, rallies, and seasonal sports participation as illustrating a ritualistic cycle in high school in the United States.[7]

CLASS STATUS

Another element in the socialization process is class status. Different socioeconomic classes socialize their young generations to differing behaviors, beliefs, and expectations; and the class, or status, is also a means for socialization.

There is a strong tendency for individuals to play, work, attend school, and associate with members of the same social class. The common language forms, behaviors, and values of a social class become marks that set the classes apart in most voluntary associations. Despite the rhetoric about mobility and equality of opportunity regardless of social status in the United States, there are long-standing barriers to mobility for large segments of the population. These barriers are part of socialization patterns that affect all of us.

Our neighborhoods are typically class-based. There is relatively little contact between members of the lowest and of the highest classes, except where that contact is unequal: the employer talks to the servant in tones and language of authority, while the servant responds in deference. Elite, private schools provide enclaves for the upper classes; gheto public schools provide enclaves for the lower classes. There is no interchange in academic, social, or athletic activities between students in these distinct forms of class schooling.

LAWS, REGULATIONS

The legal and regulatory systems in society and in schools are among the means for socialization. Laws, and law enforcement operations, are responsive to the interests of powerful groups and individuals in the society. Laws are formulated to protect the social order or to make social change manageable within the existing order. Under a capitalist economic tradition, property and profit-making are protected; under socialism, laws protect governmental control of production and distribution. In the mixed economies that dominate in the countries of the world there is a relative emphasis on protecting property or governmental rights.

Laws and regulations govern large segments of life, from traffic control to income tax to sexual activities to death. Children are socialized to law by various agencies including families, school, media, and peers. Some of the socialization is intended to build attitudes of obedience and respect for law and law enforcement. Other socialization breeds discontent with or defiance of laws.

Respect for laws is a value learned throughout the socialization process, and while it is accepted to varying degrees, rarely is disrespect for the law instilled. So, for example, elementary schools introduce "Officer Bill" to children as their protector. Officer Bill advocates law obedience. Law-related education in secondary schools intends to build strong, positive attitudes toward laws of the society. Critical views of laws, lawmakers, and law enforcement are not in the usual curriculum of the school. Civil disobedience is taught, if at all, as an historic artifact, a series of incidents involving Henry Thoreau, Mahatma Gandhi, and Martin Luther King, Jr. But disobedience on the basis of morality or conscience is usually not viewed as an appropriate behavior in current social life.

Certainly, the rules and regulations of the school are taught with the intent of socializing students to the values of that institution. Bel Kaufman, in *Up the Down Staircase*, illustrates with humor the extent to which schools convey obedience to rules and regulations, whether rational or not, to students and teachers.[8] As the novel's title suggests, one of the rules is that staircases are one-way up or down.

Society defines the nature and operation of crime. Stealing is a crime but profit-making is not. Killing another person is a crime, but not if it is in an act of war. Holding another person captive is a crime, but imprisonment following arrest is not. Some crimes are dealt with severely, while others are overlooked. Similarly, schools define social crimes: for example, tardiness, not having a hall pass, not dressing for gym, running in halls, marking in textbooks.

SANCTION SYSTEMS

Closely related to laws and regulations are the systems of sanctions that operate continuously throughout our lives in society and in schools. Sanctions can be either positive or negative, rewards or punishments. The infant learns the difference between behaviors that the parent approves or disapproves because of the sanctions the parent uses: hugging versus scolding. To a baby behaviors are relatively neutral; they take on the values of being good or bad, right or wrong, appropriate or inappropriate as these values are learned in socialization. Sanctions modify or control behavior to produce a level of conformity to the norms of society and its institutions.

In families, sanctions include comments of approval and spankings. Among peers, sanctions include isolation and selection for leadership. In society, sanctions include financial reward and imprisonment.

Socialization of individuals in school is influenced by sanctions. Looks of approval or reproach provide cues to students about the acceptability of their behaviors. But what the teacher believes is a negative sanction intended to stop a certain behavior, such as a poor grade or a threat to send a student to detention, may not always produce what the teacher expects. Some students will rebel even more against the norms; some merely desire attention regardless of the type; some will appear oblivious to the sanction; some will become more devious and surreptitious; some will entirely capitulate; and some will give differing responses in differing situations. The sanctions of different agents of socialization may compete. Getting approval from a teacher may cause disapproval from peers; similarly, a teacher who gains positive recognition from the teacher's union during a strike may be subjected to negative sanctions from school administrators.

MODELS

As indicated in Figure 10.1 socialization occurs through several means including language, laws, and sanctions. Among these means are models, ideal types that influence a person's perception of proper behavior. In a street gang the model could be the person who most fearlessly commits the most antisocial acts. In a dancing class it might be the most graceful student. In a work crew it might be the one who most easily avoids hard labor. Among teachers it could be the one with the most intelligence, the one with the most jokes, or the one most liked by students.

Models not only occur in life, they are also drawn from myth. Part of our perception of how we believe we should look, feel, or act is based upon characters in books, in comics, in films, on television, or people described to us by others. Our concepts of justice, freedom, equality, and other values are often expressed in terms of model behavior: "Barbara works as hard as any man but she doesn't get equal pay." "The boss is just like Scrooge." "Steve has his faults, but he has real integrity like Abe Lincoln." "I don't know how Mary Ann does it, she's another Wonder Woman."

The stereotypic behavior provided by models gives us guidelines, both positive and negative, for our behaviors. We want to emulate the behavior of some models and avoid the behavior of others. Some politicians want to be perceived as statesmen; some as movers and shakers; some as power brokers; some as social welfare protectors; some as tax payer advocates; some as private citizens performing a public duty; and so on. The posturing of politicians is intended to convey one or more of these model images. People in any position have some perception of model behavior that, consciously or unconsciously, they strive to communicate to others.

Social Roles
and Status

Shakespeare's remarkable ability to provide impressive insights into the human condition is illustrated by the dialogue that includes this comment on roles: "All the world's a stage, And all the men and women merely players: They have their exits and their entrances; And one man in his time plays many parts. . . ."[9]

A social role is a composite of behaviors that are expected of a person who fills it. In a sense it represents a person's interpretation of how that particular social position should be played. This is not to suggest that social roles are false or sham acting. Indeed, people usually fill social roles in great seriousness, and sometimes the role changes as a result of different people's behaviors in that role. There are times, of course, when a social role is accepted by an individual who feels compelled to act the part. The person seeks cues from others in order to ensure that the role is properly played. For example, a new father may start carrying photographs of his baby to show others because he has seen other fathers doing it and has had people ask to see baby photos. Or a newly elected student council representative may suddenly start seeking opinions of classmates about how to behave.

There is a difference between social status and social role. Status refers to a social position relative to a hierarchy. The positions of teacher, principal, and student signify differing status positions in a school. The traditional view is that principals are at the top of this status hierarchy, teachers next, and students at the bottom. That is often the case, but because individuals utilize their social positions differently, the power hierarchy in a particular school at a particular time may be quite different. It is the social role portrayal that differs. Social role is the dynamic side of social status.

Teacher is both a role and a status. Some teachers act the role as authoritarians, some as buddies; some are indecisive and baffled, and some are intelligent and thoughtful. In the interaction of roles in a social setting, traditional status hierarchies may vary. A person in the role of student may gain more power in a classroom than the teacher, and more power in the school than the principal. This is not an evaluative statement; it is only to point out that social roles may vary according to the persons who fill them, but that social expectations for the role exert great influence. Most people can contemplate a situation of role reversal where students run the school, but it is not an expected or normal institutional situation. The pressure to conform to traditional role expectations is very strong. Thus, most roles change little in basic expectations, though individual personalities provide variation in the role.

Consider a number of social roles and think of the expectations that most people have of them:

Banker

Police officer

Ballet dancer

Construction worker

Jockey

Parent

Secretary

Mediator

Campaign manager

Gang leader

The stereotypic behavior that each of these titles conjures in our minds illustrates the force of tradition in social roles. We do not expect a banker to act like a gang leader, ballet dancer, or construction worker. It is not an outrageous thought, however, that a banker could also lead a gang, dance a ballet, and work in construction. We assume different roles at different times of our lives and in different situations. The banker was once a student, may have led a gang, taken ballet lessons, and had a summer job in road construction. Similarly, the banker may also have the roles of mother, volunteer hospital worker, member of a bowling team, card player, and gardener at the same period of her life. If you thought bankers could only be men you have applied a stereotype to a role and illustrated role expectations.

In the schools are people who have several roles. Some are formally described and titled: teacher, secretary, custodian, student, nurse, guidance counselor. Others are roles related to the operation of the institution, but not formally titled: disciplinarian, friend of students, renegade, class clown, dupe, power broker, intellectual, jock, bookworm, outlaw. In different school and community situations the same person may have different roles. A teacher may be a person sought out by students for help with personal problems. The same teacher may also be a part-time grocery clerk, a member of a chess-by-mail club, tennis coach for a summer recreation program, and the uncle of a notorious local juvenile delinquent.

Norms and Values

Norms of a society, and norms of institutions and roles, are those expected typical ways of acting. Values are views of what is desirable. Norms and values are related in that most norms, and normative behavior, are based upon social values. We value privacy and have norms of conduct relating to the opening of another person's mail that derive from that value. It does not always happen that mail is kept private, but it is an expected norm where privacy is a value. Society values children, and norms govern the treatment of children. Still we value parental authority, and norms about parent treatment of their own children are different from norms about other persons' treatment of children. Teachers have more normative control of children than many other adults because teachers are perceived as parent surrogates; in law teachers are governed by the concept of *in loco parentis*, in place of the parent.

Norms provide guides for social behavior and social role portrayal. They contribute to order in society based on traditional behavior expectations. Norms are protocols for how we are supposed to act at the family dinner table, in libraries, at school, at the beach, in cars, and in any social setting. They are a sort of social adhesive that binds society and tends to prevent unexpected behavior and, at the same time, keeps people more or less in line. Norms not only provide comfort for those who understand and operate on them, they also provide discomfort for those who do not understand or do not behave according to them.

A CRITICAL VIEW

Normative behavior expectations, then, act to maintain and expand social order and social control. The creative, independent, or iconoclastic person has difficulty with norms since they circumscribe behavior. They prescribe and describe what individuals are supposed to do and say. People who are critical of or act in opposition to norms are operating at risk. They are likely to be repressed, oppressed, or ignored.

Aberrant behavior is defined in reference to norms. If a person came nude to school and made loud noises outside the principal's office window while digging up small plants and eating worms, he or she is a candidate for arrest and psychological testing because of exhibiting "abnormal" behavior. Yet these infractions of norms would not be considered as seriously if the person were only two years old. Norms differ for ages, for social roles, and for situations. As Frank, Laing and others have indicated, social norms and the tensions they create may be the greater mental illness.[10] The constrictions that socially acceptable norms put on some people seem to create their aberrant behaviors.

Rather than conform to social norms, some individuals become alienated from society. Others seek outlets through creative expression where norms may be flaunted more easily. Some take on the mantle of social outlaws. And others are classified by the society as mentally ill.

A critical view of social roles, norms, and values would assess the extent to which these were linked to socioeconomic, political, and economic ideologies in the society; that is, the extent to which normative behavior is predicated on maintaining social class distinctions, political power of elites, and competitive ambition deriving from capitalism. Criticism would address such social expectations as:

Upper-class members deserve deference from lowers.

The upper classes set the standards of appropriate behavior.

A privilege of wealth is to flaunt social conventions.

When the wealthy misbehave it is charming or eccentric; when the poor misbehave it is criminal or immoral.

If blind ambition for wealth is successful, it is socially acceptable.

Authority is to be obeyed, not questioned; the rulers have more knowledge and intellect.

Different codes of ethics and conduct are appropriate for different classes since the upper classes can be trusted to do what is best for the society.

NORMS AND CHANGE

Norms change because some individuals are willing to raise challenges to normative behavior and are persuasive enough to modify expectations. We all know of people who are "refreshing" or "exciting" because they operate differently from normative expectations. The behavior of teachers has changed over time from that of stern moralist and harsh disciplinarian to permit more relaxed and casual school behavior. Yet the basic norms for the role of teachers have not changed dramatically for most teachers. Individual teachers may exhibit variation in behavior, but general norms for teacher conduct can be observed in virtually every school. Parents expect it. Students expect it. Taxpayers expect it. School administrators expect it. And those who are preparing to become teachers expect it.

ANTICIPATORY SOCIALIZATION

Social roles, norms, and values exist as a result of a variety of traditional expectations. They are learned through socialization. We grow up in a family where everyday events provide models for social behavior. The role of infant and the roles of parents interact to modify and control individual behaviors. Feeding time, clothing, responses to crying or exploration, sleeping arrangements, fondling, and other interactions result from social traditions. As people become parents they observe, read, ask, and otherwise learn about the parenting role and normative behavior in that role. Similarly, as an infant grows the various roles of child, relative, peer, sibling, pain-in-the-neck, charmer, and others are learned from observation and interaction with others.

Anticipatory socialization describes that process by which people begin to anticipate taking on new roles and try to behave in normative ways they think are part of that new role. The younger child observes older children's behavior and begins to anticipate certain roles. A common activity among children is to dress in adult clothing and try to mimic adult conversation and mannerisms. Often anticipatory socialization is a caricature or stereotype of the actual role. It is an individual's perception of normative or expected behavior in that role. That perception is usually a rough approximation at first and is refined by interaction with others and by entry into the new role. A high-school student who plans to start college soon may adopt what he or she believes to be college-style dress or mannerisms.

SOCIALIZATION INTO TEACHING

Anticipatory socialization occurs in teacher education also. A person may start college with teaching as a goal and a certain teacher as a model. This will likely influence that student's socialization process in college. Another student may not decide to go into teaching until the junior year in college. Teacher education programs usually provide some socialization activities, such as elementary- and secondary-school observations, anecdotes and knowledge about school practice, and student teaching. These are to refine socialization into teaching. Most teacher education students have some form of anticipatory socialization. By the time they engage in student teaching they have formed a sense of norms for school teachers. Where those norms differ from the norms of their role as students in college, student teachers tend to adopt teacher role norms in anticipation of the position. Manner of speech, dress, authority, and expectations for student behavior change from those of a student to those of a teacher.

Interviews conducted with student teachers show that anticipatory socialization to teaching occurs in many realms, including political and economic views.[11] The expected political restraint censorship patterns in public schools, where controversial topics are often ignored or repressed, are accepted by student teachers as part of the role of teacher. One of the most difficult things for many student teachers is the shift from the role of college student, where certain liberties and freedom of thought and action are expected and socially condoned, to the role of teacher, where one is expected to model moral and pedagogical correctness.

Views of what is good behavior and good teaching are developed over a long period of time. Courses in teacher methodology help in the organizing of classes and in exploring differing teacher techniques, but much of the pre-teacher's concept of good teaching evolves over a long period of socialization and the influence of many teachers. Waller, in a classic work on the sociology of teaching, indicates that young teachers quickly lose the influence of teacher education classes in colleges and become more heavily influenced by older teachers, conventional wisdom, and administrators. Waller states that young teachers often experience a "gradual deterioration in their general adaptability."[12] They lose intellectual interest. Musgrove and Taylor present a more recent analysis of teacher socialization in England. They report that the "teacher arrives at a conception of his proper or necessary role through his own experience as a pupil, his experience at the job, his reading, exchange of views, and reflection—and, of course, his professional training." Musgrove and Taylor continue, "But probably the most important influence for many teachers is the staff room, the group of colleagues which he joins, with whom he must live and work, whose respect he must earn."[13]

Teacher in Society

The teacher's role, status, and social expectations depend upon the particular time, culture, and institutional setting. Although there are no certain generalizations about society's view of teachers, there is some general sense among members of a society at any one time about the status typically ascribed to teachers. The following examples illustrate varying perceptions of teachers in society:

- Socrates, known through the writings of Plato, is generally viewed as a wise man, a seeker of truth, a believer in freedom to learn, a stimulator of curiosity, and a model of courage. He had the ultimate courage to take his own life rather than sacrifice his educational principles. As a model teacher, he had great esteem and social status among the learned. His approach to discourse is still followed by many educators today.
- Ichabod Crane, schoolmaster in Washington Irving's tale, is the stereotype of a bumbling, oafish, narrow-minded teacher who appears deserving of the scapegoat role he receives. There are many in society today who perceive teachers in the Ichabod Crane tradition.
- Mr. Chips, from James Hilton's *Good-bye Mister Chips*, is the epitome of the beloved, dedicated, kindly teacher who has little money, but is rich in spirit. He is an inspiration for his students.
- Our Miss Brooks, of radio and early television fame, is portrayed as a feather-headed teacher in a school filled with incompetents. She was lovable and vital, and the best in the school, but certainly not intellectual.

Each of these teacher-types has some parallel in the schools of contemporary society. If a word-association test were given to people, and "teacher" were one of the words, the responses would probably include attributes similar to those described above. Recollections of one's own teachers vary along the same lines. Since the perceptions of people, including the students, are translated into role expectations, teachers are influenced by the stereotypic characteristics that people have in their minds about teachers in general. This influence occurs not only in the actual job of teaching, but also in the selection of teaching as a career. If teaching is viewed negatively in the society, it will be difficult to recruit talented people into the field, and those who are teachers are likely to adjust their behaviors to conform to social expectations. If teaching is accorded high social status, though not necessarily high income, it will attract talented people, and practicing teachers are more likely to adopt behaviors consistent with social expectations.

In the United States teaching has had both high and low status in different time periods. At one time teachers were indentured servants. In some towns the teachers are viewed as a rich resource and community leaders. Role performance by teachers is influenced by both the social expectations and the individual personality. John Comenius in 1700 described the teacher's role as follows: "A school is a shop in which young wits are fashioned to virtue, and it is distinguished into forms. The master sitteth in a chair, the scholars in forms; he teacheth, they learn."[14] This is a rather simple explanation of what a teacher is to do, and it implies that the teacher has the power to fashion youngsters to virtue. Many teachers would prefer to do as Comenius says, and some try it, but the dynamics of the classroom are more complex.

H. L. Mencken held, as you might expect, a more cynical view of teaching. He wrote, "The average schoolmaster is and always must be essentially an ass, for how can one imagine an intelligent man engaging in so puerile an avocation?"[15] George Bernard Shaw's oft-quoted quip that "those that can, do, and those that can't, teach," conveys another negative stereotype that some people have of teachers.[16] And Mark Twain presented a double-edged comment about the process of teaching, "To be good is noble, but to teach others to be good is nobler—and less trouble."[17] Anyone going into teaching needs to understand the perceptions that some have of those who teach. While some social expectations for teachers derive from these kinds of negative stereotypes, it is not necessary that teachers fulfill that part of the role. Henry Adams had a different concept of a teacher when he wrote: "A teacher affects eternity; he can never tell where his influence stops."[18]

FOR CONSIDERATION

1. In your own life, what were the dominant socialization agencies? Which institutions do you think had the greatest influence on you? Which individuals influenced you the most? Were there any influences that you consider highly divergent from the ideas considered the norm in your society?

2. Using a school you know as an example, analyze how the school attempts to socialize young people. Identify specific illustrations of teacher behavior, physical structure, rules, treatment of certain student behavior, and similar ongoing activities. Also, provide examples of school events, like sports or clubs, and analyze the socialization efforts of these extracurricular activities. Consider how effective these means of socialization are.

3. What examples can you identify from your teacher education program which illustrate an attempt to socialize you into the profession of teaching? Analyze these examples in terms of both a functionalist and a critical view. How is each attempt related to preserving the traditional order in teaching, and how is each related to a critical assessment of teaching?

Notes

1. Robert Merton, *Social Theory and Social Structure* (Glencoe, Ill.: Free Press, 1957), p. 265.
2. C. Wright Mills, "The Professional Ideology of Social Pathologists," *American Journal of Sociology* 49 (1943) as cited in *Toward a Sociology of Education*, ed. John Beck *et al.* (New Brunswick, N.J.: Transaction, 1978), p. 104.
3. Karl Marx, *Introduction to a Critique of Political Economy* (London: Kerr, 1918), p. 12.
4. Dennis Wrong, "The Oversocialized Conception of Man in Modern Sociology," *American Sociological Review* 26 (April 1961):183–193.
5. Colin Lacey, *The Socialization of Teachers* (London: Methuen, 1977), p. 20.
6. Eric Carlton, *Ideology and Social Order* (London: Routledge & Kegan Paul, 1977), p. 78.
7. Jacquetta Hill Burnett, "Ceremony, Rites and Economy in the Student System of an American High School," *Human Organization* 12 (Spring 1969):1–10.
8. Bel Kaufman, *Up the Down Staircase* (Englewood Cliffs, N.J.: Prentice-Hall, 1964).
9. William Shakespeare, *As You Like It*, act 2, scene 7.
10. Lawrence K. Frank, *Society as the Patient* (New Brunswick, N.J.: Rutgers University Press, 1948); and R. D. Laing, *The Divided Self* (New York: Pantheon, 1969).
11. Stuart Palonsky and Jack L. Nelson, "Political Restraint in the Socialization of Student Teachers," *Theory and Research in Social Education* 7 (Winter 1980):19–34.
12. Willard Waller, *The Sociology of Teaching* (New York: John Wiley, 1932), p. 391.

13. Frank Musgrove and Philip Taylor, *Society and the Teacher's Role* (London: Routledge & Kegan Paul, 1969), p. 9.

14. John Amos Comenius, *Orbis Sennalium Pictus* (1700), cited in Marjorie Smiley and John Diekhoff, *Prologue to Teaching* (New York: Oxford University Press, 1959), inner cover.

15. H. L. Mencken, *Prejudices*, in *The Home Book of Quotations*, ed. Burton Stevenson (New York: Dodd, Mead, 1967), p. 1971.

16. George Bernard Shaw, *Maxims for Revolutionists*, in *Home Book of Quotations, op. cit.*, p.1971.

17. Mark Twain, in *The New Book of Unusual Quotations*, ed. Rudolf Flesch (New York: Harper & Row, 1966), p. 381.

18. Henry Adams, *The Education of Henry Adams*, in *Familiar Quotations*, ed. John Bartlett (Boston: Little, Brown, 1980), p. 635.

References

Adams, Henry. *The Education of Henry Adams*, in *Familiar Quotations*, ed. John Bartlett. Boston: Little, Brown, 1980, p. 635.

Burnett, Jacquetta Hill. "Ceremony, Rites and Economy in the Student System of an American High School." *Human Organization* 12 (Spring 1969):1–10.

Carlton, Eric. *Ideology and Social Order*. London: Routledge & Kegan Paul, 1977.

Comenius, John Amos. *Orbis Sennalium Pictus*, 1700, as found in Marjorie Smiley and John Diekhoff, *Prologue to Teaching*. New York: Oxford University Press, 1959.

Flesch, Rudolph, ed. *The New Book of Unusual Quotations*. New York: Harper & Row, 1966.

Frank, Lawrence K. *Society as the Patient*. New Brunswick, N.J.: Rutgers University Press, 1948.

Greenburg, Dan. *How to Be a Jewish Mother*. New York: Price, Stern, 1965.

Kaufman, Bel. *Up the Down Staircase*. Engelwood Cliffs, N.J.: Prentice-Hall, 1964.

Lacey, Colin. *The Socialization of Teachers*. London: Methuen, 1977.

Laing, R. D. *The Divided Self*. New York: Pantheon, 1969.

Marx, Karl. *Introduction to a Critique of Political Economy*. London: Kerr, 1918.

Mencken, H. L. *Prejudices*, as found in Burton Stevenson, *The Home Book of Quotations*. New York: Dodd, Mead, 1967, p. 1971.

Merton, Robert. *Social Theory and Social Structure*. Glencoe, Ill.: Free Press, 1957.

Mills, C. Wright. "The Professional Ideology of Social Pathologists." *American Journal of Sociology* 49 (1943), as found in John Beck, ed., *Toward a Sociology of Education*. New Brunswick, N.J.: Transaction, 1978.

Musgrove, Frank, and Taylor, Philip. *Society and the Teacher's Role*. London: Routledge & Kegan Paul, 1969.

Palonsky, Stuart, and Nelson, Jack L. "Political Restraint in the Socialization of Student Teachers." *Theory and Research in Social Education* 7 (Winter 1980):19–34.

Waller, Willard. *The Sociology of Teaching*. New York: John Wiley, 1932.

Wrong, Dennis. "The Oversocialized Conception of Man in Modern Sociology." *American Sociological Review* 26 (April 1961):183–193.

Section Four: Cultural Issues and Education

T he preceding sections provided an examination of the school from a variety of perspectives. Most were derived from history and from social scientific analyses.

This section deals with several current issues that are of broad implication for society and schools. Increasing awareness of the global dimensions of everyday life are discussed in Chapter 11 on interdependence, while Chapter 13 focuses on the multicultural aspects of society and of schools, raising a number of questions about how the schools should respond to cultural diversity. Chapter 12 is devoted to an exploration of the nature of science and technology and the impact that the future holds for schools and society.

In each chapter, and for each issue, the themes of stasis and change become apparent. We are continuously caught in the struggle between the forces of stasis, with its offer of comfort, stability, and standards, and the siren of change, which holds out interest, challenge, and innovation. Whether it is a global concern or a matter of the individual student, the tension between stasis and change is evident.

Chapter 11: Global Issues and Education

Today's school children will spend the greater part of their lives in the twenty-first century. They will bear the legacy of human history and the horizon of a global society different from any that has previously existed. The shift between the eighteenth and nineteenth centuries was marked by expanding ideas of democracy, liberty, and human freedom. Revolutionary thought and action spread. At the turn of the nineteenth century, nationalism and industrialization altered life styles. Now, when we can see the outlines of the twenty-first century, the global scope of the movements toward human freedom, industrialization, and nationalism becomes clear. These movements are both conflicting and complementary. Certainly, they are global. And certainly they are subject to the same tension between pressures for stasis or for change that affect other social issues.

Secretary General of the United Nations U. Thant stated in 1969 that the member nations must "subordinate their ancient quarrels and launch a global partnership to curb the arms race, to improve the human environment, to defuse the population explosion, and to supply the required momentum to development efforts."[1] That global partnership has not occurred, but the consciousness of current generations of people around the world now includes a measure of global awareness.

We live during a period in which problems, and possible solutions, are increasingly worldwide. Pollution creeps by sea and air across national boundaries. World food supplies and global population increases are issues larger than any country can control. Multinational corporations, world monetary systems, and international competition have created massive inflation, depression, and industrialization on a global scale. Drug abuse is a global, not local, problem. The arms race continues apace and envelops more and more nations as buyers and sellers of human destruction. Decisions on national growth, economics, health, food, defense, and waste require consideration of global impact.

Yet, the schools—with some exceptions—continue to emphasize local and national studies and to avoid or ignore the dramatic changes occurring in the global environment. This chapter explores some of these global issues and their educational implications. The schools seem to strive for stasis, as though global changes will not affect them.

Functionalist versus Critical Views of the Global Society

A functionalist perspective on the current global situation would focus on the traditional institutions and systems for handling inter-nation intercourse. Recall that the functionalist view assumes (1) an order to social relations, (2) consensus on major traditional values, (3) the need to preserve and protect that order and those core values, and (4) that established institutions function to preserve and protect the social order. A critical view assumes (1) conflict is basic, (2) significant differences between socioeconomic groups in values and aspirations, and (3) that society needs continual criticism to move toward social improvement. Thus functionalism seeks stasis and gradual change, while critical views pursue rapid change with brief periods of stasis.

In analyzing the global situation functionalists would concentrate on the established world political and economic order. Systems and institutions that operate to retain stability between and among nations would be enhanced. National governments, operating through established structures of diplomacy, spy networks, the United Nations trade and monetary systems, and agencies of their initiation would strive to maintain control and coordination. The balance of power in political, economic, and military terms would be seen as precarious but subject to recognized forces from the dominating cliques. The major powers, now identified as an eastern and western bloc, seek to gain advantage over each other but fear the increasing power of the third and fourth worlds.

A functionalist perspective would view insurgent guerrillas, iconoclastic leaders, and certain grassroots transnational political movements (like Amnesty International) as dysfunctional and subject to political manipulation, economic control, and even physical force. Dominant nations, for the purpose of preserving and protecting the global structure, use political ostracism or recognition, economic boycott or support, and military intervention. Ideologies, like communism, capitalism, and nationalism, are important because they provide the major traditional values that inspire intense loyalties.

A critical perspective on the global situation would focus on the gross inequalities among peoples across the world and would point to the current world political and economic order as the primary reason. The major powers, according to the critics, exploit and manipulate the less powerful. Worldwide conditions of starvation, pollution, torture, political imprisonment, natural resource wastage, and nuclear threat to civilization are a direct result of the current global structure. The arms race, major power politics, and other actions to protect the status of those dominant nations rob the rest of the world of resources, justice, and human dignity.

The critical view sees continuing global conflict between the haves and have-nots; it sanctions guerrilla actions and revolutionary forces that strive to address the great disparities in wealth and power. Class struggle on a global scale is a part of the critical perspective.

Warfare and physical force are not the sole province of either a functionalist or a critical view. Each could support such action but for different purposes: Functionalists might see war as a last resort to maintain the global system, while the critical view would see war as a last resort to change the global system. Neither side can be said to seek the killing of others or global annihilation by nuclear warfare, although individual cynics on each side can accuse the other of this.

The main concern for this chapter is to indicate educational issues presented by the global situation. The themes of stasis and change, as illustrated by the widely divergent functionalist and critical perspectives on the global situation described above, also influence how the schools choose to treat global topics.

The Global Situation:
An Ecological System

There is a vast body of popular literature describing global issues. These books and articles present a large array of data on and interpretation of worldwide conditions. Among the most common elements expressed is the need to recognize the interdependence of factors: for example, population and food supplies, the arms race and international strife, industrialization and global pollution, human rights and political threat, international economics and politics, education and aspiration. This concept of interdependence is another way of indicating the ecological nature of things. By ecological we refer to the mutual relationships among humans and their environments. Ecology suggests that there are networks of relationships, some obvious and some hidden, and that actions in one part of a system influence other parts.

In a garden, ecological considerations include soil, water, light, minerals, air quality, seed, climate, timing, pollinization, fertilization, insects, disease, animal and human intervention, and potential consequences of each of these. Any one of these factors has an effect on the rest. This is not an argument for trying to keep the garden as it is or for making dramatic changes; rather, it is to indicate that either decision affects the garden and its environment. An attempt at stasis runs the risk of stagnation and decline; dramatic change runs the risk of disruption and damage. Yet, risk taking is necessary.

Similarly, ecological views of the globe suggest the interrelatedness of actions: political, economic, military, and educational. An environment larger than an individual's space, larger than that of a group, larger than nation, region, or hemisphere becomes the focus of global study. We are only beginning to recognize the need to take an ecological, or holistic, view of the global environment. This orientation has been advocated by individuals and organizations in the past, but now governments are showing interest.

Richard Falk, in a best-selling book published in 1971, stated:

> Mankind is passing through the early stages of its first planetary crisis. The interrelated dimensions of this crisis are population pressure, multiple forms of pollution, resource depletion, and the dangers of wars of mass destruction. It is the technological character of contemporary society that gives the planetary crisis its apocalyptic character.[2]

Falk proposed the development of "ecological politics" aimed at addressing these interrelated issues. He argued that the current sovereign state is too limited to adequately deal with any of these problems (population, pollution, resource depletion, and nuclear war), and proposed a new world order based on this ecological view. He advocated educational efforts to enlighten people about these issues. This was a very popular book on a theme that Falk and Saul Mendlovitz had treated in four volumes in 1966.[3]

In 1981, the United States Department of State and the Council on Environmental Quality published *Global Future: Time to Act*. This was an official report to the president, which followed up on the *Global 2000 Report* on global environment, population, and resources. The 1981 report shows a new government recognition of these problems:

> Resource impoverishment, environmental degradation and soaring population growth have not just been discovered for the first time as global problems. . . . What the recent reports do emphasize in a new way are the accelerating pace and scale of the problems and their interrelationships—the web of causes and effects that bind them together.

and further into the report:

> That Report [*Global 2000*] documented in detail our government's present inability to anticipate and evaluate global problems. . . . The weakness in the government's modeling abilities, described in *The Global 2000 Report*, can be cured only by a more holistic approach, achieved through better coordination.[4]

Among the actions recommended in the 1981 report was one directed at education: "There is a need for new curriculum and training aids and other educational materials to assist educators wishing to provide 'holistic' instruction emphasizing the interconnections among global population, resource, environmental, security and economic concerns."[5]

Two themes that run through much of the literature on global problems are (1) the interdependent, interrelated, ecological nature of them and (2) the great need to educate people in regard to these large-scale issues.

GLOBAL ISSUES AND GLOBAL GOALS

It would, of course, be possible to produce a long list of the problems that have beset humankind. Famine, disease, war, slavery, pollution, torture, moral corruption, terrorism, economic criminality, piracy, and denial of rights are only the beginning of such a list, and it could be multiplied by specific examples and cases. From political assassination to venereal disease, there is a virtually uncountable number of specific problems that transcend national boundaries. Although it would be appropriate to deal with the many global issues in this book, there is insufficient space. Rather, we will illustrate the dimensions of the global situation and the interrelationships among problems by a consideration of aspects of one broad category of global issue: international violence.

AN ILLUSTRATIVE GLOBAL ISSUE: INTERNATIONAL VIOLENCE   This issue may be the most pervasive of global concerns. It has the potential for immediate obliteration of all living things and the rendering of the earth sterile. Included in this category are the following kinds of problems:

War and peace-keeping

Arms race

Nuclear weaponry

Territorial expansion and protection

Religious and ideological confrontations

Terrorism

Joseph and Roberta Moore, in *War and War Prevention*, identified fifteen different kinds of war, ranging from wars for independence to wars to control economic markets.[6] The advent of nuclear weapons and the continuing capability for catastrophic disaster were initially met with the hope that war was now so blatantly absurd that it would no longer be seen as an appropriate means to resolve international conflicts. The nuclear deterrence theory was essentially that proposition; and so was the intention of keeping nuclear weapons controlled by a very small group of enlightened nations. It is now obvious that that was a Pollyanna view. The arms race, including development of even more refined nuclear weapons, has continued to expand even though we are capable of killing all people on earth many times over. We now talk of the "overkill" ratio. And small wars and skirmishes still erupt throughout the world, posing holocaust dangers for the whole world. The fraternity of governments now capable of producing nuclear arms increases, and the arsenals of nonnuclear war equipment proliferate. Arms productions and sales are a major component of international trade.

Ruth Leger Sivard records the worldwide expenditures for military and other social activities of nations in a publication entitled *World Military and Social Expenditures*.[7] Her data are drawn from national and international sources. The United States and the Soviet Union dominate other nations in these military expenditures, but developing nations have doubled their proportion of global military expenditures since 1960. They had spent about 9 percent of the total world military expenses; they now spend almost 20 percent. Total military spending is over $400 billion per year. In 1960 the total was about $100 billion.

To show how military expenditures are related to other areas of social concern, the following comparisons indicate global priorities:

- The military budget, across all nations, is greater than the annual total income of about 2 billion people in the poorest 25 percent of nations.

- The worldwide military research budget is over six times larger than the total world budget for energy research.

- Funds for military and space research exceed funds for all other research for social programs (such as health, education, food) combined.

- More is spent on military armaments in two days than is available to operate the United Nations for a whole year.

- One Trident submarine costs as much as a year's schooling for about 16,000,000 children in poorer countries.

- Worldwide military expenses per soldier are 65 times the amount expended to educate a child.

International violence, and the expenses involved in promoting and preventing it, is obviously highly interrelated with other aspects of a global environment. This is not a simple issue of good guys and bad guys. Major world leaders in virtually every country decry the waste of money, resources, and human capacity in the pursuit of military superiority. Yet, they argue that it is needed for defense, security, deterrence, protection, and national honor.

International violence presents the following global problems:

1. It risks a major nuclear war and possible human annihilation.
2. It expends huge amounts of economic, human, and mineral resources for preparation and defense, while social welfare problems are severely restricted or ignored.
3. It places excessive strain on political structures, like the United Nations, exposes their limitations in a nationalistic world, and consumes their energies.
4. It maintains a state of fear and apprehension among the peoples of the world.

Education about international violence and its impact on other areas of worldwide interest is in the best tradition of enlightened education. It is a subject of pervasive and immediate concern; it has an extensive body of literature; it can be approached from scientific, literary, social scientific, and humanistic perspectives; it provides examples of the tensions between stasis and change; and it is consistent with the most important educational goals of improving civilization and developing critical thinking.

FIVE GLOBAL GOALS   International violence is only illustrative of the variety of global issues that confront modern society. These issues can be translated into a set of global goals. People desire to be free of war, the fear of war, and the debilitating effects of the preparation for war. These desires, like desires for sufficient food, clean air, a productive job, proper education, and dignity, can be stated in terms of categories of global goals. The Institute for World Order, established as an educational organization concerned with world problems, has identified the following global goals:

Peace

Economic well-being

Social justice

Ecological balance

Political participation

These five goals were incorporated into four key processes under which major global issues can be addressed. Mendlovitz, Metcalf, and Washburn organized them as follows:

Table 11.1:
Global Issues

Processes

Minimization of Violence	Maximization of Well-Being	Maximization of Justice	Maximization of Ecological Balance
Arms policy	*Per capita* income	Participation	Population equilibrium
Peace-keeping	Life expectancy	Race equality	Pollution Control
Conflict resolution	Education and health guarantees	Human rights	Resource balance and growth

---

Source: Adapted from S. Mendlovitz, L. Metcalf, and M. Washburn, "The Crisis of Global Transformation, Interdependence and the Schools," in *Education for Responsible Citizenship*, ed. F. Brown (New York: McGraw-Hill, 1977).

The categories of global issues identified are the subject of international conferences, journal and newspaper articles, television and radio commentary, and books. From a period about four decades ago when there were relatively few people seriously concerned about global problems, these topics have become a dominating public interest. Hundreds of thousands of people march in antinuclear demonstrations; the use of food supplies as a weapon in international relations is widely debated; oil and other energy resources have become a focus of worldwide manipulation and contest; air and sea pollution are topics in United Nations conferences; the poor nations and the poor people in nations arise in protest against domination by the Old World powers; and widespread negative publicity about political imprisonment, torture, and slaughter attests to an evolving sense of the need for minimal conditions of international human rights.

There is a new global political, economic, and social environment. Schools, however, have tended to ignore these developments. Of course, they are treated in some current events lessons, or in stories appearing in weekly readers used in many schools, or in some classes where a particular teacher has a strong interest. But there is little evidence of major changes in school curricula to account for changes in the world environment. Most schools remain dominated by nationalistic education and offer very little global education.[8]

THE ISOLATIONIST URGE

The United States was preoccupied with domestic growth and internal tensions for most of the first 150 years of its existence. Our national psyche and policies were inward looking as our new nation strove to achieve its identity, to define its autonomy, and to assure its independence. In George Washington's farewell address he summarized the results of his varied experiences and offered a guide for that time and for the future. He urged his countrymen to cherish the Union and to be alert to the problems of foreign influence. Asserting that Europe and America had different interests, he declared that it must be America's policy to avoid permanent alliances. He also warned about indulging in either habitual favoritism or habitual hostility toward particular nations, lest such attitudes should provoke or involve the country in needless wars.

The United States' population was largely European in origin, and following the Civil War its educational system was designed in increasing measure to Americanize the polyglot cultures of nineteenth- and early twentieth-century immigration (see Chapter 13). During the periods surrounding the American

Civil War, the United States' westward expansion and territorial acquisition engendered clashes and border conflicts with various Native American cultures, France, Spain, Imperial Russia, and Mexico. Americans withdrew from these contacts as quickly as treaty negotiations would permit. World War I was deemed an aberration by many Americans, who generally confirmed their preference for the isolationist precedent of President Washington to President Woodrow Wilson's 1918 statement of America's "fourteen points" treaty objectives, which included:

— direct treaties for peace.

— freedom of the seas, except by international agreement.

— removal of artificial trade barriers among nations.

— sweeping reductions in national armaments.

— a general association of nations.

But the major global policies of Wilson's fourteen points were rejected, and once again the United States opted to pull back into its traditionally secure insularity by reducing its international involvements during the 1920s and 1930s.

The following events since 1941 have destroyed America's insularity:

— World War II involved American military operations in every time zone on the face of the globe;

— the atom bomb ended a war, but initiated an epoch of perpetual and worldwide anxiety and watchfulness;

— the Korean and Vietnamese wars were both local civil wars and "international civil wars" in which America was deeply enmeshed;

— the United States is a leading partner in the United Nations system that now includes scores of new nations that have only recently emerged from the chrysalises of colonialism;

— jet aircraft and communication satellites have shrunk the earth and facilitated both international sense and mischief;

— multinational corporations have stretched their strands of influence around the world;

— American and other nations' executives and heads of state find themselves involved constantly in striving to put out the tinder sparks of hostility around the world;

—world finance has become a tangle of tensions as inexorable international economic forces have intruded into national economic habits;

—newly self-conscious ethnic and racial groups in the United States have searched for identity and dignity through a rediscovery of distant areas of origin;

—energy, environmental concerns, population growth, incipient climatic crises, and possibilities of nuclear blackmail have stimulated scholars, commentators, and statesmen to sound apocalyptic alarms for the whole human race.

THE FOCUS ON EDUCATION   Since the end of World War II, education within so-called modernizing or developing nations has received a great deal of attention. One focus of attention is that of ideas or ideals; for example, in the Peoples' Republic of China, a basic idea is "China walks on two legs, redness and expertness"; in Malawi, that independent nation is being built upon "unity, loyalty, obedience and discipline"; or in Brazil, priority ideas are "security and development." These slogans set contexts within which schooling is called upon to contribute to building ways and means for creating model citizens.

A second focus of attention is growth. Between 1950 and 1970, the number of pupils in primary schools in developing countries trebled, reaching 200 million. During the same period, the number of students in secondary and higher education increased sixfold, reaching 42 and 6 million, respectively, by 1970.[9]

It is hard for guests visiting the United States to believe that Americans are still only talking about the need to expand the international component of our general school and college curricula. To be sure, America's national sense of self has been largely informed by our domestic history; by our relative self-sufficiency; by our continental frontiers; and by our emergence at the end of the Second World War as the most powerful nation in the world. But today the effects of an event on the other side of the world are likely to ripple all the way around the globe. Calculations of national sovereignty are routinely affected by the interests and needs of over 160 nations. There is no longer a country on the face of this shrunken planet that can go it alone.

WHAT UNITED STATES STUDENTS KNOW ABOUT THEIR WORLD   Several years ago the Educational Testing Service conducted a major survey of fourth, eighth, and twelfth graders' knowledge and attitudes about other peoples and other nations.[10] The results proved generally disconcerting to educators and social observers alike. The majority of the students had a surprisingly limited understanding of other countries.

But would college students understand their world any better, given their exposure to more advanced training and education? Following are some of the most significant findings of what approximately 1,000 college seniors from 185 institutions of higher learning know and perceive about global relationships and complexities.

1. Seniors achieved a mean score of 50.5 questions correct out of 101 on the test, showing a considerable lack of knowledge on topics felt important by the assessment committee.
2. Patterns of response to specific test questions indicated that important misconceptions existed. Even able students had misconceptions about the following:
   - the degree to which the dependence of the United States on foreign oil increased during the 1970s and the vulnerability of the United States economy to increases in the price of oil or decreases in its supply
   - the membership of the Organization of Petroleum Exporting Countries and the reasons it can raise oil prices
   - the causes of inadequate global nutrition
   - the United States' record on signing human rights treaties adopted by the United Nations and the major accomplishments of the Helsinki Accords
   - the comparative world membership of Islam and Christianity and the countries in which Islam predominates or constitutes a significant minority population
   - the difficulties connected with either national self-sufficiency or dependency in a world of interdependent nations
   - the historical origins of the Western sovereign territorial state and the modern state system and the emergence of nationalist movements as significant political forces in European history
   - the patterns of world birth and death rates today
   - the pattern of the world's past and possible future consumption of fossil fuels
   - the reasons for the lack of substantial progress toward world peace during the twentieth century
   - the main purpose of the recently completed multilateral trade negotiations, and the demands of representatives of developing countries in the North-South talks

3. Almost 90 percent of the seniors reported in the language self-assessment section that they had "learned or studied" a foreign language. However, despite the large number reporting foreign language study, useful levels of proficiency are being attained by very few. For example, only about one-third reported that they could quite easily "order a simple meal in a restaurant," and only 11 percent felt themselves able to "tell what I plan to be doing five years from now" using appropriate future tenses.
4. Foreign language ability was unrelated to scores on the knowledge test.
5. Fewer than one in twelve seniors had participated in formal programs abroad (only one in twenty had been in a year-long program), although almost 65 percent reported having been in other countries (mostly Canada, Mexico, and those of Western Europe).[11]

A considerable number of private educational organizations, ranging from the Institute for World Order and the Overseas Development Council to the Center for Global Perspectives in Education and the Population Reference Bureau, are developing materials and providing services to public education agencies, local school systems, and teacher-training institutions on interdependence issues.[12] Professional organizations in the field of education are also concerned with these issues and attempt to stimulate interest within their respective memberships; one recent example was reflected in the theme for the National Education Association's observation of the American Bicentennial, "Education for a Global Community."

Another example is the National Commission on Reform of Secondary Education, which includes among its various recommendations a plea for a fresh commitment to global education.

> The education of the nation's adolescents must be superior to that of their parents. Part of this superiority must be an enhanced sense of the globe as the human environment, and instruction to this end must reflect not only the ancient characteristics of the world, but emerging knowledge of biological and social unity. All secondary school students should receive a basic global education.[13]

Support for Global Education

In addition to the major efforts of individuals and organizations to stimulate educational programs about global issues, there have been a number of official statements at the level of local, state, national, and international government.

Local communities have formally advocated global studies and tried to implement programs. One example is the project "Columbus in the World and the World in Columbus," which demonstrated the large extent to which the city of Columbus, Ohio, was interdependent with global events and institutions.[14] In some states, like New Jersey, the state board of education adopted recommendations to increase global education in the schools. And the United States, in such documents as the 1981 *Global Future* report identified earlier, has advocated global education.

At the international level a number of documents, including covenants signed by most nations and reports of special commissions, have strongly supported global education on a number of topics. These United Nations' calls for educational efforts include the 1948 action of the General Assembly in proclaiming the Universal Declaration of Human Rights, which says:

> Now, therefore, The General Assembly Proclaims this Universal Declaration of Human Rights as a common standard of achievement for all peoples and all nations, to the end that every individual and every organ of society, keeping this Declaration constantly in mind, shall strive by teaching and education to promote respect for these rights and freedoms and by progressive measures, national and international, to secure their universal and effective recognition and observance, both among the peoples of Member States themselves and among the peoples of territories under their jurisdiction.[15]

And Article 26 of the Universal Declaration states:

> Education shall be directed to the full development of the human personality and to the strengthening of respect for human rights and fundamental freedoms. It shall promote understanding, tolerance and friendship among all nations, racial or religious groups, and shall further the activities of the United Nations for the maintenance of peace.[16]

UNESCO, in pursuit of this global education, adopted the Recommendation concerning Education for International Understanding, Cooperation and Peace and Education relating to Human Rights and Fundamental Freedoms. This document proposed several guiding principles of educational policy including:

> an international dimension and a global perspective in education at all levels and in all its forms; . . .
> awareness of the increasing global interdependence between peoples and nations.[17]

And another example of support for global education is the Final Document on the World Congress on Disarmament Education, a congress called by UNESCO in 1980. It starts by stating:

1. Deeply concerned by the lack of real progress towards disarmament and by the worsening of international tensions which threaten to unleash a war so devastating as to imperil the survival of mankind.
2. Convinced that education and information may make a significant contribution to reducing tensions and to promoting disarmament, that it is urgent to undertake vigorous action in these areas.[18]

Several pages of specific recommendations to implement disarmament education and to relate it to other global issues like economics and human rights follow this statement.

There is generally strong support for global education, but there may be hidden disagreements on the nature and form of that education.

Definitions and Dimensions of Global Education

Global education can be defined simply as study of the interdependence and interrelationships among actors on the world stage. Interdependence, of course, refers to the recognition that we share the global environment and are responsible to each other for its care. This suggests that no group should act independently and without consideration of global consequences and that no group is only dependent upon others and has no contribution to make to a global society. "Interrelationships among actors" refers to a variety of conditions, some of which are shown in Table 11.2.

There are at least six approaches to international or global education. Table 11.3 indicates how these approaches differ.

As Table 11.3 suggests, there are some significant differences among the approaches identified. World history tends to treat the major political and military history that preceded current governments. In the schools of the United States it is the most popular approach, emphasizing western cultural history and European ancestors and touching only briefly on nonwestern or southern hemispheric history. It also tends to concentrate on political and military actions in the past, with some excursions into traditions in the arts, sciences, and intellectual history. World history is usually fact-filled and descriptive of im-

Table 11.2:
Interrelationships among Actors

Actor	Example of World Interrelationships
Individual	Food, clothing, cars, and other goods come from all parts of the world; job depends upon international trade; affected by pollution, global inflation, health
Group	Travel across national boundaries; lobby for or against tariffs, immigration policies; exchange programs
Organizations (Scouts, Labor unions, Rotary, etc.)	International affiliates; exchanges
Companies	Multi-national corporate locations; international monetary exchange; global competition
National governments	Treaties; diplomacy; war; arms sales; boundary disputes; import/export regulations; world court; world bank; spies
United Nations	Peace-keeping; global conferences; world publicity; debates; publications; forums

portant people, events, and places. It may not offer a global perspective because of its relative ethnocentrism.

International relations is commonly taught in government or political science classes, although not extensively. Its very name indicates its heavy reliance on the nation-state as the most important element to study. Most of the work is devoted to examination of treaties, diplomacy, war, trade among nations, and similar topics that involve national governments. It is usually historical in approach, tracing developments.

Foreign policy studies also approach world problems in terms of the nation-state. As the name suggests, this field tends to see world problems from the perspective of one nation and to see others as "foreign." Thus, American foreign policy would deal with how the American government had acted on or reacted to world events and other nations in terms of American self-interest.

Table 11.3:
Approaches to World Study

Types	Key Actor	Perspective
World history	Government, military	Wars, dynasties; territory domination; religion
International relations	Nation-state	Historical; document-study; traditional
Foreign policy	Nation-state	National virtues; we–they contrast; national self-preservation
Area studies	Nation-state region	Geography; politics; history; trade; national and regional interests
Global studies	Varies from individual to global	Global values: peace, human rights, ecology, economic balance
World reconstructionism	Various	Critical theory, social activism: global problems and inequality require correction

Source: Adapted from Burns Weston, "Education for Human Survival," *Annals of the New York Academy of Science*, 261 (1975): 115–125; and Jack Nelson, "Incompatabilities Between International Studies and Citizenship Education," International Studies Association Conference, 1980.

Area studies is an approach that is larger than nations, emphasizing the regional character of world affairs. It usually concentrates on nations, however, in examining the geography, history, and trade in an area of the world. In area studies one learns of South America, the Far East, Europe, or the Communist bloc in terms of such factors as land forms, exports and imports, governmental structures, resources, climate, and the like. It tends to be descriptive, using political geography as a basis for the study.

Global studies is an approach that places emphasis on a series of values considered important in the world. The global goals identified earlier in this chapter are examples of these values. This approach assumes that people tend to share these goals throughout the world and that the study of national history or treaties is not likely to address these wider values. The key world actors, in a global studies program, need not be limited to military or national government leaders. This program tends to be more futuristic than the others. It proposes that the global values are extremely important and that it is possible for people to move toward them. It looks beyond national boundaries to a broader context, and can include science, literature, and arts.

World reconstructionism shares a futuristic orientation with global studies, but emphasizes the need to become active in addressing world problems. The main concept is to reconstruct the world to improve it. This approach can call for radical change to correct global problems of gross economic inequality, oppression of people by their governments, suppression of human rights, starvation in one part of the world while other parts waste food, manipulation by multinational corporations, protection of the elites at the sacrifice of the masses, and others. This is an activist approach, criticizing the current world system and advocating change.

There is a variety of other names that could be used to identify each of the approaches noted above. The categories, however, remain regardless of titles. And, as Table 11.3 suggests, there is a spectrum of approaches ranging from the most functionalist to the most critical—from the ones most supportive of stasis in world structures to those most supportive of change.

SUMMARY

This chapter explores the increasingly global context of human activity and indicates its implications for education. It proposes that stasis and change orientations influence perceptions of global issues and of global education. It illustrates the ecological nature of the global situation and provides an example of interrelated global goals that can serve in developing global education. Finally, it shows the level of support for education in these areas even though the schools have not made it a strong priority, and it describes differences in approaches to global education.

FOR CONSIDERATION

1. If schools are responsible for instilling national loyalties in youth, how can the concept of global interdependence be instituted? Are these compatible goals for schools?

2. How should global education be organized? Who should be able to decide what ideas are taught? Who should be required to take such courses? Who should teach these?

3. Is international interdependence based on a functionalist view of the world an attempt to maintain stasis in international relations? Or does it involve a critical perspective, one that considers and promotes change? How threatening is interdependence to the established international order?

Notes

1. U. Thant, Address to United Nations, in Richard Falk, *This Endangered Planet* (New York: Random House, 1971), p. 415.

2. *Ibid.*, p. 27.

3. Richard Falk and Saul Mendlovitz, *The Strategy of World Order*, 4 vols. (New York: World Law Fund, 1966).

4. U.S. Department of State and the Council on Environmental Quality, *Global Future: Time to Act* (Washington, D.C.: U.S. Government Printing Office, 1981), pp. xi and xxv.

5. *Ibid.*, p. 191.

6. Joseph Moore and Roberta Moore, *War and War Prevention* (New York: Hayden, 1974).

7. Ruth Leger Sivard, *World Military and Social Expenditures* (Leesburg, Va.: WMSE Publications, 1980).

8. Jack L. Nelson, "Nationalism and Education," in *Studies in International Conflict*, ed. Glenn Snyder (Buffalo: SUNY Buffalo Press, 1968), pp. 68–84; "Nationalistic Versus Global Education," *Theory and Research in Social Education* 4 (August 1976): 33–50; and James Becker, ed., *Schooling for a Global Age* (New York: McGraw-Hill, 1979).

9. World Bank, "Education Sector Working Paper" (Washington, D.C., 1974).

10. Lewis W. Pike and Thomas S. Barrows, *Other Nations, Other Peoples: A Survey of Student Interests, Knowledge, and Perceptions* (Washington, D.C.: Government Printing Office, 1979).

11. Thomas Barrows *et al.*, "What Students Know About Their World," in *Educating for the World View* (New Rochelle, N.Y.: Council on Learning, 1980), pp. 10–11.

12. Ward Morehouse and Jane Meskill, *Organizational Atlas on Diffusion of International/Intercultural Education* (New York: Foreign Area Materials Center, 1974); David H. Smith *et al.*, *Voluntary Transnational Cultural Exchange Organizations of the U.S.: A Selected List* (Washington, D.C.: Center for a Voluntary Society, 1974).

13. National Commission on the Reform of Seconday Education, *The Reform of Secondary Education* (New York: McGraw-Hill, 1973), p. 16.

14. Ohio State University, Transnational Intellectual Cooperation Program.

15. United Nations, General Assembly, *Universal Declaration of Human Rights* (New York: United Nations, 1948), p. 1.

16. *Ibid.*, p. 7.

17. Thomas Buergenthal and Judith V. Torney, *International Human Rights and International Education* (Washington, D.C.: U.S. National Commission for UNESCO, 1976), p. 90.
18. United Nations, UNESCO, *The United Nations Disarmament Yearbook*, vol. 5 (New York: United Nations, 1981), p. 1.

References

Barrows, Thomas, *et al*. "What Students Know About Their World." In *Educating for the World View*, pp. 10–11. New Rochelle, N.Y.: Council on Learning, 1980.
Becker, James, ed. *Schooling for a Global Age*. New York: McGraw-Hill, 1979.
Buergenthal, Thomas, and Torney, Judith V. *International Human Rights and International Education*. Washington D.C.: U.S. National Commission for UNESCO, 1976.
Falk, Richard. *This Endangered Planet*. New York: Random House, 1971.
———, and Mendlovitz, Saul. *The Strategy of World Order*, 4 vols. New York: World Law Fund, 1966.
Moore, Joseph, and Moore, Roberta. *War and War Prevention*. New York: Hayden, 1974.
Morehouse, Ward, and Meskill, Jane. *Organizational Atlas on Diffusion of International / Intercultural Education*. New York: Foreign Area Materials Center, June 1974.
National Commission on the Reform of Secondary Education. *The Reform of Secondary Education*. New York: McGraw-Hill, 1973.
Nelson, Jack L. "Nationalism and Education." In *Studies In International Conflict*, edited by Glenn Snyder, pp. 68–84. Buffalo: SUNY Buffalo Press, 1968.
———, "Nationalistic Versus Global Education," *Theory and Research in Social Education* 4 (August 1976):33–50.
———, and Green, Vera. *International Human Rights: Contemporary Issues*. New York: Human Rights Publishing Group, 1980.
Pike, Lewis W., and Barrows, Thomas S. *Other Nations, Other Peoples: A Survey of Student Interests, Knowledge, and Perceptions*. HEW Publication No. 78–19004. Washington, D.C.: Government Printing Office, 1979.
Sivard, Ruth Leger. *World Military and Social Expenditures*. Leesburg, Va.: WMSE Publications, 1974, 1976, 1977, 1980.
Smith, David H., *et al*. *Voluntary Transnational Cultural Exchange Organizations of the U.S.: A Selected List*. Washington, D.C.: Center for a Voluntary Society, April 1974.
United Nations. General Assembly. *Universal Declaration of Human Rights*. New York: United Nations, December 10, 1948.
———. UNESCO. *The United Nations Disarmament Yearbook*, vol. 5. New York: United Nations, 1981.
U.S. Department of State and the Council on Environmental Quality. *Global Future: Time to Act*. Report to the President on Global Resources, Environment and Population. Washington D.C.: U.S. Government Printing Office, 1981.
World Bank. "Education Sector Working Paper." Washington, D.C., 1974.

Chapter 12: Science, Technology, and Education

Introduction

There is no area of human endeavor that shows the powerful tension between stasis and change as clearly as that of science and technology. The speed with which changes in scientific knowledge and technological developments have occurred is almost unbelievable. Outside of science fiction writers, who in 1950 could have predicted space travel, the dramatic impact of computers on everday life, or the cloning of human beings? Yet, there is strong resistance to those significant changes, and to most of our high-tech lifestyle. There is a lingering resentment of the disruption of more stable living and also a yearning to return to a simpler life in a more static society.

The changes in scientific ability to know and control space beyond the planet as well as to manipulate human biology, such as altering the genes of individuals, represent a major threat to long-standing views of life on earch. The communications explosion threatens privacy; nuclear energy development threatens the totality of human existence; gene-splicing threatens our very concept of human. With each lurch forward in science and technology come cries of the destruction of values, people, and the environment. We stand on the edge of a chasm between the frontiers of science and the comfort of traditional views. Education is the bridge that can relate the two sides, but the speed of change in science and technology has outpaced the speed of educational change. In addition, stasis and change, the theme of this book, affect schooling and create forward and backward pulls that make it difficult for education to stay abreast.

Science and technology have in the past altered and are now altering our institutions, life styles, and aspirations. This chapter will argue that these transformations have occurred and are occurring without our society or our educational programs preparing us for them.

Brave New World is fiction. But how have we coped with the social impact of science and technology on our lives to date? These general inquiries need to be refined into more discrete questions. Many of the following questions which focus on technology are found implicit and explicit in our daily newspapers, television programs, and magazines. Is technology a social good? On balance does it improve the quality of human life? Does it increase our capacity to control? Has it expanded well-being? Does it decrease exploitation, suffering, pain, hardship, misery? Or is technology a social evil? On balance has it lessened the quality of human life? Has it decreased our capacity to control? Has it diminished well-being? Does it dehumanize us, alienate us from each other and the natural world? And there is a middle or neutral focus for questioning: Are we responsible for the results of the applications of technology that we see around us?

None of these questions is new. They have been asked since the rise of modern science from Sir Francis Bacon's days in the early seventeenth century through the advent of the industrial revolution in the eighteenth century and its domination of the Western world in the nineteenth and twentieth centuries. But developments since the twentieth century in such areas as travel, communications, calculating, and killing—especially killing—have made their resolution most urgent. Atomic, hydrogen, and neutron bombs were cited by President Jimmy Carter in his Farewell Address on January 14, 1981, as having been accepted by people as being like air and water, a natural part of the environment. They are taken for granted. Yet, do we take for granted the destructive capacity of these bombs to kill as many people in one minute as were killed by all the weapons during all the years of World War II? Do we accept without thought or feeling the destructive capacity of these bombs to kill as many people in one afternoon as were killed by all the weapons during all the wars of recorded history everywhere on earth?

How shall we cope with other less ominous but vexing concerns of contemporary society such as the computer revolution, fuel crises, massive pollution, and the obsolescence of work skills, among others? Pierre Teilhard de Chardin, in *The Phenomenon of Man*, wrote, "I am convinced that finally it is upon the idea of progress and faith in progress that mankind, today so divided, must rely and reshape itself."[1] Educators need to be knowledgeable about technology, the scientific basis of technology, and the impact of technology on our social institutions. Only by being knowledgeable can we devise curricula that may prepare students to cope with evolving institutions, life styles, and aspirations.

The consequences of technological advances have been pervasive, and many of them, favorable and unfavorable alike, have left today's educators, policy makers, and policy advisors seriously behind the course of events, with the result that by the time efforts have been translated into programs for action they have become unfeasible or simply irrelevant. Our social institutions, including schools, generally lag behind our technology; we do not know how to integrate such events as the technology of test tube babies and genetic engineering into timely social policy.

The Idea of Progress

Any understanding of stasis and change in American society and education requires some knowledge of selected ideas, definitions, and history. For example, the idea of progress—the belief that humankind advanced in the past, is now advancing, and will inevitably advance in the foreseeable future—is a peculiarly Western faith with a long history. In the late eighth century B.C. the ancient Greek Hesiod wrote *Works and Days*, in which he chronicled the myth of golden, silver, bronze, and iron races, which were different one from the other and which could clean up injustices, commit themselves to lives of rectitude, and progressively make life not only endurable but desirable. His belief was that Prometheus had stolen fire from Mount Olympus to give to humankind and thus generated our capacity to move from primordial deprivation and fear to eventual civilization. Hesiod anticipated progress as a result of humankind developing tools and techniques to use in controlling the forces of nature. Fire became a tool used nearly 3,000 years ago as we use atomic energy today, to provide heat, comfort, and light or to destroy our enemies.

Agricultural and the industrial-scientific revolutions engendered the only qualitative changes in social living that humankind has ever known. Modern dating techniques indicate that agriculture was established and villages developed around 7000 B.C. By 4000 B.C. population density based on diversified agriculture had expanded rapidly and urban centers had evolved in the eastern Mediterranean area. However, the agricultural base as it had evolved in, say, England or France, by the middle 1600s was not sufficient to support a good and long life. The average life span was perhaps twenty-five years and was appreciably shorter for women than for men. Infant mortality figures were high and this hazard was augmented by the scourge of killing epidemic diseases such as smallpox and cholera. Further, women had to confront the added dangers of childbearing under commonly unhygienic and frequently malnourished conditions. It was not uncommon for the greater part of entire communities to die of starvation in Europe as a result of crop failures and/or epidemic diseases in the mid-1600s. London's population fell from just over 2,000,000 in 1663 to 125,000 two years later during a seige of bubonic plague. As late as 1850 in Massachusetts the life expectancy of women exceeded that of men by 2.2 years; but women's life expectancy at birth had reached 40.5 years while men's had reached only 38.3 years.

The industrial revolution—the gradual use of machines, the employment of men, women, and children in factories, the change from a population mainly of agricultural laborers to a population mainly engaged in making things in factories and distributing them when they were made—took place in Western Europe and North America between the mid-1700s and the early 1900s. The scientific revolution as seen by the eminent British sociologist C. P. Snow is closely related to the industrial revolution and grew out of it. Snow sees the scientific revolution as dating from about 1920 "when atomic particles were first made (of) industrial use."[2] He believed that the industrial society of electronics, atomic energy, and automation is different in kind—far more deeply scientific, far quicker to change and to affect its environment, far more prodigious in its result—from the industrial revolution and will change the world much more.

If C. P. Snow is right, as we believe him to be, we must learn to understand the scientific revolution, to educate ourselves to cope with it. Not to do so may well be to watch a steep decline in our current levels of well-being. We are caught between the dead or dying industrial traditions of the past and the scientific tradition being born. To meet our cultural and practical futures our educational aims and programs will have to change.

Science and Technology

Science is commonly defined as a branch of study devoted to the observation and classification of information and with the attempt to establish verifiable general laws. The term "scientist" was first used by William Whewell, who did his pioneering work in the philosophy of science in England in the early nineteenth century. He laid stress on scientists framing of hypotheses as against simply collecting facts. The term "technology" had been coined earlier in 1772 by Johann Bechmann in Germany. The terms "science" and "technology" are commonly defined as theory and practice, with technology being seen as the practical application of scientific principles and theories. Or consider the parallels between science and technology and the concepts of intellect and intelligence. Intellect is more concerned with new ideas and with the creative and critical side of the mind. Intelligence is more concerned with knowing, understanding, and using. Intelligence seeks to grasp and manipulate knowledge; intellect creates theorizes, criticizes, imagines. The scientist uses intellect; the technologist, intelligence. People have both intellect and intelligence in varying degrees.

The development of the vacuum tube and the transistor has resulted in a proliferation of scientific theories regarding electronics just as Anton van Leeuwenhoek's technical improvements of the compound microscope resulted in new theories regarding living cell growth and development. Technological discoveries have promoted the proliferation of scientific theories and, together, technology and science have engendered in Western cultures a nearly unwavering faith in scientism—the methods of scientists—and the presumption that reality can be rationally ordered by intellect.

Auguste Comte advanced this view in 1824 and expanded upon it greatly in his *System of Positive Polity* in 1851.[3] Comte's positivism unified intellectual faculties and social sympathies. That is, our knowledge of the physical universe, of humankind, and of society were integrated to provide for a positive art of living. Science was the instrument capable of effecting this unity. The entire spectrum of facts from the physical world to the social world was incorporated into a single framework of positive inquiry—positivism. Since Comte's positivist philosophy was first popularized, modern societies' ever-increasing dependency on technology and our aspirations for technological advancement have created a nearly obsessive belief in the omnipotence of science. This belief is the dominant characteristic of the postindustrial age.

Coping with the Societal Impact of Science and Technology: The Past

Henry Adams visited the 1900 Paris Exposition of Science and Technology in the company of the secretary of the Smithsonian Institution, Samuel Pierpont

Langley. Adams was lost in the array of sights and sounds that assaulted him. Apparently Langley's presence was a good thing, in that he was able to teach Adams what to study, and why and how; while Adams, without such orientation, might as well have stood outside on a clear night and stared at the Milky Way.

In his autobiography, Henry Adams gives credit to Langley for pointing out an orienting principle that Sir Francis Bacon had striven to teach King James I and his subjects, including colonists in the Americas, in the early 1600s: that true science was the development of economy of forces, that is, the law of parsimony (the more economical a system, the better). Adams was an informed, well educated, elite representative of American civilization at the time he visited the Paris Exposition. Yet he wrote that he haunted the Great Exposition aching to absorb knowledge and helpless to find it. There was so much there that he was thus meditating chaos until Langley came by and showed his orienting principle.

Nothing in education is so astonishing as the amount of ignorance it accumulates in the form of inert facts. Adams had looked at most of the accumulations of art in the storehouses called art museums; yet he did not know how to look at the art exhibits of 1900. He had studied Karl Marx and his doctrines of history with profound attention, yet he could not apply them at Paris. Langley, with the ease of a great master of experiment, by-passed every exhibit that did not reveal a new application of force, and naturally ignored to begin with almost the whole art exhibit. Equally, he ignored almost the whole industrial exhibit. He led his pupil directly to the forces. His chief interest was in new motors to make his airship feasible, and he taught Adams the astonishing complexities of Gottlieb Daimler's new four-stroke internal combustion engine and of the automobile, which, by 1900, had become a nightmare at nearly 100 kilometers an hour, almost as destructive as the electric streetcar, which was only ten years older, and threatening to become as terrible as the steam locomotive itself, which was almost exactly as old as Adams himself.

Adams had been inducted to the world of technology. In his effort to integrate it into what he had earlier learned, Adams later wrote "The Dynamo and the Virgin," in which he drew the analogy that the energy or the force affecting human behavior had built the great medieval cathedral at Chartres. Spiritual and technological sources and forces, the Virgin and the Dynamo, both drew out the organizing and constructive genius of humankind.[4] More than three-quarters of a century later, we teachers and citizens are called upon to avoid ignorance which is no more than inert facts and develop orienting principles to guide us and our teaching and/or learning regarding technology.

Dynamos, steam engines, automobiles, and airships serve us as common-place machines that, despite their dangers and environmental impacts, no longer intimidate us; these examples of technological innovations of seventy-five years ago have been integrated into the pattern of our lives and our insti-tutions. Scientific and technological developments have profoundly altered our institutions, our life styles, and our aspirations in the last several genera-tions. What is striking about this transformation is not that it has occurred, but rather that it has occurred without preparation. Consider the culmination of thousands of years of acceleration of four human activities: traveling, com-municating, killing, and calculating. For thousands of centuries man traveled at walking pace. Then came the wheel. At the end of the nineteenth century, in Henry Adams' days, the invention of the internal combustion engine had enabled J. C. Jenatzy to reach a speed of 65.79 miles per hour. By 1945, jet aircraft were already traveling at ten times that speed. Today, astronauts move through space at speeds on the order of 23,000 miles per hour.

Twentieth-century speeds and the worldwide availability of modern ve-hicles have made travel commonplace and distance inconsequential. Last cen-tury the average person hardly ever ventured far from his or her birthplace. Modern people are nomads; in 1978 commercial airlines (not including those of the Soviet Union) flew in excess of 493,000,000 passenger miles.

In communication people were limited for thousands of years to the dis-tance their voice or a drumbeat could carry or the time it took to deliver a written message. In the 1960s hundreds of millions of people heard astronauts speaking from space and saw them within three seconds of the moment they stepped on the moon. The horror of the now primitive atomic weapon that killed between 70,000 and 80,000 people on August 6, 1945, at Hiroshima, Japan, or the current capacity of a VAX 11-780 computer to sort and manipu-late 10 to 20 million floating point instructions per second (MFIPS—an ex-ample of one MFIPS is to multiply 25.7 x 522.4 to 8 places and store the result) nearly exceed our capacity to comprehend.

Figure 12.1 demonstrates in graphic form this recent burst in acceleration.

The leap continues. Research and innovation are being institutionalized as the numbers of people working in science and applied technology soar. It is estimated that more than 90 percent of all the scientists and inventors in all human history are living and working today. Equally remarkable is the con-stantly diminishing gap between a scientific discovery and its large-scale appli-cation. Humans took 112 years to develop practical applications of the discov-ery of the principles of photography. Only two years separated the discovery

Figure 12.1 Four Leaps

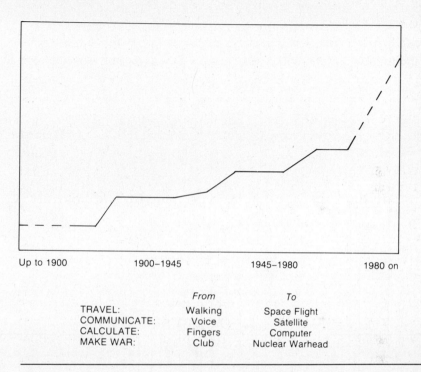

	From	To
TRAVEL:	Walking	Space Flight
COMMUNICATE:	Voice	Satellite
CALCULATE:	Fingers	Computer
MAKE WAR:	Club	Nuclear Warhead

Adapted from Edgar Faure *et al.*, *Learning to Be: The World of Education Today and Tomorrow* (Paris: UNESCO, 1972), p. 88–89; and Anthony Wedgwood Benn, London University presentation, 1971.

of solar batteries from their production. Figure 12.2 (page 270) shows the ever shorter time required for the application of eleven great discoveries made between the end of the eighteenth and the middle of the twentieth century.

Three Models for Assessing the Social Role of Technology

A vast literature is available to us on the topic of the social role of technology as it can affect stasis and change during the final two decades of the twentieth century. Bernard Gendron initiated an assessment of the social role of modern technology by dividing the contemporary literature on the subject into three

Figure 12.2 Decreasing Interval Between Discovery and
            Application in Physical Science

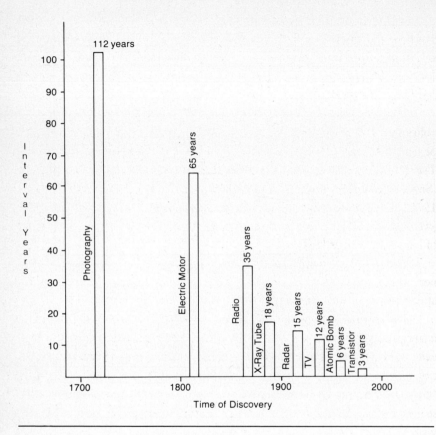

Adapted from Eli Ginsberg, *Technology and Social Change* (New York: Columbia University Press, 1964), p. 87; and from Bell Telephone Labs, Inc.

"extreme views": the Utopian view, the Dystopian view, and the Socialist view.[5] These models may serve us by presenting conceptual points of departure for coping with our near future in the 1980s.

THE UTOPIAN VIEW

The Utopian view takes the unambiguous posture that nearly all our social progress is primarily due to the rise of technology and science. Thus Utopians believe that if there were to be no interruptions, the unfettered continued development of technology would result in the erosion of all our social pathologies; that scarcity would be eliminated; and, with that, the demise of all conflicts would be assured. In this context, nationalism, sectarianism, ethnocentrism, Chauvinism, oppression, exploitation, and sexism would cease to exist. Sickness and disease would be banished to the past, and improvements in communication, transportation, and education would contribute to the extinction of parochialisms. Utopians see world problems as essentially technical, not political or ideological.

Contemporary Utopian literature dating from the end of World War II is voluminous. Due to its variety as well as abundance, the Utopian view must be assembled out of bits and pieces taken from a variety of sources. *Walden Two* (Skinner, 1948); *Utopia or Oblivion* (Fuller, 1969); *The Two Cultures* (Snow, 1964); *Understanding Media* (McLuhan, 1964); *Future Shock* (Toffler, 1970); *The Coming of Post-Industrial Society* (Bell, 1973); *Essays in Persuasion* (Keynes, 1972); and *The Affluent Society* (Galbraith, 1972) are representatives of better-known, influential Utopian works.[6]

A brief exploration of the perspectives and beliefs reflected in Burrhus Skinner's *Walden Two* and Daniel Bell's *The Coming of Post-Industrial Society* will afford us a substantial sample of the Utopianist spectrum of social concerns.

Walden Two is a novel written by a psychologist. It is not a psychological analysis of real people in a real community. The fictional setting does, however, provide a way of explaining and debating techniques of operant conditioning as used to modify and reinforce human behavior. The leader of the "Utopian" community presents the achievements of economic self-sufficiency, security, social harmony, and tranquility within the community while the visiting critic, Professor Castle, presents the limitations or flaws that he categorizes as sadistic and fascistic. Thus, readers of the novel are left with the individual responsibility of weighing out the what-one-gives and what-one-gets in Skinner's fascinating—or fascinatingly abhorrent—community.

The Coming of Post-Industrial Society: A Venture in Social Forecasting is a sociological analysis of changes that are taking place in our economy, our class structure, and our political institutions. Its points of departure are real people and real institutions. The most prominent feature of Bell's postindustrial society is congruous with C. P. Snow's scientific basis of society: the codification of theoretical knowledge that now shapes innovation in science, technology, and social policy. Bell offers a statistical and analytical picture of a new "knowledge society" that is emerging out of the older corporate capitalism. He directs our attention to the new complex patterns of conflict and compromise among technocrats, managerial elites, the military, politicians, and trade union leaders that characterize the changing society. Underlying these matters, Bell enjoins us to examine the growing tension between equality and meritocracy — the who-gets-what and who-gives-what questions raised in Skinner's novel.

A second echelon of volumes in this array of visionary literature includes *The Prometheus Project* (Feinberg, 1969); *Between Two Ages: America's Role in the Technetronic Era* (Brzezinski, 1970); *Profiles of the Future* (Clarke, 1964); *Year Two Thousand* (Kahn and Wiener, 1967); and *The Economics of Abundance* (Theobald, 1970).[7] Robert Theobald provides his readers with an economist's vision of what is wrong with modern economics and what must be done to put the United States' economy successfully into the postindustrial (cybernetic) age. He criticizes reliance on neoclassical and neo-Keynesian models as having little relation to present-day socioeconomic realities. Theobald presents a view of a new socioeconomic world where authority is not structured ("saplential"), where unemployment is not a concern, where work incentives have ceased to be meaningful, where the "simple life takes over," and we lose interest in acquiring more material goods. His vision is one in which the economics of scarcity is replaced by the economics of abundance.

This collection of works and authors represents diverse disciplinary backgrounds from architecture (Fuller) through communications (McLuhan), economics (Galbraith and Keynes), and sociology (Bell) to the three "Ps"—physics (Snow), political science (Brzezinski), and psychology (Skinner). Some of the authors cautiously address an immediate future (Snow and Bell), while others deal speculatively for far-flung features (Clarke and Kahn). Others are optimistic in carefully guarded limits (Bell and Galbraith), while still others are euphoric in their optimism (Skinner and Clarke). Finally, the dimensions of liberation to be afforded range broadly. Some envision the development of a global village (McLuhan) or the demise of ideological differences (Bell). Others see the rise of a meritocracy (Bell and Galbraith); a rising power elite of scientists and technicians (Bell); new techniques of behavior control (Skinner); and even the ultimate elimination of death (Clarke and Fuller), leading to leisure-oriented (Theobald), sensate (Toffler) cultures. They all advocate their individually preferred stasis.

THE DYSTOPIAN VIEW

The Dystopian view is the opposite of the Utopian view. Dystopians believe that technology creates more problems than it eliminates, that at some point behind us in the process of industrialization the pernicious effects or evil results of technological growth began to exceed the benefits derived.

The Dystopians constitute two echelons: in the first group are clerics, humanities teachers, and other men of letters, while in the second group are literary representatives of the counterculture. The literary works of the first group include *Decline of the West* (Spengler, 1932); *Crisis of Our Age* (Sorokin, 1941); *1984* (Orwell, 1949); *Technological Society* (Ellul, 1964); *Brave New World* (Huxley, 1969); *Notes from the Underground* (Dostoevski, republished in 1974); and *Propaganda* (Ellul, 1972). The second group includes *One Dimensional Man* (Marcuse, 1964); *The Making of a Counter-Culture* (Roszak, 1969); *The Greening of America* (Reich, 1970); and *Pursuit of Loneliness* (Slater, 1970).[8]

Orwell's *1984* is a satirical novel about a future time and a fictional place when people living in a collectivist society are persuaded by Thought Police into thinking that ignorance is strength and war is peace. The chief character, Winston Smith, is an average woman whose work in the Ministry of Truth consists of falsifying records when state policy changes. Personal liberties such as freedom of thought, freedom to love, and freedom to speak have been surrendered for assured food, shelter, and medical care. Orwell's unspoken question is, "Is what you get worth the price you pay?"

Slater's *The Pursuit of Loneliness* is his description of America and Americans as they were during the late 1960s. Slater clarifies the relationship between our self-imposed subservience to technology on one hand and the deteriorating quality of life in the United States on the other. He lays out what was happening and why it was destructive and suggests shifts in society that might possibly prevent a continuing decline in quality of life. He warns, for example, "that nothing will change until individualism is assigned a subordinate place in the American value system."

The range of views generaly concedes that technology does create affluence and does increase our power to initially control nature but at the price of undercutting freedom and democracy. That is, technology stimulates the rise of bureaucracies and fosters the use of techniques of mass manipulation and control; divorces human beings from nature, their own bodies, and fellow humans; makes work more dull, tedious, intrinsically unrewarding and unfulfilling; and increases the potential for ecological catastrophe and/or annihilatory wars. Dystopians see world problems as frequently the product of technological growth. They all advocate a morality of humanism in change and stasis.

THE SOCIALIST VIEW

The Socialist view is generally not as well known in the United States as either the Utopian or Dystopian views, because it comes mainly from the Marxist tradition, which has had few popularly read authors in this country. The ranking works in this body of literature fall into two categories: the social role of technology and science within a capitalist context as found in *Capital* (Marx, 1967), and in *Selected Works* (Marx and Engels, 1968) and the social role of technology and science within socialism and communism as found in *Selected Works* (Lenin, 1971) and *On Revolution and War* (Mao Tse-tung, 1970).[9]

Marx's *Capital* is difficult to understand in that it is at times rather turgid and opaque. It is, however, worth the effort. *Capital* is a monumental source of Marx's views on labor, alienation, and analyses of the nature of work, and it contains a vision of a fully automated society in which wealth could be devoted to the all-around development of each individual. The relationships among the phenomena of democracy, technology, private property, bureaucracy, civil society, and the state in the modern world of Marx's day are illuminated, and his "futurology" — his vision of humankind's postindustrial future — is clearly stated. Basic definitions and concepts from *Capital* are central to an ideological system that guides the destiny of half of humankind today.

Mao Tse-tung's philosophy is the result of the synthesis of multiple strands of thinking: Chinese Confucionism, Western Liberalism, Chinese Nationalism, and Marxism-Leninism. In *On Revolution and War*, Mao explains how Marx's theory of class conflict was molded into a plan of action suited to the Chinese people and culture and traces the evolution of this transformation from guerrilla warfare toward the goal of a continuing, self-sustaining revolution in society. He further details his thinking regarding revolutionary development, global policies, imperialism, and the role of the Communist party and the military in society.

Socialists agree with Utopians that technological progress is necessary for social progress and that, properly managed, it can alleviate or eliminate most, if not all, social pathologies. Socialists argue, however, the technological progress is not sufficient for overall social progress. Proper management becomes the catalyst for technological progress to be translated into social progress. Socialists agree with the Dystopians that technology results in alienating, dehumanizing, and ecologically destructive consequences in capitalist contexts. Their view is that technological growth, when controlled by the capitalist class, is, on balance, socially harmful. Thus the Socialists point out that all the scientific and technological development in the world will fail to stimulate real social progress if those developments are not preceded by a political revolution that will provide working-class ownership of technological tools.

Socialists have developed a cogent theory of the role of technology within socialist or communist societies. Presently in the People's Republic of China they are trying to implement this theory. Utopians and Dystopians have not developed a theory of the dynamic role of technology in history. Significantly more investigation and synthesis must be done before some general view of the social role of technology may merit wide-ranging acceptance. Let us here, however, use these models as points of departure for examining the world anticipated in 1985.

Announcements in the world's newspapers and on radio and television of the birth of test tube babies in England and India, or of Stanford University having been granted the first United States patent on basic gene-swapping techniques,[10] or of molecular research have refocused public attention on the immediacy of the technological and spiritual dimensions of our brave new world.

The Technological World: A Scenario

Forecasting of scientific and technological developments can provide some of the information decision makers need to accomodate the long lead-times separating the evaluation of opportunities from the implementation of specific plans.

Theodore Gordon and Robert Ament utilized ideas from participants from twenty-five separate areas of technological expertise to forecast some technological developments as of 1985.[11] These are only a few of many technological and scientific changes.

According to the forecasts, organ transplants will be commonplace and have high potential for long-lasting success due to the amelioration of the foreign-body rejection problem. Spare parts banks will be commonplace in big medical facilities. Due to shortages of parts, black markets will arise but will be constrained by both legislative regulation and the development of artificial organs such as artificial hearts with implantable power sources of five-year duration. Tissue-compatible animal research will supply additional alternatives. Overall, the emphasis in medicine will be shifting from repair to replacement. New industries, technologies, and educational goals for medical training will accompany these developments.

Human reproduction will be affected. Ninety percent certainty for non-surgical techniques for choice of sex of children will have been demonstrated and chromosome typing will permit discovery of abnormalities within weeks of conception. Because of fads in sex selection, legislative or financial incentives may be instituted to influence parents to help maintain a desirable male-female balance. Contraceptive drugs capable of being mass-administered as additions to water supplies or staple foods (as iodine is added to salt) will lower fertility rates. Public education regarding the consequences of overpopulation will contribute to societal acceptance of this practice. Surreptitious contraception will lead to a new form of warfare and efforts to create anticontraceptive pills and detection systems will be under way.

Primitive animal life forms will be engendered and protein foods will be produced, creating new industries and raising the prospect of specialized diet additives for protein-deficient populations. Large-scale desalinization plants will augment conventional agriculture. International power politics will control who gets these plants.

Immunization will protect us against most viral and bacterial diseases. The public will have access to nonnarcotic, inexpensive drugs that increase attention and effect personality change such as reducing aggression or inducing euphoria. These drugs will lead to new techniques in education, mental therapy, and rehabilitation of adjudged criminals.

Science and Technology in School Learning—
Mathetics: How Does Learning Occur?

Mathetics is the study of how human beings learn. Pedagogy focuses upon the teacher's behavior while teaching, but mathetics focuses upon pupils' behaviors while learning. Learning emphases are replacing teaching emphases. Two areas of interest in learning are internal brain functioning and external sensory stimuli or experience.

Brain growth depends at the outset upon having an abundant supply of nutritious food, especially of protein. Short periods of protein deprivation may lead to permanent defects if they occur during embryonic, neonatal, and early childhood periods. Experiments on brain growth, sensory-motor skill acquisition, task learning, and neurological and endocrine maturation have demonstrated the dependence of brain functions on having a continuous supply of protein. Vitamin B_6, pyridoxine, which is an essential cofactor for many steps in protein synthesis, is an additional indispensable requirement. Unfortunately, protein and some of the essential vitamins, including B_6, are relatively expensive and are therefore often in short supply in poverty diets. Significant losses cannot be made up and the unborn and newly born infant are so vulnerable that they readily suffer permanent underdevelopment. Maxwell Cowan states it this way.

> Assuming that the fully developed human brain contains on the order of 100 billion neurons and that virtually no new neurons are added after birth, it can be calculated that neurons must be generated in the developing brain at an average rate of more than 250,000 per minute. It is obvious here that nutritional considerations affect the brain's development during this period of rapid neurological growth.[12]

Breakthroughs achieved in recent years in our knowledge of the brain have led to a clearer and more objective understanding of human behavior, of mental mechanisms, and of the learning process. More and more attention is being devoted to this aspect of mathetics. In less than a decade the number of neurologists who are studying the brain more than trebled. The journal entitled *Brain Research* was launched modestly in 1966 for an international scientific audience. It now is a weekly, costs $1,466 a year for a subscription, and, to put that into context, is only one of about 150 scientific journals covering brain research. Another measure of growth is that ten years ago there were almost no Ph.D degrees in neurosciences. Today, more than thirty universities award them.

The average human brain, which weighs only two or three pounds, is 78 percent water, 10 percent fat, 8 percent protein, and 4 percent other materials, mainly salts. . . and you don't get much mystery out of that. The brain does differ in its high energy demands. Although it is only 2.5 percent of the normal body weight, it receives 15 percent of our blood supply and fully 25 percent of the oxygen consumed by the body. So this piece of tissue is extremely active.

Let me give you some feeling for what many people consider to be the central explanatory principle in brain research, namely, that the myriad functions that the brain performs arise out of these vast networks of neural circuits.

The analogy I'm going to make now (an update of Descartes) is to electronic devices. Just as electronic engineers can wire together a collection of transistors, resistors, capacitors, and so on to produce radios, television sets, and computers, evolution can program and shape neural circuits into devices —brains—that analyze stimuli, make decisions, and program movements. That is a hypothesis of modern brain research.

Now, a corollary of this nerve circuit hypothesis is that meaningful research about the brain must come from studies that are conducted at the level of individual nerve cells. This is called the cellular approach, and, as a result of this approach, an enormous number of specific details are now available about the structure of neural circuits.

Memory is one aspect of brain activity that holds special interest for teachers. Research has instructed us in the role of a genetic substance called ribonucleic acid (RNA), which controls protein synthesis in memory. Long-term memory is attributed to a growth process by which chemically coded neuromechanisms are recorded in the structure of brain cells. Current research is further exploring biochemical aids to learning. Many biochemical systems have been discovered in the brain, and certain nerve cells have remarkable properties that make them ideal for neurochemical research: their neurotransmitters can be treated so they fluoresce.

This means that for the first time researchers can see specific biochemical pathways in the brain. Some neurons that researchers are now able to see contain an amine transmitter. These amine-containing neurons are known to affect such behavior as mood. Many psychoactive drugs influence the amine systems in consistent ways. Substances such as amphetamine increase catecholamine synoptic activity and, as a direct result, human beings feel good, confident, optimistic, and strong. Conversely, when catecholamine synoptic activity is dramatically decreased, as it is by substances such as reserpine, we become lethargic, we feel weak, our attention spans shorten, and our capacity for learning is reduced. The general opinion today would seem to be that chemical intervention has, so far, yielded more results at the affective than at the cognitive level.

Laboratory research is currently studying the possible existence of "memory molecules" in the brain that enable information to be stored in linear fashion. If this hypothesis is proven to be correct, then the possibility exists that molecular models could be capable of expressing the learning process in other terms. Recent research has been informative on the role of ribonucleic acid (a genetic substance controlling protein synthesis) in memory. The distinction is now drawn between immediate or "telephonic" memory, as simple electrochemical coded neuromechanisms are recorded in the structure of the brain cells. Such memory involves the production of specific enzymes in the brain cells, and this can be facilitated or even provoked. More generally, it has been found that small quantities of ribonucleic acid are secreted in the brain cells during the learning process, and it would appear that any chemical sub-

Figure 12.3 Avenues to Learning

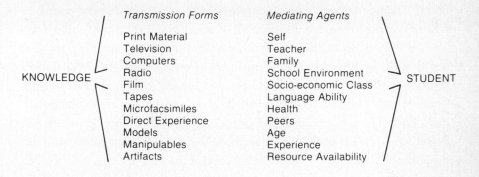

Transmission Forms	Mediating Agents
Print Material	Self
Television	Teacher
Computers	Family
Radio	School Environment
Film	Socio-economic Class
Tapes	Language Ability
Microfacsimiles	Health
Direct Experience	Peers
Models	Age
Manipulables	Experience
Artifacts	Resource Availability

KNOWLEDGE — STUDENT

stance capable of accelerating the cells' production of RNA could thereby facilitate the learning process.

Malnutrition negatively affects learning. The consequences of malnutrition are mental apathy, a shortened attention span, increased drowsiness, and prolonged sleep cycles, and all these contribute to a gross reduction of play and learning activities. Accompanying influences of malnutrition include a slowed rate of physical growth and physical, endocrinological, mental, and social maturation. Altogether these add up to a major interference with the many day-to-day learning experiences that are essential in childhood for the acquisition of thinking and linguistic tools and sensory-motor skills. Significant losses over prolonged periods become increasingly difficult to make up.

Technological tools afford present-day learners a wide array of stimuli. Prior to the invention of writing, the teacher was the principal transmitter of knowledge to be conveyed in face-to-face meetings. Writing opened a second avenue. Figure 12.3 demonstrates additional avenues including printing, film, radio, television, and machines.

Learning practices are presently affected by the disorderly and sometimes competing relations among the various vehicles for transmitting knowledge. Stimulus bombardment is massive. It is impossible to gain full advantage from communications technology without overhauling the established educational system.

Creative Forces

Henry Adams addressed the role of technology as a tool of human creativity when he wrote of the dynamo that "all of the steam in the world could not, like the Virgin, build Chartres." Technology has provided immense possibilities for mass participation in the human creative enterprise. People in earlier times left on the margins of access are, worldwide, becoming increasingly aware of their potential to participate. The revolution of rising expectations exists now. The products of technological advances constitute the means of liberating the creative genius and constructive energies of increasingly greater proportions of humanity. We, as citizens and as teachers, have an inescapable obligation to participate actively in the rapidly evolving technological and educational dynamics of the 1980s. However, as the Dystopians, we must be careful; as the Utopians, we must be open; and as the Socialists, we must be moral. Stasis and change within a moral framework of explicitly identified values combine to create our context for life-long learning—the process of education.

FOR CONSIDERATION

1. In what ways can the change from agriculture to industry to technology be understood as human progress? In what ways can these changes be understood as detrimental to life?

2. Consider Figure 12.2. Explain what the idea expressed in this figure means for education. Has education accelerated also? Should it? in what ways?

3. Review the textbooks you have used for classes during the past few years. How would you classify each: Utopian, Dystopian, Socialist, or what? What world view do they convey? Do they treat science and technology? If so, how?

STUDY QUESTIONS

1. Identify examples of current Socialist writers and what they advocate regarding the roles of science and technology in education.

2. Identify and debate ethical considerations that attend the reality of gene-swapping techniques.

Notes

1. Pierre Teilhard de Chardin, *The Phenomenon of Man* (New York: Harper & Row, 1959), p. 47.
2. C. P. Snow, *The Two Cultures* (London: Cambridge University Press, 1964), p. 30.
3. Auguste Comte, *System of Positive Polity* (New York: Lenox Hill, 1973).
4. Thomas Hughes, *Changing Attitudes Toward American Technology* (New York: Harper & Row, 1975).
5. Bernard Gendron, *Technology and the Human Condition* (New York: St. Martin's Press, 1977).
6. B. F. Skinner, *Walden Two* (New York: Macmillan, 1948); R. Buckminister Fuller, *Utopia or Oblivion* (New York: Bantam, 1969); C. P. Snow, *The Two Cultures* (London: Cambridge University Press, 1964); Marshall McLuhan, *Understanding Media* (New York: McGraw-Hill, 1954); Alvin Toffler, *Future Shock* (New York: Bantam, 1970); Daniel Bell, *The Coming of Post-Industrial Society* (New York: Basic Books, 1973); John Maynard Keynes, "Economic Possibilities for Our Grandchildren," in *Essays in Persuasion* (London: Macmillan, 1972); John Kenneth Galbraith, *The Affluent Society* (New York: New American Library, 1972).
7. Gerald Feinberg, *The Prometheus Project* (Garden City, N.Y.: Doubleday, 1969); Zbigniew Brzezinski, *Between Two Ages* (New York: Viking, 1970); Arthur Clarke, *Profiles of the Future* (New York: Bantam, 1964); Robert Theobald, *The Economics of Abundance* (New York: Pitman, 1970); Herman Kahn and Anthony Weiner, *Year Two Thousand* (New York: Macmillan, 1967).
8. Oswald Spengler, *Decline of the West* (New York: Knopf, 1971); George Orwell, *1984* (New York: Harcourt, Brace, 1949); Jacques Ellul, *Technological Society* (New York: Vintage, 1964); Aldous Huxley, *Brave New World* (New York: Harper & Row, 1969); Herbert Marcuse, *One Dimensional Man* (Boston: Beacon, 1964); Theodore Roszak, *The Making of a Counter-Culture* (Garden City, N.Y.: Doubleday, 1969); Charles Reich, *The Greening of America* (New York: Random House, 1970); Philip Slater, *The Pursuit of Loneliness* (Boston: Beacon, 1970).
9. Karl Marx, *Capital*, vol. 1 (New York: International, 1967); Karl Marx and Fredrich Engels, *Selected Works* (New York: International, 1968); V. I. Lenin, *Selected Works* (New York: International, 1971); Mao Tse-tung, *On Revolution and War* (New York: Doubleday, 1970).
10. "Stanford Wins Key Patent," *Milwaukee Journal*, December 4, 1980, II, p. 2.
11. Theodore Gordon *et al.*, *Report on a Long-Range Forecasting Study*, The Rand Corporation, Paper P-2982 (September 1964).
12. Maxwell Corwan, "The Development of the Brain," *Scientific American* 241 (September 1979), p. 113.

References

Bell, Daniel. *The Coming of Post-Industrial Society*. New York: Basic Books, 1973.

Brzezinski, Zbigniew. *Between Two Ages: America's Role in the Technetronic Era*. New York: Viking, 1970.

Clarke, Arthur. *Profiles of the Future*. New York: Bantam, 1964.

Comte, Auguste. *System of Positive Polity*. New York: Lenox Hill, 1973.

Corwan, Maxwell. "The Development of the Brain," *Scientific American* 241 (September 1979): 113–133.

Ellul, Jacques. *Technological Society*. New York: Vintage, 1964.

Feinberg, Gerald. *The Prometheus Project*. Garden City, N.Y.: Doubleday, 1969.

Fuller, R. Buckminster. *Utopia or Oblivion*. New York: Bantam, 1969.

Galbraith, John Kenneth. *The Affluent Society*. New York: New American Library, 1972.

Gendron, Bernard. *Technology and the Human Condition*. New York: St. Martin's Press, 1977.

Gordon, T. J., and Helmer, O. *Report on a Long-Range Forecasting Study*. The Rand Corporation. Paper P-2982. September 1964.

Hughes, Thomas Parke. *Changing Attitudes Toward American Technology*. New York: Harper & Row, 1975.

Huxley, Aldous. *Brave New World*. New York: Harper & Row, 1969.

Kahn, Herman and Wiener, Anthony J. *Year Two Thousand*. New York: Macmillan, 1967.

Keynes, John Maynard. "Economic Possibilities for Our Grandchildren." In *Essays in Persuasion*. London: Macmillan, 1972.

Lenin, V. I. *Selected Works*. New York: International, 1971.

Mao Tse-tung. *On Revolution and War*. New York: Doubleday, 1970.

Marcuse, Herbert. *One Dimensional Man*. Boston: Beacon, 1964.

Marx, Karl. *Capital*. Vol. 1. New York: International, 1967.

————, and Engels, Friedrich. *Selected Works*. New York: International, 1968.

McLuhan, Marshall. *Understanding Media*. New York: McGraw-Hill, 1964.

Milwaukee Journal. "Stanford Wins Key Patent." December 4, 1980, II, p. 2.

Nilssen, Jerome. *Our Church*. (Milwaukee) 53 (September 1980).

Orwell, George. *1984*. New York: Harcourt, Brace, 1949.

Reich, Charles. *The Greening of America*. New York: Random House, 1970.

Roszak, Theodore. *The Making of a Counter-Culture*. Garden City, N.Y.: Doubleday, 1969.

Skinner, B. F. *Walden Two*. New York: Macmillan, 1948.

————. *Beyond Freedom and Dignity*. New York: Knopf, 1971.

Slater, Philip. *The Pursuit of Loneliness*. Boston: Beacon, 1970.

Snow, C. P. *The Two Cultures*. London: Cambridge University Press, 1964.

Spengler, Oswald. *Decline of the West*. New York: Knopf, 1932.

Teich, Albert H., ed. *Technology and Man's Future*. New York: St. Martin's Press, 1977.

Teilhard de Chardin, Pierre. *The Phenomenon of Man*. New York: Harper & Row, 1959.

Theobald, Robert. *The Economics of Abundance*. New York: Pitman, 1970.

Toffler, Alvin. *Future Shock*. New York: Bantam, 1970.

Chapter 13: The School in a Multicultural Society

Introduction

While we might prefer to dwell on those common features of humanity that could unite us in the search for progress and improvement, there is considerable evidence in society and in schools that it is the differences between groups that receive the most notoriety. There are certainly long traditions in teaching that call for educators to rise above petty differences and to recognize the singularity of humanity. Attempts to overcome bias and prejudice through education are examples of this. And the human rights movement, now global in its interests, strives to look beyond racism, sexism, ethnicism, nationalism, religion, or other ideologies that require discrimination against people because of their heritages. Yet educational efforts to stress the oneness of humans are often considered flagrant idealism, fuzzy-mindedness, and unrelated to reality. Indeed, much of the literature advocating "oneness" is often filled with platitudes that do not seem very meaningful in light of cross-burnings, racial or sexual harassment, ethnic graffiti, and other items reported daily in the news.

From a different perspective, the effort to educate for a common humanity is seen as another example of cultural imperialism. This view holds that advocates of oneness have a particular kind of "humanity" that they want to impose upon others. This is the idea of hegemony, where the dominant group in a society controls the values and behaviors of minority groups and expects them to conform. The melting pot idea of earlier America is often criticized because some of its purpose was to force immigrants and minority people to accept the dominant culture. The idea included having the schools act to "Americanize" immigrants.

More recently, the melting pot has been seen as a myth, and there has been increasing interest in establishing and enhancing the diversity among groups in American society. Each group is rediscovering its roots and placing pressure on the schools to express more clearly the separateness of groups, their contributions, and their different customs and traditions.

Once again, the theme of stasis and change is evident. In this chapter, we explore ideas of diversity as they relate to national origin, language and other cultural factors, discrimination, and legal interpretations. We consider these in terms of schooling practice and potential. What is change in one period can become the stasis of the next. If the melting pot idea is held now by those who want to provide stasis in society and schooling, and change is represented by those who seek diversity, what happens as diversity and separateness become more static—the mainstream of ideas? Is there then hope for a larger scale change that avoids cultural imperialism but breaks down the borders between groups, or is that too naive?

Functionalist and
Critical Perspectives

There is another way to examine the current movement toward multicultural education. As suggested in earlier chapters, the functionalist perspective incorporates the concept of social order and functional relationships among social institutions. Critical views see conflict as basic, with social class disparities as paramount. In considering the information provided in this chapter, you may want to analyze melting pot and multicultural educational activities first from a functionalist perspective and then from a critical perspective. For example, ethnic studies programs can be seen as "functional" to the extent that they fit into the already-existing educational institutions: they have courses, give credit, offer credentials for those who complete, and fall within the traditional values of the society. They are "dysfunctional" when they deviate by stimulating radical activities, protesting institutional norms, or operating outside of the traditional institutions.

A functionalist explanation of the movement to ethnic studies could include the idea that it represents a step in the relatively orderly development from discrimination to equality. A critical view of multicultural education might see it as an example of diverting attention from the more basic class conflict to the more trivial concerns with national origin or derivation. Continued domination of the working masses occurs because of the focus on divergent cultural groups rather than on the exploitation of the lower classes. People become more concerned with identification as Irish or black or Jewish or female than with the larger struggle for justice. And when schools get involved in multicultural programs they avoid the socioeconomic issues and basic conflicts, while they emphasize group heroes, holidays, and historical events.

Examination of multicultural education from functionalist and critical perspectives should provide some insights into the relation between school and society in this aspect of education.

Cultural Diversity in America

It is estimated that at the beginning of the sixteenth century there were approximately one million Native Americans of some 360 language groups living on the continent of North America. European exploration and settlement led to conflicts with these Native American groups as their homelands were appropriated by the technologically more powerful invaders. The Native Americans were frequently annihilated or driven inland as the volume of European immigrants increased. Native Americans were made wards of the United States government in 1871 after more than 350 years of conflict with white settlers, including Cortez's conquest of the Aztecs in Mexico in 1518; the Seminole wars in Florida; the Black Hawk war in Illinois; the slaughter of the Plains Indians' primary source of food, shelter, and clothing—the buffaloes; and the impositions of the reservation system. In 1924, Native Americans were granted American citizenship, a right that had been withheld from them for nearly a century-and-a-half.

A black slave, Estevanico, who had been marooned with a party of Spaniards on the Florida peninsula in 1528, succeeded in walking to central New Spain (Mexico) in 1536. Because of his knowledge of Native American ways he was sent back north again as a guide for Coronado into what is now the American Southwest. Estevanico disappeared while scouting ahead of the main party, and he was killed by the Hawikuh about fifteen miles southwest of Zuni, New Mexico, in 1541.[1] Seventy-eight years later, in 1619, twenty black Africans were purchased by settlers in Jamestown, Virginia, from a Dutch man-of-war. While it appears that these blacks were treated as indentured servants similar to many whites, their color set them apart in the predominantly English ethnic context. The growth of black slavery was an outgrowth of and a stimulus for the development of the plantation system of agriculture in the South. This system rapidly expanded after the invention of the cotton gin in 1793. There were approximately 750,000 blacks in the nation at the time of the first census in 1790; some 90 percent of them were concentrated in the South. Table 13.1 presents the growth of the black population but its decline in proportion to total populations in the United States from 1790 until 1980.

Black Africans, who had been forced to come to America as slaves, came from an estimated 163 different language groups and cultural backgrounds.

Records regarding immigration were not kept until 1820 and until as late as 1907 these records were limited in scope. Thus only rough approximations of total immigration into this nation exist. The Bureau of the Census estimate is provided in Table 13.2.

The numbers of immigrants from particular countries, as they appear in Table 13.2, must be suspect, owing to changes in national boundaries during the reporting period and the fact that before 1906 the enumeration was made on the basis of the immigrant's place of embarkation rather than on his or her last permanent place of residence or nationality.

It is convenient to look at immigration in three periods:

1. *The Period from 1783 to 1830.* In 1790 the white population of the United States was predominantly of English stock. There were comparatively few Germans, Irish, and Dutch, and even fewer French, Canadians, Belgians, Swiss, Mexicans, and Swedes. Between 1783 and 1830 about 10,000 immigrants came to the United States each year.

2. *The Period from 1830 to 1882.* This period was marked by a great increase in immigration. Available land west of the Mississippi and rapid industrialization created demands for workers to work in factories and to do non-mechanized jobs, to build roads, railroads, and canals, and to build cities and towns and farms. During these fifty-two years, English, Irish, German, and Scandinavian immigrants predominated. The Irish came in

Table 13.1:
Growth of the Black Population Since 1790

Census Year	Number of Blacks	Percentage of Total Population
1790	757,208	19.3
1800	1,002,037	18.9
1810	1,377,808	19.0
1820	1,771,656	18.4
1830	2,328,642	18.1
1840	2,873,648	16.8
1850	3,638,808	15.7
1860	4,441,830	14.1
1870	4,880,009	12.7
1880	6,530,793	13.1
1890	7,488,676	11.9
1900	8,333,940	11.6
1910	9,827,763	10.7
1920	10,463,131	9.9
1930	11,891,143	9.7
1940	12,865,518	9.8
1950	15,044,937	9.9
1960	18,871,831	10.5
1970	22,580,289	11.5
1980	26,500,000	11.7

Source: U.S. Bureau of the Census. Negroes in the United States, 1920–1932, 1–2, Sixteenth Census of the United States, Population, II, 19, plus World Almanac data to 1980.

especially large numbers after 1840, when the failure of their one crop, the potato, caused famine and resultant widespread suffering throughout Ireland. For the most part the Irish settled in the tenements of American cities, in slum conditions similar to those in which southern and eastern European immigrants were to live later in the century. In contrast to the

Table 13.2:
Immigrants by Country of Origin: 1820–1963

Country	Total, 144 Years 1820–1963	Country	Total, 144 Years 1820–1963
All Countries	42,702,328	Portugal	293,420
Europe	34,896,219	Spain	188,974
Austria & Hungary	4,280,863	Sweden	1,255,296
		U.S.S.R.	3,344,998
Belgium	191,981	Yugoslavia	69,834
Czechoslovakia	129,704	Asia	1,160,758
Denmark	354,331	China	411,585
Finland	28,358	Japan	338,087
France	698,188	America	6,218,631
Germany	6,798,313	Canada & Newfoundland	3,697,649
Great Britain	3,844,058		
Greece	499,465	Mexico	1,291,922
Ireland	4,693,009	West Indies	684,175
Italy	5,017,625	Africa	53,186
Netherlands	338,722	Australia & New Zealand	84,468
Norway	843,867		
Poland	451,010	Pacific Islands	22,332

Source: U.S. Bureau of the Census, *Statistical Abstract of the United States*, 1964, p. 94.

Irish, the Germans and Scandinavians clung less tenaciously to the cities, many of them settling on farms in the Midwest. The German immigration reached its peak between 1880 and 1892, when more than 1,770,000 Germans were admitted; the Scandinavian immigration reached its height between 1881 and 1890, when more than 656,000 were admitted.

While industrial employers generally eagerly sought the cheap labor provided by this heterogeneous flow of immigrants, differences in culture often created conflicts, for example, between Protestants and Catholics, or Germans and the Irish.

3. *1882 — A Turning Point.* The year 1882 represents a turning point in the history of American immigration. It marked the climax of the movement of migrants from northern and western Europe to the United States and the beginning of the large-scale movement of migrants from southern and eastern Europe. It was also the time of the passage of the Chinese Exclusion Act, and it inaugurated the beginning of federal control of immigration in general. Included in the so-called new migration were the Italians, Poles, Jews, Greeks, Portuguese, Russians, and a varied assortment of other Slavs. Within the span of some twenty years there was a complete reversal in the proportions of immigrants from northern and western, and southern and eastern Europe. Whereas, in 1882, 87 percent of immigrants came from the former area and only 13 percent from the latter, by 1907 the corresponding figures were 13 percent and 81 percent, respectively. Italy's 2 million immigrants during the first decade of the 1900s was greater than the 1.9 million immigrants from all the northern and western European nations combined. New conflicts — conflicts between the "old" and the "new" immigrants arose. The "new" were considered less desirable than the "old." The new PIGS (*P*oles, *I*talians, *G*reeks, *S*lavs) were depricated. The "old" immigrants had been predominately Protestants except for some German and Irish Catholics. The "new" immigrants were predominately Catholic, Greek Orthodox, or Jewish.

Figure 13.1 graphically demonstrates the effects of economic and political factors on immigration between 1820 and 1960.

By the end of the 1800s America's open spaces were filling in. The better land of the West was occupied and, with the turn of the century, sentiment in favor of restricting immigration became intense. In 1907 Congress authorized an immigration commission to investigate immigration. The mood was to restrict. Categorical restrictions had been enacted earlier: Congress had enacted a law that generally prohibited Chinese immigration and a head tax on immigrants had been imposed in 1882; contract labor had been prohibited in 1884; insane persons, beggars, and anarchists were excluded in 1903. Japanese immigration was curtailed in 1907, and in 1917 a literacy test was added to immigration requirements. Finally, in a period of post-World War I isolationistic sentiment, the 1921 Immigration Act curtailed the volume of immigration and set a quota system to afford each nation an immigration allowance of

Figure 13.1 One Hundred and Forty-One Years of Immigration into the United States

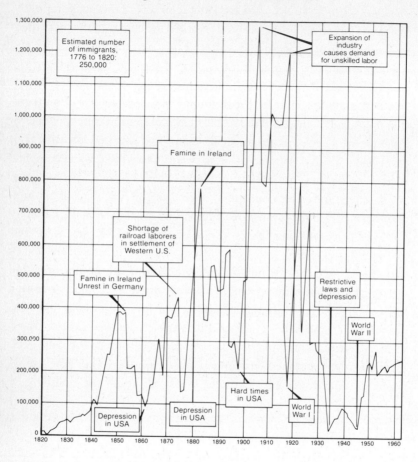

3 percent of its foreign-born in the United States, as indicated by the 1910 census. But this quota was quickly changed in 1924 to allow 2 percent per year based on the 1890 census count. This effectively favored the "old" immigrant groups. The national-origins quota system was replaced in 1968 by an overall ceiling of 120,000 immigrants being permitted to enter the United States with no single nation being allowed more than 20,000 immigrant visas.

The volume of immigrants and their cultural-linguistic variety in combination with the variety of Native American cultural-linguistic groups have created an extraordinarily heterogeneous context within which social and educational policies have developed in the United States. Policies regarding language(s) other than English in schools constitute one social issue that remains central to our consideration of the school as a multicultural system.

Linguistic Diversity and Educational Practices

Non-English and/or bilingual culture often dominated instruction and life styles in America in the nearly 300 years prior to 1900. During the 1700s school instruction throughout Pennsylvania, Maryland, Virginia, and the Carolinas was often exclusively in German. In one district in Wisconsin, one-third of the textbook funds were specified to be spent for textbooks in German; in others, school boards chose to hire only German-speaking teachers and frequently local school district records were kept in German.[2]

At the time that California became a state in 1850, 18 percent of all education in the state was private and Catholic. These private schools primarily served pupils of Hispanic cultural background. The pupils were taught in the Spanish language under the direction of the *padres*. Initially, these schools were state supported.[3]

The Cherokees had an educational system in the 1800s that produced a 90 percent literate Cherokee language population and used bilingual materials to such an extent that Oklahoma Cherokees had a higher English language literacy level than the white populations of either Texas or Arkansas.[4]

The state of New Mexico's educational laws in 1884 included the following: "Each county shall be and constitute a school district in which shall be taught . . . reading, writing . . . in either English or Spanish or both, as the directors may determine."[5]

By the turn of the twentieth century the advent of compulsory attendance laws for public schools, the elimination of public funding for church-related schools, and the dominance of the "old" immigrants combined to engender a nationwide imposition of English-only instructional policies. The "old" immigrants' assimilationist preference that unitary Americanism be created was sanctioned at the highest levels of government in the jingoistic aftermath of the Spanish-American War of 1898. Theodore Roosevelt represented this assimilationist view as follows:

> . . . any man who comes here . . . must adopt the institutions of the United States, and therefore he must adopt the language which is now the

native tongue of our people, no matter what the several strains of blood in our veins may be. It would be not merely a misfortune but a crime to perpetuate differences of language in this country. . . . We should provide for every immigrant by day schools for the young and night schools for the adult, the chance to learn English; and if after say five years he has not learned English, he should be sent back to the land from whence he came.[6]

In imposing English-only instructional policies, many states went so far as to pass statutes that formally outlawed the use of other-than-English for instruction except in foreign language classes. Nebraska, for example, promulgated "An Act Relating to the Teaching of Foreign Languages in the State of Nebraska" that stated:

Section 1. No person, individually or as a leader, shall, in any private, denominational, parochial or public school, teach any subject to any person in any language other than the English language. . . . Section 2. Languages, other than the English language, may be taught as languages only after a pupil shall have attained and successfully passed the eighth grade. . . .[7]

A similar English-only foreign language school act was in effect in the territory of Hawaii in the 1920s.

A teacher named Meyer was tried and convicted in Nebraska of the charge that on May 25, 1920, while an instructor in Zion Parochial School, he unlawfully taught the subject of reading in the German language to Raymond Parpart, a child of ten years, who had not attained and successfully passed the eighth grade. Meyer appealed to the United States Supreme Court.

The Court reasoned,

That the State may do much, go very far, indeed, in order to improve the quality of its citizens, physically, mentally and morally, is clear; but the individual has certain fundamental rights which must be respected. The protection of the Constitution extends to all, to those who speak other languages as well as to those born with English on the tongue. Perhaps it would be highly advantageous if all had ready understanding of our ordinary speech, but this cannot be coerced by methods which conflict with the Constitution—a desirable end cannot be promoted by prohibited means.

The Supreme Court concluded that "the statute as applied is arbitrary and without reasonable relation to any end within the competency of the State."[8]

The *Meyer* v. *Nebraska* decision precluded any level of government abrogating any parent's opportunity to select the language in which his or her child would be taught. It did not, however, address the issue of access or availability of other-than English as a medium of instruction. The *Lau v. Nichols* decision of the Supreme Court upheld the right of non-English-speaking students to educational programs designed to meet their language-skill needs. It did not, however, stipulate a remedy such as either teaching in Chinese or teaching English as a second language.

Lau v. Nichols was brought by Chinese public-school students against the San Francisco Unified School District in 1970. The parties did not dispute the critical facts that 1,790 Chinese students received no services designed to meet their linguistic needs and that these students suffered educationally. What was in question was whether non-English-speaking students receive an equal educational opportunity when instructed in a language they cannot understand.

The plaintiffs claimed that the absence of programs designed to meet the linguistic needs of such students violated both Title VI of the Civil Rights Act of 1964 and the Equal Protection Clause of the Fourteenth Amendment to the Constitution. They urged that equality in education goes beyond providing the same buildings and books to all students and includes intangible factors. Because they could not understand the language of the classroom, the Chinese students argued, they were deprived of even a minimally adequate education, let alone an education equal to that of other children. They claimed that their educational exclusion was a function of state action since school attendance was compulsory, the use of the English language was mandated by the state, and fluency in English was a prerequisite to high-school graduation. The difference in treatment, the plaintiffs contended, amounted to invidious discrimination because it affected a distinct national-origin group. They argued that the Constitution prohibited withholding from them the means of comprehending the language of instruction.

All these claims were rejected by the federal district court. The court ruled that the students' rights to an equal educational opportunity had been satisfied by their receipt of the same education made available on the same terms and conditions to the other tens of thousands of students in the San Francisco Unified School District. The Ninth Circuit Court of Appeals affirmed the district court decision, with one dissent. That court ruled that the uniform use of English does not constitute unlawful discrimination and declared that English-language instruction must be paramount in the schooling process.

The petitioners then presented their case to the Supreme Court. The Court considered whether students who do not understand English receive equal treatment when English is the sole medium of instruction and no additional steps are taken to teach them English. It reasoned: "Under these state-imposed standards there is no equality of treatment merely by providing students with the same facilities, textbooks, teachers, and curriculum; for students who do not understand English are effectively foreclosed from any meaningful education."[9]

The lower courts had ruled that offering identical services to all students is sufficient to meet the strictures of the Equal Protection Clause and implicitly of Title VI, even though students actually received disparate benefits because of significant differences in their opportunities to take advantage of those services. Rejecting this analysis, the Supreme Court relied on the Title VI regulations and guidelines that speak to equality in the offering and receipt of benefits: "It seems obvious that the Chinese-speaking minority receives fewer benefits than the English-speaking majority from respondents' school system which denies them a meaningful opportunity to participate in the educational program."[10] It may appear that the language question in American education has come full circle from education in various languages in the early 1800s to a fierce commitment to assimilate nearly everyone into an English-speaking-only educational setting in the early 1900s and back to various languages of instruction in the 1980s. But the debate regarding what Teddy Roosevelt called "adopting the institutions of the United States" continues.

Societal Good and
the School Curriculum

Education is an attempt by the community to form beliefs and habits that are consonant with its highest standards of knowledge and best ideals of behavior. True as this statement is, it does not mean that schools are properly directed toward indoctrination or toward the preservation of the existing culture or any one political point of view. To hold that schools are to promote one, or a few, officially approved view, or views, is to hold to the totalitarian position, and that position is inconsistent with a democratic society. On the other hand, it is as unrealistic as it is evasive to hold that the curriculum and teachers must hold fast to neutrality whenever a controversial issue is presented, leaving the matter for the individual to decide. Diversity exists within America's democratic community, and it gives rise to controversial issues. A school is supposed to prepare the student for life in the American democracy, and a school that failed openly to explore controversial questions would be a failure. It would not be a school at all, but more akin to a prison.

An indispensable function of the curriculum of the common school is to educate for good citizenship. In the American democracy this means education that is directed toward producing a mentality in all students such that they can distinguish among alternative values and can critically evaluate values and rationally choose their own. It is education directed toward achieving a responsible freedom. Specifically it means that the educational process must itself respect the principles of the American constitution while teaching those principles, especially the principles and procedures of the Bill of Rights. An educational curriculum based on these principles is not a catechism, not indoctrination in the obnoxious sense. This curriculum allows for differences of opinions and includes a fair amount of discussion about political theory, alternative economic systems, government, contemporary affairs, and literature. Its primary goal is the realization of the social purposes of American democratic society as they have been set forth in the Bill of Rights, which constitutionally protects diversity.[11]

As earlier chapters have shown, however, there is a strong tendency for schools to be agents of stasis, trying to preserve and protect certain ideas and groups in society and restraining any criticism of them. The concept of social change inherent in the United States Declaration of Independence, and permitted in the Bill of Rights through the protection of dissent and free speech, has been hampered by the continuing pressure to conform to socially approved goals, values, knowledge, and behavior. This tension between stasis and change is clearly evident in the treatment of multicultural factors in schooling.

CULTURAL PLURALISM AS AN EMERGING PRIORITY IN AMERICAN EDUCATION: CHANGING CONCEPTIONS OF EDUCATION

There is no scholarly agreement as to a universally accepted definition of multicultural education, although central tenets of ethnic legitimacy and cultural diversity pervade most definitions. The population of this country has always reflected cultural diversity. Prior to the arrival of Europeans in the sixteenth and seventeenth centuries, Native Americans consisted of in excess of 360 different language and cultural groups ranging from the Timucua in the Southeast to the Nootka in the Northwest, from the Apache in the Southwest to the Abnaki in the Northeast and the Menomini and the Winnebago in the central portion of our part of the continent of North America. The Native Americans met Spaniards and Africans who came north from what is now Mexico into the Southwest and they met Russians in our Northwest.[12] The English became dominant in the New England and southern Atlantic regions. The Scottish, Dutch, Germans, French, Danes, Swedes, Welsh, and Africans were all early arrivals during our colonial period. Religious diversity overlaid ethnic diversity to multiply the bases for identity and, at times, antipathy. The American system of public education evolved with its early roots firmly embedded in this cultural complexity.

Designing and refining a system of education to meet the needs of a culturally diverse population has been a recurring issue in American education. When the country was founded more than 200 years ago, the Founding Fathers envisioned a nation oriented toward the welfare of its people. Life, liberty, and the pursuit of happiness were inalienable rights, and to secure these rights, one of the major delivery systems that was developed was education. Education was considered necessary for the promotion of the moral, social, and economic development of the citizenry and the proper functioning of the new democratic system. The institution of a system of education, however, posed a problem, based on the realization that the citizenry was a diverse group, despite its predominantly western European origins at the time, and that this diversity encompassed class, caste, and ethnicity.

Three distinct approaches to solving the problem arose: a dual approach; a plural approach; and the focus of this chapter, a multicultural approach. The first approach, based on class and later on race, lasted with legal sanction until the Supreme Court's *Brown* decision of 1954. This approach, geared to assimilation, recognized the existence of a single dominant cultural criterion, the Anglo-Saxon. The other two approaches recognized the importance of the Anglo-Saxon ethos but also gave weight to the existence and impact of other cultures. Though both pluralistic and multicultural approaches are currently operative, the multicultural approach appears to be gaining the support of educators. The pluralistic approach is more inclined toward separatism, while the multicultural approach is more inclined toward integration.

The issue of cultural diversity during the early period in the development of the country was addressed in other than direct cultural terms. That the question of culture *vis-à-vis* education was more implicit than explicit may be due to (1) the cultural hegemony of northern and western European settlers, (2) inherited leanings toward those European traditions as preferred over others, plus the fact that the (3) existing pedagogy had not clearly established a connection between culture and education, and (4) the concept of public education had not fully evolved.

SOCIAL-CLASS BASIS OF SCHOOLING

Within these parameters, cultural diversity was addressed in terms of social class. Thus, the first phase of the dual education system emerged to meet the needs of two distinct social classes within the society. For the upper class, Latin grammar schools were designed to train scholars to provide intellectual leadership in the clergy and other professions. For the lower class, elementary schools and apprenticeship systems were instituted to provide the rudiments of learning associated with religion and the development of useful skills.

A dual system based on social class was consistent with the work ethic embraced by most of the settlers. From the vantage point of the upper class, the system did not "contribute to the growth of a poverty or vagabond class that would be a threat to the more stable elements of society."[13] For the lower class, the system appeared to help them feel that they were contributing, productive members of society and that the possibility existed for their achieving upward social and economic mobility. In addition to recognizable differences in social class, religious differences existed. The major educational issue was the problem of religious versus public control, instruction, and financing of education.

When an awareness of cultural diversity began to appear, it was reflected in issue-oriented, not people-oriented, concerns. Social class, the separation of church and state, and economic development dominated educational concerns. This attitude is plausible when one considers the fact that the population, generally, represented the Anglo-Saxon Protestant ethos common in England, Germany, and Scandinavia, with the Irish constituting a somewhat marginal group.

SLAVE EXCLUSION

The most visible "troublesome presence" was the slave, whose education was not only declared illegal but believed to be impossible.[14] Consequently, cultural diversity, as presently conceived, evoked little concern because the dominant group was representative of the established culture criterion. This belief was supported by the influential works of Spencer and others who placed European culture, especially northern and western European culture, at the top of the cultural hierarchy.[15]

American society and its cultural patterns were made all the more heterogeneous during the later part of the nineteenth century when new groups of immigrants appeared on the American scene. The Caucasians were either assimilated into the mainstream or given a place of "refuge" to live out their lives without undo interference from messengers of progress. The free blacks were "learning their places" and being relegated to them by the rise of segregated institutions. Economic development remained the major American interest and both the gradual transformation of an agrarian South and the rapid industrialization of the North created a demand for cheap labor.

Some of the "old" immigrants left the general labor force by becoming members of either the middle or upper class. Between this group and the less fortunate trouble erupted. These eruptions were based on "episodic economic decline, cruel conflicts between management and labor, and gross exploitation."[16] It was into this state of affairs that the new immigrants from eastern and southern Europe arrived. They were welcomed as new sources of cheap labor by the industrialists and subjected to hostile opposition by organized labor. In addition, they were different. Differing from the earlier Anglo-Saxons, the new immigrants tended to settle in self-contained communities that perpetuated the language, customs, practices, and standards of their home lands. A far higher rate of illiteracy was evidenced among these later immigrants causing political and educational problems of the first magnitude in the cities where they settled.[17]

RACISM IN EDUCATION

Southern European immigrants to the United States were labeled inferior and placed in somewhat the same category as blacks. "The immigrants who arrived after 1880 struck the American imagination as a dark, swarthy, inferior race; they were drawn into the orbit of the associations linked to 'black.'"[18] Many of the racist beliefs about blacks were expressed about the new immigrants. Though less obvious, violations of the civil rights of this group were widespread. The passage of the Thirteenth, Fourteenth, and Fifteenth Amendments of the Constitution provided protection for the rights of the new immigrants as well as the blacks. The Civil Rights Act of 1875 made similar provisions.

Because blacks were more numerous, more aware of the hostility of whites, and more distinctively colored, they were the most overtly harrassed and oppressed minority group in the United States. Efforts for redress sought through judicial or legislative action were easily circumvented and often reversed. The Civil Rights Act of 1875 was rescinded in principle and practice as soon as the federal troops left the South and was replaced with Jim Crow laws that stood until the latter part of the twentieth century. The doctrine of "separate but equal," based on the decision in *Plessy* v. *Ferguson* (1896), sanctioned the existence of segregation, which maintained its strongest bastion in the area of education. A dual system of education based on race became entrenched in America.

The "separate but equal" educational policy was most obvious in black/white terms. However, its effect was subtly exerted on other nonwestern European groups. For example, in the controversy over universal education, little account was taken of the long tradition of highly developed educational systems in the native lands of some of the immigrants. From an extremist point of view, a system of universal education would not only lead to "mixing" but would breed immorality and related pathologies ascribed to inferior peoples. From a more liberal point of view, it was argued that universal education should not be handled through public schools. Reactions to both points of view led to the development of a number of exclusionary institutions and devices: for example, private schools and quota systems.

When public schools were finally established, the overt and covert belief in the inferiority inherent in differences developed, consciously or unconsciously, into institutional racism. Two separate school systems were maintained, one for whites and one for blacks. Schools in other predominantly ethnic areas were only slightly comparable to those for whites. The public sector was concerned with education as the vehicle for transmitting the cultural heritage, which by then had been clearly defined in terms of the Anglo-Saxon middle class. Therefore, education became the major delivery system for "instant Americanization."

What developed was a mass system of public indoctrination. That system had two functions: first, to create a lower laboring class that adhered sufficiently to the values and myths of the American ruling class so that it was not likely to question its place in society; second, selection, the selection of those few, as needed, who possessed behavior and appearance to be adapted into the expanding middle class.[19] This system espoused cultural indoctrination leading to cultural assimilation.

In short, the ethnic/cultural question was a private matter for the immigrants who were unwilling to assimilate and the blacks who were unable to assimilate. Aware of existing inequities in the educational system but powerless to change them, these groups sought to improve the quality of the education they were receiving by establishing separate schools, attending parochial schools, and suggesting curriculum modification. Immigrant groups established private schools and maintained them by endowment. Black education received institutional support from the philanthropy of such persons as Andrew Carnegie, Collis P. Huntington, Julia Rosenwald, John D. Rockefeller, and Caroline and Olivia Stokes, who were prominent supporters of industrial and agricultural education.[20] Elementary education for blacks in rural areas was largely supported by the Jeanes Fund. Denominational groups established schools, with the Catholic school system being the strongest. Jewish groups provided religious and cultural studies during nonschool hours.

THE MELTING POT

Schools established to meet the needs of blacks and other culturally different groups were forced to exist under the aegis of the dual educational system. To achieve educational respectability or to receive accreditation, the curriculum of the schools had to conform to the cultural ethos of the dominant group. The culture of other groups—their language, history, religion, among other subjects—was treated as electives. In extreme instances "it became unlawful in many states [until declared illegal by the Supreme Court in the Nebraska case] to teach a foreign language."[21] Whether education was obtained in public, private, or parochial schools, the ultimate goal was Americanization. In short, the educational system implemented the melting pot theory.[22]

By the beginning of the twentieth century, the national effort was directed not only to building America but to creating Americans. Israel Zangwill's play, "The Melting Pot" (1909), provided the ideological label for the concept. The melting pot idea was consistent with the growing American nativism. "America is God's crucible. . . . The real American will be a fusion of all races."[23] Commager, as late as the middle of the century, pointed to the service provided by the public schools in bringing about the fusion. As he noted, each decade after 1840 saw from 2 to 8 million immigrants pour into America. No other people had ever absorbed such large and varied racial stocks so rapidly or so successfully. It was the public school that proved itself the most efficacious of all agencies of Americanization—Americanization not only of the children but, through them, of the parents as well.[24]

Though the process of Americanization appeared to work, the myth of the melting pot was gradually being proved untenable. "The American melting pot did achieve reality in some instances—initially for the western European immigrant and later for his eastern European counterpart, but for the non-European, non-white immigrant, the melting pot had little meaning."[25] To deal with the problem of the "unmeltable" immigrant, a series of immigration acts were passed. These acts set immigration quotas, restricted immigration on the basis of ethnic origin, and, in the case of Asiatics, excluded them from citizenship. These acts reflected the pervasive mood of nationalism that swept the country. They were removed from the statute books by the passage of the Reform Immigration Act during the administration of President Lyndon B. Johnson.

The problem of ethnic and cultural diversity no longer could remain either a private matter or a matter of fusion. The American population was a unique combination of diverse cultural strains. A part of and apart from the idealized American, the immigrant and migrant elements of the population settled into ethnic and cultural enclaves. The meeting of the various cultural elements, however, produced conflict instead of cohesion. As a result, cultural unity, not cultural diversity, emerged as the prevailing idealized value. A "We-They" syndrome developed.[26]

PURPOSES OF MULTICULTURAL EDUCATION

Voices in America like those of John Dewey, Julius Drachsler, and Horace Kallen were attempting to create among Americans an awareness of the richness of cultural diversity.[27] Possibly, an earlier voice was that of Booker T. Washington, who in the highly controversial Atlanta Exposition Address, used a figure of speech that, divested of the external constraints imposed by black/white relationships of the time, might well have foreshadowed cultural pluralism. Washington suggested that "we can be as separate as fingers, yet one as the hand in all things essential to mutual progress."[28] In a more universal context, the fingers could represent the distinctive ethnic cultural concerns of each group and the hand all things that operate in the general society for its enhancement and the improvement of the human condition.

Though it may be argued that interest in cultural diversity was aborted by the national concerns of the first half of the twentieth century, the fact remains that the events of the period led to greater cultural unity and greater disaffection with the mythical American dream. World War I and a great depression dramatized a cyclic movement within the country. After great bursts of patriotic endeavor in support of the shibboleth "to make the world safe for democracy," the status quo—racism, poverty, and discrimination—was resumed.

Blacks and other non-Caucasians were subjected to discriminatory practices under the court-upheld "separate but equal" doctrine. "There was nothing particularly secretive about . . . discrimination; it was an accepted way of life."[29] This way of life was, indeed, incompatible with a country that had established itself as a world power and the capstone of democracy.

It was, therefore, no mere coincidence that overt signs of disaffection and unrest began to surface from among minority groups. Reaction to the unrest was "the development of a different sense of nationality: a concept accommodating and dignifying subnationalities and contributing cultures."[30] Reflecting this new awareness, American society gradually began to move in the direction of pluralism as

> an ideology on the value level giving as an alternative to the "One Great American Culture" idea the "Many Great American Subcultures" program of pluralism, without any indication of how we are going to provide equal access to the sources of power for all or how we are going to learn each others' ways of interacting and communicating.[31]

Conditions in America in the years before and after World War II brought into sharp focus both the issues of interaction and inclusion in power. Education, reflecting the concerns of the larger society, took cues from industry and the behavioral and social scientists and developed a growing interest in intergroup education. Much of the substantive work in this area may be attributed to the endeavors of Leland Bradford and Kenneth Benne, who were primarily responsible for the development of human relations training, and to Hilda Taba, who was one of the strong advocates of intergroup education in the public schools. Though the initial target population was blacks, the results of much of the related research were applicable to other racial and ethnic groups.

Concomitant with the interest in intergroup education was an interest in the education of the disadvantaged. Again, much of the related literature dealt with the effects of deprivation and racism on blacks. Early research in the area was oriented, almost exclusively, to the pathology of blacks. Later reseach documented the fact that the disadvantaged were as racially and ethnically diverse as the American population itself. More than 15 percent of the total population was "disadvantaged," when the term was redefined to include "all persons who suffer from social and economic discrimination at the hands of the majority of the society."[32] Constituting the disadvantaged were the majority of blacks, Mexican-Americans, Puerto Ricans, Appalachian whites, and reservation Indians, all from largely rural backgrounds. Though, historically, members of these groups have been disadvantaged, it was not until they migrated in large numbers to urban industrial centers that the disadvantage became obvious. The poor had been hidden in rural areas. The two major facets of the problem were the inability to adapt to the cultural ethos of the new community and the inability to adapt to the demands of a new technology. Much research pointed to education as the most viable solution.

It would appear that the civil rights movement served as a catalyst for other racial, ethnic, and cultural groups. The movement engendered a new pride in ethnic and cultural heritages, created an awareness of the disparity of power and control, and called attention to the "culture of the powerless." In short, American culture could no longer be adequately defined as dual, either on the basis of social class or race, or on an ethnic or cultural basis. The dual concept overtly admitted the existence of a "superior" culture. From a more liberal stance, it subtly implies the existence of a "superior" culture, by juxtaposing other cultures with it on a continuum in rank order.

From Duality to Multiplicity

In terms of the educational system, the dual approach was proved to be no longer feasible. It was legally abolished by the decision in *Brown* v. *the Board of Education* (1954). Though many states resisted the change and the controversy still rages over related issues, the dual educational system has been proved incompatible with the contemporary cultural ethos. In its stead, pluralism has been embraced and implemented by a proliferation of hastily conceived, and often ineffectively implemented, ethnic studies programs that not only fostered ethnic group ethnocentrism but led to power struggles between ethnic groups. Few of the programs evolved beyond what Sizemore classifies as stage two, nationalism in the Power Inclusion Model.[33] The programs, operating adjunct to the educational program of the sponsoring institution, represented what Larry Cuban called "educational enclaves . . . without substantive changes."[34] The period of the seventies showed a decline in the number of ethnic studies programs, which appears to support Patterson's pluralistic fallacy: "Emphasis on group diversity and group tolerance . . . fails to recognize a basic paradox in human interaction: the greater the diversity and cohesiveness of groups in a society, the smaller the diversity and personal autonomy of individuals in that society."[35]

Events of the past two decades have called for a re-examination of the concept of cultural pluralism. The larger society questions not only its efficacy but its reality as an achievable goal. Ethnic and cultural groups are becoming increasingly diverse within their own ranks. The dynamic underlying the proliferation of "cultures" within homogeneous ethnic and racial groups is the individual. As the individual achieves what James Banks calls ethnic literacy, he discovers that his identity is a composite of several "cultures," ethnicity being only one. It is possible that, at one and the same time, the individual interacts with the black culture, the culture of poverty, the youth culture, and the urban culture. The central question is one of balance, that is, to what extent can our society function with many "cultures" within it and yet maintain a common ethos?

Multicultural Education

Americans are beginning to realize that, like the country itself, they are multi-cultural, not only by racial and cultural mix but by identification with mutual needs, interests, and concerns. It is to this sense of identification that education must be developed. It must function within a changing social context in which people are aware of and sensitive to cultural diversity and, at the same time, it must realize that all cultures interact with and may have implicit mutualities with all others. Education must recognize the importance of educating individuals in terms of human mutualities. This type of behavior can develop only when cultural differences are understood as different vantage points from which experiences are viewed, neither view being absolute or mutually exclusive.

To this end, multicultural education is an imperative for the American educational system. Multicultural populations, though most dense in urban areas, exist throughout the country. The schools, therefore, must concern themselves with the preparation of individuals to live in a society of varied races, cultures, and life styles, each different but interdependent. Despite this fact, educational systems continue to vacillate between ethnic and/or cultural studies and cultural pluralism. Each approach has its merits, but each sanctions a degree of separateness that is contrary to the multicultural realities of society.

Philosophically, multicultural education should have as its focus the individual in a culturally pluralistic society. Ethnicity and culture, though integral parts of the individual's identity, must be viewed more broadly than as mere labels of group membership. Individuals are developing human beings, and the dynamics of human development involves interactions that are transcultural and transethnic. Multicultural education must address itself to the student who as an individual happens to be a member of a cultural or ethnic group. On the wider continuum of American society, the basic interaction is between individuals who perceive mutual needs and goals, sharing them in the process of self-actualization.

NO ONE MODEL AMERICAN

The efforts of past and present-day theorists have produced numerous programs designed to promote cultural diversity in education. As a spin-off, many conceptualizations of multicultural education have emerged. The literature is replete with definitions that reflect the coexistence of cultures. Among the more definitive delineations are the following:

Multicultural education is education that values cultural diversity. Multicultural education rejects the view that schools should seek to melt away cultural differences or the view that schools merely tolerate cultural pluralism. Instead, multicultural education affirms that schools should be oriented toward the cultural enrichment of all children and youth through programs rooted to the preservation and extension of cultural alternatives. Multicultural education recognizes cultural diversity as a fact of life in American society, and it affirms that this cultural diversity is a valuable resource that should be preserved and extended. It affirms that major educational institutions should strive to preserve this diversity. Education for cultural pluralism includes four major thrusts: (1) the teaching of values that support cultural diversity and individual uniqueness; (2) the encouragement of the qualitative expansion of existing cultures and their incorporation into the mainstream of American socioeconomic and political life; (3) the support of explorations in alternative and emerging life styles; and (4) the encouragement of multiculturalism, multilingualism, and multidialectism.

A state of equal coexistence in a mutually supportive relationship within the framework of one nation of people of diverse cultures with significantly different patterns of belief, behavior, color, and, in many cases, with different languages requires something special: unity within the diversity. Each person must be aware of and secure in his or her own identity, and be willing to extend to others the same respect and rights that he or she expects to enjoy.[36]

Havighurst analyzes this concept to include the following meanings:

1. Mutual appreciation and understanding of the various cultures in the society
2. Cooperation of the various groups in the civic and economic institutions of the society
3. Peaceful coexistence of diverse lifestyles, folkways, manners, language patterns, religious beliefs, and family structure
4. Autonomy for each subcultural group to work out its own social futures, as long as it does not interfere with the same right for the other groups.[37]

The definitions cited have binding traits: (1) a recognition and respect for diversity among people; (2) the value of human dignity and self-esteem; and (3) the preservation of cultural identity. Strongly implied in a definition of multicultural education is the eradication of racism, along with its destructive manifestations.

SUMMARY

Schools in the United States exist in a multicultural setting. Schooling has shifted to follow the changing views of American society about how to provide for the diverse populations who inhabit, or have immigrated to, this country. Among the responses of schools have been exclusion, separation, attempted assimilation, differential treatment, and, recently, a variety of approaches to pluralistic influences. It would be wrong to argue that any of these had been successful. Certainly, exclusion and separation have come to be shown as racism or imposed deprivation. Yet these were the standards expected of schools in earlier times. The recent development of cultural pluralism has often led to a different form of separation, in which groups claim ethnicity on the basis of nation-states of their great great grandparents, or religion, or anything that seems to be a common factor in a particular group. Ethnicity is virtually impossible to define because there are no commonly accepted and clearly delineated characteristics that can be used to identify ethnicity. Cubans, Catholics, Nigerians, Jews, Blacks, and Prussians are each members of "ethnic" groups, yet these labels do not conform to a clear set of criteria for identifying what is ethnic. At the same time, "ethnic" is used in ordinary language to mean some identifiable group and its presumed characteristics. This concept of separate ethnic groups is important for self-perception and a sense of personal affiliation with others, but it poses the possibility of fracturing the society even more and creating separatist barriers. Multicultural approaches permit consideration of divergent contributions to human civilization from different cultural groups while also permitting a focus of the common element of being human.

FOR CONSIDERATION

1. What should be the role of schools in a multicultural society? Should schools attempt assimilation to a majority culture? Should they provide separate subcultures for each identifiable group? Should they impose a dominant value system or expose students to a variety of value systems?

2. Observe the level of interaction among groups in a school. Are there identifiable cultural groups? Do individuals from different groups come to school together? Do they converse socially in the halls or outside the school? Are the groups intermixed at school events like sports, dances, or dramatic activities? What groups predominate in school leadership? Is cultural group membership more important than individual characteristics in school affairs?

3. Examine school texts and other teaching materials for evidence of bias in regard to cultural groups or sexism. What criteria will you use to measure bias? What kinds did you find? Look at textbooks used ten to twenty years ago. Have the books remained static or have they changed in their treatment of minority groups?

Notes

1. Cyclone Covey, *Adventures in the Unknown Interior of America* (New York: Crowell-Collier, 1961), p. 141.
2. Arnold H. Leibowitz, "Educational Policy and Political Acceptance: The Imposition of English as the Language of Instruction in American Schools" (Washington, D. C.: ERIC Clearinghouse for Linguistics, 1971), p. 9.
3. D. Ferris, "The Founding of the California Public School System" (Washington, D. C.: ERIC Clearinghouse for Linguistics, 1962), pp. 47–48.
4. Leibowitz, *op. cit.*, pp. 51–52.
5. Josue M. Gonzales, Foreward to *Bilingual Multicultural Education and the Professional*, ed. Henry T. Tureba and Carol Barnett-Mizrahi (Rowley, Mass.: Newbury Publishers, 1979), p. 2.

6. Theodore Roosevelt, *The Foes of Our Household* (New York: Knopf, 1949), p. 12.

7. Arval A. Morris, *The Constitution and American Education* (St. Paul, Minn.: West Publishing Co., 1974), p. 281.

8. *Ibid.*, p. 285.

9. *Lau* v. *Nichols*, 414 U.S. at 569.

10. *Ibid.*, at 566.

11. Morris, *op.cit.*, p. 211.

12. Arnold Rose and Caroline Rose, *America Divided* (New York: Knopf, 1949), p. 50.

13. R. Freeman Butts and Lawrence A. Cremin, *History of Education in American Culture* (New York: Holt, Rinehart & Winston, 1953), p. 117.

14. Eli Ginsberg and A. A. Eighner, *The Troublesome Presence* (Glencoe, Ill.: Free Press, 1966).

15. Michael Cole and Sylvia Scribner, *Culture and Thought* (New York: Wiley, 1974), p. 17.

16. Michael Novak, *The Rise of the Unmeltable Ethnics* (New York: Macmillan, 1973), p. 95.

17. Butts and Cremin, *op. cit.*, p. 306.

18. Novak, *op. cit.*, p. 95.

19. Mildred Dickeman, "Teaching Cultural Pluralism," in *Teaching Ethnic Studies*, *op. cit.*, p. 6.

20. Michael Winston, "Through the Back Door: Academics and the Negro Scholar in Historical Perspective," *Daedalus* 14 (Summer 1971): 681.

21. William Hunter, ed., *Multicultural Education Through Competency Based Teacher Education* (Washington, D. C.: AACTE, 1974), p. 14.

22. Barbara Sizemore, "Shattering the Melting Pot Myth," in *Teaching Ethnic Studies*, *op. cit.*, pp. 73–101.

23. Israel Zangwill, *The Melting Pot* (New York: Macmillan, 1907), p. 37.

24. Henry S. Commager, "Free Public Schools—A Key to National Unity," in *Crucial Issues in Education*, ed. Henry Ehlers (New York: Holt, Rinehart & Winston, 1969), p. 6

25. Novak, *op. cit.*, p. 430.

26. Peter Rose, *They and We: Racial and Ethnic Relations in the United States* (New York: Random House, 1974).

27. John Dewey, "Nationalizing Education," *Proceedings of NEA* (1916): 183–189; Julius Drachsler, *Democracy and Assimilation* (New York: Macmillan, 1920); Horace Kallen, *Culture and Democracy in the United States* (New York: Macmillan, 1924).

28. Rose and Rose, *op. cit.*, p. 12.

29. Henry Abraham, "Rise: The American Dilemma," in *Crucial Issues in Education*, p. 49.

30. Dewey, *op. cit.*, p. 15.

31. *Ibid.*, p. 18.

32. John Beck and Richard Saxe, *Teaching the Culturally Disadvantaged Pupil* (Springfield, Ill.: Charles Thomas Publisher, 1965), p. x.

33. Sizemore, *op. cit.*, p. 82.

34. Larry Cuban, "Ethnic Content and White Instruction," in *Teaching Ethnic Studies*, *op. cit.*, pp. 113.

35. *Ibid.*, pp. 110–111.

36. Madelon D. Stent, William R. Hazard, and Harry N. Rivlin, "Cultural Pluralism and Schooling: Some Preliminary Observations," in *Cultural Pluralism in Education*, ed. Madelon D. Stent *et al.* (New York: Appleton-Century-Crofts, 1973), p. 14.

37. Robert J. Havighurst, "The American Indian from Assimilation to Cultural Pluralism," in *Educational Leadership*, 30 (April 1974).

References

Abraham, Henry. "Rise: The American Dilemma," *Crucial Issues in Education*, edited by Henry Ehlers. New York: Holt, Rinehart & Winston, 1969.

Baptiste, Jr., and Prentice, H. *Developing the Multicultural Process in Classroom Instruction: Competencies for Teachers*. Washington, D.C.: University Press of America, 1979.

Beck, John, and Saxe, Richard. *Teaching the Culturally Disadvantaged Pupil*. Springfield, Ill.: Charles Thomas Publisher, 1965.

Butts, R. Freeman, and Cremin, Lawrence A. *History of Education in American Culture*. New York: Holt, Rinehart & Winston, 1953.

Cole, Michael, and Scribner, Sylvia. *Culture and Thought*. New York: Wiley, 1974.

Commager, Henry S. "Free Public Schools—A Key to National Unity." In *Crucial Issues in Education*, edited by Henry Ehlers, pp. 6–12. New York: Holt, Rinehart & Winston, 1969.

Covey, Cyclone. *Adventures in the Unknown Interior of America*. New York: Crowell-Collier, 1961.

Cuban, Larry. "Ethnic Content and White Instruction." In *Teaching Ethnic Studies*, edited by James Banks. Washington, D.C.: National Council for Social Studies, 1973.

Dewey, John. "Nationalizing Education." *Proceedings of NEA* 54 (1916): 102–113.

Dickeman, Mildred. "Teaching Cultural Pluralism." In *Teaching Ethnic Studies*, edited by James Banks, pp. 5–25. Washington, D.C.: National Council for Social Studies, 1973.

Drachsler, Julius. *Democracy and Assimilation*. New York: Macmillan, 1920.

Ferris, D. "The Founding of the California Public School System." Washington, D.C.: ERIC Clearinghouse for Linguistics, 1962.

Ginsberg, Eli, and Eichner, A. A. *The Troublesome Presence*. Glencoe, Ill.: Free Press, 1966.

Gonzales, Josue M. Foreword to *Bilingual Multicultural Education and the Professional*, edited by Henry T. Tureba and Carol Barnett-Mizrahi. Rowley, Mass.: Newbury Publishers, 1979.

Havighurst, Robert J. "The American Indian from Assimilation to Cultural Pluralism." *Education Leadership* 30 (April 1974).

Hunter, William, ed. *Multicultural Education Through Competency Based Teacher Education*. Washington, D.C.: AACTE, 1974.

Joyce, William. "Minority Groups in American Society: Imperatives for Educators." In *Teaching Ethnic Studies*, edited by James Banks. Washington, D.C.: National Council for Social Studies, 1973.

Kallen, Horace. *Culture and Democracy in the United States*. New York: Macmillan, 1924.

Leibowitz, Arnold H. "Educational Policy and Political Acceptance: The Imposition of English as the Language of Instruction in American Schools." Washington, D.C.: ERIC Clearinghouse for Linguistics, 1971.

Morris, Arval A. *The Constitution and American Education*. St. Paul, Minn.: West Publishing Co., 1974.

Novak, Michael. *The Rise of the Unmeltable Ethnics*. New York: Macmillan, 1973.

Orr, Paul G., "Internationalism and Interculturalism as Concepts." In *Education for 1984 and After*, edited by Paul Olson, Larry Freeman, and James Bowman. Chicago: Study Commission on Undergraduate Education and the Education of Teachers, 1971.

Roosevelt, Theodore. *The Foes of Our Household*. New York: George H. Doran, 1907.

Rose, Arnold, and Rose, Caroline. *America Divided*. New York: Knopf, 1948.

Rose, Peter. *They and We: Racial and Ethnic Relations in the United States*. New York: Random House, 1974.

Sizemore, Barbara. "Shattering the Melting Pot Myth." In *Teaching Ethnic Studies*, edited by James Banks, pp. 73–101.Washington, D.C.: National Council for Social Studies, 1973.

Stent, Madelon, D., Hazard, William R., and Rivlin, Harry N., eds. *Cultural Pluralism in Education*. New York: Appleton-Century-Crofts, 1973.

Winston, Michael. "Through the Back Door; Academics and the Negro Scholar in Historical Perspective." *Daedalus* 14 (Summer 1971): 681.

Zangwill, Israel. *The Melting Pot*. New York: Macmillan, 1907.

Section Five:
Free Speech, Academic Freedom, Equal Access: The Constitution and the Schools

If there is one idea central to each chapter in this book, it is the necessity to understand stasis and change in a variety of settings, so that we can assist students in learning to deal with the ever-changing patterns of the modern world. If children are to grow and prosper in a democratic society, where stasis and change are in conflict, then the school must become a place where children are encouraged to make intelligent, thoughtful, and humanitarian choices. Enlightened citizens are a primary goal of—and essential to—a democracy. The schools are basic institutions, which can achieve that purpose. But, if the school is to serve the function of educating a free citizenry, then no two issues are of greater importance than student and teacher academic freedom and equal access to education.

This section is a description of the current state of constitutional law as it relates to academic freedom and equal access in the schools. It is a plea, too, that teachers and students more actively seek redress and equal access grievances concerning academic freedom through the law.

The following chapters deal with two of the greatest documents ever written in the English language: The Declaration of Independence and the Constitution of the United States, including the Bill of Rights and the 14th Amendment. Freedom and justice are among the most civilizing values, although neither have been available to all citizens equally. But one thing becomes clear from the following two chapters: the pursuit of those ideals is worth the effort.

While these two chapters ostensibly deal with constitutional law, in reality they deal with two important issues facing any institution, but particularly the school: freedom of expression and equal justice. Without these, no nation can call itself free or just, and no school can claim to educate.

This history of freedom of expression and equal justice are especially strong examples of the tension between the forces of stasis and those of change in society and schools. These continuing struggles include long periods of gradual alterations with change pulling in one direction and stability in the other, and other periods of dramatic and rapid change involving violent confrontations between different world views. As you consider these histories of the application of the ideas of freedom, equality, and justice in the United States, try to apply some of the ideas suggested in the earlier parts of the book to the cultural issues. For example, think about the following questions as you go through these chapters:

1. Are the forces of stasis or of change dominant in each period?
2. How would a functionalist explain the events described?
3. How would a critical view explain the same events?
4. Which model of analysis provided gives you the best insights into the institutions of expressive freedom and slavery?
5. What do you think was being taught in the schools about this issue during each of the time periods identified?

Chapter 14:
Freedom of
Expression:
Schools and Teachers
in a Democracy

The major premise of democracy is that people are capable of self-government. The quality of that self-government depends upon available information and ideas and the quality of reasoning. No thoughtful person would argue that democracy can work when the people are ignorant or irrational. The primary purpose of schools in a democracy is to dispel ignorance and assist in the development of rationality. Totalitarian societies stifle dissent by controlling information, censoring ideas, and banishing dissenters. The schools of a totalitarian society are agents of the government in this process of social control. Although these simple statements of principles may help differentiate democracy from totalitarianism, the actual operations of a society that claims to be democratic are, of course, much more complex. Self-government involves a variety of interpretations of what is right and wrong, what information and ideas are suitable, and what constitutes rational decisions, and these interpretations change over time and in differing situations. Despite this freedom of interpretation stability is maintained through the strength of the basic documents that convey the principles of democratic government.

Free speech, free press, and freedom of association are guaranteed under the Constitution and Bill of Rights of the United States. Yet these rights are not absolute; they have been interpreted in Supreme Court decisions to have limitations. One does not have the right to claim free speech by hollering "Fire!" in a crowded theater. Newspapers do not have the right to print, without liability, statements known to be false and libelous about individuals. And people do not have the right to associate in a conspiracy to engage in criminal acts or to overthrow the government by violence. In general these rights to freedom of speech, press, and association are protected until they conflict with other basic rights, such as personal security or privacy, or when their exercise will disrupt the public order. Despite a series of court interpretations, however, many of our rights remain unclear. For example, there is no clear and precise legal definition of obscenity.

The schools and teachers in a democracy must operate in areas where rights can conflict and obligations may appear contradictory. The schools are expected to enlighten students for adequate participation in the changing society, but they are also expected to transmit the values and traditions of that society to children. These obligations can come into conflict when enlightenment means provision and tolerance for a variety of ideas, implying the possibility of change, and transmitting means insisting on the correctness of only certain ideas, thereby supporting stasis. The right of schools to deal with controversial topics conflicts with the right of the community to be protected from topics considered alien or dangerous. The right of teachers to pursue their professional task of dispelling ignorance and assisting the development of rationality may conflict with the right of parents to control what their children see and hear. These conflicts are not entirely resolved by law and/or by court decisions. Where laws have been passed and court decisions have been made about free speech, academic freedom, and the schools, however, the issues are made much clearer. It is through the use of cases and examples that we can get some sense of the tension between stasis and change in the evolution of free speech and academic freedom in the schools.

The School's View of Academic Freedom: Stasis

Fogarty Case

John Fogarty was hired to teach English in the public schools of St. Anthony, Idaho. He was fully certified with a degree in English and teacher preparation from Idaho State University. He had been a teacher for two years. Fogarty used the book *One Flew Over the Cuckoo's Nest* in a course he taught. A group of parents complained to the principal that the book included obscene words and was inappropriate for high-school students. The principal ordered Fogarty to quit using the book. Fogarty refused. The school board then dismissed Fogarty as a teacher. He employed a lawyer and went to court to gain reinstatement.

The dismissal of English teacher John Fogarty, in St. Anthony, Idaho, was hardly a unique event. Every year dozens, perhaps hundreds, of textbooks are censored. Occasionally the censors actually burn copies of the objectionable work, as occurred recently in Warsaw, Indiana,[1] and Drake, North Dakota. Often censorship takes a more subtle form—quiet withdrawal of a book from the school library, a memorandum from the principal or superintendent warning teachers not to assign the work, or even invisible self-censorship by a teacher or librarian who decides to avoid controversy by simply not using a targeted book. Only on rare occasions like the case of Fogarty, who was willing to resist dismissal in defense of his beliefs, do issues of censorship ever get to court. For this reason there are relatively few decided cases defining the legal rights of teachers and librarians who face reprisal for using or assigning controversial literary works.

Let us take the case of John Fogarty as a starting point for an analysis of the legal issues involved.[2] Fogarty was fired by the school board after he used a book that the school principal had ordered him not to use. The position of the school board can be rather simply stated. First, it is clear under state law that local school officials and boards have the power to determine the curriculum and assign certain subjects to teachers (indeed, they are required to see that all students complete a stated number of hours of instruction in many prescribed areas; failure to do so would subject officials to legal liability). Should a teacher be hired to teach English and insist, instead, on teaching algebra or history, there would be little doubt about the propriety of not renewing the teacher's contract. The board viewed John Fogarty, who exercised his own judgment in selecting a controversial work for an assigned course, according to this general principle. As one parent in St. Anthony said, comparing farming to schooling, "If I hired an agricultural expert with a degree to help on the farm, and I wanted him to plant potatoes and he said 'no,' I'd tell him to hit the road. It's as simple as that."[3]

Second, school authorities reasonably expect a high standard of conduct and decorum from teachers, who serve in the classroom as authority figures.

Deviation from duty—especially to a degree that invites public controversy—serves in the eyes of the administration to undermine the central role of the school system. Extreme departures may also violate the often unwritten but widely accepted code of professional responsibility by which teaching has become considered a learned profession in American society. According to this code, if respect for teachers is undermined in an individual case, general respect for public education may be jeopardized.

Third, there is a continuing (and increasingly vital) need of the schools for wide community support. Most revenues for public education come from local taxes; boards are elected or appointed to represent the community; and parents have more contact with schools than with other community institutions. Surely, therefore, if a majority or even a vocal minority of citizens in a town like St. Anthony do not want *One Flew Over the Cuckoo's Nest* to be taught in the high school, the principal and the superintendent are likely to heed that sentiment. Ironically, an administration may even argue that restricting John Fogarty's freedom on this occasion will in the long run protect other teachers.

Fourth, school officials would point out that even the Supreme Court has said that children may be kept from reading some books generally available to adults. Over a decade ago, during its most liberal period, the Court held that states might apply special standards in defining obscenity for young readers and could restrict the sale and distribution to minors of works that adults have a constitutional right to read. Surely, the St. Anthony board would argue, a school may follow what law enforcement officials can do in imposing higher moral standards for minors.

Finally, school officials would claim that a basic purpose of public elementary and secondary education is subverted by a John Fogarty. From their inception, the schools have been expected to indoctrinate the youth of the nation to preserve and perpetuate basic values and traditions. To the extent that particular instruction—or even the assignment of particular materials—departs sharply from those values, a basic purpose of public education is undermined. Since it is the task of school officials to protect those values, some control over the curriculum necessarily will follow. Where John Fogarty's literary tastes and interests (and even those of some students) conflict with the basic values of American society, it becomes the duty of the board and the superintendent to preserve the latter even at the expense of the former. This is the basic argument for stasis.

The Opposing View of Academic Freedom: Change

The teacher's view of the case, as you can imagine, diverged strongly from the school's. His reply was premised on three quite different claims: (1) Persons who work for the government (including public-school teachers) may not be discharged for the exercise of freedom of speech, which the Constitution protects; (2) teachers must protect the constitutional rights and liberties of students and, therefore, their right to academic freedom should be "derivative" as well as primary, and most importantly; (3) inherent in the idea of academic freedom is that teachers enjoy a special measure of legal protection above and beyond the freedom enjoyed by other public employees. A detailed examination of these claims in the sections below will illustrate issues related to teaching and academic freedom in American schools and help clarify the implications of the *Fogarty* case for stasis and change.

THE TEACHER AS GOVERNMENT EMPLOYEE

Teachers share with other persons who work for the government certain protections not available in the private sector.[4] A teacher in a private school, for example, has no *constitutional* right to comment publicly on the policies of the school administration, but a public-school teacher does.

Pickering Case

A decade ago the United States Supreme Court held that an Illinois public-school teacher named Pickering could not be fired for writing an open letter critical of the conduct of school finances.[5] Even though the letter contained several errors, the Court held that the teacher could be discharged only if he had shown reckless disregard of the truth or had acted with malice. The *Pickering* decision has been applied in hundreds of other public-employment settings and has been a cornerstone for the protection of the free speech of persons who work for the government. The underlying principle is simple enough: While no person has a right to obtain or to keep a government job, the Constitution does not allow the government to condition its hiring upon the willingness of persons to give up the rights of citizenship they would otherwise enjoy. Since the right to criticize government is basic among those liberties, persons who work for the government must be as free to speak publicly (even about the policies of their employer) as is anyone else.

A pair of cases in the early 1970s extended the safeguards for government employees into the public-school classroom. Two teachers in New York state were dismissed, one for refusing to lead her students in the daily pledge to the flag, the other for wearing a black armband in class to protest the Vietnam War. Both teachers took their cases to the federal courts, and both were successful.[6] The court both times found the conduct well within the protection of a public employee's right to protest government policy; in the black armband case, the court applied to teachers essentially the same standard as the Supreme Court had applied to student protest in the landmark *Tinker* case,[7] where rights of free expression were extended to students (see page 327).

The public-employment cases do, however, contain important qualifications. In *Pickering*, the Supreme Court warned that some kinds of critical speech might be punished if they disrupted the effective working of the agency. Other kinds of speech might exceed the bounds of the constitutional privilege through sheer irresponsibility or because of their particular personal nature. Taking company time or defaulting on assigned tasks could also result in a sanction, even if the content of the speech were otherwise protected. While these qualifications may not seem troublesome for the school teacher, one post-*Pickering* decision is highly pertinent. An American civilian had been hired by the federal government to instruct Vietnamese military personnel. During one of his classes he departed from the assigned topic, military weapons, to express some personal views about the role of the United States in the Indochina war. For this deviation he was dismissed, and his dismissal was upheld by the federal courts. Such a departure from the assigned material, said the court, was not only a breach of duty but threatened to disrupt sensitive relations with the foreign personnel who, in this case, were the students.[8] Thus there are limits to the value of *Pickering* and other public-employment cases for a teacher.

THE TEACHER AS REPRESENTATIVE
OF STUDENTS' RIGHTS

It is sometimes suggested that a public-school teacher should be allowed curricular discretion in order to protect the freedom of students to learn. Professor Sheldon Nahmod of Duquesne University Law School has thoughtfully stated the case for this sort of "derivative" teacher's freedom in the classroom:

An unbalanced presentation on a controversial subject . . . may be harmful to the education of students. It deprives them of the opportunity to consider as many relevant facts and opinions as possible. Moreover, a classroom is one of the few places where controversial subjects can be discussed in a supervised and reasonably thorough manner. In making an unbalanced presentation, a teacher impedes the development of critical and other faculties; the point of view espoused and perhaps received so uncritically may in fact be erroneous and ultimately harmful to the students. Although this may also occur in the context of a balanced presentation, students at least will have had the opportunity to decide otherwise.[9]

Student Rights Case

One recent case illustrates the way in which a teacher's rights may be reinforced by the interests of students.[10] An Oregon political-science teacher arranged to invite four speakers into his senior high-school classroom. Three of the speakers —a Democrat, a Republican, and a John Birch Society member—appeared without incident. An invitation was extended to a Communist and was approved by both the principal and the school board. Community pressure soon developed, however, and the board not only cancelled the invitation but imposed a broad ban on all "political speakers" anywhere in the school system. The teacher and a group of his students went to federal court to challenge the ban, asking that the Communist be allowed to speak and complete the series. The federal district court held the school policy unconstitutional—in part because it violated general First Amendment principles developed in college speaker ban cases, but also because it prevented the students from receiving information to which they had a constitutional right. The ban was declared a violation of the First Amendment rights both of the teachers and of the students.

The nature of this case suggests the rarity with which the "derivative rights" argument will in fact be available to the teacher. Only where the wishes of the students are clearly parallel is there the necessary certainty about the factual basis for the claim. Much more often, the views of students will either be unknown to the court, or will actually be opposed to those of the teacher. Where student interests are not directly reflected in the case, it is likely that either the parents or the school board (acting *in loco parentis*) will assert contrary views. Take the *Fogarty* case as an example. It was apparent from newspaper reports that many students either enjoyed *One Flew Over the Cuckoo's Nest* or at least did not find it offensive. Such views could possibly be introduced in evidence—although they would conflict with claims of the school administration, presumably reinforced by parental testimony, that students of impressionable ages should not be exposed to such material. Where a teacher argues that students want to read the book, but the principal and the parents insist that they should not (at least not in class), the court is likely to defer to the latter set of derivative rights rather than to the former. This may seem a contradiction, because the *Fogarty* and Oregon cases appear similar.

ACADEMIC FREEDOM FOR THE TEACHER

If the general rights of public employees do not fully protect embattled teachers, they must then seek special protection. College and university professors have long enjoyed such a special status under the doctrine of academic freedom. The contours of the doctrine have been well stated by the American Association of University Professors in a 1940 statement that now has the imprimatur of the courts as well as of major colleges, universities, and professional and learned societies. It says:

> Institutions of higher education are conducted for the common good and not to further the interest of either the individual teacher or the institution as a whole. The common good depends upon the free search for truth and its free exposition.
>
> Academic freedom is essential to these purposes and applies to both teaching and research. Freedom in research is fundamental to the advancement of truth. Academic freedom in its teaching aspect is fundamental for the protection of the rights of the teacher in teaching and of the student to freedom in learning.[11]

The uncertainty is the extent to which academic freedom is available to elementary and secondary teachers—and that is really the central issue in the *Fogarty* case. Had the same dispute arisen at the University of Idaho, no action would have been taken; had reprisal even been threatened, any court would have held that a university professor enjoys a constitutional right to assign to his or her classes any material that is not obscene or otherwise unlawful. (Even when material could be banned at newstands or drugstores, its dissemination and study in a university classroom or laboratory may well be protected—but that is a question beyond our present scope.)

The *Fogarty* case is difficult because of a subtle tension between the high-school setting and the nature of the course. The students would be in college the following year, and the course in which the assignment was made had many qualities of a college-level course. Elective study of literature in a college-preparatory track closely resembles a college course—and, in fact, may be more demanding or sophisticated in content and depth than many literature courses offered to college freshmen. On the other hand, the expectations of the public-school system from kindergarten through senior high school are profoundly different from those of the college or university.

Even the teacher of senior literature courses typically comes through a quite different preparatory route and has different duties and responsibilities from those of the college professor. So, for example, the public-school teacher is expected to watch the lunchroom one day a week but is not expected to do advanced research. Thus, despite the similarities in *content* between Fogarty's course and an introductory literature course at the University of Idaho, there are significant differences in *context*.

Some concise views of academic freedom in public schools have been offered. They at least have the virtue of simplicity and perhaps that of consistency as well. For example, Professor Stephen Goldstein, a sensitive student both of free expression and of teacher's rights, argues that academic freedom really does not belong in the elementary or secondary classroom.[12] Certain aspects of the elementary and secondary school—the teacher's position as an authority figure, the importance of inculcation of values as a school function, the relative immaturity of the student, and the rather structured nature of the curriculum (all stasis values)—militate against the downward extension of concepts developed at the collegiate level. On this basis, Goldstein seemingly would give academic freedom to an instructor in secretarial skills or remedial English at a junior college but would deny it to the high-school teacher of a senior elective course in comparative literature, government, or religion. For him the structure and organization are basic; the need to sustain the authority of the school officials (and ultimately that of the community that supports the school system) is paramount. Since the tension between the two forces must be resolved in some way, Goldstein argues for a standard that will apply across all levels of elementary and secondary education. Some support for his view comes from the relatively small number of cases addressing the issue. In order to assess the soundness of this position, we must now turn to the courts.

The Courts and Academic Freedom

It should be pointed out that while Professor Goldstein's argument is legally compelling, there are a number of social scientists who might feel that it reflects a position on schooling and the schools that is no longer viable. The basic emphasis of this book has been to show the conflict between stasis and change. The social context of the school, which maintains the teacher as the authority figure, the school as an inculcator of values, and perceives the student as basically immature, may be dysfunctional in a world where adherence to any authority without question may be the quickest road to error, inaccuracy, and debilitation. Because political, technological, and sociohistorical values change and because greater information is available to students through the increasing speed of communication, students may be more mature and thoughtful at any given age than their teachers were at the same age, requiring a change in the concept and context of the school. This is not to deny the importance of the values placed on the school by Professor Goldstein, but only to point out that it might be necessary to introduce into the school values that more closely resemble the reality of the world outside of the school. Although this issue is not of particular relevance to the courts, they have handed down some decisions that relate to it.

It is always wise to begin with the relevant decisions of the United States Supreme Court. These decisions are of somewhat limited value, however, because the justices have never considered a curricular issue under the free-speech clause of the First Amendment, from which the academic freedom claim derives. But the Court has shown its concern for and commitment to the principle of academic freedom in other settings. In a series of decisions going back to the 1950s, the Court struck down loyalty oaths on First Amendment grounds. In several of these cases, most of which involved college or public-school teachers, the Court recognized that members of the academic profession made a special claim to freedom of thought and inquiry. The clearest such statement came in the 1967 case striking down a New York loyalty law:

> Our Nation is deeply committed to safeguarding academic freedom which is of transcendent value to all of us and not merely to the teachers concerned. That freedom is, therefore, a special concern of the First Amendment, which does not tolerate laws that cast a pall of orthodoxy over the classroom. . . . The classroom is peculiarly the "marketplace of ideas." The Nation's future depends upon leaders trained through wide exposure to that robust exchange of ideas which discovers truth "out of a multitude of tongues, [rather] than through any kind of authoritative selection."[13]

While most of the loyalty oath cases involved college professors rather than school teachers, their principles do have a more general application. These decisions really defined the rights and liberties of all public employees, and since oaths have been generally invalidated, no special dispensation for the teaching profession has been sought or granted. The most that can be said with confidence is that such statements about academic freedom are helpful, though they are not decisive.

ACADEMIC FREEDOM IN THE CURRICULUM

Other cases, relating to such issues as the curriculum in the schools, may be even more helpful to the development of a claim of academic freedom. The origins of the Supreme Court's concern with the public-school curriculum, for example, go back to the 1920s.

Meyer Case

Nebraska, like many other states, shortly after World War I enacted a law that forbade the use of German in any classroom in the state. When in 1925 a German-speaking teacher in a Lutheran school appealed his conviction to the Supreme Court, a majority of the justices held the Nebraska law unconstitutional.[14] The Court recognized the legitimacy of the state's desire to promote assimilation among its people by requiring a common language. But the Court felt that the means Nebraska had used violated the teacher's right to teach and the right of parents to engage him to instruct their children—a right protected by the due-process clause of the Fourteenth Amendment. Two questions remain: (1) To what extent did this decision—*Meyer* v. *Nebraska*—apply to public schools; and (2) what elements of the curriculum did it protect?

The first question posed by the *Meyer* case has been partially answered in the intervening years. Although the facts and much of the reasoning of the *Meyer* case would limit its effect to private schools, the Supreme Court has read it more broadly. In two cases in the late 1960s, both involving public schools, the justices simply assumed that *Meyer* applied quite as much to public as to private schools. The Court characterized the Nebraska statute as an "arbitrary restriction upon the freedom of teachers to teach and of students to learn" and as a "restriction upon the liberty of teacher and pupil." The other question—to what parts of the curriculum does *Meyer* apply—remains unsettled. The Supreme Court recognized in 1923 "the power of the State . . . to make reasonable regulations for all schools, including a requirement that they shall give instruction in English. . . ." The Court also disclaimed any disparagement of "the State's power to prescribe a curriculum for institutions which it supports."[15] Later cases have reaffirmed this general language.

The possible relevance of *Meyer* to the curriculum and to the teacher's claim of academic freedom was measurably enhanced in 1968 by the case of *Epperson* v. *Arkansas*. The Supreme Court there struck down state laws banning the teaching of evolution, although on the grounds of religious freedom and with no explicit mention of academic freedom or teachers' liberty of expression. In *Epperson* the Supreme Court underscored what was said in *Meyer* about the "state's undoubted right to prescribe the curriculum for its public schools. . . ." The problem here, according to the Court, was that Arkansas had sought to prohibit "on pain of criminal penalty, the teaching of a scientific theory or doctrine where that prohibition is based upon reasons that violate the First Amendment."[16] These elements were important to the decision: the law contained criminal sanctions, it completely excluded from the schools a whole body of scientific thought, and the basis for the exclusion was a particular religious point of view.

Some additional guidance comes from the concurring opinion of Justice Black. He would have struck down the law because of the vagueness of its key provisions. He also offered a critical distinction:

> It is plain that a state law prohibiting all teaching of human development or biology is constitutionally quite different from a law that compels a teacher to teach as true only one theory of a given doctrine. It would be difficult to make a First Amendment case out of a state law eliminating the subject of higher mathematics, or astronomy, or biology from its curriculum.[17]

Justice Stewart, who wrote another concurring opinion, reinforced Justice Black's distinction:

> The States are most assuredly free "to choose their own curriculums for their own schools." A State is entirely free, for example, to decide that the only foreign language to be taught in its public school system shall be Spanish. But would a State be free to punish a teacher for letting his students know that there are other languages in the world? I think not.
>
> It is one thing for a State to determine that "the subject of higher mathematics, or astronomy, or biology" shall or shall not be included in its public school curriculum. It is quite another thing for a State to make it a criminal offense for a public school teacher so much as to mention the very existence of an entire system of respected human thought.[18]

It is not quite clear what troubled Justice Stewart. Perhaps, as Professor Goldstein suggests, he was more concerned about a state's attempt to forbid a teacher from even mentioning Darwinism in class than with totally banning a particular subject from the curriculum. Stewart, on the one hand, would grant that a state could decide not to offer biology in its public schools. On the other hand, he would uphold the lower federal court that reinstated the North Carolina teacher for giving Darwinian answers to student questions about evolution.[19] It is less clear whether Justice Stewart would allow school officials, for example, to require some materials—and forbid others—on the basis of their views of the evolution controversy.

ACADEMIC FREEDOM AND STUDENT RIGHTS

The cases addressing curricular issues provide limited guidance on academic freedom—but only that. The other possible source of the Supreme Court's views on academic freedom is the case of *Tinker* v. *Des Moines School District*,[20] which involved student rather than teacher rights.

Tinker Case

Several students had worn black armbands to class, in clear violation of a school rule, to express their opposition to the Vietnam War. They were suspended and brought their claims into the federal courts. The Supreme Court eventually held that, in the absence of any actual or seriously threatened disruption, the students could not be disciplined for peaceful protest of this sort. Although the case was concerned chiefly with the rights of students vis-à-vis the authority of the public schools, the majority opinion contained a vitally important statement about the Constitution's protection of the freedom of inquiry even at the secondary-school level:

> In our system, state-operated schools may not be enclaves of totalitarianism. School officials do not possess absolute authority over their students. Students in school as well as out of school are "persons" under our Constitution. They are possessed of fundamental rights which the State must respect, just as they themselves must respect their obligations to the State. In our system, students may not be regarded as close-circuit recipients of only that which the State chooses to communicate. They may not be confined to the expression of those sentiments that are officially approved. In the absence of

a specific showing of constitutionally valid reasons to regulate their speech, students are entitled to freedom of expression of their views.[21]

The Court in the *Tinker* case suggested that activity protected by the First Amendment—such as the wearing of antiwar protest symbols—may be prohibited only where there is a clear threat of disruption. As we noted earlier, one federal court of appeals applied that reasoning to the case of a teacher wearing a *Tinker*-like black armband in class. There is reason to believe that the Supreme Court would also apply the *Tinker* reasoning to a curricular case like *Fogarty*, although the absence of cases in point must make any such judgment speculative.

The Supreme Court decisions, in fact, do no more than refine the issues. Professor Thomas Emerson, in his lengthy treatise on First Amendment law, offers two observations about the limited value of the Supreme Court cases bearing on academic freedom:

> The first is that the Supreme Court has touched upon only a small fraction of the total area of academic freedom. . . . None of them considers the rights of individual faculty members [or teachers] vis-à-vis the administration of their own institutions or vis-à-vis their colleagues. . . . The second conclusion is that the Supreme Court has never undertaken to establish academic freedom as an independent constitutional right. . . . All that the Court has done is to say that academic freedom considerations are relevant in the application of standard doctrine; it has not held that they possess any constitutional dimension of their own.[22]

Decisions in the Lower Courts

Since the Supreme Court has not spoken, we must look for closer precedent in the lower courts. Important, though not conclusive, is the pair of cases we discussed above that dealt with teacher conduct and expression. In one case a teacher was discharged for refusing to lead the morning salute to the flag; in the other, it was the peaceful display of a black armband in class that brought the sanction. Both cases involved mature high-school classes, and there was no evidence of disruption or any other harmful effect. Thus the appellate court (both cases went through the same federal circuit) ordered the reinstatement of both teachers on First Amendment grounds. Given the circumstances, these were really general public-employment cases that happened to involve teachers, and they did not attempt to define the scope of allowable expression in the classroom. We must, therefore, turn to a group of cases that did more precisely address the content of the curriculum through teachers' claims of redress.

Baltimore and *Brave New World*

The first modern reported case, in the mid-sixties, had an ironic quality. A high-school teacher in Baltimore had assigned *Brave New World* to her senior English class. When parental complaint about the content of the book brought the matter to the principal's attention, the teacher was asked to cancel the assignment. She refused to do so and found at the end of the spring that her contract for the following year had not been renewed. She went to court, claiming that her constitutional liberties had been violated. The court found in favor of the school board, with some suggestion that First Amendment activity was not centrally involved. The court of appeals, however, affirmed the decision solely on the ground that "a probationary teacher simply had no right" to continuing employment, and declined to establish the merits of the case.[23] Thus, the first opportunity to establish relevant precedent aborted on procedural grounds.

Keefe Case

The next reported cases came in the late 1960s. Two judgments of the federal court of appeals for the first circuit have important factual similarities and should be considered together. The first involved a teacher named Keefe in Ipswich, Massachusetts, who gave his senior English class copies of an article in a current issue of the *Atlantic Monthly* to read. Written by the noted psychiatrist Robert Jay Lifton, the article discussed the mounting wave of student protest in the larger context of radicalism and revolt. Lifton used at one point the word "motherfucker" for illustrative purposes, and during discussion of the essay in class Keefe drew attention to that word. He also told the class that any student who found the assignment distasteful could choose an alternative. Apparently in response to parental protest, Keefe was summoned before the school committee and asked to defend his use of the word. He was also asked whether he would agree never to use that word again in class, but he declined to make such a commitment. He was then suspended, and his discharge was in prospect at the time he sought the aid of the federal courts.

In the *Keefe* case, although the district court held for the school committee, the court of appeals reversed the decision. The way in which the higher court posed the question anticipated its answer:

> The question in this case is whether a teacher may, for demonstrated educational purposes, quote a "dirty" world currently used in order to give special offense, or whether the shock is too great for high school seniors to stand. If the answer were that the students must be protected from such exposure, we would fear for their future. We do not question the good faith of the defendants in believing that some parents have been offended. With the greatest of respect to such parents, their sensibilities are not the full measure of what is proper education.[24]

The court then referred to the *Brave New World* case, which it found procedurally inapplicable. Keefe's case was stronger for several reasons. First of all, the cited word was available in at least five books in the school library. Said the judge who overturned the decision, "It is hard to think that any student could walk into the library and receive a book, but that his teacher could not subject the content to serious discussion in class." While acknowledging the need for restraint in the classroom, he went on to state, "We find it difficult not to think that its application to the present case demeans any proper concept of education. The general chilling effect of permitting such rigorous censorship is even more serious."[25]

It may be premature to ask whether the *Keefe* case really applied academic freedom to the high-school classroom. There is partial support, however, for a positive answer. When the school committee argued that Keefe could be fully vindicated by seeking money damages, and that judges, therefore, need not intervene to protect his interests at an earlier stage, the court of appeals responded cryptically, "Academic freedom is not preserved by compulsory retirement, even at full pay." Nevertheless, other portions of the opinion stop short of a clear commitment to academic freedom for secondary-school teachers. But since the issue was resolved in the teacher's favor, the rationale may seem less important than the result.

Mailloux Case

The following year, the same legal issue returned to the court of appeals in a slightly different form.[26] Another Massachusetts high-school English teacher had been dismissed for using a taboo word in class, and he too sought the aid of the federal courts. The discussion had revolved about a Jesse Stuart novel of life in rural Kentucky. The issue was the role of taboos in the school context, triggered by the discussion of sex-segregated seating in a rural one-room schoolhouse. The teacher, Roger Mailloux, suggested to the class that many taboos persist. He illustrated the point by writing on the board first the word "goo," which the students agreed was meaningless, and then the word "fuck," which the students recognized as meaningful but impolite. After one student offered a definition of the word, the discussion turned to other matters. Mailloux was, however, summoned to the principal's office and proceedings were set in motion that led to his dismissal. It was this personnel action that brought the dispute into the federal courts.

The district judge first thought the *Mailloux* case was controlled by *Keefe* and on that basis summarily ordered the teacher reinstated. The court of appeals sent the case back for a full hearing, warning that *Keefe* should not be read "to do away with what, to use an old-fashioned term, are considered the proprieties, or to give carte blanche in the name of academic freedom to conduct which can reasonably be deemed both offensive and unnecessary to the accomplishment of educational objectives."[27]

Despite the caution, the district judge found again for Mailloux. Central to his thinking was evidence on several points: that the teaching method involved was relevant to the subject and to the students; that the approach was deemed by experts (for example, education professors from Harvard) to serve a serious educational purpose; that the teacher had acted in good faith; and that the general policies of the school district had not adequately warned him that such conduct would jeopardize his job. According to the district judge, the case for at least qualified academic freedom was persuasive in the context of a senior high school literature class:

The Constitution recognizes that academic freedom is necessary in order to foster open minds, creative imaginations, and adventurous spirits. Our national belief is that the heterodox as well as the orthodox are a source of individual and of social growth. We do not confine academic freedom to conventional teachers or to those who can get a majority vote from their colleagues. Our faith is that the teacher's freedom to choose among options for which there is any substantial support will increase his intellectual vitality and his moral strength. The teacher whose responsibility has been nourished by independence, enterprise, and free choice becomes for his student a better model of the democratic citizen. His examples of applying and adapting the values of the old order to the demands and opportunities of a constantly changing world are among the most important lessons he gives to youth.[28]

On the other hand, the district judge was troubled by the context within which the case arose, and the uncertain relevance of the collegiate model:

> The secondary school more clearly than the college or university acts *in loco parentis* with respect to minors. It is closely governed by a school board selected by a local community. The faculty does not have the independent traditions, the broad discretion as to teaching methods, nor usually the intellectual qualifications, of university professors. Among secondary school teachers there are often many persons with little experience. Some teachers and most students have limited intellectual and emotional maturity. Most parents, students, school boards, and members of the community usually expect the secondary school to concentrate on transmitting basic information, teaching "the best that is known and thought in the world," training by established techniques, and, to some extent at least, indoctrinating in the mores of the surrounding society. While secondary schools are not rigid disciplinary institutions, neither are they open forums in which mature adults, already habituated to social restraints, exchange ideas on a level of parity.[29]

These two conflicting themes had now to be resolved, and the district court relied heavily on the procedural fairness issue in doing so. The court of appeals affirmed a judgment in the teacher's favor, but solely on the procedural ground, agreeing that the school system's regulations failed to give proper warning. The appellate court restated its concern about the possible overreading of *Keefe*, warned that each case must be decided on its own facts, and confessed that "we are not of one mind as to whether [Mailloux's] conduct fell within the protection of the First Amendment."[30] It was only the fair notice issue that resolved the case, leaving the substantive question of academic freedom open.

Illinois and a Poem

A 1974 case in another federal court of appeals illustrates a similar ambivalence about the issue of academic freedom.[31] Three Illinois teachers were discharged for distributing to their classes a poem about Woodstock, the rock festival held in upstate New York. The poem contained some taboo words and could be read as condoning or even encouraging drug use and sexual freedom. School officials focused on such phrases as "a place to take acid," and "we're a big fucking wave," among others. Copies of the brochure containing the poem were distributed in one teacher's eighth-grade classes and were displayed on the bulletin board in the classroom of another. When several students took the brochure home, parents complained, and the superintendent initiated the dismissal of the teachers. They promptly took to the federal court a claim of violation of constitutional rights.

As opposed to the decision in *Mailloux*, the district judge ruled in favor of the school board in the Illinois case, and a panel of the court of appeals (three of eight judges) affirmed that decision. Despite some testimony that the brochure as a whole was "an admirable teaching tool," the facts of this case made it substantially different from the earlier cases in several respects. For one, the students wre much younger—eighth-graders rather than seniors (in *Keefe*) or juniors (in *Mailloux*). Another obvious difference was the relationship between the suspect material and the teacher's regular assignments. One of the three plaintiffs was a French teacher, and little connection between the Woodstock festival and French could be claimed. Of the other two, one had just completed a study of the history of rock music and the other was exploring in class the construction of musical instruments; the relationship of the Woodstock brochure to these themes is a bit closer but still tenuous. A third difference has to do with the nature and weight of the exculpatory evidence. In the earlier cases, teacher-plaintiffs brought forth substantial testimony either on the value of the material itself or on the validity of the teaching technique that provoked the controversy. Finally, there was in the Illinois case a lurking issue of illegality—the "admitted invitation," in the court's phrase, to the use of drugs in violation of state law. Without suggesting that any of the teachers could be criminally charged for circulating the brochure, the presence of the drug laws undoubtedly undermined any claim of academic freedom.

The case is still not an easy one, however. Four of the eight judges of the full court would have found in the teachers' favor, though we know the reasoning of only one (the dissenter on the original panel). An excerpt from the dissenting opinion may suggest the strength of the countervailing argument:

> Particularly where the school board has not formulated standards to guide him, academic freedom affords a teacher a certain latitude in judging whether material is suitable and relevant to his instruction. . . . These instructors did not exceed the bounds which germaneness places on protected classroom speech. . . . More importantly, however, the appropriateness of a particular classroom discussion cannot be gauged solely by its logical nexus to the subject matter of instruction. A teacher may be more

successful with his students if he is able to relate to them in philosophy of life, and conversely, students may profit by learning something of a teacher's views on general subjects. Academic freedom entails the exchange of ideas which promote education in its broadest sense. [The dissenting judge then discussed the "fair notice" issue and argued that here, as in *Mailloux*, the teachers had not been adequately warned that such conduct could cost them their jobs.][32]

North Carolina Elementary-School Case

A later and consistent footnote to the Illinois case comes from another federal appellate court.[33] A fifth-grade teacher in North Carolina had been demoted (to the position of tutor) because she had read to two of her classes a note she found circulating among her students. The note contained several taboo words that she stressed, but she apparently warned against their use in other interstudent communications. A parent complained of the incident, and the teacher was demoted after a hearing. Although the applicable school-board rule forbade conduct no more precisely defined than "neglect of duty," the court of appeals felt the teacher had adequate warning that such language might jeopardize her position. The tender age of the students undoubtedly contributed to the result. There was also something in the way the offending language was used; a concurring judge remarked that the teacher "gave [the note] stature by reading it to the class and later rehearsing it before another class, each time accenting the vulgarities."[34]

If John Fogarty (or his attorney) read either the Illinois or North Carolina case, he would surely share our confusion. Using "motherfucker" in a class discussion may be protected if the course is respectable and if the word is found in books already in the school library. On the other hand, writing the word "fuck" on the blackboard may not be protected, although the teacher may still win reinstatement on procedural grounds. And distributing a poem with drug and sex references and other taboos may or may not be protected, depending on which panel of the court of appeals happens to hear the case. Of course, the law is not wholly without guidance. Certain important factors do begin to emerge: for example, the age and sophistication of the students; the relationship of the suspect language to the teacher's assigned tasks; the availability of those same words in the school library; and the "educational value" of the discussion or material (an issue on which the courts are apparently willing to receive expert testimony from professors of education).

It is also true that none of these decisions deals precisely with the issue in the *Fogarty* case — that is, the selection and assignment of literary works. Several other cases do come closer to that issue and will help to round out the discussion. We have already noted the inconclusive judgment in the 1965 *Brave New World* case, which might have given some early guidance. Now we shall turn to a later example.

Parducci Case

The next such case, decided in 1970, involved a Montgomery, Alabama, teacher named Parducci, who was dismissed for assigning Kurt Vonnegut's short story "Welcome to the Monkey House" to her eleventh-grade English class.[35] The principal and the associate superintendent called the teacher to account for the use of what they described as "literary garbage," which, in their view, promoted "the killing off of elderly people and free sex." The teacher brought suit in the federal court, asking both for reinstatement and for monetary compensation for damages.

The case happened to come before Judge Frank Johnson, the author of a number of major civil rights and civil liberties decisions. "That teachers are entitled to first amendment freedoms," he began, "is an issue no longer in dispute." While the legal status of academic freedom remained uncertain, "the Supreme Court has on numerous occasions emphasized that the right to teach, to inquire, to evaluate and to study is fundamental to a democratic society."[36] The *Tinker* case, then recently decided, had obvious relevance to the classroom environment, and Judge Johnson quoted extensively from the majority opinion. Applying *Tinker* to curricular issues, he asserted that a court must first decide whether the material in question was "inappropriate" reading for high-school juniors. Despite the presence of taboo words and "vulgar terms," the assignment of the story could not be thought inappropriate when judged in a larger literary context:

> The slang words are contained in two short rhymes which are less ribald than those found in many of Shakespeare's plays. The reference in the story to an act of sexual intercourse is no more descriptive than the rape scene in Pope's "Rape of the Lock." As for the theme of the story, the Court notes that the anthology in which the story was published was reviewed by several of the popular national weekly magazines, none of which found the subject matter of any of the stories to be offensive. It

appears to the Court, moreover, that the author, rather than advocating the "killing off of old people," satirizes the practice to symbolize the increasing depersonalization of man in society.[37]

The validation of the assignment on the basis of its content was reinforced by the classroom experience. Where *Tinker* required evidence of "disruption," in Parducci's case only 3 students had asked to be excused from the assignment and "there was no evidence that any of [the teacher's] other 87 students were planning to disrupt the normal routine of the school."[38] Thus, in applying *Tinker* to this case, there was not that degree of interference with the educational process or with classroom decorum that would warrant restricting First Amendment freedoms. Dismissal of a teacher might be justified either on the basis of the demonstrated inappropriateness of the material or by actual or threatened disruption; since the school board could show neither condition, the dismissal violated the teacher's constitutional rights.

Several other cases decided during the 1970s, unfortunately, add little to our understanding of the issue. A federal district court in Iowa, not surprisingly, held that a drama teacher could not be discharged for allowing students to recite the words "damn" and "son of a bitch" in rehearsal of a play—although she had made them substitute "son of a biscuit" in the public performance.[39] A federal judge in Texas ordered the reinstatement of a high-school civics teacher who had been discharged for using somewhat controversial but professionally acceptable material dealing with race relations and antiwar protest, remarking that "a responsible teacher must have freedom to use the tools of his profession as he sees fit."[40] In none of these cases did the opinions add measurably to the understanding of the legal issues, and for that reason the brief summary given here should suffice.

Through the course of these decisions, two important elements went almost unnoticed. First, little attention was given to the educational purposes of the course and of the broader curriculum. And, second, not much was made of the issue of governance—the level at which, or authority by which, vital decisions are made in the public-school system. It remained for a 1978 case to first draw critical attention to those issues.

Censorship in a Denver Suburb: The Cary Case

This 1978 case involved a school district in a Denver suburb.[41] The school board had ordered that ten titles—works of beat poets like Allen Ginsberg and Lawrence Ferlinghetti, and novels dealing with the supernatural—could no longer be used in junior and senior courses in contemporary literature. At the same time the board approved 1,275 other titles. The next day, a further directive explained that the ten proscribed works "will not be purchased, nor used for class assignment, nor will an individual be given credit for reading any of the books."[42] It appeared that even reading aloud or causing to be read aloud any of the ten books, or discussing any of them in class, would violate the board's order. None of the works on the proscribed list was legally obscene.

A group of teachers brought suit in federal court, claiming that the board's order abridged their free expression and their academic freedom.

The court was troubled at the outset by an implication of the case, stating that "the logical extension of plaintiff's contention is that they can teach without accountability to their employer." On the other hand, the court was also troubled by the board's claim of unfettered authority to direct the teachers' activities: "The logical extension of [this contention] is that they have the power to cause teachers to teach from a prepared script." Nor did the court find the earlier cases relating to teachers especially helpful. As far as they were concerned, *Keefe* and *Parducci* had but "limited value" here for two reasons. "First, the existence of the constitutional right of academic freedom in the high school context is not self-evident." Second, "the courts must not assume the role of arbiters of the appropriateness of material for use in a classroom."[43] And that was about as far as the earlier cases had gone. A more basic issue of governance—the extent to which the Constitution imposes limits on the locus of curricular decisions—posed the central task of the court here. Having defined the issue in this way, the court recognized that curriculum and instruction in the *elementary* schools should be shaped by persons directly responsible to the community. At the *secondary*-school level, however, the court was troubled by the implications of full community control of curricular content:

> That view is the essence of tyranny, because it imposes a collectivist control on the individual's thoughts and actions. The tyranny of the majority is as contrary to the fundamental principles of the Constitution as the authoritarianism of an autocracy. Consider the possibility that the plurality in a given community may decidedly differ from the national majoritarian principles. What would be the reaction to a school board's decision to teach nothing but Maoism in the public schools? Can there be any teacher dissent to that societal value if it is representative of the plurality of the voting electorate in a given school district?[44]

Apart from the level of instruction, the nature of the course was considered relevant to the degree of school-board control. While many subjects, even at the high-school level, properly fell within the "implantation or indoctrination stage," others were by their nature less readily subject to administrative domination. The fact that the board itself had declared the senior literature course an elective argued strongly for constitutional protection. Finally, and most significantly, the court distinguished those tasks and responsibilities of a teacher that were regulable on the "employer-employee model": taking attendance, getting students to assembly, coming promptly to class, and performing myriad other extracurricular and co-curricular tasks. There was, however, a core of intellectual activity that could be restricted only to the extent that it was "inconsistent with or counter-productive to the objective of producing effective citizens," or to the extent "it breached the bounds of professional responsibility." (Here the judge cited as an example a recent unreported case in which he had upheld the discharge of a teacher who "turned an innovative graffiti exercise into a verbal attack upon the junior high school principal.")[45]

The activity involved in the present case was precisely the kind that the Constitution protects: "The selection of the subject books as material for these elective courses in these grades is clearly within the protected area recognized as academic freedom." The board's decree was the "kind of broad prior restraint which is particularly offensive to First Amendment freedoms." On this basis, one would naturally suppose that the teachers won their case—and so they would have but for one final ironic twist on the basis of which the court ruled against them. During collective bargaining the previous year, there had been discussion of a possible academic freedom provision in the contract between the board and the union, under which the Teachers Advisory Council would have final authority on the selection of instructional material. That draft provision was eventually replaced by the declaration that "the final responsibility in the determination of [issues of academic freedom] rests with the Board." Under this clause, the court now held that the teachers had bargained away their First Amendment rights, including an otherwise clear primacy in the selection of materials for the literature course. Since the teachers had voted for an exclusive bargaining agent and were thus bound by the contract, the court found that "they may not now seek to avoid it by calling up a constitutional freedom to act independently and individually."[46]

On the final point, the Denver case seems quite at variance with Supreme Court precedent. Many years ago the Court held that white workers and the unions they controlled could not bargain away the interests of black members of the employment unit. More recently, the same principle has been applied to First Amendment rights as well, the Court holding that a dissident teacher could not be prevented from speaking out at a school-board meeting on an issue that was then under discussion at the bargaining table. Thus the final point of the case is probably erroneous as well as ironic. The major premise of the decision is, however, its analysis of the restriction imposed on the text selection process and the striking conclusion that *some* secondary-school teachers enjoy academic freedom with regard to *some* judgments in *some* courses.

The court was careful to qualify the holding in several respects, not only regarding the grade level and the type of course to which it applied but also the activity that was in dispute. Had the same teachers failed to maintain discipline or refused to take attendance—or perhaps even allowed their students to read fewer than a prescribed number of novels—the case would almost surely have fallen on the other side of the line. Change any of the critical factors, this court warned, and the outcome would no longer be certain. That, surely, is the meaning of the reference to a teacher's use of graffiti to lampoon the junior-high principal in front of his students.

The court of appeals reversed on both issues. After holding—quite properly in light of labor-law precedents—that union members could not bargain away their First Amendment rights, the court turned to the substantive issue that the district judge had resolved in the teachers' favor. The central issue was which of two groups—the school board or the teachers—had ultimate authority to choose textbooks. Since the board could decide whether or not to offer the course and could select a major textbook, then why (the court asked) "may it not go further and exclude certain books from being assigned for instruction in the course?"[47] The board had in fact approved a very long list of permissible texts and had proscribed only the ten titles that led to the suit. Moreover, the board's rule did not forbid mention of the ten books in class, nor their citation as examples of contemporary literature, but only their formal assignment. Under these conditions, the appellate court concluded that such a ban lay within the powers of the school board and did not abridge the First Amendment freedoms of the teachers.

The *Cary* (Denver) case represents a significant refinement of earlier precedents. In place of the monotonous focus on "relevance" and "disruption," other criteria now entered the picture. Two absolutely central issues began at this time (the late seventies) to receive proper attention—first, the question of the governance of education and the allocation of decisional authority or responsibility; and second, the purpose or nature of the educational experience.

The question of who may decide what issues is surely central to such cases and, Goldstein and others have argued, should have received attention in the courts much earlier. Perhaps the issue has been blurred because the earlier cases involved a single (admittedly familiar) model: the community protests the use of certain material, the board or administration orders it removed from the curriculum, and a teacher protests. In such a case it may be unnecessary to separate the governance issue—who may decide—from the substantive issue of what is being decided. But, in conclusion, we should consider one other case that involves a quite different model.

Ohio and the Spoon River Anthology

In the spring of 1972 a teacher in northern Ohio bought for and gave to her ninth-grade English students new paperback copies of Edgar Lee Masters's *Spoon River Anthology*. The students soon discovered that two pairs of facing pages had been neatly removed from the anthologies. When they asked the teacher for an explanation, she told them that she had decided that certain poems were "inappropriate" and that their language might be offensive to some. (She made no attempt to tamper with copies that students had bought on their own.)

Several students, with the aid of the Ohio Civil Liberties Union, brought suit against the district and the principal for having approved the deletion.[48]

The federal judge was perplexed by the novel issue presented by this case and cast about for helpful analogies. There was, he recognized, no issue of obscenity, since the reason given for deleting the questionable pages was the general subject matter rather than the impact of particular words. None of the familiar precedents seemed to fit. *Tinker* did not help because the students in this case "were not refused permission to express an opinion. . . ." The cases involving teachers (*Keefe, Parducci,* and *Mailloux*) did not really apply either because there "the stifled party [was] a teacher," and here the teacher was doing the stifling to the displeasure of the students. As the court said, "What a teacher chooses to teach is not equivalent to what a student decides to learn."[49] Finally, the court rejected a claim that would have given the students their strongest support—the right to receive information, which at the time of the decision (1974) was far less well developed than it has since become. As there was no constitutional basis on which to challenge the teacher's action, the students were left with only a tort claim, that is, unconsented destruction of their property (since the books had been bought with money they gave to the teacher). The case was then dismissed because the federal courts lack jurisdiction over such nonconstitutional issues.

The *Spoon River* case squarely raises the governance issue. Suppose, for example, the teacher had been discharged (under pressure from a group of liberal parents) for engaging in an act of censorship, and she had brought suit for reinstatement. A court would then face the issue that had been conveniently avoided in the earlier cases—whether the critical question is *who does the act* complained of (teacher, administration, or board), or whether instead the critical issue is the act itself (excising nonobscene material from an anthology). If, for example, a court felt that a teacher could not be dismissed for *refusing* to remove the suspect pages because that would constitute censorship of the *Keefe/Parducci* sort, it might also hold that the teacher could no more readily deprive the students of access to those pages on his or her own initiative. Conversely, the court could say that the teacher may "edit" the book even though the principal might not force him or her to do so. Such a decision would say, in effect, that a judgment to delete the pages is within the scope of the teacher's academic freedom, even though it denies students access to constitutionally protected material and even though the board could not have forced the teacher to delete the material.

The difference between the two focuses—who decides and what is decided—emerges from the *Spoon River* case. If removing the pages is something that *no one* may do, then the teacher would fare no better than would the board. Indeed, if one believes (as Goldstein appears to) that curricular judgments are essentially administrative, then the teacher might fare even less well than the board. If, on the other hand, one differentiates according to the locus of the decision—as the federal judge in the *Cary* case did—the outcome may depend on the identity of the actor as well as on the action taken. One might conclude that the board may not remove the pages—nor may it compel a teacher to do so—but that teachers may do so on their own. (In the actual *Spoon River* case, of course, the board and the administration approved what the teacher had done, so this issue did not arise. But in the event of disagreement over such editing of materials, a court would have to decide whether such action is within the province of the teacher's academic freedom, or whether it is an act permissible to neither teacher nor administration. The source or level of the action, the lurking issue of governance, becomes central under such circumstances.)

Apart from the focus on governance, *Cary* also brought to the fore the issue of educational mission or purpose. Earlier cases, notably *Parducci*, did consider such matters as the appropriateness of challenged material in the school setting, or the relationship of classroom discussion and its content to the works in the school library. But *Cary* posed a more basic inquiry: the nature of the course or part of the curriculum responsible for the controversy. To the *Cary* court a persuasive factor in the teachers' favor was the board's own listing of the course as a senior elective, thus implying the board's own view that orthodoxy should be minimized and freedom of choice should be encouraged. For the board to restrict the teacher's freedom of choice after encouraging student freedom of choice would be as inconsistent as would forbidding a teacher to discuss in class words found widely in books available in the school library. If the school board decided no longer to offer an advanced elective course in contemporary literature, that would be a different matter; but so long as the course was available to college-bound seniors who opted for an enriching experience, restrictions of the kind imposed in the *Cary* case were simply unsuited to the educational goals declared by the very authority that imposed them. Freedom of choice could be curtailed, to be sure, by simply discontinuing the course (and in fact that step has been taken by other communities seeking to stifle controversy in the classroom). But so long as the elective curriculum remains intact, its effectiveness cannot be undermined by winnowing out titles.

Such a conclusion is comforting, and partly reduces the conflicting pressures we spoke of at the beginning of this chapter. Academic freedom in the high-school classroom clearly is not absolute. Its scope, in fact, is to some degree subject to the judgment of the school board and the administration. It is the elected and appointed officials who shape the curriculum and decide in broad terms what shall be taught. If a district chooses to offer only basic required subjects, teachers in that district will enjoy very little freedom of expression, save in those areas in which the speech of any public employee may not be curtailed. If, on the other hand, school authorities (presumably in response to parental as well as student pressure) decide to enrich the curriculum and to offer advanced courses in literature, drama, government, or economics, they must accept the consequences. Teachers hired to teach such courses therefore enjoy a degree of academic freedom that is properly denied to their colleagues who teach manual arts, typing, and basic grammar. The school board can somewhat vary the scope of academic freedom available within the sytem—not by silencing particular teachers because it dislikes the words they write on the blackboard or the novels they select but rather by reshaping the curriculum. If school officials, for whatever reason, will not tolerate the liberties essential to an open curriculum, the remedy available to them must be general (eliminate all elective classes) rather than selective (stop particular behaviors of particular teachers).[50]

And now, perhaps we have reached the heart of the problem, which is not the legal question of academic freedom but rather the social and educational one — what is the proper role of the schools? Is the purpose of education in the present crisis of our society training for stasis or training for change? If we wish stasis, then certainly the schools should opt for a closed and structured curriculum. If we believe change should be the nature of things in our students' lives, then an open, elective, and less restricted educational program is called for.

Those who would apply the law to the school as an institution face the same questions as do the people involved in any other area of modern education: For what world do we prepare future citizens, and what philosophy and practice may best suit that goal? The law cannot and will not decide that issue. Education must.

FOR CONSIDERATION

1. How would you define academic freedom? What would you use as criteria to measure whether or not it existed in a school? Should all teachers have academic freedom? all students?

2. Review the cases described in this chapter. Which decisions do you agree with? With which do you disagree? In each case, what reasons do you have for your view?

3. Observe how controversial topics are treated in a school you are familiar with. Is there a procedure for inviting speakers to the school, or using certain teaching material? Is the procedure restrictive? Are there district policies on academic freedom? on teacher and student rights? on textbook selection? on handling complaints by parents or others in the community? Have there been examples of censorship or political restraint in the school recently? What do the teachers think of their academic freedom?

Notes

1. *Zykan* v. *Warsaw Community School Corp.*, 631 F.2d. 1300 (7th Cir. 1980).
2. *Los Angeles Times*, March 12, 1978, pt. IV, pp. 1, 16–19.

3. *Ibid.*

4. See R. O'Neil, *The Rights of Government Employees* (New York: Avon Books, 1978).

5. *Pickering* v. *Board of Education*, 391 U.S. 563 (1968).

6. *Russo* v. *Central School District No. 1*, 469 F.2d 623 (flag salute); *James* v. *Board of Education*, 461 F.2d 566 (2d Cir. 1972) (black armband).

7. *Tinker* v. *Des Moines School District*, 393 U.S. 503 (1969).

8. *Goldwasser* v. *Brown*, 417 F.2d 1169 (D.C. Cir. 1969).

9. Sheldon Nahmod, "Controversy in the Classroom: The High School Teacher and Freedom of Expression," *George Washington University Law Review* 39 (1971):1032, 1050.

10. *Wilson* v. *Chancellor*, 418 F. Supp. 1358 (D. Ore. 1976).

11. American Association of University Professors, *AAUP Policy Documents and Reports* (1977):2–3.

12. Stephen Goldstein, "The Asserted Right of Teachers to Determine What They Teach," *University of Pennsylvania Law Review* 124 (1976):1,293.

13. *Keyishian* v. *Board of Regents*, 385 U.S. 589 (1967).

14. *Meyer* v. *Nebraska*, 262 U.S. 390 (1925).

15. *Ibid.*

16. *Epperson* v. *Arkansas*, 393 U.S. 97 (1968).

17. *Ibid.*, p. 105.

18. *Ibid.*, p. 111.

19. *Moore* v. *Gaston County Board of Education*, 357 F. Supp. 1037 (W.D.N.C. 1973).

20. *Tinker* v. *Des Moines School District*, 393 U.S. 503 (1969).

21. *Ibid.*, p. 511.

22. Thomas Emerson, *The System of Freedom of Expression* (New York: Random House, 1970), pp. 609–610.

23. *Parker* v. *Board of Education*, 237 F. Supp. 222 (D. Md.); affirmed, 348 F.2d 464 (4th Cir. 1965).

24. *Keefe* v. *Geanakos*, 418 F.2d 359, 361 (1st Cir. 1969).

25. *Ibid.*, p. 362.

26. *Mailloux* v. *Kiley*, 436 F.2d 565 (1st Cir. 1971).

27. *Ibid.*, p. 566.

28. *Ibid.*, 323 F. Supp. 1387, 1391 (D. Mass.), aff'd., 448 F.2d 1242 (1st Cir. 1971).

29. *Ibid.*, p. 1392.

30. *Mailloux* v. *Kiley*, 448 F.2d 1242, 1243 (1st Cir. 1971).

31. *Brubaker* v. *Board of Education*, 502 F.2d 973 (7th Cir. 1974).

32. *Ibid.*

33. *Frison* v. *Franklin County Board of Education*, 596 F.2d 1192 (4th Cir. 1979).

34. *Ibid.*, p. 1194.

35. *Parducci* v. *Rutland*, 316 F. Supp. 352 (M.D. Ala. 1970).

36. *Ibid.*, p. 355.

37. *Ibid.*, p. 356.

38. *Ibid.*, p. 356.
39. *Webb* v. *Lake Mills Community School District*, 344 F. Supp. 791 (N.D. Iowa 1972).
40. *Kingsville Independent School District* v. *Cooper*, 611 F.2d 1109 (5th Cir. 1980).
41. *Cary* v. *Adams-Arapahoe School District*, 427 F. Supp. 945 (D. Colo. 1978).
42. *Ibid.*, p. 948.
43. *Cary* v. *Adams-Arapahoe School District*, p. 950.
44. *Ibid.*, p. 952.
45. *Ibid.*, p. 955.
46. *Ibid.*, p. 956.
47. *Cary* v. *Adams-Arapahoe School District*, 598 F.2d 535, 544 (10th Cir. 1979).
48. *Kramer* v. *Scioto-Darby City School District*, Civil Action 72-406, Southern District of Ohio, March 8, 1974 (not officially reported).
49. *Ibid.*
50. See *Zykan* v. *Warsaw Community School Corp.*, 631 F.2d 1300 (7th Cir. 1980).

Chapter 15:
Integration:
The Quest
for Equal
Justice

Introduction

There is perhaps no greater danger facing the United States than the internal danger of self-destruction through discrimination and denial of freedoms. Gunner Myrdahl, in *The American Dilemma*, warned us that if we could not learn to live together without the racial and ethnic hatred that has so often marred our quest for freedom and justice, there was good reason to believe that our country would not only fail in its mission of freedom and justice, but that, indeed, it would cease to exist in the way that we know it.[1]

Although things are certainly better than they were 150 years ago, there is no great reason to rejoice. A look at the 1980 census maps clearly indicates that there is continuing segregation in this country in major cities and along belts of population stretching between cities. Many of the census tracts in these belts show the population to be largely black, while other tracts show no blacks in the population. The potential for racial tension and violence is obvious.

In this chapter we are not interested in what caused the bigotries and segregation, but only in recognizing their essential evilness both morally and societally. Specifically, this chapter reviews the legal history of slavery, abolition, segregation, desegregation, and the hope for integration. There is no issue of greater social concern or danger to the United States. There is also no issue in which the schools have been more centrally involved. When schools choose to desegregate—and it is a choice since teachers and administrators can make the process smooth or difficult, successful or unsuccessful—then we as educators are on the forefront of social change. While the values of equality begin in the home, actual institutionalization of inequality or equality begins with the schools.

An End of an Abomination: The Abolition of Slavery

Almost every culture has had slaves, some occasionally, some as a way of life. Perhaps only the far northern cultures were virtually without slavery. This is not because the far northern cultures were more virtuous, but more that slavery must be economically feasible. For slavery to work, there must be a need for large numbers of very low skilled workers, usually mine or agriculture workers. Further, the work must be year round work. Slavery is not economical if slaves work only during the summer. A small part-time mine or farm does not need slaves and would find them economically unfeasible. The family or clan could handle the work. Slavery only works, then, in areas where the growing or working season is long, where the need for workers is large, and where the work is unskilled. Whether this be the Egyptian pyramids, Greek copper mines, or cotton fields in the southern United States makes no difference. Slavery is an economic feasibility in these places while it would not be in Scandinavia or the farms of Minnesota, Vermont, or Wisconsin.

Two cultures based on slavery were the ante-bellum South and the West Indies. In both places the growing season was long, the work was hard and dirty, there was a need for large numbers of people to work at the lowest possible expense, and there was a large expanse of land with few people to work it, among other factors. However, slavery had lost some of its economic appeal in the South by the time of the Civil War due to the depletion of the soil, the lack of new territories open to the growth of cotton, and the growing dependence on industry. Slavery itself, however, had been a major legal issue in the United Kingdom and the United States for almost 100 years.

Slavery in the
British Isles

Slavery had never been very popular in Great Britain largely because the population was very large in comparison to the land area and the land was used either for small family-owned farms or industrial development. It is therefore no great surprise that the fight against slavery should not have begun in the Colonies or, later, the United States where slavery was both popular and economically useful, but in Great Britain where it was not really economically feasible anyway. In Great Britain, there was neither positive nor negative law regarding slavery, that is, there were no laws on the books that allowed or denied slavery. There was no law at all. This is not surprising. One interpretation of history is the growth of public awareness of the morality of social issues. Slavery was accepted before the eighteenth century because very few people saw it as particularly evil. It was only with an increase in awareness, and thereby an increase in conflicts between the forces of stasis and change, that law was needed. That awareness emerged in the seventeenth and eighteenth centuries.

Because there was no law, the way was therefore open to a decision not on the basis of law, but on the basis of morality. The question had to be asked, "Should slavery be allowed to exist?" This period from the mid- to late 1700s was a period of growing industrialization that led, as it so often does, to growth in the demands for civil and social rights. With the growth of a well-to-do mercantile class, there was less emphasis on birth rights and more emphasis on personal rights. In this atmosphere it is not surprising that questions should be raised regarding the rights of others as well as the self. Such did indeed happen in the case of *Somerset* v. *Stewart*.

Somerset v. Stewart (1772): The First Case

Stewart voluntarily brought a slave named Somerset from Virginia to England in November 1769. Somerset escaped from Stewart and, in time, made the acquaintance of a number of free blacks in England as well as some of the emergent Quaker abolitionists. Somerset did not wish to return to the service of Stewart. Stewart recaptured Somerset and had him placed on board the ship *Ann and Mary*, in the care of a Captain Knowles, bound for Jamaica where Somerset would be sold. As the *Ann and Mary* was about to set sail, Somerset was removed through a writ of *habeas corpus*. It was at this point that Lord Mansfield entered the case.

Lord Mansfield, Court of the King's Beach, the judge in the case, was to determine the question, "Whether a slave, by coming to England, became free?" England had no laws regarding slavery at all and it had been the practice of Americans to bring a household slave with them both to aid them and as a mark of prestige. Lord Mansfield was to determine whether or not slavery would be tolerated in England. It was true that slavery had positive law in America. The question was whether or not the laws of America should be held valid in England where no such laws existed. Lord Mansfield was very clear on both questions.

> The state of slavery is of such a nature, that it is incapable of being introduced on any reasons, moral or political; but only positive law, which preserves its force long after the reasons, occasion, and time itself from whence it was created, is erased from memory: it's so odious, that nothing can be suffered to support it but positive law. Whatever inconveniences, therefore, may follow from a decision, I cannot say this case is allowed or approved by the law of England; and therefore the Black must be discharged.[2]

The inconvenience, by the way, was not inconsequential. There were 14,000 to 15,000 black slaves in England, valued at about 700,000 pounds sterling. Even so, Lord Mansfield made it eminently clear that, from June 22, 1772, any slave who was voluntarily brought to England, would be free from the time that he or she stepped off the boat. It was a masterful decision.

The Slave Grace (1827): A Step Back

In 1822, fifty years after the *Somerset* case, a Mrs. Allen of Antigua came to England with her female attendant, Grace, a slave by birth. Grace voluntarily returned to Antigua with Mrs. Allen in 1823 and continued with Mrs. Allen until August 8, 1825, when Grace was seized by the Port Authority of Antigua as having been illegally imported in 1823. The authority for the seizure was *Somerset* v. *Stewart*, since the slave, Grace, had become free by being on English soil from 1822 to 1823. The case was heard before Lord Stowell, High Court of the Admiralty in 1827.[3]

Lord Stowell, who seemed to be interested in property rights (England was going through a conservative period at the time), used a number of arguments, for example, the hardship to slave owners of not being able to come home to England with their house servants because the slaves would be free even if they returned with their masters to their place of servitude; and the disruption of having large numbers of slaves freed at one time, that is, all those who had been to England at any time since the *Somerset* decision. These are largely proprietary arguments and certainly would be rejected by the Quakers and abolitionists of the *Somerset* era. Lord Stowell said that *Somerset* was not a precedential case in the matter of Grace because Grace was not in England at the time of her seizure. Lord Stowell said, if effect, that Grace would have been free if she had desired it in England, but because she had voluntarily left and returned to a place where slavery was legal, she was no longer free.

Although the case was decided in favor of the slave owners, its precedent was not to last long.

The Act Abolishing Slavery in the Colonies (1833): The English Solution

The full title of the act was "An Act for the Abolition of Slavery throughout the British colonies; for promoting the Industry of the manumitted Slaves; and for compensating the Persons hitherto entitled to the Services of such Slaves."[4] When, in August of 1833, the statute took effect, all slaves in British colonies were to be freed and slavery was over in half the English-speaking world. A war would have to be fought to end slavery in the other half.

The American Solution: We Aren't Done Yet

The problem was far more severe in the United States than in the United Kingdom. We had a long history of economically feasible slavery, far more territory, a better climate, and a much higher percentage of black slaves than did the United Kingdom. There were many areas in the South where black slaves outnumbered white owners by twenty to one. Blacks still outnumber whites in many parts of the South. The entire South had opted both philosophically and economically to retain agriculture. It was a clean, profitable, and graceful pursuit for the landowners. Industry was not clean or graceful, though it was profitable. The South was living in the past, but it should be pointed out that that past was indeed both beautiful and graceful if one was not a black slave. There were more universities and colleges in the South than in the North, more writers and artists and scholars and scientists in the South than in the North. Slavery had led to a gracious and intellectual life in the South, albeit one based on the dirty immorality of slavery. In brief, slavery was not just an economic problem, it was a way of life and a philosophical problem. Because the problem was severe in this country, the solution would also be more severe and take a good deal longer.

JEFFERSON AND THE DECLARATION OF INDEPENDENCE

The first clear indication of the problem came with the ratification of the Declaration of Independence. In Jefferson's original version, there was a relatively clear statement about slavery:

> He [King George III] has waged cruel war against human nature itself, violating its most sacred rights of life and liberty in the persons of a distant people [Africans] who never offended him, captivating & carrying them into slavery in another hemisphere or to incur miserable death in their transportation thither. This piratical warfare, the opprobrium of *infidel* powers, is the warfare of the *Christian* king of Great Britain. Determined to keep open a market where *Men* should be bought & sold, he has prostituted his negative for suppressing every legislative attempt to prohibit or to restrain this execrable commerce. And that this assemblage of horrors might want no fact of distinguished die, he is now exciting those very people to rise in arms among us, and to purchase that liberty of which he has deprived them, by murdering the people on whom he also obtruded them: thus paying off former crimes committed against the *Liberties* of one people, with the crimes which he urges them to commit against the *lives* of another.[5]

Even though Jefferson did not say that slavery should be abolished or even terminated in the future, the very concept that slavery was wrong was not allowed to remain in the Declaration. The slave states would not allow it and since a unanimous vote was required for the Declaration, it was finally removed. The battle lines, however, were drawn.

STATE CONSTITUTIONS

Some of the American Colonies never did find slavery particularly attractive. New England was both economically and philosophically unattuned to it.

Small farms or businesses, industry, and trade dominated its economy and slavery does not function well in areas where people believe in individualism and where the family can and must take care of its own needs.

The first clear indications of individual state actions concerning slavery came as the states wrote their own constitutions. Vermont was the earliest when in 1777 its constitution stated that no male over twenty-one and no female over eighteen shall be a slave—a stereotypical straightforward New England statement. Pennsylvania followed soon after, but was somewhat more circumspect about it. In 1780, Pennsylvania enacted a statute stating that no one born in Pennsylvania from March 1, 1780, onward would be a slave.[6] All slave children were to be indentured servants until the age of twenty-eight. Massachusetts followed also in 1780, and Rhode Island in 1784. New York, of course, had a two-step plan. Any child born of a slave after July 4, 1799,[7] would be "born free." The child was to be an apprenticed servant until age twenty-five for females and twenty-eight for males. The 1817 statute[8] stated that any slave in New York born before July 4, 1799, would be free as of July 4, 1827. A number of other New England and northeastern seaboard states affected similar constitutional provisions or statutes before the turn of the century.

THE CONSTITUTIONAL CONVENTION

The United States Constitution was somewhat more complex because it had to satisfy both the South and the North. There are three pertinent articles in the original Constitution:

Article I, section 2, is the three-fifths rule. The slave states wanted to count black slaves for representation in the House of Representatives. However, the nonslave states said that if blacks could not vote then they should not be counted for representation. The apocryphal story is that Ben Franklin said that since there were nine States and territories that allowed slaves and wanted them to be fully counted, and six that did not want them counted at all, that they should be counted as three-fifths of a person (9 is 3/5 of 15). That is as reasonable a story as any other since three-fifths is certainly a peculiar number.

Article I, section 9, states that Congress shall not make any law prohibiting the importation of slaves until 1808, thereby assuring the slave states that there would be no interference with their practices at least until that year.

Article IV, section 2, is the infamous escaped slave clause. It states that:

No person held to Service or Labour in one State, under the Laws thereof, escaping into another, shall, in Consequence of any Law or Regulation therein, be discharged from such Service or Labour, but shall be delivered up on Claim of the Party to whom such Service or Labour may be due.

The Constitution of the United States said that any escaped slave had to be returned even if the slave was in a free State. For this reason the Underground Railroad had to take slaves to Canada, where slavery was illegal due to the English Abolition Act, rather than just to the free states. It would be pointed out, however, that the return of a slave captured in a free state is different than the situation in the *Somerset* case where the slave was voluntarily brought into a free country, that is, where the slave did not escape to the free territory but was brought there by his or her master. This distinction becomes important in the first major court case in the United States on the possible rights of slaves.

Somerset Visits America:
Commonwealth v. Aves (1836)

The case took place in the Commonwealth of Massachusetts.[9] A Mr. Aves had brought his personal female slave servant to Massachusetts. When he wished to return to New Orleans with his slave, the slave refused to go. Judge Shaw was in exactly the same situation as Lord Mansfield had been almost seventy years before, namely, the slave had been voluntarily brought into a free state and wished to be free. There was no question of the slave's having escaped to a free state, which would have fallen under article IV, section 9, of the Constitution. The case was clear; unfortunately the law was not. The first finding of Judge Shaw was the same as that of Lord Mansfield, shocked that there was no law, either positive or negative, regarding slavery in Massachusetts. Slavery had been abolished in the state by its own Constitution before the adoption of the United States Constitition. In the state Constitution slavery was ". . . abolished, as being contrary to the principles of justice, and of nature, and repugnant to the provisions of the declaration of rights, which is a component part of the constitution of the State."

Judge Shaw saw the relationship between *Aves* and *Somerset* and based his decision on *Somerset*. The United States courts based many of their precedential cases on English Common Law, which is the basis of the law of both countries. Judge Shaw was, however, very careful to point out that he was not including the situation where slaves were being transported across state lines, but only the case in which an owner voluntarily brought a slave to reside for some time in Massachusetts and then wanted to forcibly remove the slave from that free state.

By 1836, Massachusetts was at the same point as England had been in 1772. Slaves were now free if they were moved voluntarily to free states and resided there for an extended period.

Jackson v. Bolloch (1837)

The following year a similar case occurred in Connecticut, *Jackson* v. *Bulloch*. In even stronger language than in *Aves*, Connecticut courts stated that from the precedent of both *Aves* and *Somerset*, a person who wishes freedom shall have it in the state of Connecticut regardless of previous condition of servitude:

> That every human being has a right to liberty, as well as to life and property and to enjoy the fruit of his own labour; that slavery is contrary to the principles of natural right and to the great law of love; that it is founded on injustice and fraud, and can be supported only by the provision of positive law, and positions, which it is not necessary here to prove.[10]

We were on our way. Unfortunately, just as the British had a setback in the case concerning the slave Grace, so the United States would have two setbacks, one relatively unknown but an augury of the future, the other justifiably infamous. The first is *Roberts* v. *City of Boston*. The second is *Dred Scott* v. *Sandford*.

The First Desegregation Case:
Roberts v. City of Boston (1850)

Charles Sumner (not to be confused with William Graham Sumner, a racist Social Darwinist of the late nineteenth and early twentieth centuries), a leading abolitionist, aided in the suit of a Mr. Roberts of Boston.[11] Boston had segregated schools and a colored child was not allowed to attend a white school even though the colored school was substantially further away than the white school. Sumner and Morris pleaded for the plaintiff that separate schools and segregation are a violation of the spirit of both American institutions and the Constitution of Massachusetts; exclusion of black children from white schools is an inconvenience which white parents are not forced into and therefore is a violation of equal protection of the laws; and, segregation by race is in the nature of a caste system and a violation of equality.

The arguments sound exceedingly modern and were to be used again 104 years later in *Brown* v. *Board of Education*. The question raised and answered by the Supreme Court of Massachusetts was whether separate schools for colored students are inherently unequal. The answer in 1850 was "No." The added distance traveled by colored children is not sufficient to say that they are not given equal protection of the law. Further, said the court, education is a local concern and the school committee will have to make the best judgments that it can.

Roberts is interesting because the arguments both in favor of segregation and opposed to it would be used so often in the latter half of the twentieth century. The case was an attempt to solve a social problem before society really recognized that the problem existed. It was an attempt to move forward in time. The *Dred Scott* decision was an attempt to go backward in time.

Pre–Civil War Reaction:
Dred Scott (1857)

In 1834 Dred Scott, a slave belonging to an Army surgeon, Dr. Emerson, was taken to Rock Island, Illinois, a free state that prohibited slavery. In 1836, Scott was taken to Fort Snelling in the Louisiana Territory north of the line 36 degrees 30 minutes, which made it a free area according to the Missouri Compromise. In 1838 Scott was brought back to Missouri and in 1847 brought suit in Missouri courts to gain his freedom. He based his action on *Aves* and *Somerset*.[12]

Chief Justice Taney wrote the majority decision, though each of the justices wrote a separate decision either concurring or dissenting. Justice Taney pointed out that Negroes were not intended to be "members of the society" and "citizens" by the framers of the Constitution and that neither the Constitution nor the Declaration of Independence indicates any rights given to Negroes that whites are bound to respect. Further, and absolutely central for Taney, was that the Missouri Compromise did not intend to, nor could it, deprive a person of his property without due process of law (Fifth Amendment to the Constitution). Freeing the slave, Scott, would be deprivation of property without due process as guaranteed by the Fifth Amendment to the Constitution of the United States. Taney never referred to *Aves, Somerset*, or *Jackson*. The Dred Scott decision remained in effect for ten years, when it was abrogated by the Fourteenth Amendment.

Legal Equality Comes Home: The Thirteenth and Fourteenth Amendments

The Fifth Amendment to the Constitution guarantees us certain rights: the right to a grand jury; not to have to incriminate ourselves; protection against double jeopardy; and possibly most importantly, ". . . nor be deprived of life, liberty, or property without due process of law. . . ." The due process clause has been the basis of a large number of civil liberties cases. However, the Fifth Amendment does not apply to the states but only to the federal government. It was the Fourteenth Amendment that made the Fifth Amendment applicable to more than federal territories. The Fourteenth Amendment went even further, because it not only guaranteed that all of the Bill of Rights would be applicable to citizens of states, but also that both due process and equal protection of the laws ("equal protection" is not included in the Fifth Amendment) were guaranteed by the federal government. The Thirteenth Amendment (abolition of slavery) and the Fourteenth Amendment were passed in the very liberal period immediately following the Civil War. The attempt was to guarantee that every citizen of every state would be able to avail himself (women were not counted at this point; that came in the Nineteenth Amendment in 1929) of equal protection before the law and due process of the law. The Dred Scott decision had been overturned. It took a war to do it.

IS SEPARATE, EQUAL? THE FIRST TEST

In the period immediately following the Civil War there was a general liberal feeling and a more general willingness on the part of some whites to include blacks in the mainstream of American life. One case can be directly traced to this more positive feeling.

Railroad Company v. Brown (1873)

Catherine Brown, who was a passenger on a train in the District of Columbia, was forcibly ejected from the "whites only car." Since Congress, which is the ruling legislative body for the District, had enacted a set of laws abolishing "separate but equal" facilities in the District in the liberal period following the Civil War, suit was brought before the Supreme Court. The Supreme Court granted relief on the grounds that the "separate but equal" doctrine was discriminatory and therefore a violation of the law passed by Congress.[13]

If the railroad were to continue operations in the District of Columbia, discrimination by race would have to cease.

THE INTERVENING YEARS

Following the Civil War, federal troops were stationed in the South to make sure that newly freed black Americans would be given all the protections guaranteed them by the Thirteenth and Fourteenth Amendments. Blacks voted in large numbers and a number of black legislators were elected both on the state and federal levels. Both black voting and the election of black officials ended when federal troops were removed. There was no longer any agency to enforce the provisions of equal protection and due process. In both the South and the North, the values gained in the Civil War were going into retreat. It was during this time that "separate but equal" schools were developed in much of the country. Although this was particularly true of the South, it was by no means limited to that area. Not only education was affected. Education, frankly, was not very important in the largely rural, nontechnological sections of the United States. The first case that would challenge "separate but equal" facilities was not an education case at all. It was, again, a railroad car case. This time the decision would overturn *Railroad Company*.

Plessy v. Ferguson: Sixty Years Wrong

In 1892 Plessy, a citizen of Louisiana, who was one-eighth "African blood" and seven-eighths Caucasian, boarded a train from New Orleans to Covington, both in Louisiana (this is important because it is not an interstate case). He was ordered out of the whites only railroad car. He refused and was arrested, jailed, and convicted on July 10, 1890, of violating a state statute that required separate accommodation for white and colored passengers.[14]

The difference in attitude between 1873 (*Railroad Company*) and 1890 is quite striking. The federal troops had been removed from the South by this time and blacks were no longer voting or in positions of power. "Jim Crow" laws separating the races had been instituted in a number of states and would be instituted in more. *Plessy* v. *Ferguson* came to the Supreme Court when Plessy sued Ferguson, who was the judge of the criminal district court that had convicted him.

The question before the Court was whether "separate but equal" facilities violated the Thirteenth and Fourteenth Amendments to the Constitution.

There is little doubt that the Court immediately following the Civil War would have said that it was indeed a violation. In point of fact, that is what the Court did say in *Railroad Company* v. *Brown*. That case was not even mentioned as a precedent in *Plessy*. The Court simply reversed itself and said that "separate but equal" facilities were not a violation.

There is good reason to believe that some of the decision was based on the writings of the major Social Darwinist of that day, William Graham Sumner. One of his major works was published in *The Forum* in 1894: "The Absurd Effort to Make the World Over" in which Sumner said that it is not possible to make changes in society through the use of laws or the courts or social programs because folkways, or societal behavior patterns, arise naturally and can neither be encouraged nor discouraged by government.[15] Further, he said, basing his ideas both on Spencer's Social Darwinism and the growing belief in eugenics, some people are, indeed, inferior and should be separated socially. These inferior peoples could not be aided by social programs because their inferiority was not social, but hereditary. These are the same arguments being raised in the last quarter of the twentieth century by those who feel that test scores show that blacks and other minorities are inherently inferior. Therefore, social and educational programs designed to aid minority children are of no value.[16] In the case of *Plessy* v. *Ferguson* the arguments were used by the Court and they were to maintain legal segregation in the United States for sixty years.

After quoting from *Roberts* v. *Boston* at some length to show that separate has always been considered equal and pointing out that the District of Columbia had segregated schools (but not quoting from *Railroad Company*), Judge Brown concluded as follows in the majority opinion:

> We consider the underlying fallacy of the plaintiff's argument to consist in the assumption that the enforced separation of the two races stamps the colored race with a badge of inferiority. If this is so, it is not by reason of anything found in the act, but solely because the colored race chooses to put that construction upon it. The argument necessarily assumes that if, as has been more than once the case, and is not unlikely to be so again, the colored race should become the dominant power in the state legislature, and should enact a law in precisely similar terms, it would thereby relegate the white race to an inferior position. We imagine that the white race, at least, would not acquiesce in this assumption. The argument also assumes that social prejudices may be overcome by legislation, and that equal rights cannot be secured to the negro except by an enforced commin-

gling of the two races. We cannot accept this proposition. If the two races are to meet upon terms of social equality, it must be the result of natural affinities, a mutual appreciation of each other's merits and a voluntary consent of individuals. . . . *Legislation is powerless to eradicate racial instincts or to abolish distinctions based upon physical differences*, and the attempt to do so can only result in accentuating the difficulties of the present situation. If the civil and political rights of both races be equal one cannot be inferior to the other civilly or politically. *If one race be inferior to the other socially, the Constitution of the United States cannot put them upon the same plane.*[17] [Emphasis Added]

Plessy made it clear that all colored peoples were now legally separate and that if that made them inferior, that was a problem of *folkways* and could not, and should not, be interfered with by the Court. Education, transportation, housing, and society were to be separate but equal; "equal" was to be defined later in a most peculiar fashion (see *Cumming*, page 360).

The decision in *Plessy* was not unanimous, however. Justice Harlan wrote a strong and stirring dissent that also has modern-sounding arguments. It is sometimes difficult for us to realize that the issue of racism is not new and the arguments are not new on either side. Justice Harlan spoke for equality:

. . . But in view of the Constitution, in the eye of the law, there is in this country no superior, dominant, ruling class of citizens. There is no caste here. Our Constitution is color-blind, and neither knows nor tolerates classes among citizens.

After showing the hideousness of the *Dred Scott* decision, which was finally overturned by the Thirteenth and Fourteenth Amendments, Justice Harlan continued:

. . . Sixty millions of whites are in no danger from the presence here of eight millions of blacks. The destinies of the two races, in this country, are indissolubly linked together, and the interests of both require that the common government of all shall not permit the seeds of race hate to be planted under the sanction of law. What can more certainly arouse race hate, what more certainly create and perpetuate a feeling of distrust between the races, than state enactments, which, in fact, proceed on the ground that colored citizens are so inferior and degraded that they cannot be allowed to sit in public coaches occupied by white citizens? That, as all will admit, is the real meaning of such legislation as was enacted in Louisiana.

The sure guarantee of peace and security of each race is the clear, distinct, unconditional recognition by our government, Nation and State, of every right that inheres in civil freedom, and of the equality before the law of all citizens of the United States without regard to race.

And finally,

. . . We boast of the freedom enjoyed by our people above all other peoples. But it is difficult to reconcile that boast with a state of the law which, practically, puts the brand of servitude and degradation upon a large class of our fellow-citizens, our equals before the law. The thin disguise of "equal" accommodations for passengers in railroad coaches will not mislead any one, nor atone for the wrong this day done. . . .[18]

What more can be said? For the next sixty years, "separate but equal" would be the law of the land. And it would get worse. The Social Darwinists and the emerging eugenicist psychologists would give scientific validity to racial and ethnic separation.

IT GETS WORSE: CUMMING V. RICHMOND COUNTY BOARD OF EDUCATION

Just three years after *Plessy*, the Supreme Court decided its first educational case in fifty years. Education was not very important at the turn of the century. Most of our population lived in rural areas, was not technologically oriented, and really did not need to be particularly well educated. For that reason, there are very few education cases until the later half of the twentieth century. What few cases there were, were a disaster. *Cumming*, the first of these cases, involved the definition of "equal."

Cumming v. Richmond (1899)[19]

In Richmond County, Georgia, the school board had closed the black high school while still maintaining the white one. The ostensible reason for closing the black high school was a lack of funds. The black parents brought suit. However, of concern to us is the definition of "equal" that comes out of *Cumming*. Evidently, an equal amount of money was spent by the Richmond County School Board for black and white children. Unfortunately, there were many more black children in the county than white children. This is what necessitated the closing of the black high school. The money was needed to educate the larger number of black elementary-school children. The

funds were allocated by race, not per child. Justice Harlan accepted this definition of equality before the law. So long as equal monies were spent on both
races, the Fourteenth Amendment had been satisfied as determined by *Plessy*.
In the *Plessy* case, as well, there was no interest in how many blacks as opposed
to whites ride the train, but only that there be an equal number of cars and
that they be equally appointed. It was not a *per capita* decision.

Justice Harlan wrote the majority decision and there is some historical interest in the change in his attitude between 1894 when he wrote the dissent in
Plessy and 1899 when he wrote the majority decision in *Cumming*. Some say that
the Social Darwinists got to him and changed his mind about the role of the Constitution in maintaining equal rights for all citizens. Others, the present author
included, feel that Justice Harlan believed in the law and the law had spoken
in *Plessy* and it is the jurist's duty to uphold and interpret the law, not to make it.

Justice Harlan's opinion is based on two constructs: First, education is a
state right and except in extreme circumstances decisions should be left to the
states. Therefore, if the State of Georgia wants to maintain "separate but
equal" educational facilities, it has every right to do so. The Constitution does
not mention education and since all issues not mentioned in the document are
relegated to state control, education is a state prerogative unless an individual
constitutional right has been violated. The second construct then is whether
the constitutional right of equal protection has been violated in separate but
equal schools. On the basis of *Plessy*, Justice Harlan said "No."

Even Worse: Gong Lum v. Rice (1927)

Gong Lum lived in Mississippi and his daughter, Martha, wanted to go to the
all-white school, which was a substantially better school than the all-black
school. The laws of Mississippi stated that colored people should be educated
separately from whites. The Supreme Court decided that being Chinese was
not being white and therefore Martha Lum would have to go to the all-
colored school.[20]

The racism was now more or less complete. White was white, and everything else was not.

Between the Wars

As has been implied, racism in the United States extended beyond blacks: The
emergent eugenicist psychometricians who had developed a series of standard-

ized intelligence tests were able to "prove," to their own satisfaction at least that, aside from blacks, who were considered the dumbest people in the world, the Jews and the Chinese, were certainly next. This was determined by giving Jews and Chinese standardized intelligence tests in English. The Jews were tested with other immigrants at Ellis Island in New York harbor as they got off the boats from Europe, while the Chinese were tested in California, where they had often been excluded from English-speaking schools. By the test, the next dumbest groups were the so-called PIGS. This acronym stood for *P*oles, *I*talians, *G*reeks, and *S*lavs. They were also tested at Ellis Island and came out only slightly brighter than the Jews.

A much more liberal period began with the 1930s and 1940s in politics, economics, and social arrangements. The New Deal changed many poor people's attitudes about their economic condition. It also changed the attitude of many toward government. While before the New Deal many of us may have thought of government as a necessary evil, these people now came to view it as our aid in time of need. It was only with the coming of the Second World War and the realization of the evils of eugenics whether used by the Nazi's or by American psychometricians, that the whole eugenics movement went into a hiatus.

The Second World War, as is so often the case with wars, increased our awareness of the diversity of peoples and life styles. Further, with the end of the war came one of the greatest social revolutions to occur in the United States, the GI Bill of Rights. In one generation, the country moved from a largely agricultural and nontechnological society to a college-educated white-collar society. After the experiences of our soldiers, white and black, in dealing with each other and with other cultures, the GI Bill, and the economic and social changes of the New Deal, the United States would never be the same. Once the war was over, the country was ready to move forward with the social business at hand. The armed services had been desegregated in the late 1940s and so would graduate professional university education. By 1954 the country would finally be ready to end legal subservience and inferiority in education. Once and for all, "separate but equal" would be defined as inherently unequal. Eighty years after *Railroad Company* v. *Brown* another Brown would bring us full circle.

On Freedom's Road: The College Cases

While the Second World War changed the United States in an irreversable fashion, there was a reaction to this liberal and open-world view: the paranoia and hysteria of McCarthyism. While that movement was most violent and ruined many lives and reputations, it was more a diversion than a stream. The stream, almost river, was a demand on the part of the disenfranchised for a part of the American Dream. This was the success of the G.I. Bill of Rights, which provided free education to all those veterans who wanted it. Some of those who wanted it were black and they could not get it because there were few black colleges and fewer black graduate and professional schools. It should be remembered that America had just left the era when Marian Anderson, the great black contralto, was not allowed to sing on the only stage in Washington D.C. (the auditorium of the Daughters of the American Revolution building) and was invited by Eleanor Roosevelt to sing at the Lincoln Memorial instead. It was the same in 1948. The next twenty years would see educational desegregation, voting rights acts, civil rights acts, and a general opening of the society with an understanding that, finally, race has no place in the Constitution of the United States.

As early as 1938 the Supreme Court had begun the process of equality of educational opportunity on the professional school level. In *Missouri ex rel. Gaines* v. *Canada*,[21] the Court had ruled that Lloyd Gaines, a Negro graduate of all-black Lincoln University, had to be allowed to attend the University of Missouri Law School since there was no black equivalent law school in the state. Had the Second World War not brought more immediate problems to the fore, this might have been the first case in the fight against segregation. However, the fight would have to wait ten years.

The first of the postwar college cases occurred in 1948 in Oklahoma. The case has received very little attention, but it was the opening shot for the new battle. The NAACP and other groups dedicated to equal protection knew that they would have to build a case to have schools desegregated and that it would be easier to make on the college and professional school levels than on lower levels. States would find it difficult, if not impossible, to maintain two totally separate and fully equal professional schools in every discipline. The expense would be overwhelming. For this reason, it would be easier to desegregate graduate and professional schools where the states could not show some equality as in *Plessy* and *Cumming*.

Sipuel v. Board of Regents of the University of Oklahoma

Sipuel was denied admittance to the University of Oklahoma School of Law solely because of her race. She appealed to the Supreme Court saying that she was not being given equal protection since whites were allowed to go to law school and she was not. The Court agreed and said that "the State must provide it [law school education] for her in conformity with the equal protection clause of the Fourteenth Amendment and provide it as soon as it does for applicants of any other group." They quoted *Gaines* in their decision.[22]

Sweatt v. Painter

Sweatt, a black student, was denied admission to the University of Texas Law School solely because of his race. Texas, being richer than Oklahoma, then established a separate law school for black students. That law school, to no one's surprise, was not on an academic par with the law school at the University of Texas. Sweatt said that he was being denied an equal law school education and was therefore being denied equal protection of the laws. The Court again agreed and ordered that he be admitted to the University of Texas Law School.[23]

McLaurin v. Oklahoma State Regents

G. W. McLaurin, a black student of education, wished to receive a doctorate in that subject at the University of Oklahoma since no black institution in the state offered such a degree. He was denied admission but filed a complaint. A three judge district court ordered him admitted. The Oklahoma State legislature then passed a law saying that although blacks must be admitted to the University of Oklahoma, they would still have to be totally segregated in their education. Mr. McLaurin, therefore, while admitted for doctoral work, was required to sit outside the door of all of his classes, use the cafeteria only when other students were not present, and use a special desk on a special floor of the library among other indignities.[24]

Unfortunately, this law could not be struck down on the grounds of stupidity; rather the question was whether differential treatment of one student because of his race is a violation of that student's equal rights protection. The Court said yes and ordered that the differential treatment be stopped.

These three cases demanded equal protection of black students who wanted college and professional education. They did not question the concept of "separate but equal," which had withstood the test of some sixty years. They did set the stage. Would it now be possible to ask the obvious question asked 100 years before in *Roberts*, "Is separate ever equal?" That question would be far more difficult to answer. It would mean overturning *Plessy* and the Supreme Court is very hesitant to overrule itself. It believes in precedent because it is based on precedent. The evidence would have to be overwhelming.

Free At Last! Free At Last!
The *Brown* Decisions

It was not black children who were made the most free by *Brown*, it was education itself. No longer would Americans be required to maintain the myths of superiority and inferiority or the myth of the need to separate and segregate children. Education could finally join the twentieth century with its multi-cultural and pluralistic world view. Children could be taught in a setting that was more similar to the real world, namely, a setting that was black and white and yellow and red and brown. It is important for children to see and respect differences. *Brown* allows education that freedom.

Brown is actually four cases: *Brown* v. *Topeka Board of Education* (Kansas, 1951)[25]; *Briggs* v. *Elliot* (South Carolina, 1951)[26]; *Davis* v. *County School Board* (Virginia, 1952)[27]; and *Belton* v. *Gebhart* (Delaware, 1952)[28]. The laws in the four cases are so similar that they were combined into the one *Brown* case. Why *Brown* was chosen is not entirely clear. The Supreme Court often takes the cases in alphabetical or chronological order, either of which would have placed *Brown* first. However, it is interesting that the case picked by the Court to represent all the cases comes from a state that was free territory during the Civil War, is considered a northern or midwestern state, and was the home state of the then president of the United States, Dwight Eisenhower.

There is striking similarity between the cases.

Briggs v. Elliot

The court was asked to enjoin enforcement of the state constitution and statues that enforced segregation. The district court denied the injunction, citing *Plessy*, but said that the black schools were inferior to the white ones and that they should be equalized.

The Supreme Court asked the district court to determine the progress made in equalization and the district court found that substantial equalization had indeed taken place. This was important because the Supreme Court wanted to rule on whether the "separate but equal" doctrine promoted equality under any circumstances. If the schools were unequal, then *Plessy* would take precedence. If the schools were equal, then either there was no case because according to *Plessy* equality means there is no violation of the Fourteenth Amendment; or *Plessy* must be overturned because equality in spending is not enough. There must be true social equality and no artificial separation of the races.

Davis v. County School Board

In the second case, black students again asked the Court to enjoin the enforcement of Virginia state constitution and statutes that permit, but do not require, segregation. Again the Court told the schools to equalize their programs for black and white students "with due diligence."

Belton v. Gebhart

This case was slightly different in that elementary and high school students sought to enjoin the enforcement of mandatory segregation laws of the state of Delaware.

The lower state court held that segregation results in inferior education for black children and that the black schools were not substantially equal. It ordered the white schools to admit black students. The Supreme Court of Delaware, while affirming the lower court's ruling, did not declare segregation unconstitutional. The state of Delaware asked the Supreme Court to overturn the lower court's and the the state Supreme Court's rulings on the admission of black students to white schools.

Brown v. Topeka

Brown was divided into two parts: *Brown I* was the finding of fact, that segregation is a violation of the Fourteenth Amendment protections; and, *Brown II*, which would present the broad methodology for a redress of grievances if *Brown I* finds that a violation does exist. The case finally chosen as the consolidation of all four cases is *Brown* v. *Topeka Board of Education*. In this case, black elementry-school children sought to have the courts enjoin the enforcement of a Kansas statute that allowed, but did not require, cities with a population of 15,000 or more to maintain separate school facilities for black and white children. The Topeka public schools opted to have separate schools.

The federal district court found that segregated schools did, indeed, have a detrimental effect upon black children, but refused to grant relief because the two school systems were substantially equal. Moreover, the district court said, segregation is not in and of itself unconstitutional unless there are substantial inequities.

This case was clear. Kansas has no history of slavery; it is not a southern state; there was no attempt to undereducate the black children; there was equality of education—but education was separate. There were no ancillary issues to interfere with a clear test of *Plessy*. The American courts had indeed come full circle: It was *Roberts* v. *City of Boston* and *Railroad Company* v. *Brown* for the second time around. The time was right. It would take the Supreme Court three years to rule, and the decision would be unanimous.

BROWN v. TOPEKA BOARD OF EDUCATION

Because of the importance of this case, we will again quote from the decision. The Supreme Court under Chief Justice Earl Warren made a host of impressive and critical decisions related to individual freedom and justice: the right to a lawyer in a criminal trial; the rights of arrested persons; the civil rights of juvenile defendants in criminal proceedings; voting rights; ending segregation in public places; the rights of women; equality of employment opportunities; and ensuring "one man, one vote." The country's awareness had indeed been raised. Justice Warren said that in his opinion the most important decision that his Court handed down was the "one man, one vote" decision. That may be true, but certainly no decision had a greater immediate effect on education than *Brown*.

The separate but equal test of *Plessy* was applied to each of the four cases. In *Gebhart* the black children were admitted to white schools but only because the black schools were substantially unequal. It was now the Court's turn to try to define "equal." The first test was in terms of "tangible" assests of the schools. It was immediately determined that the definition of *Cumming* that all that was necessary was an equal expenditure regardless of the *per capita* expenditure, was inadequate. Black children often had substantially less spent per child than white children. The Court compared number of pupils per school, room, and teacher; it considered physical facilities ranging from the number of water fountains and rest rooms to auditoriums and gymnasiums. The discrepancies were obviously great between black and white schools even if the total dollars spent on black and white schools was the same, because there was substantial *per capita* differences.

But that was not the real issue. The real issue revolved about the "intangible" variables. Even if the schools had been completely equal in terms of tangible facilities, would black children have suffered anyhow just because they were segregated? Was Justice Harlan right in his dissent in *Plessy* when he said that "the evil done this day" would place the Negro in a position of legally sanctioned inferiority just because of segregation itself?

To answer this question, the Court received testimony from psychologists and sociologists, all of whom agreed that segregation, in and of itself even in absolute tangible equality, was detrimental to the mental, educational, and financial growth and health of black children. the financial argument was necessary to show that the black children suffered a tangible injury due to segregation. If no loss could be shown, then it would be difficult to prove violation of equal protection of the law.

The Court rendered its verdict in 1954 based on five questions placed before it: (1) Did the Congress contemplate the abolition of school segregation when it framed the Fourteenth Amendment in 1865? (2) If not, could Congress abolish segregation under section 5 of the Fourteenth Amendment, which states that Congress shall have power to enforce, by appropriate legislation, the provisions of this article? (3) Had the situation changed so drastically since 1865 that no matter what the framers of the amendment had in mind regarding educational segregation, their thinking could not be the basis for a current-day decision? (4) If none of these points would end segregation, could the Court eliminate it anyway? (5) Did the Court have the power to eliminate a social evil that was not even mentioned in the Constitution or its amendments? Questions 4 and 5 dealt with implementation if any of the first three questions could be answered positively.

Those who wished to maintain segregation argued that the framers of the Fourteenth Amendment never had educational segregation in mind. They claimed that segregation was common at the time and that therefore the framers could not have contemplated interference with a commonly accepted social practice.

The Court countered with data of its own. It sent a questionnaire to each of the state archives, historical societies, and governments asking for information as to how difficult it had been to get the Fourteenth Amendment passed and the history of legal and statutory, or *de jure*, segregation in their schools.

According to the Court, the evidence was inconclusive, which is no great surprise since education was not particularly important to most people in 1865. The Court found that there were almost no free public schools in the South in 1865 and almost all the blacks were illiterate since it had been against the law to teach blacks to read in many of the southern states. Public education was at a rudimentary stage in the South and there was little in the history of the Fourteenth Amendment about it.

The Court went on to say, however, "We must consider public education in light of its full development and its present place in American life throughout the nation. Only in this way can it be determined if segregation in public schools deprives these plaintiffs of the equal protection of the laws."

Education, according to the Court, regardless of what it was in 1865 or at the time of *Plessy* in 1894, is critical in the contemporary world. It is the foundation of good citizenship, it is doubtful that a child can succeed in life without it, and the Court said that if the state is going to provide public education at the state expense, then it must do so for all children equally. Further, the court said that even if both tangible and intangible assets of education are equal to both races, segregation deprives the minority children of equal education opportunties because:

> The impact is greater when it has the saction of law. For the policy of separating the races is usually interpreted as denoting inferiority of the Negro group. A sense of inferiority affects the motivation of a child to learn. Segregation with the sanction of law, therefore, has a tendency to retard the educational and mental development of Negro children and to deprive them of some of the benefits they would receive in a racially integrated school system.

The Court, after citing *Sweatt* v. *Painter* and *McLaurin* v. *Oklahoma*, stressed the importance of qualities of education that are incapable of measurement. It said that these intangibles apply to elementary and high school children as well as university students. The Court said that separating children solely on the basis of race "generates a feeling of inferiority as to their status in the community that may affect their hearts and minds in a way unlikely ever to be undone." The doctrine of "separate but equal" has no place in modern American education. A single sentence from the decision sums it up: "Separate educational facilities are inherently unequal."

BROWN II

Again, *Brown I* was the finding of fact. *Brown II* was a determination of process. *Brown II* said that all those schools that were legally segregated at the time should:

1. make a prompt and reasonable start toward desegregation
2. carry out the ruling in an effective manner
3. be consistent with good faith compliance at the earliest possible date
4. develop local plans to meet local desegregation problems

The Court also said that local courts should be in charge of the local desegregation plans and they should consider problems of administration arising from physical conditions of school plant, transportation, personnel, and revision of school districts and attendence areas.

As an interesting side note that would continue to play a role in education, the Court did not overturn the concept of "separate but equal" in the *Plessy* decision. It said that *Plessy* could not be applied to education because separate is inherently unequal in education. Everything else in education, segregated or not, still had to be equal.

Legalized segregation was finally over. There would be those who would fight it, but they would lose. Little Rock, Arkansas, Central High School would have troops placed in its halls because Orville Faubus, the governor of Arkansas, used desegregation as a political ploy and stirred up the populace (a second high school in Little Rock had been desegregated for five years before the *Brown* decisions with no difficulty at all; *Cooper* v. *Aaron*, 1958)[29]; Prince Edward County, Virginia, would attempt to close its schools and then use tax and tuition credits and vouchers to reopen the white schools as private schools while keeping the public schools closed entirely (*Griffin* v. *County School Board of Prince Edward County*, 1964)[30]; Knoxville, Tennesee, would be so slow that the district court would finally tell them to desegregate immediately (*Goss* v. *Board of Education*, 1962)[31]; so called "freedom of choice" plans in which parents were allowed to choose the school their children would attend (the re-segregation that would result was to be considered a "folkway" of the people) were declared unconstitutional (*Greene* v. *County School Board of New Kent*, 1969),[32] among other instances. There were others who would try other legal maneuvers, but none would work. The Court had forced education to join the twentieth century and there was no turning back.

However, just as Americans of the eighteenth century had to recognize the evils of slavery, so those of the last half of the twentieth century had to be made aware of the evils of segregation. The *Brown* decisions, rather than ending the fight, only made other inequities in education more obvious. It was time for *Brown* to move north and west. (The two *Brown* decisions are usually referred to as *Brown* unless specific reference is to be made to one or the other case. We will use *Brown* to refer to both.)

Desegregation Moves North

Brown affected only those schools that had *de jure* segregation. By 1973, almost twenty years after *Brown*, although most northern schools did not have *de jure* segregation, they did have *de facto* segregation. The question was, was segregation acceptable where there was no law, either positive or negative, about it.

As was the case in all northern desegregation cases if there was no positive or negative law regarding segregation, two questions had to be answered before relief could be granted by the courts: (1) Does segregation exist? (2) Was it deliberate? If questions could be answered in the affirmative, then, and only then, could a case be made for a violation of equal protection. The first case occurred in Denver, Colorado.

Keyes v. School District Number 1
(Denver, 1973)

Two areas of Denver were heavily segregated: Park Hill and the core area. It could be clearly shown that the Park Hill area had been intentionally segregated and therefore fell under the aegis of *de jure* segregation. The core area, however, was not intentionally segregated. Here, the residential patterns had just simply emerged and there was no intent on the part of the school district to make the schools black or segregated. This area, therefore, was *de facto* segregated.[33]

The district court ruled that the Park Hill area had to be desegregated immediately since it was a clear case of intentional *de jure* segregation. The court, however, said that since there was no intent in the core area, the schools there would not have to be desegregated, but, because the schools in the core area were inferior, Denver would have to make them equal! The court pointed out that while *de jure* segregation did not exist, inequality did. Therefore, *Brown* did not apply, but *Plessy* did.

The case went to the Supreme Court, and although the Court had changed drastically with the retirement of Earl Warren and the appointment of Warren Burger to replace him, there were still enough justices on the Court who saw the issue in terms of individual equality and justice and not property rights and states' rights. Justices Powell and Douglass wrote opinions concurring with the majority that said that the distinction between *de jure* and *de facto* segregation should be eliminated in regard to equal protection and school desegregation for both practical and social reasons. First, it is difficult to prove *de jure* segregation where there are no laws or statutes. Second, there were differences between the North and South that would lead to different decisions in each area of the country. Justice Powell, in particular, wanted one standard to be used throughout the country.

On the basis of the majority opinion, Denver was told to desegregate all its schools regardless of whether the segregation had been intentional. The problem to be solved was segregation, not intent. There was, however, a dissenting opinion that augured a less positive future. Justice Rehnquist, who had been recently appointed by President Richard Nixon, indicated in the dissent that the distinction between *de jure* and *de facto* segregation should be maintained and that changing the evidentiary rules so that it was easier for the plaintiff to prove segregation, was also unwarranted. That position would become the majority position as more of the Warren Court was replaced by justices appointed by Presidents Nixon and Ford.

The Reaction: A Pullback from *Keyes*

As we have seen throughout the history of slavery, abolition, segregation, and desegregation, there is a tendency to move forward decisively in the expansion of human and civil rights, and then to retrograde somewhat as though we had to catch our breath. This happened again with the end of the all-too-brief Warren Court. Within a very brief time of the *Keyes* decision, the first major test of how the Court would react to future claims of inequality came forth.

San Antonio Independent School District v. Rodriguez (1973)

The Rodriguez case was the watershed. Mexican-American parents in the Edgewood Independent School District, an urban school district in San

Antonio, requested that all the children in Texas who attended school in poor districts having low property tax bases be given relief.[34]

Here the Court would have had the opportunity to eliminate inequality not only within school districts, but among them as well. If equality is to have meaning, then all children should be afforded the same educational opportunities. Partially, that opportunity can be defined in terms of an equal amount of money spent per child regardless of where the child goes to school. Up to this point, the Court had been willing to say that there could be no discrimination within a district. *Rodriguez* went one step further and asked the Court to rule that Texas must finance education equally on a *per capita* basis in all school districts and that local property taxes, which paid for education, could not be used to provide children in poor districts with less education than those from richer districts paying higher property taxes. The plaintiffs, in brief, asked that educational financing be made equitable regardless of the living conditions of the child.

The majority of the Burger Court ruled that interdistrict differentials in financial ability were acceptable and not a violation of Fourteenth Amendment equal protection rights. It said that the only time that school financing could be based on interdistrict funding was when the inequality had been caused by redistricting to make one district rich and the other poor. That was not the case in San Antonio. Residential patterns had caused the distinctions, not any redistricting plan. On the basis of *Keyes* the Court could have ruled that *de facto* injury, whether it is intended or not, is sufficient reason for a remedy, that is, the injury has taken place and is just as severe as if it had been intended. The Court did not.

There was again a dissent from the more liberal members of the Court. Thurgood Marshall said,

> But this Court has never suggested that because some "adequate" level of benefits is provided to all, discrimination in the provision of services is therefore constitutional. The Equal Protection Clause is not addressed to the minimal sufficiency but rather to the unjustifiable inequalities of state action.

Further,

> That education is the dominant factor in influencing political participation and awareness is sufficient, I believe, to dispose of the Court's suggestion that, in all events, there is no indication that Texas is not providing all

of its children with a sufficient education. . . . [It] should be obvious that the political process, like most other aspects of social intercourse, is to some degree competitive. It is thus of little benefit to an individual from a poor district to have "enough" education if those around him have more than "enough."

The next major case also involves the differential treatment of children in the affluent suburbs and poor inner-city sections of the same urban area: Detroit.

Milliken v. Bradley (1974)

In April of 1970, the Detroit Board of Education adopted a desegregation plan. The Michigan state legislature enacted a statute that would have prevented the implementation of the plan. *Milliken* v. *Bradley* declared the statute unconstitutional. Before the desegregation plan could be put into effect, however, a new board of education was elected and the original pl· n was rescinded. A suit was initiated and the district court found that the school district was indeed segregated. However, the remedy might not be possible in Detroit alone because Detroit was 60 to 70 percent black. Further, there was some evidence that the segregation had been partially caused by state actions, for example, the 1970 legislation attempting to stop the desegregation plan; segregative school construction sites approved by the state board of education; denial of transportation allowances, which forced Detroit to maintain a neighborhood school system while other districts were given the transportation allowance, among others. There was sufficient cause for suspicion.[35]

Both the district court and the court of appeals held that the only way to bring about desegregation in the Detroit schools was to include some of the eighty-five suburban, largely white, more affluent school districts through manditory busing of students across district boundary lines.

In the Supreme Court, in a five to four vote (which was to become all too familiar), the majority said that it was not within the province of the Supreme Court to deny local control and local custom. School district lines cannot be casually ignored or treated as a mere administrative convenience. Even if the state might be partially responsible, there was no constitutional justification for an interdistrict remedy.

The dissent stated that the Michigan State Board of Education was at least partially responsible for interdistrict segregation, that there was good reason to believe that Detroit would soon be all-black if some remedy were not instituted, and that the state, because of its role in segregating, was responsible for eliminating vestiges of segregation in the state. Thurgood Marshall saw the decision as a "giant leap backward."

Keyes Modified: The Dayton Case

Dayton Board of Education v. *Brinkman* extended over more than five years. In 1972 the district court found that *de jure* segregation existed in the Dayton schools because: (1) the schools were racially unbalanced; (2) two high school optional attendance zones had had demonstrable racial effects in the past; and (3) the current school board had rescinded the previous school board's action taking responsibility for the segregation. The board took the case to the Supreme Court.[36]

The Supreme Court treated two major issues: (1) What standard should be used to determine the existence of constitutional violation? and, (2) What standard should be used to decide the scope of the remedy? In the *Keyes* decision both questions were decided, that is, segregation was an injury regardless of intent and should be remedied, and the solution should involve the problem, not the intent, that is, both Park Hill (*de jure* segregation) and the core area (*de facto* segregation) should both be remedied. The new Burger Court would not agree with the *Keyes* decision. The majority said that the distinction between *de jure* and *de facto* segregation is an important one regardless of the injury, and that the remedy must meet the *de jure* problem. Since in Dayton only the two high schools had been shown to be *de jure* segregated, the remedy could apply only to those two schools regardless of where the problem was. This decision was based on two discrimination cases that had nothing to do with education.

Washington v. *Davis* was an employment discrimination case involving an employment test that was not job related but that discriminated against minorities. The test was a verbal skills test for a police officer training program. The lower court ruled that the test was unconstitutional because of its obvious bias and because it was not directly job related.

The Supreme Court, in a seven to two ruling, reversed this decision, saying that:

Disproportionate impact is not irrelevant, but it is not the sole touchstone of an invidious discrimination forbidden by the Constitution. Standing alone, it does not trigger the rule that racial classifications are to be subjected to the strictest scrutiny. . . .[37]

The Court ruled that racial discrimination alone was not enough. Intent had to be proved to show an equal protection violation.

Arlington Heights v. Metropolitan Housing Development Corp.

In this case, the Chicago Metropolitan Housing Development Corporation applied in 1971 for a permit to put up low-cost housing in Arlington Heights, a suburb of Chicago. Arlington Heights refused a rezoning permit. The MHDC sued, saying that the refusal to issue a rezoning permit violated the rights of potential residents of the housing project, who were largely black. Here again the lower courts ruled that discriminatory effect is sufficient to show that an equal protection violation exists. The Supreme Court again reversed the lower courts and said that segregation alone was not enough to show an equal protection violation.[38]

These two cases in conjunction with *Dayton* have slowed the process of desegregation in areas where it is difficult to prove *de jure* segregation even though it is patently clear that *de facto* segregation exists. There have been a number of similar cases, such as those in Austin, Texas, and Omaha, Nebraska, among others.

One Success of Many

We tend to think that desegregation has been a difficult and violent process because the cases with which most of us are familiar are Little Rock, Boston, Pontiac, Louisville, and Prince Edward County. It should never be forgotten that for every place where there has been enough trouble to make the newspaper headlines, there have been many places where desegregation went smoothly. Perhaps we should look at one such success where the schools improved consistently since the advent of desegregation.

In Milwaukee, Wisconsin, history, the power structure, the attitude of the people, the school personnel (both administrators and teachers), the school board, the district court judge, and an educational plan that had the education of the children of Milwaukee at its center, all combined to make not just desegregation, but possibly even integration, work.

The Milwaukee Case

The Milwaukee case was unusual in a number of ways. In the first place the names on the case changed over the period that the case was in court. Second, the case took an inordinate amount of time, 1965 to 1974. Third, not only was there a class of black students named as plaintiffs, but there were also three non-black students named. In January of 1974, Judge Reynolds presented his decision in which he stated that the policies of the Milwaukee School Board had consistently and uniformly adhered to a "neighborhood school" policy that was developed in 1919 and that the board knew was increasing the segregation of black and white children in separate schools. The district court went on to say that the school authorities engaged in practices with the intent to maintain segregation. The issue was segregation since no one stated that the all-black schools were inferior in staff or facilities to the white schools. The schools truly were as equal as segregated schools could be. In point of fact, some of the older schools in the inner city had recently been completely refurbished and redecorated. However, while the schools were being redone, the black students from those schools were bused in intact classes to white schools. At the white schools, the black children had their own faculty, cafeteria hours, playground hours, assemblies, and other activities. Black children were totally segregated from white children while they were in a white school.

The school board appealed the district court decision. The appeals court upheld the district court, but the Supreme Court remanded the case back to the district court for revision. The district court held its ground and stayed with its original finding.[39]

While all this was going on, the superintendent, teachers, and board were quietly putting into effect a plan that had been developed by the superintendent, who had been hired the previous year. The plan did not involve geographical desegregation. Rather it stated that each school should be desegregated regardless of the geography. Children should be moved as little as possible and what movement there was should be voluntary as often as possible. Children should come from anywhere in the city and go to anywhere in the city that they and their parents chose. This was to be accomplished in two ways: (1) a system of specialty or magnet schools was to be established in the inner city to attract white children, and (2) an open and immediate transfer policy was established whereby any parents could demand that their child be transferred from a nonintegrated school to an integrated school (the opposite was not true, i.e., a parent could not demand transfer to a nonintegrated school). The emphasis would be on integration, not on desegregation; on education, not on moving children about.

Over a three-year period, more than 85 percent of the children in the Milwaukee public schools either were placed in or opted for integrated schools. During that same period a number of studies were completed to determine the attitudes of the children and the parents about the Milwaukee public schools, integration, and other races. Those parents and children who were involved in the specialty-integrated schools praised both the education that their children were receiving and the process of integration. There were some black and white parents and children who objected to their opposite number, but they were rare. Where there were disputes in schools, they were minor and were healed quickly. Since 1976, educational achievement as measured on standardized tests has improved slightly. The superintendent is quick to point out that this was not caused by integration but it was not hurt by it either. Education is what was important. The superintendent, the school, the community, and its leaders in general feel that part of education for the latter half of the twentieth century should, and must, include the ability to work with, and understand, children and adults who are very different from each other. Desegregation is an attempt toward that. Integration is better yet. Milwaukee is certainly not the only place where desegregation was the order and integration became the fact, but it is one example that has been extensively studied.

SUMMARY

Not all the important cases have been covered in this chapter, partially because the history of this form of inequality before the law is so extensive. One thing becomes clear—we have come a long way since 1772 when it was difficult to bring the evils of slavery to the consciousness of the citizens of the United Kingdom. While there have been retrogressions, the overall pattern has been "up." There are more children going to school now than ever before and they are going to school without the legally sanctioned stigma of segregation. White children are as much the beneficiaries of this desegregation as black children, for the white, American middle-class children of today will be citizens of the world tomorrow. The only way that the schools can prepare the youth of today to be those world citizens is through the integration of society in the schools. We, as educators, in the thirty years since *Brown* v. *Board* have carried the burden of much of this social upheaval. In most cases we have shouldered it well.

There have been retrogressions in the Burger Court and recalcitrant schools, teachers, administrators, and school boards. But in general, teachers, administrators, and school districts have not just followed the letter of the law and desegregated the schools. Rather we have often seen the opportunity and have attempted to integrate our schools and our students into the multicultural twentieth century. When we were at our best, we did what we have always done as educators when we were at our best: We have taught the children of this generation so that they may become the citizens of the next. At our best, we have not viewed the children as coming from particular social classes, races, national origins, or sexes, but only as the representatives of the future who are our responsibility. We may be justly proud.

FOR CONSIDERATION

1. How would you define integration? Does it have socioeconomic and religious aspects as well as a racial one? What would be a good legal definition? a good educational definition?

2. Do you think that you, as a teacher, should try to enhance integration in your school? What can you do to enhance it?

3. What other social justice issues do you think the schools will have to confront in the next few years? How will you, as a teacher, confront those issues?

Notes

1. Gunnar Myrdal, *An American Dilemma* (New York: Harper, 1944).
2. *Somerset* v. *Stewart*, Court of King's Bench 98 Eng. Rep. 499, 1 Lofft (1772).
3. *The Slave Grace*, High Court of the Admiralty, 166 Eng. Rep. 179 (1827).
4. "An Act for the Abolition of Slavery throughout the British Colonies; for promoting the Industry of the manumitted Slaves; and for compensating the Persons hitherto entitled to the Services of such Slaves"; 3 & 4 W:11. 4, c. 73 (1833).
5. *The Autobiography of Thomas Jefferson*, Introduction by Dumas Malone (New York, Capricorn Books, 1959), p. 39.

6. Pennsylvania Statute, Act of March 1, 1780, c. 146.

7. New York Statute, Act of March 29, 1799, c. 62.

8. New York Statute, Act of March 31, 1812, c. 137.

9. *Commonwealth* v. *Aves*, Supreme Judicial Court of Massachusetts, 35 Mass. (18 Pick.) 193 (1836).

10. *Jackson* v. *Bulloch*, Supreme Court of Errors of Conn. 12 Conn. 39 (1837).

11. *Roberts* v. *City of Boston*, Supreme Judicial Court of Mass., 59 Mass (5 Cush.) 198 (1850).

12. *Dred Scott* v. *Sandford*, Supreme Court of the U.S., 60 U.S. (19 How.) 393 (1875).

13. *Railroad Company* v. *Brown*, 84 U.S. 445 (17, Wall.), (1873).

14. *Plessy* v. *Ferguson*, Supreme Court of the U.S., 163 U.S. 537 (1896).

15. William Graham Summer, "The Absurd Effort to Make the World Over"; reprinted in *War and Other Essays*, Albert G. Keller, ed., (New Haven: Yale University Press, 1911).

16. William Graham Summer, *Folkways* (New York: Dover Publications, 1959).

17. *Plessy* v. *Ferguson*.

18. *Ibid.*

19. *Cumming* v. *Richmond County Board of Education*, 175 U.S. 528, 545 (1899).

20. *Gong Lum* v. *Rice*, Supreme Court of the U.S., 275 U.S. 76 (1927).

21. *Missouri ex rel Gaines* v. *Canada*, 305 U.S. 337 (1938).

22. *Sipuel* v. *Board of Regents of the University of Oklahoma*, 332 U.S. 631 (1948).

23. *Sweatt* v. *Painter*, 210 SW 2nd 442 (1947).

24. *McLaurin* v. *Oklahoma State Regents for Higher Education*, 339 U.S. 637 (1950).

25. *Brown* v. *Topeka Board of Education*, 347 U.S. 483 (1954).

26. *Briggs* v. *Elliot*, 1347 U.S. 497 (1954).

27. *Davis* v. *County School Board of Prince Edward County*, 347 U.S. 483 (1954).

28. *Belton* v. *Gebhart*, 347 U.S. 483 (1954).

29. *Cooper* v. *Aaron*, 358 U.S. 1 (1958).

30. *Griffin* v. *County School Board*, 377 U.S. 281, 234.

31. *Goss* v. *Board of Education*, 373 U.S. 683, 689.

32. *Green* v. *County School Board of New Kent*, Supreme Court of U.S., 391 U.S. 430 (1968).

33. *Keyes* v. *Denver School District No. 1*, 1, 93, S. Ct. 2686 (1973).

34. *San Antonio Independent School Dist.* v. *Rodriguez*, 93 S. Ct. 1278 (1973).

35. *Milliken* v. *Bradley*, 94 S. Ct. 3112 (1974).

36. *Dayton Board of Education* v. *Brinkman*, 433 U.S. 406 (1977).

37. *Washington* v. *Davis*, 462 U.S. 299 (1976).

38. *Village of Arlington Heights* v. *Metropolitan Housing Development Corp.*, 429 U.S. 252 (1977).

39. *Amos* v. *Board of School Directors of Milwaukee*, 408 F. Supp. 765 (E. D. Wis.) (1976).

Epilogue

We have now come full circle. In the prologue we said that this book was a history and status of education's role in the struggle for freedom and justice. We began with history and models for analysis, passed through the present situation of society and education's role in it, looked at the multicultural and worldwide perspectives of education, and concluded with two issues that are so terribly central to education in any free society: freedom of expression and to learn; and equality of justice and access to education.

When we look at the history and status of education, we have reason to be both optimistic and pessimistic. There has been a great deal of backsliding in freedom and in justice in education and society. But in general, the pattern has been toward greater freedom and greater justice. Although the struggle against those who would limit the acceptability of books, ideas, and concepts never ends, there is still greater acceptability of difference of opinion and thought now than at any time in our history. Similarly, although the struggle for equality of minorities, women, the handicapped, the older student, and so many others must continue, there have been battles won.

There are always those who would limit either who can be educated or what they may learn. But, in general, all students of all ages, sex, race, and level of ability are more free to read, explore, and discover than in the past, and teachers are more free to teach and encourage freedom of thought and expression than in the past.

We in education have been in the forefront in some of these struggles. In others we have been remiss in our defense of all the students, of all the people, of all the ideas. But without us, those who wish to teach, this relatively free and just society would not be as well educated, as free, and as just as it is.

This should be a cause neither for complacency nor for a lack of vigilance. The struggle for a free and just education is never won for there are always new battles to fight with those who would limit us or our students. Nor is the struggle ever lost, for so long as there are teachers who wish to teach and students who wish to learn, repression and tyranny will always have an adversary.

Index

About the Authors

FRANK BESAG has been professor of cultural foundations of education at the University of Wisconsin, Milwaukee since 1970. Previously he was assistant and associate professor of sociology of education at the State University of New York at Buffalo and associate professor of sociology of education at the University of Washington. He taught junior and senior high school from 1959 to 1963. He received his Ph.D. in Educational Sociology and Sociology from the University of Southern California in 1965. In 1981 and 1982 he was Vice President of the American Educational Research Association for Division G (Social Context of Education) and was founder and first editor of *Issues in Education: A Journal of Research and Opinion*. Professor Besag is the author of eight other books and many articles, but views teaching as his most important activity. He has served on many state and national councils and boards including the Wisconsin Council on Criminal Justice. Dr. Besag was born in Amsterdam, the Netherlands in 1935 and escaped from there with his parents and two brothers in 1940.

JACK L. NELSON is Professor II (Distinguished) in the Graduate School of Education at Rutgers University. His undergraduate degree is from the University of Denver; his masters from California State University at Los Angeles; and his doctorate from the University of Southern California. He has taught in public schools, at California State University at Los Angeles, and at SUNY, Buffalo, in addition to having had visiting faculty positions at Colgate University, the University of Colorado, City University of New York, and Cambridge University in England. He has also been a Visiting Scholar at the University of California, Berkeley, and at Stanford University. Professor Nelson's publications include over 100 articles and fourteen books on education and social issues. Among these are *Patterns of Power, Sociological Perspectives in Education, Radical Ideas and the Schools, Values, Rights and the New Morality,* and *International Human Rights: Contemporary Perspectives.*